ELLA
FITZGERALD

By the Same Author

JAZZ: THE MODERN RESURGENCE

ELLA FITZGERALD

A BIOGRAPHY
OF THE FIRST LADY OF JAZZ

STUART NICHOLSON

Charles Scribner's Sons
New York

Maxwell Macmillan International
New York   Oxford   Singapore   Sydney

For my mother

Copyright © 1993 by Stuart Nicholson

First American Edition 1994

Charles Scribner's Sons
Macmillan Publishing Company
866 Third Avenue
New York, NY 10022

Macmillan Publishing Company is part of the Maxwell Communication Group of Companies.

Library of Congress Cataloging-in-Publication Data
    Ella Fitzgerald: a biography of the first lady of jazz / Stuart Nicholson. — 1st American ed.
      p.   cm.
    Includes bibliographical references, discography, and index.
    ISBN 0-684-19699-9
    1. Fitzgerald, Ella.   2. Singers—United States—Biography.
I. Title.
ML420.F52N5   1994
782.42165'092—dc20
[B]   93-34359   CIP
                      MN

Macmillan books are available at special discounts for bulk purchases for sales promotions, premiums, fund-raising, or educational use. For details, contact:

Special Sales Director
Macmillan Publishing Company
866 Third Avenue
New York, NY 10022

10 9 8 7 6 5 4 3 2 1

Printed in the United States of America

CONTENTS

PREFACE

Legends are lies that become history in the end.

JEAN COCTEAU

THEY SAY THAT WHEN New York taxi drivers know your name, you've made it. Well, New York taxi drivers, so I'm told, have known the name Ella Fitzgerald since the early 1940s. By the 1990s, these most hard-boiled of men and women speak of her with genuine affection. But it isn't only the New York taxi drivers; Americans in general regard Ella with the kind of affection that the British reserve for Queen Elizabeth the Queen Mother.

The extent of this affection gradually revealed itself to me while I was in the United States researching this book, and it came, I must confess, as a surprise. It crossed over the arbitrary boundaries imposed by age and ethnicity. Ella's popularity was such that it seemed to transcend categories. She was beyond jazz, she was beyond popular music, yet paradoxically she remained limited by them, as much through our received notions of one or the other as through the way she applied her great talent to both.

Yet Ella's whole career has been full of paradoxes, some almost hidden from view, some not, as I discovered when I became progressively more involved in this project. I quickly realized it was going to be very different from what I had imagined it would be. Quite apart from anything else, I found I had to delve into much more material than I had previously envisaged. While there was plenty that had been written about Ella, there was also plenty that I discovered was patently incorrect. And as I solved one enigma, there always seemed to be another to take its place, like a nest of Russian dolls. As my knowledge of Ella's story grew, it gradually began to dawn on me that I was in the midst of trying to strip away the myths that made the legend.

There were vast inconsistencies about her early years, for example. Since Ella has steadfastly refused to talk in anything but the most superficial terms about her childhood and the time that preceded her membership in the Chick Webb Orchestra, writers and journalists over the decades have filled in the missing details in the best jazz tradition: They improvised. To paraphrase that immortal line from *The Man Who Shot Liberty Valance*: When the woman became a legend, they printed the legend.

And certainly legend and fact didn't always go hand in hand. Very often I found that the "when, where, and with whoms" of basic journalism had never been checked out. I soon discovered why. Obtaining this sort of information, some of it seventy-five years after the event, took a remarkable amount of time and research. Here, I am grateful for the enthusiasm and determination of Marsha Saron Dennis in unearthing a wealth of previously unpublished facts about Ella, particularly her early years, and for tracing her childhood friends. Marsha started out a researcher and ended a dear friend.

Although I tried to arrange an interview with Ella, Mary Jane Outwater of Salle Productions told me several times it was impossible; indeed, she even succeeded in blocking an interview I had set up with one of Ella's friends while I was in New York. Why?

Now that I was forced to do my own thing, a curious paradox emerged: By going my own way I probably discovered more about Ella than I ever would have had I spoken to her. If I had, I am sure that, like those who have interviewed her in the past, I would have seen no reason to doubt what she said. And, also, it is difficult to imagine a scenario where, on seeing me, she would suddenly have been overcome with the desire to confess her correct date of birth or clarify longstanding mysteries, such as her alleged marriage to Benny Kornegay (which she has frequently denied ever took place). Those are the kinds of things you have to find out for yourself, it seemed.

After finding certain anomalies in the Ella legend, I moved from being a believer to being an agnostic, curious about the past she would never talk about. Where did she go to school? What was the influence of school and church on her singing? When did she leave school? Could that old chestnut about being taken to sing at Yale with Chick Webb's band be true? Surprisingly, nobody had taken the trouble to find out. The record books are not much help; much of what they tell us about Ella is either incomplete or incorrect. The date of her debut at the Apollo, for example, has never been given, and other important dates in her life, such as her marriage to Ray Brown and her first appearance with Jazz at the Philharmonic, have, I discovered, always been wrong.

However, the interviews I managed to get with her childhood

friends (the first time they have ever been traced and gone on record), the surviving members of the Chick Webb band, and countless musicians who played regularly with her or know her well—such as the ever gracious Mel Tormé—provide, I think, a unique perspective on Ella's career.

Why then should there be such inconsistencies in her past? Perhaps the answer lies in her difficult childhood. It now seems clear that she has simply replaced memories that are painful to her with an idealized version that she can live with. This is by no means unusual; countless people who have experienced difficult episodes in their past have done, and are doing, the same thing. It is a way of coping with life. But separating those strands can make the biographer feel at times, I must confess, like a person calling a minister a liar mid-vespers.

Sweeping generalizations about Ella's career abound, not the least the accumulated wisdom about her years with the Decca Records label. This would have us believe that all she recorded in the years leading up to 1955 were forgettable commercial pops. When one commentator wrote, "Ella Fitzgerald spent the first twenty years on the Decca plantation, and the percentage of the 300 sides she made that remain palatable remains pitifully low,"[1] I doubt whether one voice was raised in protest; at the time, certainly not mine.

Yet when I managed to hear much of that (now rare) Decca material myself—largely through the generosity of Ed Berger at the Institute of Jazz Studies at Rutgers University in New Jersey—I was astonished at the consistency and diversity of Ella's output. There were dismal numbers, to be sure, but by no means enough to write off this period of her career as an artistic no-go area. It seemed to me that the years 1939 to 1955 were in need of a fresh reappraisal, and so began another fascinating voyage of discovery.

In fact, listening to as much of Ella's vast recorded output as I could proved to be a major task in itself. Michel Macaire in France provided some rare 1940s concert material for which I am grateful, while Terri Hinte of Fantasy Records in Berkeley, California, made sure that I had all Ella's Pablo output. Similarly, Cees Schrama at Polygram Jazz, Polygram International Music BV, The Netherlands, provided me with every available Verve release. Thanks also to Pete Harvey of Panther Records for Ella's early material on Decca and to Jo Pratt and Joanna Nagle of EMI for Ella's Capitol output. Obviously in a discography as vast as Ella's it is impossible to discuss every record. I have attempted, however, to cover as much of her recorded output as space permitted.

Throughout the book I have used interview material from prime witnesses. This, I hope, has had two advantages. First, I believe it has helped me to avoid becoming a victim of my own subjectivity by forcing me to keep all lines of input open. When talking, both on and off the record, to the many people who have known Ella over the years, I found they very quickly disabused me of any preconceptions I might have had and that their knowledge of Ella took me in new and unexpected directions. Second, and most important, these people were there at the time; I wasn't. Their recollections seem to me to have an immediacy that speaks across the decades. I have also quoted from Ella's concert reviews throughout her career. I think they, too, help build a picture of a remarkable singer at work through nearly half a century, and show how she was perceived at the time.

The list of interviewees is long, and since they appear in the text and chapter by chapter in the Notes, I will not attempt to list them here. Without exception they fielded my questions with courtesy and insight and willingly gave of their time with great generosity. I am most grateful to one and all. I am also greatly indebted to tenor saxophonist, bandleader, and musicologist Loren Schoenberg for taking time from his busy schedule to interview Milt Gabler, Tommy Flanagan, Ram Ramirez, Hal Austin, Beverly Peer, and Heywood Henry on my behalf. He also arranged numerous interviews for me and checked and rechecked details, poring over interview material and old copies of the trade press to prove or disprove some theory or idea I always seemed to be trying to develop. Thanks also to Phil Schaap, dubbed "The Dean of Jazz Radio" by *The New York Times*, for his insights, helpful hints, suggestions, and the most complete Ella discography yet.

Many other people kindly gave me important leads, set up interviews, checked information, and generally, I hope, kept me on the right track. I am especially grateful to Dan Morgenstern of the Institute of Jazz Studies, Rutgers University; Dr. Wolfram Knauer of the Jazz-Institut Darmstadt; Will Friedwald; John Chilton; Max Harrison; Brian Rust; Max Jones; Michael Krog for his super research work in Denmark; Michael Hashim; Ken Peplowski; Al Wagner for keeping the clippings coming; and to Carolyn Williams for her vital help in researching Ella's career in the 1940s. Thanks also to Jed Williams, who read the typescript and made countless timely suggestions. My editor, Richard Wigmore at Victor Gollancz, London, was a model of patience, understanding, and insight, for which I am grateful.

For this, the American edition, I am truly grateful to Bill Goldstein of Charles Scribner's Sons for the precious gift of twenty-twenty hindsight in permitting me to rethink, revise, and update the text right up to the eleventh hour. His patient understanding allowed the inclusion of much new research data that turned up too late for the European editions. I am also grateful for the time and trouble Norman Granz took to help me prepare the final draft for the American edition.

Finally, much gratitude to my family: my wife Kath, the in-laws for their nonmusical help and generosity, and my brother for his consistent encouragement, insight, and willing assistance. Finally, thanks and love to my mother, to whom the book is dedicated.

WOODLANDS ST. MARY, BERKSHIRE, ENGLAND
SEPTEMBER 1993

PROLOGUE

Ella has no great ego, no sense of having accomplished all
she has.

BENNY CARTER[1]

ON MONDAY, FEBRUARY 12, 1990, American Express Gold Card presented a tribute to Ella Fitzgerald at Avery Fisher Hall, New York
City. Headlined "Hearts for Ella," it was a fund-raiser for the
American Heart Association. "For 56 years Ella Fitzgerald has been
singing her heart out," ran the advertisements. "On February 12, a
few of her admirers will return the favor." If it seemed an excuse to
indulge in nostalgia, no one said so and no one objected.

Here was a woman whose singing had won her practically every
honor she might have dreamed could come her way: countless prestigious critics' and listeners' polls as top jazz singer; Grammy Awards;
a Kennedy Center Award; the National Medal of Arts presented to
her by the President of the United States; honorary doctorates in
music from such bastions of the establishment as Yale, Dartmouth,
the University of Maryland, and more. She had been presented to
heads of state and feted by the rich and famous, and had collaborated
with the very best artists in jazz and popular music, from Louis
Armstrong and Duke Ellington to Frank Sinatra and Nat King Cole.
She was, quite simply, one of the most celebrated jazz musicians of all
time.

Assembled for the "Hearts for Ella" tribute was an impressive roster of celebrities and jazz greats. The singer and entertainer Lena
Horne and the classical violinist Itzhak Perlman co-hosted the
evening, which began with the mayor of New York, David Dinkins,
presenting Ella with a symbolic apple made of crystal and declaring
"an Ella Fitzgerald Day." Composer, arranger, alto saxophonist, and
multi-instrumentalist Benny Carter directed an orchestra that com-
prised Stan Getz, Phil Woods, David Sanborn, Jimmy Heath, and

Nick Brignola, saxes; Al Grey, Urbie Green, Slide Hampton, and Jack Jeffers, trombones; Clark Terry, Red Rodney, Jon Faddis, and Joe Wilder, trumpets; a rhythm section of Herb Ellis, guitar, Ray Brown, bass, and, at different times, pianists Hank Jones and Tommy Flanagan and drummers Louis Bellson and Roy Proctor. Even the urbane Carter, one of the most universally respected of all jazz musicians, who had consistently worked with the music's finest since the late 1920s, was sufficiently impressed with such a remarkable lineup of talent to comment in an aside to the audience: "This is what you *really* call a dream band."

There were appearances by pianist George Shearing; tap dancers Honi Coles and the Copasetics and Savion Glover; singers Joe Williams, Bobby McFerrin, Cab Calloway, and Melissa Manchester; tenor saxophonist James Moody; vocal group Manhattan Transfer; jazz and pop legend Quincy Jones; a subdued but still clownish Dizzy Gillespie; and an unscheduled appearance by Oscar Peterson.

Janis Siegal and Cheryl Bentyne from Manhattan Transfer joined Melissa Manchester in a re-creation of the Boswell Sisters in concert. The Boswells, and Connee Boswell in particular, were singers ahead of their time in the early 1930s. Throughout her life, in interview after interview, Ella Fitzgerald always credited the Boswells as her original inspiration, upon whom she modeled her singing style.

Finally, after sitting in an aisle seat for nearly four hours, Ella Fitzgerald was escorted to the stage by Joe Williams. Although she was unsteady, and would later cancel her appearance at the post-concert party, she launched into "Honeysuckle Rose" to a huge ovation from the sold-out audience. She thanked everyone "very humbly," and then, with a shrug of her shoulders, turned to Benny Carter and said, "We could do another one." It was George Gershwin's "Lady Be Good," a number that had virtually become her own special property. Joe Williams joined her, and down from the trumpet section came Clark Terry in the guise of his alter ego Mumbles, the manic scat singer, to create a three-way scat finale. "Such a feeling of spontaneity peppered the evening," said the *Daily News*.

It was the second time that night the audience had heard Gershwin's "Lady Be Good." The first was when Benny Carter's All Star Big Band played an arrangement of it by Billy Byers, based on Ella's 1947 recording of the tune. "We played exactly what she had sung," said Carter later. "When she goes into her improvisations on that record, everything she does following the opening chorus is composition. It's so exciting, so creative, so wonderfully melodic and swinging. She has such an uncanny sense of hearing; she seems to hear every chord change there is. When she scats, she doesn't miss anything, and when she's singing something straight, it's pure. It's fantastic."[2]

ELLA
FITZGERALD

CHAPTER ONE

1917–1930

When you consider, well, her beginnings, very poor beginnings, you know, very poor . . .

GEORGE WEIN

ELLA FITZGERALD HAS LIVED to sing. Nothing else in life has meant as
much to her. It has been the focus of her whole being, sustaining her
career at the top of her profession through seven decades. Her vocal
style, widely acknowledged as a touchstone of excellence, has been
admired for its purity of tone, clarity of diction, harmonic imagination, and a highly refined sense of swing. Seemingly impervious to
the unrelenting shocks announcing the new that periodically swept
both jazz and popular music, she had the ability to fill concert halls
around the world, whatever the prevailing musical trend.

Even in the notoriously fickle record business, where the slightest
downturn in an album's sales usually means deletion from the catalogue faster than you can blink, her *Songbook* series, made mostly in
the 1950s, remained almost constantly in print, and *The Cole Porter
Songbook* along with the two *My Fair Lady* albums (with the original
cast and Shelly Manne's) became the largest-selling record albums in
history. To paraphrase Robert Graves, Ella Fitzgerald was really very
good, despite all the people who said she was very good.

Her consuming desire to perform has continued well into her third
age, even though she has long since become a millionaire and could
have retired in comfort in the 1960s. Despite failing eyesight and fee-
ble health she has willingly submitted herself to grueling tour schedules, intercontinental one-night stands, and demanding concert sets
in the world's most famous auditoriums. Recalling her 1990 appearance at Radio City Music Hall in New York City, for example, internationally respected jazz commentator Dan Morgenstern observed:
"She can hardly see and she's frail now. She has to be walked on stage
and she sits, of course. But boy, does she still have energy. *And she*

1

just does not want to let go! That was a long show, and she was on all the time. And *no* rest between songs. Some singers will do a little patter between each song, but she goes *boom!* right into the next number. That's the way she likes to do it. God knows she doesn't need to perform anymore, she's a multi-millionairess. But she wants to. She wants that applause. It's her life."

Music has meant everything to Ella. Friends and musicians close to her spoke of how she constantly turned songs over in her mind or hummed them to herself, imagining how they might turn out during performance. The guitarist Joe Pass, a frequent collaborator since the early 1970s, recalled: "Since I've known her she's always had a melody on her mind—sitting in the car, backstage, in a restaurant, she's humming! She always has a tune on her mind. It's like a preoccupation with her. She's always got a melody going on in her head. It's always a piece that you've forgotten all about, haven't played in a long time or heard in a long time."

Ella's love affair with music is a common thread that emerges from the recollections of all the musicians with whom she has worked. For example, Jimmy Rowles, her pianist from time to time since the 1950s and her regular accompanist in the 1980s, recalled: "She was always either singing or listening to music. Music was going on around her. Everything is music. Music comes out of her. When she walks down the street, she leaves notes. Pete Cavallo was her road manager. When we were up in a plane, I would go to sleep. And I'd wake up to the sound of her calling out, 'Pete, Pete!' She'd heard a song she liked. 'Pete, get the name of that. Write that down. I want it.' We added so many songs to the book that we never got a chance to do them all."[1]

For most of her career she dominated the annual readers' polls conducted by the influential music magazines; when she was displaced by Roberta Flack as Best Female Vocalist by five votes in the 1971 *Down Beat* readers' poll, it ended an almost unbroken run that had begun in 1937. Equally she enjoyed similar unanimity among the critics. From the first *Down Beat* critics' poll in 1953 until the mid-1970s, she was regularly voted Number One Female Vocalist. No other artist in jazz has enjoyed such unanimous approbation over such a long period from both public and critics, critical acuity and popular opinion for the most part seeming to converge only by accident.

Always at heart a shy and self-effacing woman, Ella disappeared into the words and music of a song so completely that it transcended her matronly appearance, leaving just the purity of her voice. It was the voice of everywoman. Just as advertisers portray the feminine image as young, slim, and beautiful, Ella's voice, half girl's, half woman's, was its aural equivalent. Its perpetually youthful timbre gave it a universal, timeless appeal. It evoked straightforward and uncomplicated emotions, the emotions of adolescence rather than the complex "grown-up" emotions of, say, loneliness or the discovery of infidelity. The values she communicated were simple, even optimistic; her yearning became the adolescent's yearning, her dreams the adolescent's dreams of "boy meeting girl, falling in love, marrying, and living happily ever after." This ingenue quality of her singing was perhaps its most endearing characteristic, as singer Mel Tormé, a personal friend for almost fifty years, observed in 1991. "She's never lost that girl-woman quality. She still sounds—even at her age, and I guess she's in her early seventies now—she still sounds like a little girl when she sings, she's still got that 'A-Tisket, A-Tasket' sound of innocence." All Ella ever wanted, as she said so often, was that no matter what she sang, people might say, "She's still singing a pretty tune."[2]

Ever since she started singing in public, Ella Fitzgerald has remained a private person. Mario Bauza, the trumpet player with whom she worked for the first four years of her professional career, said, "She didn't hang out much. When she got into the band, she was dedicated to her music. . . . She was a lonely girl around New York, just kept herself to herself, for the gig."

Since those early days, little changed in terms of Ella's personal relationships. Few people ever had access to her private world, as Mel Tormé observed: "I adore Ella. Every time we see each other, there's a lot of hugging and kissing, and she's come to see me several times and I've seen her more than she could ever see me. But I don't really *know* her very well, and she lives about six blocks from me. . . . And by the way, I'm not sure if anybody does, except perhaps the people who work for her, you know. She's insular, she's very, very insular. She keeps to herself."

Throughout her life Ella has remained uncomfortable about giving interviews and would become even more uncomfortable if pressed to discuss her past in anything but the most general terms. On such occasions she fell back on a standard story dreamed up by a press agent early in her career. It was of a we-were-poor-but-happy childhood and of a mother always on hand with homespun philosophy to soothe the growing pains of childhood. The story was repeated again and again until it became standard journalistic copy, but all along it was just another song into which she could disappear.

Ella Fitzgerald's enigmatic life began a year earlier than the date shown in all the reference books, which say she was born on April 25, 1918, in Newport News, Virginia. The state registrar for Virginia confirms she was born Ella Jane Fitzgerald on Wednesday, April 25, 1917, in Newport News City, Warwick County, in the Commonwealth of Virginia. She was the firstborn child of William Fitzgerald and Tempie Williams Fitzgerald; although the couple was not married, William acknowledged paternity. Tempie, an abbreviation of Temperance, was the name Ella's mother always used.

The family lived in rented accommodations at 2050 Madison Avenue in Newport News City. In the 1920 United States census for the household of William Fitzgerald, taken on January 17, William was then thirty-five, able to read and write, and was a wage earner driving a transfer wagon. Tempie was twenty-six, could also read and write, and her occupation was given as laundress, "working out." Both were native Virginians, as apparently were their parents. The age of their only daughter, Ella, was given as "2 $^{8}/_{12}$ years old." The census required the race of every member of the household, and each was designated a "mulatto" by James Jenkins, the census taker.

Within a year, however, William Fitzgerald had apparently disappeared from the scene, and Tempie was with a new man, Joseph Da Silva. Joe, as he was known, was a first-generation immigrant from Portugal who was later described by a family friend as "a big fellow, a heavy man, and a hard worker." With Tempie's young baby in tow, the couple moved to the city of Yonkers in Westchester County, New York. Like thousands of members of America's disadvantaged black community, they were responding to the stories then rife of better employment and housing prospects in the northern urban centers. For most the move, in what was known as the Great Migration, would be a bitter disappointment; the stories of a better life were at best exaggerated and simply meant replacing one ordeal of squalid poverty with another.

With no work and unable to afford an apartment, Tempie and Joe moved into one room at 27 Clinton Street, a big red-brick building of twenty-eight rooms, probably found for them by the Austrian Lutheran Church in the immediate vicinity; it frequently placed foster children and whole families in temporary shelter with people who lived on Clinton Street. Both soon found jobs in the neighborhood,

Tempie at the Silver Lining Laundry and Joe at a sugarhouse. In 1923, Tempie gave birth to another daughter, Frances, who took her father's surname. Until Frances's death in the 1960s, Ella remained exceptionally close to her half-sister; it was one of the few enduring relationships she formed in her lifetime.

In September 1923, Tempie took Ella to begin her education at Public School 10, on the corner of Prospect and Clinton. When she registered her tall, gawky six-year-old, she gave her daughter's date of birth as April 25, 1917, which was correct, but gave the name of the parent or guardian with whom Ella was residing as William Fitzgerald,[3] which was not.

Just after the 1925 New York State census in June, Tempie, Joe, Ella, and Frances moved five blocks east, to 72 School Street. Their new neighborhood had a significant minority of blacks amid a majority of Italians, with just a sprinkling of eastern Europeans, Irish, and Greeks.[4] "We were *all* poor in that neighborhood then," said Josephine Attanasio, who knew Ella as a child. "Where I lived was mostly Italian, and where Ella lived was with the black kids down below. . . . It was a little rough. We were just a street above; Ella lived down on School Street in Yonkers, and I had moved to the street above her on Waverly. We were all in the same boat, whites and blacks. I guess people don't realize we were poorer than the poor today. But we all got on, that's the difference. Today it's a different story. On the west side of School Street there were a few vegetable markets. My stepfather worked there. Across from the fruit markets were apartment houses mostly rented by the black families. Toward the south of the street lived the Italians and other nationalities." Annette Miller (formerly Gulliver) lived in the apartment block on School Street with her father, mother, grandmother, and brother Charles.[5] "We all grew up together. I was three or four years older than Ella. My brother Charles was the same age as her. We all lived there at 70, 72, 74 School Street. It was a big apartment house. Ella lived in 72, same as us. I knew her mother, Tempie, very well. All the kids used to play together, and her mother would come home from work and she would stop and talk with us all. She was a very nice lady, a very fine lady who used to work very hard. She came home, cooked her dinners, and kept her house, and would mind her own business."

Annette Miller remembered Ella as shy but very ambitious. Apparently even from a young age she was determined to hit the big time. "She would tell us, 'Someday you're going to see me in the headlines. I'm going to be famous.' We'd all laugh, 'Oh yeah, sure!'"

In September 1926, Ella entered fourth grade at Public School 18 on Park Hill Avenue near Chauncey (the street no longer exists). "She was as thin as a rail at that time," recalled Josephine Attanasio. "I remember having a little spat with her. We had a little fight, and she gave me a bloody nose. She intimidated my younger sister and she came home crying, and I ran down and had it out with her!"

Despite childhood squabbles, Ella seems to have adjusted to the emotional upset of Tempie and William's separation and the introduction of a stepfather. Annette Miller described her as a very jolly person, very happy-go-lucky, while Rose Sarubbi, a young Italian girl who befriended Ella at P.S. 18, said, "When I think of Ella, I think of a very happy girl who loved to dance and sing. Despite her poor upbringing she always remained positive and jolly."[6] Rose Sarubbi lived two blocks away on Linden Street and remained close to Ella for the next six years of their school lives. Even though she was a white girl from a middle-class Italian family, she felt no racial barriers. Ella was a frequent visitor to her home, where she grew fond of Rose's father. She also developed a taste for Italian cooking. "Ella would always come to our home and loved eating my mother's spaghetti," recalled Rose.[7]

Around third grade Ella started to dance, and this grew into an enthusiasm that was much more than a childhood craze. "It was just that she loved to sing and dance," said Annette Miller, "dance more than sing. She was crazy about dancing, her and my brother Charles." In Charles Gulliver, Ella found a kindred spirit. They used to hang out constantly, practicing steps in the streets and urging their older teenage neighbors to show them the latest dances from the ballrooms and dance halls of Harlem. All their spare time was spent dancing, and as Annette Miller recalled, they developed a remarkable empathy. "We'd all play in the streets," she said. "We'd have like an amateur show. We'd all take turns. She would get up and sing and dance—her, my brother, and my nephew would dance, the three of them. It was then that we'd say Ella was going to go places, as a dancer!"

Although bitten by the dancing bug in general, and the swivel-hipped dancer Snake Hips Tucker in particular, Ella also liked to sing. From quite a young age she attended the Bethany African Methodist Episcopal Church. Initially the Bethany AME was situated at 6 Woodworth Avenue, a good half-hour walk north from School Street, but in 1925 the church moved to new premises at Maple Street near Nepperhan Avenue, just around the corner from the north end of School Street. Here Ella attended both the Sunday service and

Sunday school and joined in the usual activities organized by the church for its youngsters, such as hymn singing and Bible class.

The church provided Ella, like countless other children, with her first active participation in formal music-making. Indeed, it is impossible to overstate the role the Church has played, and continues to play, in establishing and shaping a sound musical foundation for young children. The Church has been a training ground for some of jazz's most important vocalists, such as Ethel Waters, Sarah Vaughan, and Dinah Washington, and some of soul music's most vibrant singers, including Sam Cooke, Aretha Franklin, Patti LaBelle, and Whitney Houston.

Annette Miller recalled that all the kids on the block went to each other's churches, so Ella never became particularly involved in Bethany's activities. Even so, certain rudiments of singing would have rooted in her subconscious. Simply by imitating and following the example of her peers—as any child would do in church—she would have become aware of voice projection, intonation, simple harmony and part singing and, not least, rhythmic phrasing. "Gospel singing," wrote the critic Whitney Balliett, "is jazz gussied up and dressed in the clothes of a lamb. Gospel singers use jazz rhythms and inflections, and they often use them outrageously."[8]

In June 1929, Ella completed sixth grade, and in September she attended Benjamin Franklin Junior High School on Poplar Street, which was one of the first junior high schools in the area when it opened in 1925. Josephine Attanasio recalled Ella regularly dancing and singing on the way to school for any of the school kids who might care to stop and watch. "It would be at lunchtime or in the morning when we were outside the building. She would be standing up against the wall, and she would be popping and shaking and swaying, dancing to herself. She wasn't anybody then, just one of the kids from school. She would just be out there, and we'd just hang around watching her. She just smiled all the time, just shaking her shoulders and singing. She had dangling earrings, those big hoops, and broken-down shoes. We were poor in those days."

It is possible that around this time Ella gained a rudimentary knowledge of the piano, perhaps from a short series of lessons arranged by her mother during a period when she had funds. It all helped to build and broaden her musical experience and confidence. She was as yet unaware that she possessed certain gifts, which she would describe in later life as having come "from God," but throughout her childhood and early adolescence, unmarked by any specific commitment to singing, these gifts gradually came to the surface of her consciousness. Neither her family environment nor the educational system offered any specific help to focus such talents, however. Indeed, Yonkers public school archives have no record of Ella singing or even taking part in a school play.[9] Rather, her gifts emerged through her childlike joy in wanting to sing and, especially, dance.

As a child Ella was among the first generation of youngsters to grow up with both the radio and the phonograph. For the first time music for the masses was freely available, revolutionizing popular song and popular singing, changing and transforming people's lives forever. Like the emergent cinema in relation to theater, records and radio brought music within everybody's reach. But just as in the movies, classically trained actors struggled with the medium, so, too, classically trained singers had difficulty handling the popular song convincingly. It ushered in the age of the vernacular performer, but it did something more: It gave the audience a license to dream, to imagine that they, too, could become one of those performers, become famous, become a star.

The radio boom got under way in the early 1920s. There was not much to listen to initially other than whistles and screeches, but Americans took to the radio with gusto and stayed up into the night in the hope of "logging" radio stations hundreds of miles away. The phonograph industry, which had originally brought music into the homes of the well-to-do, was forced to react to the encroachment of radio by producing cheaper hardware; by 1921 it had an annual production of a hundred million records in the United States.

These sales were greatly boosted by the popularity of jazz. Since the end of World War I, young people, keen to break with prewar social conventions and strictures, adopted jazz, the popular music of the day, for their own expressive purposes. In August 1921, the *Ladies' Home Journal* posed the question: "Does jazz put the sin in syncopation?" From now on, popular music would become synonymous with the youth culture as a means of self-expression, offering the opportunity to express an identity, to dream, and to obtain a distance from reality. For girls, particularly, listening to popular music and singing along with the current hits provided an accompaniment to domestic tasks such as baby-sitting and housework. Even girls with minimal musical ability found that during their adolescence music became closely linked to their emotional lives. And still today most women can remember the pop song that was being played at the time of a first romance, the breakup of a relationship, their first kiss, and so on. By 1938, Dorothy Baker was able to observe, through the eyes of Jeff Williams in her novel *Young Man with a Horn*: "The only records that pay for themselves are the new ones with a vocal. People buy them to learn the words. . . . Who buys records is the high school girls."[10] Ella was no different from any other girl of her generation— or succeeding generations—in singing along with the current pop songs. To her it was easy, something she did well, made all the more so because she had the gift of relative pitch.

Relative pitch is different from perfect pitch—a term for the ability, on hearing a note, to identify it by name—in that the possessor of relative pitch knows the precise relationship of every other note to the note sounded and can hit them perfectly in tune. This is far more useful to a singer than perfect pitch, and in the case of Ella Fitzgerald, it developed to the extent that it became greatly admired by both musicians and singers alike. As Mel Tormé observed, "I'm still trying to find an Ella Fitzgerald record where she sings one single note out of tune, and I'm failing. I can find plenty of my own that way, but I can't find an Ella Fitzgerald that way!"

It is also clear that Ella had an ear for imitation. Annette Miller recalls her singing Louis Armstrong's 1929 version of "Ain't Misbehavin'": "It didn't take long for her to catch on to any of those songs." It was this ability to mimic songs so accurately that made Ella stand out among her friends. They loved it and encouraged her. She was big for her age, gawky and self-conscious, and although she had a ready smile, she was a rather plain-looking girl to whom boys never gave a second glance. So when she tried snatches of the current hits on her friends, she discovered that singing was a way of courting popularity, as much among the girls as the boys.

As soon as Ella heard Louis Armstrong, she was attracted to his singing style. Even years after she became an established artist she included an imitation of his vocal style in her act. Armstrong was a crucial early influence. He literally spelled out what a jazz vocal was all about, even though it was through his trumpet playing that he single-handedly turned jazz into a legitimate art form, an achievement that became obscured by his later clowning and hits such as "Hello Dolly" and "Wonderful World."

On every conceivable level—technically, rhythmically, harmonically, and conceptually—Armstrong was laying the foundation of jazz as we now know it. His influence was such that jazz critic and author Gary Giddins could quite rightly point to him as being the only major figure in Western culture who influenced the music of his time equally as instrumentalist and singer.[11] In emulating Armstrong, Ella's musical subconscious was being shaped by the most important vernacular vocalist of the twentieth century. Armstrong's singing has been overshadowed by his instrumental prowess simply because there has been a tendency to assume it was an extension of his instrumental personality. But it was Armstrong's concept of improvisatory liberty with lyrics, the way he made them *swing*, and his variety of attack and inflection that had a profound effect on both jazz and popular singing of the day.

Armstrong broke the rhythmic straitjacket that was based on European precedent by singing as he played and playing as he sang. If a word could not be broken down into the rhythmic and melodic patterns he had in mind, he simply substituted an onomatopoeic equivalent, and in so doing made scat a household word. At the time Ella was imitating Armstrong, there was no one else in jazz or popular music who could make the lyrics of a song leap off the printed page to assume a rhythmic vitality of their own.

As Ella kept listening and learning, the burgeoning art of popular singing gathered momentum; while Armstrong's inimitable style was the first to make an impression on her, she was drawn in turn to the singing of Bing Crosby and the Boswell Sisters, and to their lead singer, Connee Boswell, in particular. "She was tops at the time," said Ella in 1988. "I was attracted to her immediately. My mother brought home one of her records, and I fell in love with it. I tried so hard to sound just like her."[12]

By listening carefully and imitating, Ella was instinctively following the method by which all young musicians become proficient in jazz. Just as the young composer learns much about his craft by listening to music while following the score, the aspiring jazz musician learns the nomenclature of his craft by committing to memory the work of its master musicians. Studying their solos and style provides a deep understanding of how jazz musicians work and how they approach the process of improvisation. Once technique and tone are in place, the best musicians emerge from their apprenticeship with a mixture of their mentor's ideas, and experiment with their own until finally the very best manage to shed assimilated influences and develop their own individual voice.

In this way Ella Fitzgerald, attracted to the singing style of the Boswell Sisters, gradually absorbed their style from the radio and from records until she found that she could sing non-Boswell material in the Boswell manner; by a mixture of God-given ability and circumstance she was unwittingly providing herself with a foundation from which to advance her career as a singer. In jazz and popular music at that time there could hardly have been a better choice for a role model than the Boswells; author Will Friedwald has described them as the greatest of all jazz vocal groups.[13]

The Boswell Sisters grew up in New Orleans. Martha and Connee were born in Kansas City in 1905 and 1907, respectively, and Helvetia (Vet) in Birmingham, Alabama, in 1911. They came from an exceptionally musical middle-class family; all three girls learned to play several instruments to a high level of proficiency, and all of them performed at some time with the New Orleans Philharmonic. But they became captivated by jazz and began working out three-part vocal arrangements that impressed some of the top New Orleans jazz musicians, including Tony Parenti and jazz legend Emmett Hardy. It was Hardy who encouraged the sisters to pursue a career as a vocal group after they won a talent contest in 1925. They made a few early recordings, toured in vaudeville, appeared from time to time on the radio, and were finally offered a major label deal by Brunswick Records, then home to the biggest stars of the day, when they arrived in New York in 1931 to appear at the Paramount Theatre.

Their first Brunswick release was "Wha' Dja Do to Me?" coupled with "When I Take My Sugar to Tea." It caused a sensation. The Boswells' vocal arrangements, usually by Connee, the group's lead singer, were minor miracles of recomposition. Connee was not only one of the outstanding singers of the 1930s, she was also, along with pianist Mary Lou Williams, among the first important women composers and arrangers in jazz. In the space of a three-minute arrangement she might completely recast a tune by altering its harmonic framework, change its rhythmic characteristics with up to six or seven tempo changes, insert completely new interludes of her own, and introduce an infinite number of highly original vocal devices that might include the "instrumental" use of voices, scat singing, and elements of blues and gospel music. The Boswells were so far ahead of their time that the breakthrough quality of their art is still apparent from their recordings today.

The Boswells became extremely popular in the early 1930s; in 1931 they could be heard on coast-to-coast radio on Fleischmann's Yeast Hour; by 1932 they alternated with Arthur Tracy in a prime-time radio slot on the Chesterfield "Music That Satisfies" show, and followed this by a move to the Woodbury Program where they joined the biggest name in popular music, Bing Crosby, then also with Brunswick Records. With their frequent radio shows and regular record releases, the young Ella Fitzgerald would have had plenty of opportunity to hear them and latch on to their style.

Ella drew heavily on the Boswells' rhythmic impetus, a hard, swinging sound that stayed with her throughout her career and grew more pronounced as she got older. The modern, swinging feel of Connee Boswell's singing translated well into her arrangements, and Ella clearly picked up on this from numbers such as "Heebie Jeebies," "Shout, Sister, Shout," "Hand Me Down My Walking Cane," and, as composer, author, and educator Gunther Schuller noted,[14] the quite remarkable "Everybody Loves My Baby." Significantly, Ella was not the only one who caught on to the Boswells' style; other singers were influenced by it, too, including Mildred Bailey, Peggy Lee, and Lee Wiley.

Although the Boswell Sisters' memory was reawakened during the 1980s by groups such as the Pfister Sisters, Jazz Babies, and the Sweet Hots, among others, plus the 1981 off-Broadway musical *Heebie Jeebies* which featured their music, their standing in jazz today remains curiously equivocal. Ella, however, was in no doubt about their significance: "When I was a girl, I listened to records by all the singers, white and black, and I know that Connee Boswell was doing things that no one else was doing at the time. You don't have to take my word for it. Just check the recordings and hear for yourself."[15]

CHAPTER TWO

1931–1935

She always knew she was going to be someone someday because she kept on saying, "I want to do something. I want to make something of myself." And she did.

CHARLES GULLIVER

ELLA'S SCHOOL RECORDS confirm she was an excellent student. She was bright, and she had a retentive memory. Her education was interrupted, so the records say, through illness during her last years at Benjamin Franklin Junior High School.[1] Occasionally there was live music in the neighborhood, and according to Annette Miller, Ella was not above playing hookey. In later years Ella herself recalled how she was captivated by the singer Dolly Dawn with the George Hall Orchestra;[2] her glamorous stage presence left an indelible impression on the young teenager and her friends when the orchestra appeared in Yonkers. Josephine Attanasio recalled their performances at the Armory on North Broadway and at Columbus Hall on Waverly as big events in the locality.

At this stage in her life Ella saw her future as a dancer. She listened to records and the radio, and she could imitate her favorites, such as the Boswell Sisters, Louis Armstrong, and Bing Crosby, and could sing from memory many of the popular hits of the day. It was something that came easily to her. But she had her heart set on dancing. "She didn't sing so much at all then, really," said Charles Gulliver, "but she loved to dance. She was some dancer, oh yeah! She was a terrific dancer!"

As they got older, Charles and Ella used to sneak off to the Savoy Ballroom in Harlem to pick up the latest steps. "We used to go down to one of the dance halls in New York a lot called the Savoy," said Gulliver. "We'd learn all the latest dances. Sometimes we'd go together. We took the trolley car to the subway station, then the subway to New York, and we come out at 125th Street. . . . You could go almost anywhere, to all those clubs and the Savoy. I'd come back and teach all the kids the steps. I was like a dance teacher. I taught them all the latest steps, the Shuffle Off to Buffalo, the types of dances they were doing in those days. Then Ella and I, we'd be out there on the street corner just practicing different steps, and people would stand there and watch us."

By the time they were fifteen they began getting dance jobs in the clubs around Yonkers. "I had taught Ella a dance that was very popular in those days, the Susie Q. Out of the Susie Q we developed a routine, and we went out and did one-night stands. We went out and did dancing and got paid for it at little clubs. Different organizations would give a dance on a Saturday night, and you'd pay maybe a dollar or seventy-five cents to get in, and they'd have entertainment. They might have somebody who could sing, somebody who could dance, somebody who played an instrument or a comedian. We danced, and that's what we did to earn a few pennies."

Then, without warning in early 1932, the hardworking Tempie had a heart attack and died suddenly. She was just thirty-eight. Ella has claimed that her mother died from injuries sustained when trying to save a child from being run down by a car.[3] Neither Charles Gulliver nor Annette Miller has any knowledge of this. They did confirm, however, that Ella single-mindedly continued her small dancing jobs with Charles. "Ella was still young when her mother died," said Annette Miller. "She was always around my brother Charlie." Their dancing excursions had become part business, mostly pleasure.

One night not too long after Tempie's death, they got home late. "We were fifteen," recalled Charles Gulliver. "We weren't supposed to be going or be out late. But I remember her stepfather punishing her for being out at one of these dances. He made her stay in the house for quite a while for staying out at that particular time." But that was not all. Rumor was spreading of Joe's ill treatment of his stepdaughter: "He wasn't taking good care of her" was how Charles Gulliver put it.[4] It is difficult not to rule out the possibility that Ella was a victim of child abuse, but whatever happened in Joe Da Silva's household, it was sufficient for Tempie's sister, Virginia, to step in abruptly and take Ella into her own family. "She went with her aunt and Georgie [Ella's cousin]. They lived in Harlem," said Annette Miller. "We never saw much of her after that. She used to come back to Yonkers sometimes on the weekend to see everybody, but we sort of lost touch." Ella's school records show that she left Benjamin Franklin Junior High on April 21, 1932: "Family moved to NYC."[5]

At Virginia's home on West 145th Street, Ella became close to her cousin Georgiana, who in later years became her traveling companion and wardrobe mistress. She also remained in close touch with her half-sister Frances, and it was mainly to see her that she returned to Yonkers. Those visits ceased, however, when Joe died fairly soon after Tempie, also from a heart attack, and Frances joined Ella in Virginia's home.

The next two years were difficult ones for Ella. She found herself competing for Virginia's affection, and she became fractious, concealing her natural self-consciousness with petulance and aggression. Ella dropped out of school, keeping house when her aunt was at work and running numbers—"to make extra money," she explained later in life.[6] The Mafia-run numbers racket, an illegal lottery, had been ubiquitous in Harlem and the adjacent black communities since the 1920s. Originally it was a chance for poor blacks, at the cost of only a penny, a nickel, a dime, a quarter, or half a dollar, to have their pockets suddenly filled with cash. After the stock market crash of 1929, poverty extended to millions of whites as well, and the "policy racket" quickly spread to every poor neighborhood in the country. By 1933 it was estimated that in New York City alone the racket was grossing $100,000,000 a year. It was run along ruthless lines, with commissions and salaries paid to operators who risked violent summary justice if impropriety with the proceeds was even so much as suspected.

For a while Ella also worked as a lookout for a "sporting house," knocking on the door to let the women inside know if the police were around.[7] Skirting the fringes of the law and persistently absent from school, she was eventually caught by the authorities. "She went to a kids' school on the Hudson River before she went out onto the streets in Harlem," said Charles Linton, who in a few months' time would have a crucial role in Ella's career.

Ella was sent to Public School 49, which had formerly been the Colored Orphan Asylum at Riverdale-on-Hudson until the New York City Board of Education took it over in February 1911.[8] Founded by two Quaker women in 1836 as the Association for the Benefit of Colored Children Institute and Foster Home, it was originally located in a cottage on West Twelfth Street near Sixth Avenue. After two moves the orphanage bought a tract of land in Riverdale overlooking the Hudson River in 1905, and the campus at 5901 Palisade Avenue, at West 261st Street, finally opened on June 27, 1907. In 1911, Dr. Mason Pitman, a physician and psychiatrist, took over the administration, and shortly afterward the name was changed to the Riverdale Children's Association. Almost from the start Ella disliked Dr. Pitman's regime intensely. Determined to make her way in show business, she ran away in the fall of 1934, never to return. And although in later years many eminent performers played at fundraisers for the association, including Duke Ellington, Ella's bitter memories were such that she never wanted anything to do with the place again, refusing to even speak about her experiences.

Unable to return to her aunt's, where the authorities could trace her, Ella now had to make her own way in the world and was forced on hard times. She hung out on Seventh Avenue in the area known as "Black Broadway," between 130th and 140th streets. Here, dancers, jugglers, novelty acts, and all kinds of street entertainment abounded during the Depression years. She earned tips and got by as best she could. Ella tells of deciding along with two friends, Frances and Doris, to put their names in for one of the talent auditions that were in vogue in Harlem at the time. Theoretically it was possible to enter a talent contest every night of the week at a major theater such as the Regent (116th Street) or Loew's Victoria (125th Street), or at clubs and vaudeville houses, following the success of the Wednesday night auditions at the Lafayette Theatre, at Seventh Avenue and 131st Street.

Ella drew the short straw. She decided to try her luck at the Apollo Theater, situated at 253 West 125th Street. The Apollo had instituted its own Wednesday Amateur Night in January 1934, with Ralph Cooper as the master of ceremonies, following his move from the Lafayette. The Apollo had at one time been Hurtig & Seamons Burlesque Theatre, where white men watched white women strip down to body stockings; it was closed down in 1932 by then-Congressman Fiorello La Guardia. It was the first theater to break the 125th Street color barrier when, under Sidney Cohen's ownership and Morris Sussman's management, it reopened on January 26, 1934, as a Negro vaudeville theater.

In Harlem at 125th Street, Seventh Avenue hit an anomaly: an all-white neighborhood where segregation was practiced harshly. Today the area is Harlem's main street, but at that time it was a shopping center for the mostly Irish residents of neighborhoods surrounding Columbia University, Barnard College, and City College. When the Apollo opened, it was the first theater to offer live entertainment for black audiences on 125th Street.

When Ralph Cooper got the go-ahead for the Amateur Night from Morris Sussman, he immediately began making announcements at the end of the theater's other presentations. He invited members of the audience to test their own talents or to get their friends to try their luck. Word soon spread, helped by Sussman's advertisements in the local press for the theater's regular productions which now included a brief note at the bottom announcing "Wednesday Night: Ralph Cooper's Amateur Night in Harlem."

Cooper's Apollo Amateur Night was different from all the others in Harlem. Competitors who had not been booed off or removed by the "Official Executioner" were brought back onstage at the end. Each act would take a bow, and the one receiving the biggest response was the winner. And, as Ralph Cooper described it, "we decided that the winners would be awarded something better than prize money—further opportunity. Amateur Night winners would be given a week's engagement at the Apollo Theater. Someone who came onstage Wednesday night and won would appear in the next week's show."[9]

Potential contestants were required to attend the Monday auditions before appearing on the Apollo stage the following Wednesday. Here, keys were set for singers, suitable music was agreed upon for the dancers and other specialty acts, and a final running order was decided. The contestants who survived this initial screening process won cash prizes of up to $10. They then returned on Wednesday night, assembling in the Green Room beneath the stage, nervously waiting for midnight when the band struck up the Amateur Night theme "I May Be Wrong" and Ralph Cooper called on each contestant in turn to perform and broadcast over Radio WMCA.

With all the publicity and interest this new talent showcase generated, it was hardly surprising that it attracted the ambitious young Ella Fitzgerald. In its press advertisements, the Apollo boasted "High Fidelity RCA sound equipment, the same used by Radio City Music Hall and an innovation in public address systems,"[10] which meant that at the time the Apollo had one of the finest sound systems in the world. There could scarcely have been a better venue for a first public appearance, but for a nervous young girl who had spent the last few months on the streets, the glamour and bright lights must have been disorienting. Indeed, for decades artists have spoken of how nerve-racking an appearance at the Apollo Theater can be. Its audiences are forthright in their shared belief of what constitutes a good performance. Even established artists are not immune to the audience's wrath if it suspects a below-par performance. For an amateur artist waiting in the wings the tension must have been unbearable.

Ella made her stage debut at the Apollo on Wednesday, November 21, 1934, and was among the first contestants in what subsequently became a Harlem tradition that survived into the 1990s. Her intention had been to perform as a dancer, but at the Monday audition she discovered she was in competition with the Edwards Sisters, a hot dance duo currently making a big name for themselves after being trained by their father, himself a professional dancer.[11] "When I got the call to audition at the Apollo, I was very surprised because there were two sisters who were the greatest dancers at that time, and they were closing the show," said Ella later.[12] Insecure and wearing cast-off clothing and men's boots, she found the presence of the Edwards Sisters demoralizing as much for their professional appearance in sequined dresses and proper dancing pumps as for their dancing ability. When asked to perform her dance routine, Ella suddenly changed her mind and entered as a singer.

It was hardly surprising that when Ella walked onstage, she was, according to emcee Ralph Cooper, "jumpy and unnerved." When she started to sing, her voice cracked, and sensing the audience beginning to "rumble," Cooper stopped her singing, allowed her to compose herself, and started her again.[13] Now in control, and in spite of her appearance, she created such an impression that she went on to win.

Ella's musical accompaniment was provided by the Benny Carter Orchestra, although Carter himself was watching the show from the wings. It was the theater's policy to use whatever big-name orchestra was booked into the theater that week. "That way," recalled Cooper, "the amateurs not only got to perform before a sophisticated audience, they had the added treat of singing onstage with the Count Basie Orchestra or Jimmie Lunceford's band or Duke Ellington's or Louis Armstrong's."[14]

Carter had taken most of the musicians from Fletcher Henderson's great "Decca" orchestra with him into the Apollo that week since Fletcher's band had broken up because of lack of work. The Apollo booking was Carter's first with this new band, the *New York Age* reporting: "Benny Carter with his red-hot jazz band playing fast, famous, and noisy tunes—especially noise."[15] Carter subsequently went out on the road to tour around Detroit, but his band ultimately folded during the Depression when bookings became hard to come by.

Countless books and magazine and newspaper articles over the years have stated that Ella sang two Connee Boswell numbers, "The Object of My Affection" and "Judy," when she entered the Apollo talent show. According to discographer Brian Rust,[16] however, these songs had no association with Connee Boswell at the time of Ella's audition. Rust points out that the earliest recording of "Object of My

Affection" was not until November 1934, so no commercial recording of the song could have existed at the time of Ella's debut, and in any event, it was not until December 1934 that the Boswell Sisters recorded it. In addition, Rust also says that neither the Boswell Sisters nor Connee Boswell herself ever recorded "Judy."

Clearly, to have used these songs on November 21, 1934, Ella Fitzgerald would have had to pick them up from somewhere, either on the radio or, as musicologist Phil Schaap suggested, in a movie theater. "In those days movie houses had live entertainment as well as films, so for a few nickels you could stay in a movie house for maybe ten hours if you wanted to. They had their own records which they played between features, but they weren't allowed to play regular 78s, so the movie theaters would get a regular transcription service. There was also a thing called 'Hits of the Week.' They still survive—laminated cardboard and plastic records for theaters to play. So in a theater you might remember a song even though there's no documentation of it. If you're in a theater all day, you hear this song like thirty-seven times, and it stays in your mind forever!" And it is quite possible that while living on the streets, Ella sought refuge in movie houses from time to time, her admission paid from tips earned by dancing in the street.

However she picked up these songs, it now seems clear that, using her gift for mimicry, she sang them in the manner of Connee Boswell, her favorite singer. Indeed, Ella herself has confirmed that she tried to sing like Connee Boswell at the Apollo Amateur Night,[17] and Benny Carter, who was watching from the wings, is sure she sang "Object of My Affection" and "Judy." "I heard her," he recalled. "My orchestra was playing at the Apollo, and the amateur show followed us."[18] He was particularly struck by Ella's emulation of Connee Boswell: "As a matter of fact, I even likened her approach to Connee Boswell," he confirmed in 1991.

To Ella's delight and surprise, she brought the house down. When she was called onstage at the end, the roar of the crowd made it clear she was the winner. But she was never given the prize of a week's work: "I was promised a week at the Apollo, but that never came through," she told writer Joe Smith.[19] Charles Linton explained why: "She had won first prize. Now Ralph Cooper should have given her the week following the first prize, it should have been arranged. . . . But she lived in such a way that Ralph wouldn't give it to her . . . how she was dressed and everything that goes with not being clean because she didn't have a place to live." The theater was beginning to attract the top movie, radio, and stage stars of the day in its audience, including Bob Hope, Joan Crawford, and Betty Grable, and image counted.

However, Benny Carter was impressed by her talent, and took her for an audition with his former boss, bandleader Fletcher Henderson, at his house on "Striver's Row," West 138th Street. "I remember the occasion very well," confirmed Carter. But Henderson was immediately put off by Ella's appearance. Later the trumpeter Mouse Randolph corroborated the story, explaining why Ella was never offered a job: "Fletcher was high on looks at that time."[20] Ella had to return to her life on 125th Street. "After she won first prize," said Charles Linton, "I guess, like some of the old dancers who were by now walking around. . . . They lived wherever they could."

In later years Ella's press office circulated a story suggesting that during this period she auditioned successfully for Arthur Tracy's popular radio spot on Chesterfield's "Music That Satisfies." Tracy, known as the Street Singer, had a radio audience of millions and a huge hit record, "Marta (Rambling Rose of the Wildwood)." The story suggests that only the death of Ella's mother prevented her from appearing on the show since Ella could not sign the contract as a minor. But Tempie had died in early 1932, and Ella's Aunt Virginia could have signed *in loco parentis.*

The issue became a piece of show biz apocrypha that was finally resolved by Tracy himself in 1991: "Ralph Wonders, who was the manager of the artists bureau of CBS, had come to me and said, 'Arthur, I'd like to put on so-and-so.' I could run through a list of names and put on so-and-so because my program was well attended. That would be a beautiful introduction for new artists, and of course they would be introduced by me, the Street Singer, which was of much more value. I refused everyone. I never had anyone on with me. I refused him for no reason other than I wanted to prove to myself I could go solo, all through the years."

In June 1934, Leo Brecker and Frank Schiffman took over the management of the Harlem Opera House at 211 West 125th Street after a dispute with the American Federation of Musicians (the musicians' union) had prevented stage shows for a number of weeks. Brecker and Schiffman already owned the Lafayette Theatre, which had suffered a considerable loss of business during the six months the Apollo had been open. They had been forced to reduce the admission price and to cut back on production costs to such an extent that newspaper reviewers took to ridiculing the once grand theater for putting on mediocre entertainment that was an insult to the "scattered few."[21]

In December 1934 the Lafayette was finally forced to discontinue stage shows and become a movie theater, but between Ella's November Apollo debut and the winding up of stage presentations the following month, she appeared on one of the final amateur nights. It was not an auspicious evening for Ella. Jazz critic Leonard Feather says she was booed off the stage.[22] Ella has also referred specifically to the Lafayette as the place where she was unceremoniously dispatched by the crowd when she got lost singing—and here there is a suggestion of a press agent's pen—"Lost in a Fog."[23]

When Brecker and Schiffman acquired the Harlem Opera House, a new front opened in the Harlem theater wars; their intention was to offer the Apollo direct competition by producing shows of similar style and content to those being offered with such success just half a block away. Ralph Cooper said Brecker and Schiffman tried to copy everything the Apollo did, even down to using similar press advertising.[24] With the success of the Apollo's Wednesday amateur night, the Harlem Opera House management soon instituted its own Tuesday amateur night during the fall of 1934, again copying the Apollo by offering a week's work rather than a cash prize.

During December, Ella began hanging around the Harlem Opera House after putting in an entry for its amateur night. "I used to tell her to come down there Thursday afternoon when the band rehearsed, and I'd introduce her to the bandleader," said Tom Whaley,[25] who was then the theater's music director. Although she never took him up on the offer, she was called for the "Amateur Hour" at the end of January 1935. Again she won first prize. Journalist Bob Bach, who was in the audience that night, recalled: "The song was 'Judy.' The theater went wild, and Ella won the contest and with it a week's engagement at the theater."[26]

Her achievement was noted in the *New York Age*. In listing the forthcoming acts to appear at the Harlem Opera House, the reviewer referred to "Ella Fitzgerald, the last name a prize winner at a recent audition contest at the Harlem Opera House."[27] It was her first mention in the press.

This time Ella's prize of a week's work was honored, and she was booked for the week commencing Friday, February 15, 1935, along with the Tiny Bradshaw Band, Mae Alix, and others; her name appeared in small print on a Harlem Opera House poster announcing the acts for that week. Trumpeter Otis Johnson was in Bradshaw's band at the time and recalls the week vividly. Apparently Ella caused a sensation but even so was not paid by the Harlem Opera House.[28] This could well have been because the autocratic Frank Schiffman insisted on suitable clothing and deducted the cost from her pay. In later years Ella's press office came up with a story of how the chorus line chipped in to pay for a dress, but this stretches credibility; we are talking about the Depression, after all. The hardworking chorus line would have had no interest in yet another prizewinner, the lowest of the low in the theater pecking order.

It is generally assumed that Ella made the rounds of talent showcases at this time, but there is a remarkable absence of firsthand witnesses to substantiate this, other than her appearances at the Apollo and at the Harlem Opera House and her own recollection of her unsuccessful entry in the Lafayette Theatre's talent night.

Significantly, Ella's early career contrasts markedly with the degree of corroboration that exists for singer Billie Holiday's early struggle for recognition. Born in 1915, Holiday was a young hopeful who had started to make her way just a couple of years before Ella. Yet when Ella Fitzgerald first gained public recognition, it seemed as if she had come from nowhere, illustrated by an incident from jazz historian John Chilton's archives. Trombonist Benny Morton, present on Ella's record date for Teddy Wilson in early 1936, was part of a small backing group that included Frankie Newton on trumpet. Morton clearly recalled Newton walking into the studio on the day of the recording session and, on seeing Ella, doing a double take and asking him, "Who the hell's she?"

Newton was surprised because aspiring musicians and singers normally did the rounds of talent showcases, clubs, and after-hours spots to sit in with established musicians. This was known as "paying dues." It provided both valuable on-the-job training and a form of self-advertisement, a way of building a reputation that might attract a potential employer such as a bandleader or club owner. Newton, a *bon viveur* and habitué of these places, prided himself on his knowledge of the Harlem music scene and of any up-and-coming talent. He had never heard of Ella Fitzgerald.[29]

The reality was that Ella's age, her gauche appearance, and the way she was living conspired to prevent her from getting work. "She hadn't had a bath and smelled like it could have been a year. This is fact, meaning she had no job *anyplace*," said Charles Linton. "You ask how did she eat. She lived with people she talked to, and she ate with them, and she slept wherever she could—that's how she was living."

In the end it was Ella's remarkable voice that enabled her to step off the streets into the big time in one stride. It needed an incredible stroke of luck—and that, in February 1935, was just around the corner. "I don't know how to say this," observed singer Sylvia Syms, a contemporary of both Ella and Billie Holiday, who herself had come up the hard way through the Harlem clubs. "Everybody had to go out there and really stick their nose to the grindstone, as it were, to get that big break. But Ella was, from the very beginning, blessed."

1935

Charlie Linton is the one who got Ella Fitzgerald with
Chick Webb.

RAM RAMIREZ[1]

IN EARLY 1935 the Chick Webb band was continuing a seemingly
unending round of Harlem's main theaters and dance halls. In January
and February they had played two revues for the Lafayette, and on
March 1 were due to head the bill at the Harlem Opera House for a
week. After years of scuffling, Webb had built a reputation as one of
the top bandleaders in Harlem. But even so, he still remained relatively
unknown to audiences below 125th Street. Despite nine years of striv-
ing, a breakthrough to a national audience, such as Duke Ellington and
Cab Calloway had achieved, seemed as far away as ever. But Webb was
undaunted. An immensely proud and determined man, he never for a
moment doubted he would make the big time, even though he was
temperamentally unsuited to the role of leading a band.

Throughout his life Webb had battled to overcome terrible physical handicaps. He was, as *Down Beat* magazine described him in 1939,
"deformed, dwarfish, and delicate."[2] During the last four years of his
life he endured terrible pain through the steadily debilitating effects
of tuberculosis of the spine. Yet despite such personal adversity, he
was regarded by his contemporaries as the finest drummer in jazz.
Webb was both an inspirational player and an innovator. He linked
bass drum patterns played with his right foot to snare drum and tom-
tom figures played with his hands, and in so doing pointed the way to
modern jazz drumming and the experiments of Kenny Clarke and
Max Roach. He also used accents and fills to a greater extent than had
been the custom in jazz. "To my knowledge," said Garvin Bushell,
who played alongside Webb from 1937 to 1939, "Chick was the first
drummer that became publicly known to drum the arrangement."[3]

But during that warm spring of 1935, Webb was frustrated and impatient, willing to try anything that might increase his popularity. Although he didn't realize it at the time, a young girl who had asked for his autograph just a few months earlier, when the snow was on the ground, was going to play a remarkable role in moving his career out of the doldrums and establishing the Chick Webb Orchestra as one of the nation's top big bands. That young girl was Ella Fitzgerald.

William "Chick" Webb was born in Baltimore in 1909, the youngest of three children who were raised in very poor circumstances. By nine he had left school and was earning his living selling newspapers. Webb was captivated by the drums after seeing a parade band every Sunday on the way to church. By the time he was ten he had his own drum set and was soon playing alongside established semiprofessional musicians. "All he knew is that when he heard music he played," said Alan Paley, a drummer who knew Webb well in the thirties. "He couldn't read a thing. Untrained, he learned by playing, listening, and allowing his great talent to grow."[4]

Webb arrived on the New York music scene when he was sixteen, after gaining experience in his hometown working with the Jazzola Band on excursion boats crossing the Chesapeake Bay. Despite his youth, he impressed a circle of young up-and-coming New York musicians, including Duke Ellington, Benny Carter, Coleman Hawkins, and trumpeter Bobby Stark. After much freelancing and a job with the Edgar Dowdell Orchestra, he graduated from sideman to bandleader in 1926. He was just seventeen. It was a step he took with great reluctance and only at the behest of Duke Ellington. Ellington had been offered a booking at the Black Bottom Club after the resident band led by Harry Cooper suddenly departed for a more lucrative engagement elsewhere. Ellington, committed at the time to the Kentucky Club, responded by contracting a five-piece band under Webb's nominal leadership.

The job paid $200 a week, from which Ellington took $30 as a commission fee, and it lasted five months. When it was over, Ellington gave Webb another booking at the Paddock Club below Earl Carroll's Theatre on Seventh Avenue at Fiftieth Street. Here they caused a minor sensation, attracting celebrities such as bandleader Paul Whiteman. Their popularity enabled them to expand to an eight-piece band, but they suddenly found themselves out of work at the end of 1926 when a fire closed the club down—a dramatic incident in which Webb's pianist carried out a girl dancer who had fainted.

Despite his small but growing reputation, Webb was still a young man and very green, remaining uncomfortable in the role of band-leader. When offered work in January 1927 by Jay Faggen of the Savoy Ballroom, he hesitated. It took much persuasion by his cousin, alto saxophonist Johnny Hodges who was then playing in his band, to make him accept. The band members were offered $67.50 each per week and Webb $70 as leader. On seeing Webb's surprise at being offered more than his men, the management took advantage of his naïveté, telling him not to be such a "wise guy" by taking more than he was entitled to. Webb apologized and accepted $67.50.

This incident marked the beginning of Webb's enduring relation-ship with the Savoy, a second-story ballroom that stretched the length of the block between 140th and 141st streets on the east side of Lenox Avenue. He was offered a twelve-month contract for his eight-piece band, now called Chick Webb and His Harlem Stompers. It was a measure of his rising stature as a bandleader that the eighteen-year-old held his own in what was billed as a "Battle of Jazz" at the Savoy Ballroom on Sunday, May 15, 1927. Webb's outfit was pitted against three top bands of the day: Fletcher Henderson, Fess Williams, and King Oliver. The *Amsterdam News* stated that "thou-sands [were] unable to gain admittance." It seems Webb's little combo was by no means outclassed by the big guns: The *News* reporter said it was "difficult to determine who won this historic bat-tle of music."[5]

When the Savoy contract expired, Webb spent a brief period on the road, and on his return he asked the Savoy management to expand the band. The Savoy refused, so he took a residency with two more musicians at the Rose Danceland at 125th Street and Seventh Avenue from the end of December 1927. On Sunday, May 6, 1928, he was involved in another battle of bands at the Savoy, this time a six-header dubbed a "Jazz War" with Webb, Lloyd Scott, Alex Jackson, Charlie Johnson, Fess Williams, and Fletcher Henderson. "Chick had such amazing musicians in his band and they played with so much feeling and fervor that they swung the crowd right over to them, astounding everybody," reported *Down Beat* a few years later."[6]

While at Danceland, Webb's naïveté was again exposed when he was approached with a deal to play several months of vaudeville. Rose Danceland offered Webb a considerable raise if he stayed, but he went on the road. It was a "phony" deal, possibly to get a rival bandleader the Danceland job. Within weeks Webb and his musicians were out of work. The Danceland suffered a considerable loss in turnover when he left, and the management was so incensed with Webb that they told him he would never work there again.

Since the Webb band was unemployed, bandleader Fletcher Henderson approached Webb to "borrow" two of his musicians, including Webb's key trumpeter, Bobby Stark. Webb agreed, with the proviso that they return for an upcoming audition at the Arcadia Ballroom. Needless to say, when the audition came around, Henderson made Stark an offer he couldn't refuse, and without his key brassman, Webb failed to land the job—another lesson for the greenhorn bandleader.

During this period of inactivity he continued to play one-night stands but desperately needed a residency to keep his band together. A measure of the band's desperation came when trumpeter Cootie Williams, then part of Webb's struggling band, visited the Alhambra Ballroom one night in October 1928. He publicly belittled the resident band led by George DeLeon in an attempt to induce the management to give Webb the job, saying, "A good orchestra was in the street and a ham-fat bunch working."[7] DeLeon brought Webb and Williams before the musicians' union, which saw to it that the two would never work together again. The union's Local 802 has a bylaw forbidding its members "to commit any act tending to injure the reputation of a fellow member in his or her calling as a musician."

By now Webb was becoming quite intense about his ambitions as a bandleader and was getting a reputation for spotting and developing talent. He declined offers from Duke Ellington and Fletcher Henderson to join their bands and instead stayed with a nucleus of musicians who were all desperate for work and who had thrown in their lot with him, rehearsing regularly and hoping for that elusive break. "For months on end the group endured starvation regimens. Relying on occasional gigs to pay the rent, they would hole up in one room and refuse to separate," said Helen Oakley-Dance, who would later act as press agent for Webb.[8]

A change in Webb's fortunes came when he signed with the Moe Gale office, then known as Consolidated Radio Artists at the RKO Building, 48 West Forty-eighth Street, in late 1929. Gale, one of the stockholders in the Savoy Ballroom, would now play a key role in shaping Webb's career that had so far been marked by a spectacular lack of business acumen.

Even so, Duke Ellington, then resident at the Cotton Club, continued to give his young friend work. From time to time Ellington undertook touring engagements outside the club, and Webb substituted for him in July 1929, after making his recording debut the previous month as "The Jungle Band" for Brunswick. It is hardly surprising, therefore, that his ten-piece band played in a style evoking Ellington's then current "jungle" sound—indeed, one side, a twelve-bar blues, is called "Jungle Mama." Webb's slick cymbal breaks feature on "Dog Bottom," an uptempo romp also indebted to the Duke's "jungle" style.

Under Gale's management, Webb was booked into the swanky downtown Roseland Ballroom on Broadway at Fifty-second Street for an engagement at $1,500 a week, which was big money in 1929. Playing for the all-white clientele, they appeared there regularly over the following two years. But Webb still got the call from the Savoy when they had their Battle of the Bands. On May 14, 1930, they ran their most ambitious promotion to date, heralded somewhat incongruously as the "Battle of 1812." Along with Webb, the lineup included Duke Ellington, Fletcher Henderson, Cab Calloway, Cecil Scott, and Lockwood Lewis. This was fast company. Ellington, Henderson, and Calloway were the top black bands in New York.

But Webb still remained naïve in his personal relationships, exhibiting a degree of trust in his sidemen that didn't allow for their putting business before friendship. At the end of March 1931, while at the Roseland where they had been for several months, the alto saxophonist Benny Carter joined the Webb band in an unusual swap with bandleader Fletcher Henderson. "Fletcher Henderson released his first sax and trombone player, Chick Webb ... released his first sax and trombone player," reported the *New York Age*. "Fletcher hired the two men from Chick's band, and Chick took Fletcher's two men. None of the musicians lost a day's work, and both principals are satisfied and think their orchestra is strengthened by this unprecedented incident."[9]

Carter recorded three sides for Vocalion with the Webb band, now consisting of twelve pieces, at the end of March. Once again a trademark sound, so important in making a breakthrough with the public, remained beyond Webb's grasp. Gale remained suspicious of Carter's intentions, however, and advised Webb to get rid of him. Webb, always loyal to his men, refused. Then, in August 1931, Carter abruptly left to join the Detroit-based McKinney's Cotton Pickers, taking alto saxophonist Hilton Jefferson with him. The loss of two key figures of the stature of Carter and Jefferson tore the heart out of Webb's band. It took a while for Webb to shake the band down with new musicians, at which point Gale booked him into the Savoy again. By October 1932, Webb was back on course, setting an attendance record of forty-six hundred at a breakfast dance there, along with the Cab Calloway and Fletcher Henderson bands.[10]

Once again Webb had gathered a talented group of musicians around him, and by 1933 he had assembled another powerful lineup that included, among those with whom he would break into the big time, Taft Jordan on trumpet, Sandy Williams on trombone, and saxophonist Edgar Sampson. Also joining them in 1933 was trumpet player Mario Bauza, a vastly experienced musician who had previously played woodwinds in the Havana Symphony Orchestra before emigrating to New York. Initially Bauza had difficulty adjusting to the conventions of jazz phrasing. Even though Webb couldn't read music, he memorized every arrangement the band played. He took his promising young trumpeter aside and rehearsed him separately until he felt comfortable phrasing in the jazz idiom.

Although the band recorded for Columbia that year and again in 1934 as "Chick Webb's Savoy Orchestra," the results still did not square with its reputation in live performance, where it was taking on all comers at the Savoy's battle of the bands. Webb was clearly aware, however, that his band lacked a specific musical identity, and so around this time, between 1933 and 1934, he began investing heavily in new orchestrations. His saxophonist, Edgar Sampson, provided some key charts, while others came from established arrangers such as Benny Carter, Charlie Dixon, and Don Redman. But his heaviest investment was in about fifty arrangements from George Bassman, a white arranger who had worked for Fletcher Henderson. "Sometimes he didn't have room rent because he had to pay arrangers—the top guys—to write for him," said Bauza.[11]

Yet even though Webb had still not defined the personality of his band on record, he could justifiably claim to be one of the most popular bandleaders in Harlem. On Thursday, March 2, 1933, he opened at the Dixie Ballroom on 125th Street at Seventh Avenue with a floor show straight from Connie's Inn. On Saturday, March 11, to celebrate seven years of "the finest entertainment ever presented in Harlem," he played a breakfast dance at the Savoy Ballroom with Fletcher Henderson, Luis Russell, the Savoy Cotton Pickers, and Clark's Missourians, rushing from the Dixie as soon as they closed their doors at 2:00 A.M. When the dance finished at 8:00 A.M. the following morning, Webb was judged the winner.

Curiously, the Savoy Ballroom had begun a policy of mounting revues in the early part of 1933, but when the Leonard Harper Revue flopped in mid-April, the management decided to return to the tried and tested policy of booking big bands. They reduced their prices to sixty cents for men and thirty-five cents for women and booked the Chick Webb and Fess Williams bands to attract the crowds back again. Yet, perhaps surprisingly today, they were outdrawn by the nationally famous Isham Jones Orchestra the following month. "Isham Jones pulls the largest crowd to Savoy since the shows closed," reported the *Amsterdam News*.[12]

In June, Webb had moved to the Lafayette, headlining a revue that boasted a cast of forty-five. For the occasion his band was fronted by Valaida Snow, "conducting Chick Webb's band, playing on her silver cornet, singing and dancing, demonstrating her versatility."[13] Snow gave a boost to the Webb band that his regular front man, Bardu Ali, did not, sowing the seed that maybe a girl vocalist was what the band needed now. In July, Webb was booked into the Harlem Opera House, but he was back at the Lafayette in August. "Chick Webb's band, with the likable Ralph Cooper leading and acting as master of ceremonies, is another real feature of the revue," reported the *Amsterdam News*.[14]

Webb was now alternating at the major Harlem entertainment centers; in October and November he was at the Harlem Opera House, and in January 1934 he was back to head a major revue at the Lafayette. "Chick Webb and his boys are furnishing the music for the show . . . with Bardu Ali fronting," said the *Amsterdam News*.[15] But these theaters were in tough competition and were looking for exclusivity. Webb, on the other hand, was forced to take work wherever he could and suddenly found himself in the middle of what was becoming known as the "theater wars."

While Webb was in Philadelphia doing one-nighters between the Harlem Opera House revue and the Lafayette opening, the undercurrent of distrust and suspicion among the theater owners erupted. The *Amsterdam News* reported: "Chick Webb was stopped by a number of gangsters and an attempt was made to make him gorge up monies he had received to pay off musicians. It is further claimed that they hoped by this move to prevent Webb's entire band from moving into the Lafayette Theatre."[16] Webb refused to be scared off; Moe Gale had his connections, too. But it brought home the fact that Harlem was becoming too small for him. It was time to make a play for the national stage.

A significant step in achieving that end came when Moe Gale

negotiated a deal with the newly formed Decca Recording Company and signed Webb as one of the first artists to go with the label in July 1934. When the band went into the studios on September 10 and November 19, 1934, it was to record several arrangements by the band's alto saxophonist, Edgar Sampson, whose hallmark staccato brass and flowing reed lines can be heard on classics such as "Blue Lou," "Blue Minor," "What a Shuffle," and one of the anthems of the swing era, "Don't Be That Way."

With Webb's drumming mediating the orchestral dynamics from *pianissimo* to a shouting *treble forte*, they were among perhaps only a dozen or so sides from the whole Webb discography that captured the coiled-spring intensity that must have been so riveting in live performance. Indeed, jazz historian Robert Parker points out that contemporary drummers are often astonished to discover Webb frequently drove his band through loud, uptempo numbers using only brushes and a snare drum, as he does on sections of "Don't Be That Way."[17]

Webb's income was now such that he was able to rent a house on "Striver's Row" at 120 West 138th Street,[18] ironically near his great rival and admirer, bandleader Fletcher Henderson. His self-reliance had increased, too, now that he had his own car and chauffeur-cum-valet Joe Sanders to take care of tasks that were difficult for him because of his deformity. Yet, despite his record contract with Decca, Webb knew his career had reached a significant crossroad.

Four years later, in 1938, when Webb was hitting the big time, *Down Beat* magazine summed up this crucial period in his life:

Now followed what is in a sense the most interesting period of Chick's career, in that it is now possible to see in what manner his former experiences had worked upon his mind and what conclusions he had drawn from them. Up until this time he had always had astoundingly good bands about which there was certainly nothing commercial. He had a style, but it was purely a musical style and not one which would be easily recognized by the general public. He had seen Fletcher Henderson and Duke Ellington and Cab Calloway work out their futures and he observed the manner in which business was conducted. He began to understand that it was the finished product that mattered both to the booker and the general public, that it did not matter very much . . . as long as it had something about it to which the public could respond.[19]

A measure of Webb's box office value at the Apollo during 1934 illustrates just how far he had to go to catch up with his main competitors who had broken through to a national audience: Duke Ellington commanded $4,700 for a week, Earl Hines $1,400, while Webb got just $950. To help break this impasse, Charlie Buchanan, the black manager of the Savoy Ballroom who acted for Moe Gale, began urging Webb to add a female vocalist to his lineup. Buchanan could see the commercial potential a girl singer might make in creating a bridge between bandstand and audience. It was an idea not lost on Webb. He had seen the effect Valaida Snow had on audiences when she fronted the band in June 1933 and was well aware of the commercial potential that vocalists offered. Indeed, on his very first recording session in 1929 he had trumpeter Ward Pinkett take a scat vocal on "Dog Bottom." Since then he had included at least one vocal on every one of his subsequent recording dates. Initially, they came from one of the band's instrumentalists, but by 1933 he could afford to add the baritone crooner Chuck Richards to his payroll.

In 1934, Richards was replaced by Charles Linton, whom Webb had heard singing at the Hollywood Restaurant near 122nd Street. "He was a very good singer," said tenor saxophonist Teddy McRae, who joined Webb in 1936, "a nice-looking fella. Looked like an Indian. And he could sing pretty good."[20] Linton sang in the fashionable falsetto style of singers like Harlan Lattimore with Don Redman's band, Dan Grissom with Jimmy Lunceford's band, and drummer Sonny Greer with Duke Ellington's Orchestra—who on occasion was asked to sing pop tunes like "Dinah." Linton didn't sing uptempo numbers, however, and this was just the area Buchanan thought a girl vocalist might score for Webb.

In turn, Webb, highly ambitious and now desperate for success, was willing to try anything that might give him the breakthrough with the public he had been working so hard to achieve. "He'd spend his last cent [on the band]," said Teddy McRae. "He was a self-made man, and he knew where he wanted to go way before I joined him. . . . He was going to do this, he was going to be here by this time; next year I want to be here and the next year I want to be there. He told Charlie Buchanan, 'Oh, you got a Caddy. I'm going to get one, too.' Two years later he got his Cadillac. . . . This was the great part about this man. He was on his way."[21]

Webb was immensely proud of Charles Linton. His good looks projected the right image with the dancers, and he was able to act as emcee when the band's regular front man, Bardu Ali, who combined tumbling and conducting to crowd-pleasing effect, was not present. When Webb learned that Linton had an offer to go with the Ink Spots, "he raised hell," said Linton. "'You're going to go with them Ink Spots? Who are those Ink Spots? You're with *Chick Webb's band*.' He wouldn't let me go!" Linton, who was tall, suave, and remarkably self-possessed—he never in his life smoked or drank, for example— was delegated the task of finding a suitable girl singer. The reason was simple: Linton attracted the ladies in droves wherever he went and knew his way around the Harlem nightclub scene.

It was March 1935 when Linton first began passing the word around that he was looking for an attractive girl to audition as vocal- ist for the Chick Webb band. "We were opening up at the Harlem Opera House—that was a theater between Seventh Avenue and the Apollo Theater on 125th Street. We were doing a show there for a week. The office [Moe Gale and Charlie Buchanan] asked me to find a girl vocalist. I did the classics and the ballad tunes, and they wanted me to find someone that I liked to do the swing tunes. They left it to me because they knew I knew all the women that were, well, you know, beautiful.

"At the theater I knew an Italian girl in the chorus so I asked her, 'Do you know of a beautiful girl who does swing tunes?' 'No, I don't,' she said, 'but there's that little girl who won first prize at the Apollo, and her name's Ella.' And I said, 'All right. Do you have a telephone number?' She said, 'No.' I asked her for her address, and she said, 'She doesn't have a place to go. She plays out on 125th Street every day; she's out there every day.' So I said, 'When you see her, bring her to me.'

"A couple of days later after the show she came and said, 'I found her, I found her.' I had forgotten. She said, 'You know, Ella, the girl that I told you sings.' And she brought Ella in and we sat down. I sat in front of her. I got right up on Ella, and I said, 'They tell me you won first prize at the Apollo Theater,' and she said, 'Yeees,' very shy, and I said, 'Sing me the song you won first prize with,' and she sang 'Judy' all the way through, which was good but very bashful and very hoarse. I said to her, 'Well your voice is soft, but that's all right. The mike will bring it out.' These are my exact words to her. And I said, 'Do you have an encore?' and she said, 'Yeees,' and I said, 'What did you do?' and she started another tune, and she was five or six bars into it when I said, 'That's all right. Come on up and I'll introduce you to Chick.'

"So we went upstairs to Chick's room, and Bardu and Chick were standing there talking. Chick was a big talker, you know, and Bardu, too. Chick was very comical. I pushed the door open, walked in, and said, 'Chick, I want you to meet—' He said, 'Look at him, he's robbing the cradle.' Now he knew better. Chick loved to joke. Ella wasn't the type I'd go for. So I said, 'No. I want you to listen to her sing.' And that did it! He came over to me and grabbed my collar and whispered real close, 'You're not puttin' that on my bandstand. No, no, no. Out!' He was whispering. All of a sudden we're off over behind the door, and Ella was sitting on the side. When he said that, Buchanan pushed the door open and came in. He was the fellow who was responsible for all the bands that played the Savoy Ballroom. He was really head guy for the Moe Gale Agency. So Chick looked at Buchanan and said, 'Look what Charles wants to put on my bandstand.' Buchanan took a look and said, 'No, no. Out!' He didn't want her either. *Out!*

"Ella knows nothing of this. She's sitting at the other end of the room. And when Buchanan went to turn—I don't know what it was, I didn't know the girl—when he turned to walk away, I knew if he walked away that would be the end of it. I said, 'If you don't listen to her—' before he got too far, because if he got *too* far— I said, 'If you don't listen to her, I will quit!' I wasn't going to quit the job, but it was the only thing that came to me when he went to walk away. And he said, 'Oh, no. Okay, okay. When you finish the theater, you've got two weeks at the Savoy Ballroom. Bring her up. Let her sing along with the band, and if the public likes her, we'll keep her. And if not, *out! No pay!*' And I said okay, and so I took Ella back down with me.

"I lived with some German people at that particular time, and there was an empty room over mine and I put her in there. That was 122nd Street at Seventh Avenue. I said to her, 'Now, if you don't go with us, I'll make arrangements for you to eat at the Hollywood Restaurant, and I'll pay when I come in each month or whatever.' She stayed there two weeks until Chick decided to keep her on. Now, doing all this, I don't know the woman. I know that she won first prize, which don't mean anything. Many people won first prize and don't get anywhere. But if it hadn't been for the Italian girl, we wouldn't have any Ella because she wasn't in any condition to accept any job anyplace. She was scuffling and didn't have any place to go."

Moe Gale told jazz critic Leonard Feather that when he first saw her, "she looked incredible. Her hair disheveled, her clothes terrible."[22] Even so, while the band was completing their engagement at the Harlem Opera House, Linton took her every day to watch the show from the wings and had her listen to the numbers she was to learn for her trial run at the Savoy. "I used to take her up every day as long as we were at the theater. I said, 'You watch me and do what I do'—like this, you know. There was one song I did that was in her key, the only fast tune I did. I said, 'Do your best now.' I took her up to the Savoy—I didn't introduce her to anyone, I just took her in, and Chick accepted that because Buchanan was in control of Chick's band and everything, all the hiring and everything. So she got up, and she was all right! She did well!"

Webb, however, remained ambivalent about adding Ella to his payroll. "She was a big girl," commented *Down Beat* three years later, "and knew nothing whatsoever about how to dress or talk to strangers."[23] Webb began soliciting the opinions of musicians in the band and those who stopped by the Savoy to hear him perform. Over the years many musicians have claimed a role in Ella's discovery, and it is probably a result of Webb's seeking a consensus of opinion that so many felt they played a part in making musical history. It was only when Webb spoke to Kaiser Marshall, the great drummer from the Fletcher Henderson band and the man who invented the hi-hat cymbal, that he finally made up his mind. Hal Austin, then a busy young drummer on the Harlem scene and a friend of both Webb and Marshall, recalled: "[Chick] didn't want her 'cause she was ugly. He said she was too ugly! 'I don't want that old ugly thing!' Kaiser Marshall said, 'You damn fool, you better take her!' She was smart. And that's how he raised so much sand with Chick until Chick took her. And that's how it happened."[24]

When Webb finally made the decision to add Ella to the band, the Gale office agreed to pay for a room for her at the Braddock Hotel at 126th Street and Eighth Avenue. "The first few years Moe Gale bought her a room at the Braddock. She was a— They look after themselves, put it that way," said Mario Bauza. Contrary to legend, Ella was not adopted by Webb, nor did she live with him and his wife Sallye. "Chick had a small place, and he couldn't take anyone in, he and Sallye," said Charles Linton. "He didn't adopt her. Later he said to me, 'I'll say that I adopted her, for the press people.' When Buchanan and Chick gave her money to live at the hotel, that's when the German people cleaned her room out and burned everything; cleaned the room out and painted it after her, which they had to do, it was so dirty. After she was there [the Savoy], she didn't look the part, so the hosieress, Helen, used to take her into the bathroom and comb her hair and make her look nice."

The band members also tried to straighten her out by teasing her about her appearance. "We all kidded her," said Edgar Sampson. "It would be 'Hey, Sis, where'd you get those clothes?'—we all called her Sis—and 'Sis, what's with that hairdo?'"[25] Finally, it was the unlikely figure of the gruff trombonist Sandy Williams, who had told Webb not to hire Ella, who took her in hand: "Sandy Williams took care of her like a father," said Linton, "and I mean take care. She didn't use soap and water. That's what I'm talking about. It had to be someone to know what they were doing to take care of her 'cause she was in bad shape."

Ella quickly responded. She was well aware of the opportunity that had suddenly opened up for her. "In less than two weeks she had proven what she could do, and the dancers at the Savoy Ballroom were made [sic] about her," reported *Down Beat* in February 1938. "By this time the situation began to look a little different. Chick's manager sent for her and asked if she would like to sign a contract."[26] Ella signed. But she was still conspicuously short of experience and was very much, as Mario Bauza put it, "a diamond in the rough."

At this time trombonist Clyde Bernhardt was working at Harlem's Renaissance Ballroom for bandleader Vernon Andrade. "I remember in early 1935 when Ella Fitzgerald used to come up to the Renny two and three nights a week. She was working with Chick Webb who was on and off at the Savoy . . . " he recalled. "Webb didn't pay her a regular salary but let her have a couple of bucks now and then. She always sang in her street clothes because that's all she had. Andrade wouldn't let her work formal dances without an evening gown. We always felt sorry for her and always gave Ella money before she left."[27]

Within weeks Ella had settled into her new role as vocalist with the Webb band. In May 1935 a young George T. Simon of *Metronome* magazine was sent to review the Webb band at the Savoy for his new column, Simon Says, and was mightily impressed with Webb's young girl singer: "I had just joined *Metronome* in February of 1935. I didn't know anything [about her] until I went up there and was so knocked out by her, knocked out not only by the way she sang but the spirit and the way she would lead the band by throwing kicks on the side of the bandstand. She used to move her arms around for certain trumpet riffs and so forth. She sang quite a few numbers. I'm sure she didn't record all the numbers she sang—during the course of an evening they did a lot of numbers. . . . Ella was very demonstrative; she was sort of a shy gal. I remember she had very thin legs, as I recall, spindly legs. She wasn't terribly heavy at that time."

Simon gave the Webb band a B-plus rating in the June edition of *Metronome*, concluding: "Miss Fitzgerald should go places."[28] It was her first review and something she would remember for the rest of her life. In later years when Simon was in the audience, Ella would always make him take a bow, which resulted in one amusing incident, described by Simon: "One time she was playing Basin Street East. . . . There were long tables going away from the bandstand. And she made a couple of remarks: 'I hope you like this one, George,' and 'The man who gave me my first write-up, a dear friend, I want you to acknowledge him—George Simon.' And she pointed to a guy who also didn't have too much hair, sitting two or three seats closer than I was. And the guy didn't know what to do, so I said, 'Here I am, Ella,' and she said, 'Oh, I gotta wear my glasses from now on when I work!'"

Ella threw her all into her new role as band singer. From the start she could memorize lyrics with phenomenal ease. "When I came into the band [in early 1936], I flipped," said Teddy McRae. "I knew she could catch on. . . . She could sight-read better than any of the singers. She was real fast. . . . I was thinking to myself, now how many songs has she got in her? She could sing this and this, she can remember lyrics, a million songs. . . . When she went over a song in rehearsal, she had cards. Maybe she took the cards home with her. Just sing the song down, and she'd go home and memorize the lyrics. And when she came back in the night when we were going to play the arrangements rehearsed that day, perfect. There would be no stumbling or 'I forgot the lyrics.' I never heard her say, 'I forgot the lyrics' or nothing."[29]

Ella's infallible ear also enabled her to learn melodies just as quickly. "Nobody told her how to sing or do nothing," said Mario Bauza. "I don't know where she learned it, but she read music. When I met her she read music. . . . She used to go to the piano with a lead sheet and ding-a-ding-a-ding and learn all the songs. She knew exactly what she had to do. She was smart. Give her a piece of sheet music, and she'd read it. The band, when they went to a band rehearsal, they'd say, 'Ella, we're ready for you!' And she's straight in!"

After his initial misgivings, Webb soon realized he had a valuable asset in Ella. Within weeks of her joining the band she was on the road when Webb pinch-hit for some Willie Bryant dates around Boston.[30] Back by June 1 for rehearsals, she was in the recording studio featuring on two of the four numbers the band cut on June 12, 1935. Ella's vocal on "Love and Kisses," coupled with "Are You Here to Stay?" with a Charles Linton vocal, was issued a few weeks later. There could be no doubting Webb's intentions. "Love and Kisses" was a commercial dance band arrangement with no pretensions to jazz. Webb, on recordings at least, was intent on appealing to the broadest possible audience.

Indeed, after Ella joined Webb, he recorded only fourteen further instrumentals with his full band, as against over sixty vocal numbers, of which more than fifty were by Ella. "Chick had been totally immersed in the *band*, and the guys stood behind him 100 percent," said Helen Oakley-Dance. "But after he got Ella, it was different because his point of view had changed. He began to see that there could be a commercial future for the band."[31]

CHAPTER FOUR

1935–1938

I think it's a wonderful thing to know that you can live in the streets here in America and pull yourself up with a little help from someone and make it to the top. I think that's a wonderful thing.

CHARLES LINTON

FROM THE VERY BEGINNING of Ella's professional career, musicians were impressed by her remarkable rhythmic security. "She could swing," said drummer Hal Austin, who witnessed her early performances at the Savoy. "She came into this business swinging."[1] This combination of rhythmic ease and clarity of diction was at once disarming and endearing in its purity. Mary Lou Williams, who also heard Ella shortly after joining Webb, said it was a voice that sent chills up and down her spine.[2]

Ella's first recorded vocals on "Love and Kisses" and "I'll Chase the Blues Away" from June 1935 projected a strong sense of rhythmic impetus, of swing, by compressing or expanding the words ever so slightly to give her vocal line momentum. This subtle syncopation, even though slight, was closer to Louis Armstrong than to Connee Boswell and might even have been inspired by Billie Holiday's style. However, as Holiday did more than merely gargle at the well of Louis Armstrong, it is difficult to say whether she was an important formative influence or not. Even so, Ella's intonation was good, she had great clarity of diction, and she swung. "She was a commercial singer," said Mario Bauza, "very commercial. She knew how to pull a thing here, there. She was commercial; she could sing melodies good."

Ella uses throat tones, the initial tendency of all untrained singers, which restricts range and gives the voice a harder edge. Indeed, she has a little difficulty covering the lowest notes of "Love and Kisses," and it would be some years before she mastered singing from the diaphragm, which would have the effect of extending her range. However, for an eighteen-year-old with an absolute minimum of professional experience, her work as a dance-band singer was more than merely competent, it was surprisingly accomplished.

On July 10, 1935, she began a week at the Apollo with the Webb band. Significantly, her raw talent continued to stand up to scrutiny. "During the Chick Webb band presentation," said *New York Age*, "Charlie Linton, vocalist, sings rather well, but it takes Ella Fitzgerald to send the audience into a vociferous display of enthusiasm. Her voice is seemingly tinged with honey, and she sings with a rhythmic tempo that puts her over with a bang."[3] Ella appeared again with Webb at the Apollo the following November. On each occasion the demanding Apollo crowd brought on an extreme attack of nerves. "She was pacing up and down, wringing a handkerchief and dabbing constantly at sweat trickling down her brow," recalled Jack Schiffman.[4]

But Ella was on her way. Her rise from obscurity had been swift. Within nine months of her debut with Webb, *Metronome* magazine's George T. Simon was confident enough to make this prophetic prediction about her in January 1936:

> During the past year or so, this column has emitted various toasts and raves about various heretofore unknowns. . . . Here's number one for 1936: *Ella Fitzgerald* . . . the seventeen-year-old gal singing up in Harlem's Savoy Ballroom with Chick Webb's fine band . . . unheralded and practically unknown right now, but what a future . . . a great natural flair for singing . . . extraordinary intonation and figures. . . . As she is right now, she's one of the best femme hot warblers . . . and there's no reason why she shouldn't be just about the best in time to come.[5]

In March 1936, Billie Holiday was out of town touring with the Jimmie Lunceford Orchestra. The year before, at the behest of jazz entrepreneur and critic John Hammond, she had begun an enduring relationship on disc with pianist Teddy Wilson that produced some of the finest jazz vocals ever, set against a backdrop of some of the most engaging small-group jazz to emerge in the 1930s. In Billie's temporary absence, Ella was invited to take part in a forthcoming session on March 16 with a band comprising Teddy McRae on tenor saxophone; Frank Newton on trumpet; Benny Morton on trombone; Jerry Blake, alto and clarinet; John Trueheart, guitar; Lennie Stanfield, bass; Cozy Cole, drums; and of course Wilson on piano.

Teddy McRae had recently joined Webb's band after the breakup of Lil Armstrong's combo with which he had been touring, replacing Elmer Williams. Wilson's budget sessions did not allow for anything but minimum preparation. "We'd walk in and tune up and skim down the stuff one time and one take," said McRae. "That was it. No two or three takes. We'd run it down for the vocalist, then run it down once more together. And boom, let's make it."[6]

Ella's appearance on the session was another significant measure of her progress, as McRae pointed out: "They would only call like the top musicians around to record. They'd pick certain guys that they knew they wouldn't have any trouble with [musically]."[7] As an interesting aside, Dan Morgenstern observed that despite the many critically acclaimed records cut by Wilson and Holiday, Wilson did not much like Billie's singing. He much preferred Ella's! "In Teddy Wilson's aural history here [at the Institute of Jazz Studies, Rutgers University] . . . he said he didn't like Billie because she copied Louis. He liked Ella better!" In any event, Ella's records sold as well as Holiday's. Clear and secure, she quietly suggested Billie Holiday's characteristic vocal inflections at one or two points, particularly on her entry to "All My Life" and the tenth bar of her second chorus of "Melancholy Baby."

However, there was no reciprocal admiration. Holiday, herself not fully established in 1935–36, found it difficult to accept that Ella had all but come from nowhere and was sharing the stage with Chick Webb, one of the top Harlem bands. "Billie Holiday didn't like her at that time," said Charles Linton. "She used to come into the Savoy and I'd look from the bandstand. She'd have a big coat on, and she would walk and look, just a look. What I figured was that she was surprised to see Ella with Chick Webb's band. 'A great band like that with Ella,' she used to say, 'that bitch,' turn around, and walk out."

Meanwhile, Webb was continuing to use all his vocal options on the bandstand and in the recording studio. Although Ella was used on every record session, Charles Linton was given a few songs, trumpeter Taft Jordan was given "I May Be Wrong," and a vocal trio of Ella, Linton, and Louis Jordan was featured on "Wake Up and Live" and "There's Frost on the Moon," with its prophetic tag ending "Re-bop!" leading to much speculation as to whether in 1937 it was Ella who gave jazz the term "re-bop," which eventually mutated into "bebop." "When Louis Jordan came in, we decided to do 'Frost on the Moon' like a trio thing," said Teddy McRae. "I think Van Alexander wrote that. . . . I liked it, and I liked the trio. . . . This is one of the things we featured at the Apollo Theater."[8]

Webb spent the winter of 1935–36 at the Savoy, and after an opera-tion in April to remove an abscess from his arm, he went on the road for a series of one-night stands between the beginning of June and the end of October 1936. "We stayed out there for about six months," said Teddy McRae. "We came back to the Savoy Ballroom. . . . We had moved the band on a little bit, a step up. . . . Ella Fitzgerald had devel-oped; she was singing much better after the road trip."[9]

It is possible to put McRae's contention to the test; the road trip was sandwiched between two recording sessions, on June 2 and October 29. Certainly Ella's voice seems to have matured by the October session; her tone is round and fuller, and her projection has improved. Her confidence must have increased, too, because October yielded "You'll Have to Swing It," Ella's ode to "Mr. Paganini," with tempo changes and two moments, each a bar and a half, of scat singing that the youngster, a professional of only about sixteen months' standing, handles with aplomb. "We did a thing called 'Mr. Paganini,'" said McRae. "They [other big bands] don't ever do noth-ing like 'Mr. Paganini,' but Ella could do those types of things, novel-ty types of things. She could do them good! And she put style into them. The girl had talent!"[10]

Coincidentally, both sessions also yielded Ella's first hits. "Sing Me a Swing Song (and Let Me Dance)" from the June session reached number eighteen in the charts for one week in July, and "You'll Have to Swing It" peaked at number twenty for a week in December. With "Sing Me a Swing Song" Ella finally began to attract attention as a singer in her own right rather than merely as the "Webb band vocal-ist." Benny Goodman, who had recorded the song with his own band on May 27, listened with great interest to the rival version. When Helen Ward, his regular vocalist, took a two-week leave of absence to obtain a divorce in November, Goodman asked Ella to substitute for her on three numbers—"Goodnight, My Love," "Take Another Guess," and "Did You Mean It?"—on his November 5 session for Victor Records. When "Did You Mean It?" was released on November 25, all kinds of legal problems ensued. Decca claimed Ella was under contract to them; she had been in the studios for Decca on November 18 as "Ella Fitzgerald and Her Savoy Eight" with a pickup group from the Webb band, and prior to that she must have signed a separate contract in her own right. Consequently, "Did You Mean It?" was withdrawn from the Victor catalogue on January 20, 1937. Until the reissue of the Benny Goodman–Ella sides in the 1960s, the original was a collector's item. The BG-Ella collaboration didn't end there. On November 10 she appeared on Goodman's coast-to-coast radio show, "Camel Caravan," then the most popular music show in America. Later he offered Webb $5,000 to buy out her contract. Ella's star was now in the ascendant; even the phlegmatic Webb bandsmen sat up and took notice. "Then Benny Goodman took her, too," said Mario Bauza. "Led her away for a couple of records and broadcasting. Then everybody wanted that lady, everybody." Rival bandleader Jimmie Lunceford came in with an attractive offer to join his band; whatever Ella may have thought of it, she had to turn it down because of her contract with Gale.

According to Mario Bauza, Ella's involvement with the Benny Goodman band resulted in a brief affair with Goodman's Italian tenor saxophonist Vido Musso. But in December, Ella was suddenly absent from the Webb band. "Mystery surrounds the departure of Ella Fitzgerald from Chick Webb's band—but we bet you she'll be back in a month or two,"[11] said the English magazine *Melody Maker*.

Meanwhile, Chick and the band finished their winter season at the Savoy and had a week at the Apollo at the end of January 1937 before going out on the road for a long series of one-nighters. Their place at the Savoy was taken by the Teddy Hill band. Ella, who allegedly had left for an abortion, was too frail to join Webb on the road when she recovered. (The operation reputedly had gone wrong; she would never have children, something that in later life was the cause of great sadness.) Instead of rejoining Webb, Gale suggested she return to the Savoy to work with the Hill band where at least she could return to the comfort of home after work.

Throughout January and February she was broadcasting weekly for Moe Gale's "Good Time Society" with the Hill band: "Teddy Hill's Orchestra replaced Webb, and Ella sounded as great as ever with Hill,"[12] reported *Melody Maker*. Just prior to Webb's road trip, however, Ella had recovered sufficiently to join him in the recording studios, on January 14, 1937, for a split recording session with the big band and the Mills Brothers. The cuts with the Mills Brothers, "Big Boy Blue" and a version of "Dedicated to You," done the following month, hit the charts in successive weeks in April 1937, at numbers twenty and nineteen, respectively.

With Ella's return to the Webb band in March 1937, a problem that had been simmering below the surface was again highlighted. It was becoming clear to the Webb bandsmen that Ella had a difficult streak. "Most of the musicians didn't care much for her personality," said Webb's bassist Beverly Peer. "I don't think she was really nasty, but she was insecure and came off as being nasty."[13] Perhaps this was hardly surprising. She had had a difficult childhood, and now she was very much a young woman in a grown man's world, having to prove herself in front of demanding audiences night after night for what one report described as "coffee and doughnut spendings."

Even now, jazz remains essentially a chauvinistic music, and like it or not, a woman has to prove herself more than an equal of her male contemporaries to become accepted in their domain. For example, writer Gene Lees has pointed out that the fine alto saxophonist Vi Redd told him she suffered far more discrimination as a woman than as a black.[14] Jazz is also a notoriously demanding and precarious profession, for a woman most of all. But Ella never allowed the pressures to force her to retreat into drink or drugs. Instead, she developed a steely edge that enabled her to look after herself in a man's world. She was determined and ambitious. There was no one to stand up for her, so she did it herself, using all the feminine guile at her disposal. When a ballad feature was passed to Charles Linton, for example, there were tears and a tantrum because she wanted to do it herself. "This is a song that, well, she wanted to do it, and I liked the song first, you know," said Linton. "And then she wanted to do it, and then I wind up letting her do it. . . . She got a little pushy, you know what I mean? So when she gets like that, she always has her way."

Ella was doing what she had to do to get ahead. Pianist and composer Ram Ramirez, a member of her band in 1940, pointed out: "Oh, man. One thing I know, she's not as nice as people say or think that she is, you know. When she came up she was tough. . . . *Yes she was!*"[15]

During the thirties, radio exposure was the most important single factor in making it into the big time. Webb had begun broadcasting in the fall of 1934, and in April 1935 he secured three slots a week on Radio WJZ, broadcasting from Radio City, to which was added a spot on the Moe Gale production "Good Time Society" on NBC in the winter of 1935. The program featured the Webb band, Ella's and Charles Linton's vocals, plus various guest singers, dancers, and combos. The program was broadcast coast to coast on Saturdays at 10:00 P.M., also from Radio City in midtown Manhattan. *Down Beat* described the content as "always top-notch guests, talented colored combos."[16]

Most music broadcasts in the 1930s were live and often captured the in-person excitement of the big bands and their vocalists. Every bandleader sought and welcomed such exposure, often accepting low wages to play venues with a radio wire in the hope of running into surplus with subsequent one-night stands and theater tours.

Along with radio exposure came the song pluggers who were anxious to get air time for their latest "plugs." They wanted to get their songs onto the charts, which were based on the number of times a song was played on the air during a seven-day week; this had a big bearing on whether the tune would rank on the overall "hit parade" survey. No other medium, not even records, offered as much impact as radio. The song pluggers knew it; good, bad, and indifferent tunes were often advanced by bandleaders in exchange for an "inducement." It was a crazy marketplace, but it was the way to get ahead.

Webb's reputation began taking off fast during 1937, and the main reason was radio exposure. He had eight slots a week, more than any other big band at the time, white or colored. He had a weekly sustaining program for NBC that produced over five thousand fan letters a week; Moe Gale's "Good Time Society," which had continued since 1935; three slots a week from the Savoy Ballroom; and from March 11 he took over the "Lucidin" program from jazz violinist Stuff Smith, which provided another three weekly slots. (Lucidin, incidentally, was a mouthwash.)

Many of the broadcasts were made downtown, a journey that Charles Linton recalled making frequently with Ella. "Traveling from Radio City Music Hall back to Harlem, riding in the subway, her action when people looked at her. . . . She was self-conscious, you know, because her hair was real short. She was very self-conscious. She must have had a hard life. . . . If someone turned to look at her and turned to one of their friends and said something, that was it, kid! Oh! *That was it!* I'd say they're not saying anything. You're a star now. They're saying, 'I saw her at the Savoy Ballroom. I saw her at the Apollo Theatre.' But that didn't change anything, she was so conscious of herself."

Ella began to be featured more and more as Webb's policy of covering the pop tunes of the day began to pay off. The more popular Webb became, the more popular Ella became, and in November 1937, she was voted Number One Female Vocalist in the first-ever *Down Beat* and *Melody Maker* readers' polls, ahead of her main rivals Billie Holiday and Mildred Bailey.

Most of what Ella was singing were pop and novelty songs, and not especially memorable ones at that. "Having seen from his own experience that good music did not really pay," commented *Down Beat* in 1938, "Chick decided that in order to make a living he would be forced to compromise. He therefore set about to prove that the band could play commercial music in a very creditable fashion."[17]

Artistically, Ella was unconcerned about the quality of the material she was asked to perform. Her motivation, like that of Webb, was to land a hit record. The songs she sang (many of which were never recorded) came through an arrangement Teddy McRae had made on behalf of Webb with song publisher Jack Robbins. McRae was also a songwriter in his own right. The Robbins office published his compositions, including "You Showed Me the Way" with lyrics by Bud Green, recorded by the Webb band with an Ella vocal on March 24, 1937.

Robbins had begun to follow the fortunes of the Webb band, and more particularly of its girl vocalist, with great interest. "Jack talked to me about a deal where he would support us with arrangements. It was like song plugging. . . . So Jack said, 'We'll take care of the arrangements, and all you have to do is broadcast. . . . We're going to give you the hit songs that come out before anybody . . . because we feel Ella Fitzgerald is about the top thing right now. We think she's really going to be tops.' I told Chick Webb, 'Look, Jack wants to give us a deal. He's going to give us the top songs, and whatever the cost, they'll [absorb] it themselves because they have song pluggers all around the country plugging songs, and this will be a way they can be plugged.' So he began to give us all these top songs. And we began to move Ella Fitzgerald . . . into pop. . . . We were going commercial. Chick felt that we did all we could where we were. . . .

"And we began to give Ella Fitzgerald most of the broadcast time. Like, she used to do just one song, we would have her doing three, sometimes four. And this moved her up. And then people started taking notice. . . . Then Chick Webb and her made like a double attraction. That was the beginning of her—when we put all that music behind her, all those big pop songs, all those big hits."[18]

Putting Ella in the spotlight to the extent Webb did was to play a vital role in establishing her early popularity. At that time bandleaders used their singers sparingly. Most had established their reputations with muscular, riff-laden instrumental numbers, and singers were used as a change of pace, to spare the brass section whose lip muscles took a pounding over the course of a night's work. Singers were paid less than musicians, reflecting their status in the band's hierarchy. Many bandleaders regarded them as an afterthought, handing them arrangements that were not in their ideal key or giving them inappropriate tempos to cope with. The prominence that Webb now gave Ella, making her "part of the band," was almost unprecedented, particularly in a band like Webb's which had developed a powerful instrumental personality of its own.

Webb's commercial stance surprised and disappointed many of the band's admirers, including John Hammond. He had followed Webb's progress since the 1920s and could not work out why, at the height of the big band era, when killer-diller arrangements were all the rage, Webb did not stick to the powerhouse brand of jazz with which he had built his reputation in Harlem. In November 1937, after a season at Kimball's Indoor Ballroom in Boston, Hammond publicly berated Webb in *Down Beat*: "Chick Webb's standard of musicianship is far too low. . . . At least partly because of Ella Fitzgerald the band is extremely popular these days. . . . On the stage Chick exhibits the best and the worst in the band . . . elaborate, badly written 'white' arrangements, a 'comedian' saxophonist, and an athletic director who mimes around and contributes not a whit to the proceedings. . . . But Chick is such a swell performer and Ella so great a personality that crowds usually overlook such deficiencies."[19] Indeed, the crowds did overlook such deficiencies; Ella's two duets with Louis Jordan, "If You Should Ever Leave" and "All or Nothing at All," charted at twelve and twenty in July and August 1937, respectively.

Hammond was not the only person to comment on the poor arrangements and how they made the band sound "white." While the deal with Jack Robbins brought quantity, it was not providing quality. Critic Dave Dexter, who saw the band at Fairyland Park, Kansas City, in the summer of 1937, said, "The Webb band never sounded really black. . . . It was the charts mostly."[20]

Even Webb's own sidemen were impatient with some of the arrangements. "For some reason Chick wanted his band to sound like a first-class white band," said Garvin Bushell, "so he used arrangers like Al Feldman [who used the stage name Van Alexander] that he thought were great. But they didn't write for colored bands, they didn't write the things we played. . . . What really made the band, though, was Ella."[21]

Apart from the specific potboilers for his audience at the Savoy, Webb made a conscious artistic choice to use the "white"-sounding arrangements at the expense of experienced and imaginative writers like Edgar Sampson and Charlie Dixon who had provided some of the band's best instrumentals. Rather than developing an indigenous repertoire of originals, as bandleaders like Duke Ellington, Count Basie, and Jimmie Lunceford did, jazz considerations were now no longer paramount for Webb in his pursuit of commercial success. It was a curious irony that when Artie Shaw wanted his own band to sound "black," he approached Teddy McRae, Webb's tenor saxophonist, who duly obliged with two million-selling hits, "Back Bay Shuffle" and "Traffic Jam."

"I felt Chick had given the go-ahead to Ella. She really *dominated*," said Helen Oakley-Dance. "The band played a smaller role, and its character was changing. I used to argue with Chick about it all the time, but he was committed to going his own way."[22] Perhaps this is the key to the Webb-Fitzgerald relationship. Webb's bias toward a "white" sound could well have been the key factor that endeared him to the raw, inexperienced Ella when he took her under his wing in 1935. John Chilton pointed out that Ella's voice sounded as if it could just as easily be from a white singer. In commercializing his band for the broadest possible appeal, Webb was focusing on white America, the constituency that could provide the biggest paychecks.

Ella was now playing a significant role in helping the Webb band establish a national profile. Her income was such that she moved to rooms at 2040 Seventh Avenue and was able to afford her own maid. (This address was a popular haunt for musicians; also living there at the time was saxophonist Chu Berry.) Ella was beginning to put on weight, a problem that would dog her throughout her life, but in the fall of 1937 it was the cause of an amusing story in the pages of *Down Beat*: "Ella Fitzgerald stuck in an elevator rushing to make a Swing Club broadcast with four minutes to spare. Trap at top of cage opened and 220 lbs. of songstress pulled out by three men."[23]

Toward the end of 1937, Ella moved again, this time to the Woodside Hotel at 2424 Seventh Avenue at 142nd Street, to be close to Jo Jones, the drummer from the Count Basie band. The band had recently hit town and was playing the Roseland Ballroom, and most of its members were staying at the Woodside, which achieved a kind of immortality with Basie's hit "Jumpin' at the Woodside." For a while Ella and Jones were an item.[24] It was Ella's first major love affair. Jones—handsome, immaculately groomed, articulate, and sophisticated—attracted the girls in droves. Ella fell in a big way, entranced as much by his looks as by his strong, worldly wise personality. But a musician's life provides little opportunity for a romance to flourish. In time the affair burned itself out, and Ella and Jo Jones became ships that passed in the night. For a long time afterward, however, Ella remained smitten; a photograph that was taken backstage at the Apollo[25] several years later shows a picture of Jones on her dressing table. Drummer Hal Austin remembered Ella at the

Woodside: "When she was living in the Woodside Hotel, 'Jumpin' at the Woodside'! Eddie Durham wrote that tune. That was a good-time building!"[26]

Perhaps the three most exciting events in jazz during 1937 were Webb's legendary band battles at the Savoy: against Fletcher Henderson on February 28, against Duke Ellington on March 7, and against Benny Goodman on May 11. Webb lost to Ellington, but the Goodman battle was one of the greatest events of the swing era. More than four thousand broke the attendance record at the Savoy, and five thousand were turned away. The fire department, the riot squad, mounted police, and reserves were all called out to control the crowds. Goodman was the biggest thing in music in 1937, but it was Webb who won: "Chick Webb Defeats Ben Goodman!" shouted the headline in *Metronome* magazine.[27]

"It was a helluva night," said Mario Bauza. "Chick told everyone the night before, 'Fellas, tomorrow is my hour. Anybody that misses notes, don't look for notice—don't come back to work!' That was a big night. Everybody in Benny's band, they were congratulating Chick. And Gene Krupa—Chick was like a father to Gene Krupa." According to *Metronome*'s reporter, George T. Simon, one of the highlights of the evening was "Ella Fitzgerald's singing, with the crowd locking arms and swaying to and fro before her."[28]

At the end of 1937, Webb was back on the road. When they played in Cleveland in December, a week at the Palace Hotel and Christmas night at the Cleveland Hotel, the press reports were no longer filed under the heading "Chick Webb and his Orchestra" but, significantly, as "Chick and Ella." In January the band was back in the Savoy Ballroom, and on the night of the 16th, Webb was confronted with perhaps the most formidable challenge of his career. He was to battle with the fast-rising Count Basie Orchestra, fresh from Kansas City and today considered one of the finest ensembles in the history of jazz.

Earlier in the evening Basie had appeared at Benny Goodman's legendary Carnegie Hall concert, the first major, formal, bona fide jazz concert in history. Afterward the Goodman family and most of the Goodman band, together with other jazz notables including Mildred Bailey, Red Norvo, Teddy Hill, Willie Bryant, and Duke Ellington, gathered uptown to see Webb and Basie battle it out. The occasion was a significant challenge for Ella. The girl vocalist in the Basie band was Billie Holiday, who represented for many the epitome of jazz singing. Ella could have been under no illusion about what was in store: On April 11 the previous year she had been in the audience at the Savoy, along with Louis Armstrong, Benny Goodman, John Hammond, and Lionel Hampton, to see Billie and the formidable Basie aggregation perform.

When the crunch came on that cold January night in 1938, *Metronome* credited Webb with the spoils of victory, while *Down Beat* decided they had been taken by Basie. When the ballot was taken to decide on the winning vocalist, however, Ella was "well out in front over Billie Holiday.... Ella Fitzgerald caused a sensation with her rendition of 'Loch Lomond,' and Billie Holiday thrilled fans with 'My Man.' When Ella sang, she had the whole crowd rocking with her.... Handkerchiefs were waving, people were shouting and stomping, and the excitement was intense."[29]

On February 7 the band moved to Boston for a five-week stay at the Flamingo Room of Levaggi's Restaurant. It caused a sensation. "Business in what is one of the worst slumps Boston night life has ever experienced is downright stupendous," said *Down Beat*. "Chick himself is exciting as hell. Ella Fitzgerald is fine, of course.... Her appeal to the public is an amazing thing. Every time she sings she stops things cold, and if the patrons at Levaggi's are any indication, she's far and away the most popular songstress in the business today."[30]

Chick and Ella were on a roll. Their version of "Rock It for Me" had gone to number nineteen on the hit parade chart that month, and almost immediately their stay at Levaggi's was extended to May 2. *Down Beat* reported that "Chick Webb's Savoy Orchestra with the First Lady of Swing, Ella Fitzgerald, has proved a veritable sensation."[31]

It was the first time that Ella's famous "First Lady" nickname was used in print, but as Teddy McRae pointed out, its origins were not an allusion to the distaff side of the presidency. "Jack Robbins used to give us all these hit songs.... A lot of publishers would come up and give us songs, top publishers—Mills Music, Robbins, Shapiro-Bernstein, you name them, all top publishers. Everybody was trying to get Ella to do the top hit songs.... That's why they made her the First Lady of Swing, because we were ahead of everybody in getting material for Ella."[32]

Ella, as center of attraction for the Webb band, had quickly learned that there was no shortage of men trying to catch her eye. Clearly she loved the attention: "She wasn't a good-looking girl, see," said Charles Linton. Ella was beginning to have the time of her life. "She was always with some man," said Beverly Peer. "All the good-looking guys hung around her because she could sing."[33] At Levaggi's many in the audience were young college kids from nearby Harvard University, whom Jack Levaggi continually tried to discourage because his policy of no minimum charge meant that they could dance all night without spending much.

Here Ella attracted the attention of one young admirer who was a little different from all the others. "Roosevelt's son was in love with Ella," recalled Mario Bauza. "He used to come every night with a chauffeur to take Ella home. And I would say, 'What're you doing?' and he would say, 'I'm a steady son, and going to be the future of this country.' And I'd say, 'What is that?' 'Psychology.' He used to come and pick up Ella every day. He waited at the same time to see that she got home, and the chauffeur took him home. And every night he was there. Sometimes it was, 'Where's your boyfriend? Is he coming tonight?' 'He'll be here before we finish. He won't be late!'"

Chick Webb's physical frailty was beginning to catch up with him. On April 4, 1938, he was admitted to the hospital for two weeks, leaving his friend Scrippy substituting on drums at Levaggi's. On their return to New York the band went into the Savoy, followed by a few weeks at Roseland. "This is when that hard work began to tell on Chick," said Teddy McRae, "because every time we closed a stage down at Roseland, the valet had to go and pick him up and bring him off the stage. That hump was beginning to tell on him."[34]

On May 2, Chick and Ella went into the Decca recording studios in New York for a session that produced "A-Tisket, A-Tasket." "That was Ella's own thing," said Teddy McRae. "It was her own idea. That was her thing that she would sing up in Yonkers.... 'A-Tisket, A-Tasket,' that's a nursery rhyme.... We had nothing to do with that. We called Van [Alexander] to put it down on paper for her, and Van made the arrangements."[35]

Ella had worked out the outline of "A-Tisket, A-Tasket" at Levaggi's and taken it to Van Alexander. "I was terribly busy at the time," he recalled, "so I did nothing about the tune. But Ella approached me again after about a month, and I went home and put the melody and her lyrics together, copying all the parts myself, and took it to Webb. He rehearsed the song for about an hour in the afternoon, and that very night, from the Savoy, he broadcast it. And that's how 'A-Tisket, A-Tasket' was born and popularized."[36]

"A-Tisket, A-Tasket" came from a nursery rhyme that dated back to 1879, and at first the Decca executives flinched at the idea of recording it. "That recording of 'Tasket,'" said Beverly Peer, "we almost didn't take it. Bob Stephens [recording engineer at Decca] didn't want to take it. Chick started to pack up his drums and forced the issue. If he hadn't bothered, there'd be no 'Tasket.' That was down to Chick."[37]

The song went on the charts at number ten on June 18, 1938, and hit number one two weeks later; it stayed on the hit parade for a total of nineteen weeks. It eventually became a million seller in 1950, its sales helped after it was revived in the 1944 movie *Two Girls and a Sailor* starring June Allyson, Gloria DeHaven, and Van Johnson, with specialty numbers by Lena Horne, Harry James, and Xavier Cugat.

With a hit as big as "A-Tisket, A-Tasket," Chick and Ella had finally arrived. The band was now a national attraction. "The band was a success all the way back," said Teddy McRae, "all to the coast and back. We broke record after record. People just lined the streets. . . . People brought their kids into the ballroom, the little girls. Chick gave them prizes. . . . There was $100 he gave away. They had little girls singing 'A-Tisket, A-Tasket.' Whoever won the first prize, the second prize, Chick would pay out of his pocket. . . . She became like a feature attraction with this 'A-Tisket, A-Tasket' where we played. . . . Everybody would bring their little girls, dressed up, and sing 'A-Tisket, A-Tasket.'"[38]

Between May and August, when he left the Webb band, Ella had an affair with alto saxophonist and singer Louis Jordan. "She had a boyfriend. . . . It used to be Louis Jordan," recalled Mario Bauza. "Louis was in the band, and I didn't like the way he was acting. I said, 'Louis, are you taking advantage of this girl here? I'm like her father. I don't want you to not respect this lady or nothing like that.' 'No, no, no. I'm a married man.' I said, 'I *know* you are a married man.'" Jordan's intentions may not have been entirely honorable, however, for he was thinking of forming his own band and was actively canvassing other band members to leave Webb with him. It is possible that his affair with Ella may have been a way of getting her to follow him. "We used to go out to the theaters," continued Bauza. "He was a good showman. He used to stop the show."

Jordan's performances were a major attraction with the band. "What really made the band, though, was Ella," said Garvin Bushell. "Chick was smart enough to see that. But Ella's one problem was that she didn't have a tremendous stage presence. . . . Louis was overshadowing Ella, so Chick decided to fire him."[39] It was the best thing that happened to Louis Jordan. He went on to become a key figure in the history of popular music, the link between jazz and rhythm and blues, the early precursor of rock and roll.

By May 1938, Webb was off the sick list. The band played a week at the Apollo at the end of the month, but on May 29 they appeared at Randall's Island Stadium for an outdoor swing session, a benefit for unemployed musicians. Hosted by Martin Block, it was broadcast by Radio WNEW, and airchecks of Chick and Ella's performance apparently still survive. In June they began an extensive run of one-nighters. When they appeared in Chick's hometown of Baltimore in July, they were mobbed, although surprisingly they could only manage a draw in a band battle at the Savoy against Horace Henderson on Sunday, July 31. In August they toured the West, playing two nights in Kansas City's Fairyland Park: one night for a white audience, the following night for a colored one. In St. Louis they were booked for a $750 guarantee against 50 percent of the gross; they earned $1,600 against a total gross gate of $3,200, which was big money, but it was being creamed off by the Gale office. Then, in September, they set an attendance record at New York's huge Paramount Theatre, breaking a five-year all-white record for the house. At the time, Webb's was only the third black band ever to play the Paramount, following Louis Armstrong and Cab Calloway.

Ella was beginning to have her own ideas about Webb's choice of programming, however. "Ella wanted her way," said Beverly Peer. "She kept on at Chick about the program. We played the Paramount. Ella chose the show. It didn't go down so well. Then Chick chose the program; it brought the house down."[40]

That same month Moe Gale received an offer from Warner Brothers for Chick, Ella, and the band to appear in a forthcoming Dick Powell picture, but advance bookings prevented them from appearing. In October they went back into the Paramount with $1,000 more than their previous guarantee. The following month their take of $25,000 in Chicago's Regal Theatre broke Benny Goodman's record, and in Camden, New Jersey, they created another box office record with a $3,500 take for a one-day performance.

With "A-Tisket, A-Tasket" Ella was now the most popular female vocalist in America. In three short years she had risen from obscurity to stardom, and although she was only twenty-one, she had the world at her feet. Her needs were simple: All she wanted was to sing and have a good time, and these were being fulfilled beyond her wildest dreams. "We used to go to nightclubs," said Charles Linton. "When she came out in the morning, she would have the shoes hanging across her shoulders, and as we were walking down the street, she was walking barefoot. She was cute, you know, but she also had a side. I just don't know what made her like it."

Ella had every reason to be happy and, especially, to be grateful to Chick Webb who had provided her with her big break. "One day we were at a rehearsal, and Chick was so happy she was doing well," continued Linton. "Ella was— We were standing off together side by side, and Chick was on the drums and they started a swing tune. Chick was looking at Ella with a big smile, and she turns and says, 'What the hell are you grinning at me for?' Right then I knew her disposition, when she says to her boss, 'What the hell are you grinning at me for?'"

CHAPTER FIVE

1938–1942

That was the one thing that Chick had in mind to do, that he wanted to do, to make Ella a star. I guess he had the foresight to see that something was going to happen to him.

TEDDY MCRAE[1]

IN NOVEMBER 1938, Chick and Ella were riding high. On the 11th, three of their records hit the charts. "I Found My Yellow Basket," a follow-up to "A-Tisket, A-Tasket," went on at number three, "Wacky Dust" at thirteen, and "Macpherson Is Rehearsin' (to Swing)" at fourteen. A week later "F.D.R. Jones," from the Broadway musical *Sing Out the News*, went to number eight. In December they played to record crowds in Galveston, Texas, and after a sellout week at the Apollo from January 18, 1939, they were at the exclusive, all-white Cocoanut Grove of the Park Central Hotel from January 25, 1939. They were the first black band booked there since the Noble Sissle Orchestra several years before. On their opening night Ella was spotted wearing a large diamond engagement ring. Speculation was immediately rife in the music press. *Down Beat* reported, "Ella to Wed! Plump chanteuse with Webb will go to the altar this month while band is at Park Central. . . . Ella won't reveal man's name."[2]

Elsewhere it was reported that the groom was to be Heywood Henry, the baritone saxophonist in the fast-rising Erskine Hawkins Orchestra: "Clarinet Iced Man! Heywood Henry of Erskine Hawkins courting Ella. Gave her ring!"[3] The Erskine Hawkins band, also represented by Moe Gale, was establishing itself at the Savoy Ballroom. It had arrived in New York fresh out of college as the 'Bama State Collegians in 1934. But in 1937, with a change of name when trumpeter Erskine Hawkins assumed leadership, the band signed with Gale and soon had fifty weeks of work a year, appearing regularly at the Savoy until the late 1950s.

"We all used to live at the Woodside Hotel during those early days," recalled Heywood Henry. "Most of the guys in the band stayed there, and so did Ella, and we started socializing together. We'd been hanging out together for quite a few weeks. We were working in the Royal at Baltimore, a theater, and Chick was in the Hollywood Theatre in Washington.

"So we had a little time off, and Ella came up to Baltimore to see me. Billy Rose, the writer, saw us sitting in a little bar, sitting in a booth together talking, and she had a ring on, so she told Billy Rose it was from me. So he wrote up we were engaged, and it was in all the papers. Later she sent me a telegram saying did I mind all the publicity. I sent her one back saying it didn't make any difference, so that's the way it went down. It wasn't the truth, but we were going around together.

"She was a very nice person. I had just come off a college campus, and she wasn't up to the kind of conversation that I liked to talk about. But Chick Webb used to encourage my friendship with Ella because he used to say I was a nice guy, fresh out of college. Those days everyone in Harlem smoked reefers, and you could get a shot of whiskey for five cents, but we were clean-living guys. I had represented my college running; I could even-time a hundred-yard dash.

"She digged being around guys that were well cultured because she wasn't cultured herself. Chick saw me with her. He told others I was the right type of guy because she didn't know nothing about nothing. She didn't know nothing about no man. She was no one when she came off the amateur hour; nobody paid her any attention. The guys in the band didn't pay her much attention until 'A-Tisket, A-Tasket' came along. Nobody thought much of her singing, but she was a natural! Not to learn it, just a natural, just like Frank Sinatra. You got to be a natural to learn all those damn songs! They don't know about no mathematical formulas of music, but they do it right.

"It turned out that I went by to see Ella one night. She told me she was tired and didn't feel like talking. She told me she was working down at the Park Central Hotel all night, and I said, 'Hell, I've been working up at the Savoy playing baritone.' Well, she said, 'you don't sing!' and I said, 'You don't play baritone, either.' I didn't think too much of singing. I thought playing the horn was more important than singing. When I grew up, everybody in town could sing, so that wasn't saying anything!"[4]

Soon their romance fizzled: "Ella Wasn't Wed," reported *Down Beat*. "Diamond ring she has been sporting of late is Xmas gift from

Moe Gale, personal manager. . . . Would not comment on diamond, marriage false tip."[5] Once again, it was the problem of a romance in the entertainment business: Two people working unsocial hours, each with different schedules, grabbing time together when they could, and often tired; friction was inevitable. In 1967, Henry gave author Gene Fernett a rare portrait of Ella taken in a dime-store automatic photo machine in Boston, a souvenir of their long-past affair.[6]

However, while the Park Central engagement provided speculation about Ella in the music press, more sinister forces were at work: "I hope the last-minute flash rumors are erroneous," reported the *New York Age*. "Chick Webb and Ella (Tisket Tasket) Fitzgerald, 'First Lady of Swing,' are the objects of ill effect at the swank Cocoanut Grove, Park Central Hotel on Broadway, along with the Four Ink Spots, NBC (male) songcasters. Evidently the loathsome serpent, race prejudice, has cropped up out of the darkness; the dirty viper, he will find his domain in hell, not in New York. Certain 'cheap,' jealous Nordics are supposed to have functioned an ouster. I heard the grand opening on Wednesday night, right after the fight [Joe Louis KO'd John H. Lewis], and Ella began her program with 'Just a Kid Named Joe,' far from the Harlem jive, and her rendition of the sensational bit of 'F.D.R. Jones' was a solid killer. Moe Gale, the manager, says they'll fight to a finish."[7]

The Park Central booking, set to be an indefinite engagement, ended shortly afterward. Gale hastily assembled a series of one-nighters to keep the band working, and in mid-February the band was in Memphis, but Webb was experiencing great pain and was frequently spelled by Hal West, formerly of Roy Eldridge's band. "Webb one-nighting while under the weather so played few numbers himself. Ella knocked them for a wow!" announced one press report.[8]

Even if Webb's failing health was causing his playing to become inconsistent in live performances, the hits kept coming. On March 18, "Undecided" was on the chart at number eight, and the following week "'Tain't What You Do (It's the Way That 'Cha Do It)," another tune Ella tagged with "Re-bop," went on for one week at nineteen. At the beginning of May a composition by Ella, "Chew, Chew, Chew, Chew Your Bubble Gum," charted for a week at fourteen.

"We were really on our way then," said Teddy McRae, "with a double attraction, Ella and Chick Webb's band. The band was really on its way."[9] Webb was now enjoying unprecedented popularity. His gamble in backing Ella had paid off; he'd made the breakthrough to both black and white audiences to such an extent that *Down Beat* was now calling it "one of the best known and most popular swing bands in the country."[10]

But dark clouds were looming on the horizon. In April, Webb finally surrendered to the terrible pain he was enduring and entered the Johns Hopkins Hospital in Baltimore for treatment. "That fluid in his back, something was happening with that," said Teddy McRae. "So they figured they had to have it drained. Chick [went] to the hospital and they operated on that, they drained it. The doctor took some fluid out of it or something, you know. And it made him worse. So then we brought in Big Sid Catlett . . . and [Bill] Beason and others [to] rest him up. . . . We went on the road and did a couple of one-nighters. We took Big Sid Catlett with us."[11]

When Webb was discharged, the band returned to Park Central, this time to no controversy, and in May they went into the spot just vacated by Louis Armstrong at Boston's Southland Café where they did "bang-up business, chiefly because of the drawing power of Chick and Ella."[12] The Southland had a radio hookup, and a broadcast from May 1939 has enjoyed frequent reissue on both vinyl and compact disc. In their half-hour show, Ella is featured on four numbers, contrasting the band's killer-diller spots with ballads. The arrangements that feature her are really quite poor by 1939 standards and serve only to highlight that at this stage of her career she is still an immature if nevertheless effective ballad singer. Her "rhythm singing," however, is excellent, and on the novelty number "Chew, Chew, Chew" her infectious swing brings an awful number alive. Another Ella original in the childish-charm mold of "A-Tisket, A-Tasket," she shows her ability to "sell" a song, right down to the crazy voice she assumes for laughs in the final chorus.

In contrast, the Webb band swings mightily on the snatch of Webb's theme, "Let's Get Together," giving a portent of what was to come on "Poor Little Rich Girl" and "Break 'Em Down." Once again these arrangements are not especially well written, but there is electricity in their interpretation that still manages to communicate across the decades. It is impossible not to listen to these numbers without wanting to move in time with the music, and a lot of credit for this must go to Beverly Peer's bass playing, the rock on which the Webb band was built. Webb acts as a colorist, supercharging certain phrases with perfectly timed accents, yet is content for the band to swing around him while he keeps relatively simple time. Only on the out choruses does he flex his muscles, giving us a hint of how he built his reputation at the Savoy Ballroom in Harlem. Nothing Webb plays is extraneous or overly complicated, yet in the scheme of the arrangements, what he does play assumes an almost frightening logic; like all great jazz musicians, Webb had the capacity to edit his playing for maximum impact.

Following their stay at Southland, the band embarked on an exhausting round of one-nighters. But with each booking Webb was clearly getting worse and in need of hospital treatment. In Washington, D.C., when the band was about to travel south, he left to return to Johns Hopkins Hospital in Baltimore. "I sat out in front of Keyes Restaurant [with Chick], and we were talking in the back of his Cadillac," said McRae. "His wife was sitting in the car. . . . He was driving back. He sat in front of the Keyes Restaurant, there at Seventh and T. That's the eatery, the famous eatery . . . around the corner from the theater.

"And he was telling me, 'Anything happens to me . . . take care of Ella. Don't let the guys mess up. Just take care of Ella.' I said, 'Ah, man, come on. You're going to be all right. You know everything's going to be all right.' He said, 'Nah. I got to take care of this business. Take care of Ella. . . . ' I said, 'Okay. I'll see you. Go back and have the operation, and I'll see you in Florida in four or five days.' 'I'll be down there,' [said Webb]. I hollered at his wife: 'All right. I'll see y'all later.'"[13]

During the first few days of June, Chick made a guest appearance at a swing concert at the Hippodrome, sponsored by the National Swing Club of America. On June 9 he was again admitted to Johns Hopkins Hospital. He was now having problems with his kidneys, compounded by the difficulties he was having with his spine. On June 16, 1939, he finally gave up the struggle and died quietly in his mother's arms.

Meanwhile, with Bill Beason substituting on drums, Ella and the band had reached Alabama on the southern leg of their tour. They were unaware of Webb's death. After playing four sets they had the bizarre experience of receiving no reaction from the audience. "Nobody clapped or nothing," said McRae. "Everybody just stood there and looked at us. . . . So the road manager called Taft [Jordan] inside. . . . When he came back out he told us: 'You know, Chick Webb died today. Passed away this afternoon.' Now we didn't know that, we never knew that; we hadn't heard. We were traveling all day long. We came straight off the road right into the ballroom. . . . Everybody in town knew it. Everybody heard it on the radio all over the country. But the band didn't know it."[14] Afterward they made the sad journey back to Baltimore and waited for the funeral.

"Just once toward the end Chick was a little pitiful," recalled trombonist Sandy Williams. "'When I was young and playing for peanuts,' he told me, 'I could eat anything you guys eat, but now I have all this money and can eat certain things. I can't even take a little nip when I want to.' In my estimation, Chick was the top drummer. I guess Gene Krupa was the closest competition in his last years. . . . Krupa and Buddy Rich used to hang around Chick in those days. Of course Sidney Cadett was hell of a drummer, too. But Chick didn't take no from anybody. He thought he was the best, and he'd tell you he was the best, right quick. He couldn't read a note, but he was a top-notcher."[15]

In Baltimore, people gathered in the thousands to mourn Chick. "I went out to the little house where Chick often stayed with his uncle," said Garvin Bushell. "The casket was on view there, and Gene Krupa—who was playing in town then—was sitting by the casket and sobbing. He idolized Chick. Later I came back, and Gene was still sitting there. He stayed all day. The following day they stopped all the traffic all across the city for his funeral. They hadn't even done that for the mayor, but they did it for Chick and paid their respects."[16]

Webb, who had battled long and hard to get to the top, had enjoyed his triumph for only a few months. The vast crowds that turned out for his funeral now seemed somehow ironic. "His funeral was memorable, and perversely this was success beyond his wildest dream," said Helen Oakley-Dance. "Thousands lined the streets for the procession, and thousands more viewed him in the AME church where he lay. . . . Ella Fitzgerald sang . . . few listened unmoved as she paid final tribute with 'My Buddy.'"[17]

Within two weeks of Webb's death Ella and the band were back in New York and in the recording studios. "She never skipped a beat, was back the next day," said Beverly Peer. "She was thinking about her future."[18] Of the five numbers recorded on June 29, 1939, "I Want the Waiter (with the Water)" continued Ella's run of hits, charting at nine for three weeks in September. Initially, the Gale office's main concern was honoring the existing bookings for the band and finishing the potentially lucrative southern tour. To prepare, the band went into the Savoy where it worked up a new program centered around Ella. "We played there about a week," said McRae, "just to rest the band and add Bill Beason to the band. . . . For a show we had to reset everything because Chick Webb was a big part of the band."[19] Then followed a profile appearance at the Paramount Theatre, billed as Ella Fitzgerald and the Famous Chick Webb Orchestra, where they alternated with the movie *Wuthering Heights*.

After a guest appearance on "George Jessel's Celebrities" on NBC's Red Network on August 23, where she shared the airwaves with boxer Jack Dempsey, Ella and the band went back on the road. "We were booked all the way down into Florida and all through the Midwest. Those dates were still pending," recalled Teddy McRae. "We went to Chicago . . . and played the Grand Terrace while Earl Hines was out. We stayed there about four weeks. We worked our way back into New York and played the Roseland Ballroom. Then we went to the Famous Door. . . . We stayed there about four weeks; we broadcast from there."[20]

At Chicago's Grand Terrace in September, Chick's name was dropped. The billing became Ella Fitzgerald and Her Famous Orchestra. An unusual consequence was that Ella now had to join the musicians' union; in those days singers, who were not considered musicians, belonged to the actors' union!

Ella's name was big business, and Gale intended to capitalize on it. But she hadn't a clue how to run a big band, to motivate or discipline thirteen mature men, rehearse them, decide on repertoire, and all the other sundry tasks that bandleaders found themselves doing. These duties were taken on by trumpeter Taft Jordan, who had been with Webb since 1933 and had directed the band when Webb was indisposed. "After Chick died, I had charge of the band for a while, but I was young. A bit later there was a lot of resentment."[21] This finally blew up at the end of the long tour when the band went into the Roseland Ballroom in December 1939. As a result Gale asked Benny Carter, a musician who commanded respect throughout the world of jazz, to take over the band.

"They couldn't come to any agreement with Benny," said Teddy McRae, "because Benny said it would be Benny Carter's band featuring Ella Fitzgerald. And Moe didn't want that. He wanted Ella to have the band. So Benny said, 'Why don't you give the band to Teddy McRae?' So he called me in, and we made an agreement."[22] As a result there were several personnel changes: "Shake-up Hits Ella's Band; Bob Stark Out," reported *Down Beat* in January 1940. Among the changes was the addition of pianist Ram Ramirez, who came in to replace Tommy Fulford who had been stricken by pneumonia.

Almost as soon as Ramirez joined, the band traveled to Baltimore to play a concert in aid of the Chick Webb Memorial Recreation Fund. "We went down there and we did our thing to pay tribute," said Ramirez. "It was a great big thing because Chick was from Baltimore. It was a huge stadium and all the acts were there. Everybody came over to play. Billie Holiday. The city of Baltimore gave their respects to Chick."[23] The governor of Maryland, the state senator, Joe Louis, Chick's wife, Sallye, and Chick's grandfather were among an audience of eight thousand who paid $1.15 each, raising a total gross of $9,200. Ella and her band performed "Oh Johnny," and other artists included the Ink Spots, Peg Leg Bates, the Nicholas Brothers, and Teddy Hill.

In May Ella and the band went into the Famous Door on Fifty-second Street, by which time trombonist Sandy Williams and two more of the original band had gone, disenchanted since Webb's death. Ironically, the Famous Door went bust the following month; its owners, Felshin and Brooks, left without paying the Gale office for the booking.

The problem that beset Ella's band from the start was money, as Taft Jordan explained: "The higher-ups . . . didn't want to pay anybody any money. I think we were making $75 a week while guys in other big orchestras that were not drawing as much as we were were making $25 to $35 a week more."[24] John Chilton reported that admission charges to see Ella's band at this time were just as much as for the top bands of the day, such as Ellington, Lunceford, and Basie.

Clearly Gale was holding down the wages of the band to increase his profit margins, which made for dissension among the band members who wanted a fairer split of the take. During Chick's lifetime there was a feeling of fraternity among the sidemen because of the loyalty the little drummer inspired, but after he died the group became purely a business venture run by Gale. "It was a way for me to work," Ella once explained.[25] And the band was beginning to see it that way, too. Men who happily accepted low wages under Webb had felt they were part of a team, but now they no longer shared this feeling of camaraderie. They quickly became conscious that they were an anonymous backup group for Ella, a fact underlined by having to play some fairly dire stuff at times, such as "My Wubba Dolly," which went to number sixteen on the charts in November 1939.

In 1940, Ella became one of the youngest members of the American Society of Composers, Authors and Publishers (ASCAP). The songs she was credited with composing, either by herself or in collaboration with others, included: "A-Tisket, A-Tasket," "You Showed Me the Way," "I Found My Yellow Basket," "Once Is Enough for Me," "Betcha Nickel," "Please Tell the Truth," "Oh! But I Do," "Spinnin' the Webb," "Chew, Chew, Chew," and "Deedle-De-Dum." Most were novelty songs that flowed in the wake of "A-Tisket, A-Tasket" and were custom-made for the hit parade charts. Indeed, Ella's entire repertoire at this time was motivated by commercial rather than artistic considerations. No song was too trite or banal, as "My Wubba Dolly" proved when she affected a baby-girl voice, and it is easy to see why Mario Bauza described her as a commercial singer.

Ella's popularity continued through much of 1940. "The Starlight Hour" and "Sing Song Swing" were on the charts at numbers seventeen and twenty-three in successive weeks in April; a cover version of Clyde McCoy's "Sugar Blues" went to twenty-seven for one week in June; "Shake Down the Stars" went to eighteen in July, and "Five O'Clock Whistle" went to nine in December.

Ella and the band remained at Roseland until the end of April, broadcasting regularly over an NBC wire. There are several airchecks available that reveal the band was a lot tighter than during Webb's time but that it had no specific identity other than that projected by Ella's voice. What is also immediately apparent is how little the style of the band had changed since Ella made her recording debut five years earlier. Bands such as Ellington, Goodman, Basie, Lunceford, Calloway, Glenn Miller, and Artie Shaw had continually refined and improved the quality of their arrangements, and over that same relatively short period they had become increasingly sophisticated.

In contrast, Moe Gale was not interested in raising his overhead with better orchestrations to frame his star singer but was content to milk Ella's commercial potential for all it was worth. Gradually this nearsighted policy began to catch up with Ella's band at the box office. In October 1940, for example, the Jay McShann Orchestra, which only twelve months previously had been a seven-piece group playing in obscurity in Kansas City, outdrew her three to one at River View in Des Moines, Iowa.[26]

The problem was that no thought had been given to creating a context for Ella's singing by employing sympathetic arrangers and expanding her role within the band with suitable, specially arranged material. She continued to operate as she had done with Webb, as a band singer, albeit with the band in her name, grinding out the pop songs with no apparent discrimination between good and bad. Much of her recorded output was marred by poor arrangements that sounded no better than music publishers' stock arrangements of the kind that could be bought over the counter at most music stores.

Given Ella's proven hit parade and box office success and the revenue this was generating, her career should have been moved forward at this point with more sensitive management and investment in her potential; after all, she was still only twenty-three. Indeed, a sense of artistic direction from Ella herself might have helped focus her talents. Instead, both band and singer began to wither on the vine, using many tired formula arrangements that would have sounded dated even at the beginning of the swing era.

The potential of framing a singer within sympathetic orchestrations, instead of band performances "with vocal refrain" (as the old 78s used to say), remained unresolved until, as Gunther Schuller has pointed out, the very capable Helen Forrest joined the Harry James Orchestra at the end of 1941. It was then that James had the foresight to instruct his arrangers to create special musical frameworks for Forrest that supported and enhanced her voice and created, as a result, many "magical performances."[27]

But Ella was happy to sing anything, particularly if she or her advisers thought it would sell. "She was a poplike singer at that point," said Milt Gabler, who would later take over her recording career at Decca. "She was a jive singer, and the kids, the whites and blacks, used to love to dance to that kind of thing. She was a jive singer, and they kept her in that damn groove a long time, even when I started to work for Decca."[28]

Consequently, it is difficult to see her as a jazz singer per se during her big-band period. The term implies a certain aesthetic direction that is lacking in her work. For example, as early as 1939, Lee Wiley began recording 78 albums by composers such as George Gershwin, Cole Porter, and Richard Rodgers, backed by sympathetic jazz musicians. Meanwhile, Mildred Bailey had completed a series of almost perfect sides with her husband Red Norvo that sported some brilliant arrangements by Eddie Sauter, and Billie Holiday's small-group recordings from 1935 to 1939 with Teddy Wilson are among the enduring classics of jazz.

Between her recording debut with Chick Webb and the demise of her own big band in 1942, Ella cut almost 150 sides, but many of these were pop or novelty songs that were of dubious merit. It brings to mind critic Whitney Balliett's wry comment that only about a quarter of Frank Sinatra's work with Tommy Dorsey's orchestra between 1940 and 1942 is worth hearing more than once.[29] In Ella's case it was even less than a quarter. Certainly some of her more popular work, such as cover versions of "Undecided," "'Tain't What You Do," and "The Dipsy Doodle," with her first outing in extended scat, or pop songs such as "A Little Bit Later On" (a favorite of George T. Simon) and "Rock It for Me," still in her repertoire in 1961, were pleasant. But in the context of jazz during this period, or indeed the swing era as a whole, Ella's work barely warrants a mention. Her early period is really remembered for just one song, "A-Tisket, A-Tasket," a fun number of great charm but little artistic merit.

In May 1940, while at the Famous Door, Ella cut four titles for Decca, among them "Gulf Coast Blues" which was included by *Metronome*'s Gordon Wright (a pseudonym for George T. Simon) in the top fifty discs of the year and by *Esquire*'s Carlton Smith in his top ten of 1940. In June the band went on tour to capitalize on several months of coast-to-coast broadcasting; Ella was mobbed by a crowd of four thousand in New Orleans who "tore the clothes off [her] . . . when she left the stand and made her way to an exit in the New Rhythm Club."[30] At the end of the year Universal opened negotiations with the Gale office with a view to featuring Ella in a forthcoming Abbott and Costello movie.

For a long period during the following year, 1941, Ella was involved with Benny Kornegay, one of the many hangers-on she attracted wherever the band performed. "That's who she went off with in between shows," said Beverly Peer. "Everyone called him Cigarette. I don't know why; he wasn't tall and thin. He was a quiet, private guy."[31] After a while the couple appeared to be serious, and Kornegay began going on one-night stands in the band bus. "He traveled with us, picked up the checks," said trumpeter Mousie Randolph, who was with the band from late 1939.[32] Toward the end of the year it was clear that Ella was smitten with Kornegay. He had moved in with her, and when the band was on the road, he shared a room with her. As with Heywood Henry, the thought of marriage had begun to loom large in Ella's daydreams. Kornegay, for his part, saw a chance of a regular paycheck. Things were going well between them. When Benny "borrowed" a few bucks from money he had collected from promoters, Ella made up the difference.

Another time when he "lost" a few more bucks, Ella stuck up for him. He was sure he had a goose who was going to lay countless golden eggs, and he asked her to marry him. Ella was delighted. The band was out on the road, and she simply couldn't wait until they returned to New York to fulfill her greatest ambition: On Friday, December 26, 1941, Ella and Benjamin Kornegay were married in St. Louis, Missouri.

However, the marriage was not mentioned in the music press, which was ever alert for the slightest gossip in the band business; within days of returning to New York it was hushed up. As soon as he learned of the nuptials, Moe Gale, taken aback at Ella's sudden and unexpected rush to wed, decided to find out a little more about the mysterious Mr. Kornegay. He had heard about the cash discrepancies and immediately put private investigators on the case. What they came up with was not good. Kornegay had a criminal record: He had been convicted of drug charges in the 1930s and had served time. To make matters worse, he was becoming increasingly assertive and insisting on greater involvement in his wife's career.

Moe Gale was appalled. A normally compliant client had become a major headache overnight. Kornegay was "persuaded" to back off. But it took several weeks to persuade Ella that things were not what they seemed and to break with Kornegay, by which time she had given an interview to Sidney Shields describing the domestic bliss she was now enjoying, a story carefully designed by her press agent. It spoke of Benny listening to Ella's records while she was on the road and of his going out to listen to her on jukeboxes. Kornegay, for his part, made it clear that he had no intention of divorcing his golden goose. The only alternative to fighting a potentially messy and damaging divorce was to seek an annulment, but New York State was particularly strict on such petitions. In the end, Gale instructed his lawyers to proceed on the basis that Benjamin Kornegay married Ella on false pretenses, that he had withheld from her the information about his criminal record, and that the marriage was motivated by criminal intent. In the end this provided sufficient grounds for the annulment Ella sought, which was granted in mid-1942.

Ella's press office papered over the cracks. They released a statement designed to make the whole affair sound like a silly, childish foible, claiming that the judge said, "You go back to singing 'A-Tisket, A-Tasket' and leave the boys alone." The truth could hardly have been more different. The case was closely contested, and in the climate that then prevailed in the New York judiciary, Ella was fortunate to have succeeded in her suit.

A photograph exists of Ella leaving the court after the action; she is beaming from ear to ear. But when Moe Gale had initially spelled

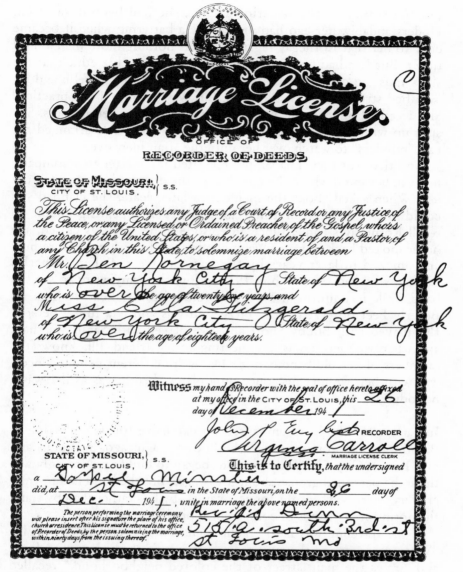

The speculation about whether Ella's first marriage to Benny Kornegay actually took place has often been compounded by her apparent inability to remember Kornegay's name. This copy of their marriage certificate, dated December 26, 1941, in St. Louis, Missouri, removes the doubt once and for all. The "C" in the top right-hand corner denotes "colored."

out the reality of the situation to her, she had been devastated. Understandably, her ego had undergone a battering when it became clear to her that Kornegay regarded her as nothing more than a meal ticket. But Ella had been raised on the strict show biz ethic that the show must go on, as personified by her mentor Chick Webb and his dignified struggle against the odds. Ella was nothing if not practical. She accepted philosophically what she was told by her advisers. She split up with Kornegay with little fuss, and Moe Gale arranged for two "minders" to watch over her until the affair blew over.

And that was that. Ella simply relegated the matter to a compartment in her mind where she could close the door and throw away the key. When asked about the incident in later years, she claimed she could not remember anything about it, even appearing unable to recall Kornegay's name. Once an episode in her life was closed, she never looked back. Former Webb bandmates, for example, were hurt and amazed in later years by the way she treated them. Charles Linton, who had left Webb in 1938 to join the army, went to see the band while in uniform in 1939. Ella refused to say hello to him. As Beverly Peer observed, "Ella Fitzgerald was and is a funny person. I've played with Bobby Short and I've played with Sarah Vaughan, and when we met, it was like meeting an old friend. Ella knows the members of her old band, yet it's like we're different people. Since I was with her, we met just once on a plane; then it was as if I was a nobody."[33]

In early 1941 the band embarked on extensive touring, starting in Pittsburgh, and going through the Midwest, Chicago, St. Louis, and into Kansas City. Gradually tensions began to build up. Not only was there the perennial grouse about low wages, but the band had to travel everywhere—except the longest hauls—by bus rather than by train, the norm for big bands of comparable popularity.

If the traveling was hard on the men, it was even harder on Ella. "When we get in [to the city where we're playing], the bus goes down and circles the main street of the colored neighborhood," recalled Teddy McRae, "and everybody was standing with their little girls waiting to meet Ella Fitzgerald. Now, we've been riding all day long. And Ella maybe couldn't come out of the bus because her hair was all down; we had to keep her in the back. Then she got dressed. She had a welcome committee. She almost had to get dressed on the bus. It was really rough on a girl traveling with a band, especially in the summertime."[34]

Not only was travel made harder by the incessant bus trips, but the members of the band also had to find their own band suits, something many other bands provided free. And on top of that, they still had to pay for their lodgings. Eventually bad feelings began to surface. "A guy called Frenchie worked for Moe Gale," said Teddy McRae. "He was a road manager. Frenchie says, 'Can I talk to you for a minute . . . before we leave here tonight? I want to tell you something.' He called me over to the side and said, 'You know, we're going to pick up a new drummer in Kansas City.' 'A new drummer? Why?' I say. 'Well, you heard the argument on the bus with Beason and Ella. You know they got into a little argument on the bus. Beason said something to Ella, and Ella said, 'Well, you can go home if you want to.' So that was a couple of days before we had to play. . . . Jessie Price agreed [to replace Beason]. Moe Gale must've made him a good offer, so he agreed to join the band [when we got to Kansas City]."[35]

Price was impressive. It took just one hearing for him to play all the band's numbers faultlessly and with the flair of Webb himself. "When we got to California, there was nothing you could tell this man," continued McRae. "He was just sensational on stage. . . . We played in Los Angeles. Ella did *Ride 'Em Cowboy*. Abbott and Costello. We were sitting out there doing nothing waiting for Ella to finish doing the picture for a week. . . . We were on the coast about a month. We played up and down the coast."[36]

Ella sang two numbers in *Ride 'Em Cowboy*, which was released in March 1942. A Universal rodeo extravaganza directed by Arthur Lubin, featuring Abbott and Costello, it proved to be an otherwise forgettable film. However, Ella's performance provides some explanation of her remarkable popularity. She projected a light, frothy, easygoing humor that simultaneously communicated and was endearing. In contrast to the come-and-get-me sexuality of Lena Horne or the vamplike bandleader Ina Ray Hutton, Ella seemed innocent, unsullied, and playful. From her recordings we get only half the story; on the film version of "A-Tisket, A-Tasket" she goes through a complete little-girl-lost routine that fits the lyrics perfectly. Even on "Rockin' 'n' Reelin'," sung with the vocal group the Merry Macs, she is full of ingenious, girlish mischievousness—a fascinating glimpse of the young Ella as much an entertainer as a singer.

While in Los Angeles in July the band recorded six numbers. Included was the dire "Melinda the Mousie," in stark contrast to Ella's remarkably mature vocal on "When My Sugar Walks Down the Street." Here she presages much of her subsequent postwar work on the Decca label: an assured, swinging but relatively straight first chorus (Beverly Peer's powerfully swinging bass was as vital to Ella's band as it was to Webb's), returning for an out chorus where she takes just enough rhythmic and harmonic liberties to give the song a real feeling of "lift." In this instance the momentum her vocal line generates is spoiled by an unsatisfactory coda, lurching briefly into half-time, a difficult obstacle course for any singer but negotiated impeccably by Ella. This contrived effect serves only to highlight the functional rather than the inspired quality of arrangements used by the band. Although "Sugar" failed to get on the charts, it remains, despite its shortcomings, one of the better cuts of the period. Nineteen forty-one did provide three minor hits, however: "Louisville, K-Y," number twenty-three in February; "Hello Ma! I Done It Again," twenty-six in March, and "The Muffin Man," twenty-three in August. A hundred copies of "Muffin Man" were sent to war-torn London later in the year in response to requests for records to help pass the interminable hours spent by the public in bomb shelters.

After the filming and recording, the band continued with a long series of one-nighters. But despite the unrelenting grind of long bus trips from coast to coast, Ella could still produce truly memorable performances. Her stature as an artist was growing; her performances in front of a live audience were reaching a level of intensity she had not achieved in the recording studio. "One night, around eleven or twelve o'clock," recalled Teddy McRae, "Ella started singing a medley of things, and she had everybody in tears. She was singing her heart out that night. That's one of those nights, I guess, she was thinking about Chick. I guess something hit her. Boy, this was half an hour, and the ballroom was quiet, and Ella was going through these songs. She just tore the place up."[37]

On their return to New York on September 1941, the band went into the reopened Famous Door on New York's celebrated "Swing Street," followed by a week at the Apollo. In October they traveled to Boston for a stay at Levaggi's Restaurant. "After I left Cab Calloway in 1941," said trumpeter Dizzy Gillespie, "I went to Levaggi's in Boston with Ella Fitzgerald. . . . Teddy McRae was in charge of the band then."[38] Gillespie, brash and enthusiastic, had been sacked from the Calloway band under controversial circumstances. Calloway's was then one of the top black bands in the country, so working with Ella was something of a step down. Even so, Gillespie was glad of the work. "Dizzy agreed to go up and play with us . . . made four weeks with us," said McRae.[39] But the strange setup in the

Fitzgerald band totally bemused Gillespie: "Teddy McRae was the leader who took charge of everything," he said. "Ella just sang. It was Ella's band, but the money went to the Gale agency which paid Ella, but the musical directorship of the band was in the hands of Teddy McRae, and he hired me. . . . After that, they fired him!"[40]

McRae had taken up the matter of pay with Moe Gale; the issue had simmered bitterly beneath the surface during the long tour. "I wanted more money for the musicians because they had worked their hearts out," he explained. "On the road you'd be working a long time. . . . And they're making all that money, and they don't want to divide, you know. Look, give the guys a raise. This band should get more money!"[41] As McRae discovered, Moe Gale met dissension with dismissal. "He came up the last day, it was Saturday night. . . . Moe Gale comes in after the second show, and he has with him my friend Eddie Barefield. . . . So Barefield took over the band. . . . That night, 12:05, I came back to New York. That was the end of it with Ella."[42]

Eddie Barefield was a much-respected musician who had an impressive track record. An alto saxophonist and accomplished clarinettist, he had played with leaders such as Bennie Moten, Cab Calloway, Les Hite, Fletcher Henderson, Don Redman, and Benny Carter by the time he took over Ella's band. He had even played briefly with Ella for a couple of months, from the end of 1939 to April 1940, as a replacement for Garvin Bushell. "We went out to Chicago . . . several road trips. Took several road trips down to Florida. . . . We came back and then I quit. . . . I had a little band . . . went to Boston with Benny Carter, and when I came back, worked with Don Redman. Then finally I ran into Charlie Buchanan who had the Savoy. And he said, 'When are you going to work for me?' I said, 'Well, I don't want to come back up there, but if you want me to do something, get me the job conducting Ella.' So he did. And I went down and talked to them, and they gave me the job leading the band. So I had to go to Boston and hear the band and everything, and then we brought the band back into New York and rehearsed for a couple of weeks.

"I ran the whole thing. She sang whatever I called for her to sing, and I made arrangements for her and Dick Vance, and a few others made arrangements. And we took a trip after I got the band in shape because I added some more men, different things—enlarged the band a little bit. . . . Instead of the regular three trumpets and two trombones, I had three trombones and four trumpets and five saxes."[43]

Yet Barefield was also to find the problems of pay with the Gale office intractable. Musicologist Phil Schaap has pointed out that "as a leader he had to come to terms with the fact that he wasn't much more than an ant on the ground as far as management was concerned. Both Barefield and Taft Jordan were both very bitter about this. It really wasn't the job it seemed. All they did was coordinate the musicians. Moe Gale really demeaned the importance of the bandleader and I guess by extrapolation the band, so it wasn't a great gig to have. Money was one of the problems, but it was also what you got to play."

Barefield inherited a divided band, and bad feeling persisted about money. As one band member recalled: "The booking office that handled us, it was rumored, was giving certain of its bandleaders bonuses to 'cool' the demands of the men for more money. Now that story kept persisting, and that didn't help morale. Although we trusted Eddie Barefield . . . it made us all mad to be working under such a setup."[44]

In any event, the band's days were numbered. In March, April, and July 1942, Ella recorded a series of numbers with the instrumental/vocal group the Three Keys. There was immediate speculation in the music press about Ella's future. According to *Orchestra World*, "Conflicting stories have been circulating about Ella Fitzgerald giving up her band."[45] *Metronome*'s front page announced: "Ella Drops Band, Works with Trio,"[46] while *Music and Rhythm* reported, "Ella Fitzgerald Will Quit as Leader: Moe Gale . . . revealed that Miss Fitzgerald would appear exclusively with a new Philadelphia vocal instrumental group using the name 'Three Keys,' comprising the Furness brothers who sing and play piano, bass, and guitar."[47]

The first discs by Ella and the Keys went out in May, while the band was on the West Coast. Several weeks of bookings had been canceled so that the band could tour army camps to entertain the troops. Eight weeks before the band finally broke up, it was at the Trianon Ballroom, South Gate, California. It sounded "rough in spots"; Barefield "had a wealth of ideas on clarinet"; Ella was "still as fine as ever" and "especially at home at slow tempos."[48]

Eventually Ella Fitzgerald and Her Famous Orchestra completed their final commitments, and at the end of July they played their last date together at the Earl Theatre in Philadelphia, sharing the bill with Bill Robinson. By then Eddie Barefield had become dissatisfied with the whole setup: "I just got disgusted," he said.[49] By the end of the week the musicians went their separate ways, and the band was no more. "The best thing that ever happened to it," said bassist Beverly Peer.[50]

CHAPTER SIX

1942–1946

[Milt] Gabler, a man of empyrean standards . . . brought a
wide intelligence and a good ear to the music.

WHITNEY BALLIETT[1]

ELLA SURVEYED a brave new world when she made her first public
appearance with the Three Keys at the Aquarium Theatre in New
York's Times Square in September 1942. Things had changed radically
since the heady days of 1940. Then she had been voted Number One
Female Vocalist in both the *Down Beat* and *Metronome* polls and was
at the peak of her popularity. Now she had slipped to seventh in the
Metronome poll (she was ineligible to compete under the rules of the
Down Beat poll because she was a bandleader in 1941), and falling
box office receipts had forced Moe Gale to disband her orchestra.

Wartime restrictions made travel difficult, and from August 1942
the American Federation of Musicians imposed a recording ban.
They were claiming the right to a fee for every record played over the
air. The strike dragged on for a year, and musicians were forbidden to
enter the studios. It meant that other than stockpiled sides, which
clearly were not the popular songs of the day that could be heard live
on radio, nothing new was appearing on record from the big bands
during the strike. To fill the void, record companies turned to the
only musicians who were not members of the union: the singers.
Backed by vocal trios, quartets, quintets, sextets, and every possible
permutation up to full choirs, singers were suddenly thrust onto center stage. As long as no musicians were used in the recording session,
the union ban was not infringed. Ironically, however, Decca did not
turn to Ella. They considered her popularity to be on the wane.

No one knew it at the time, but the big band era was effectively
over. The buoyant optimism and excitement of the big bands that
epitomized Roosevelt's "New Deal" was giving way to the somber
realism of a country at war. Singers were more in keeping with the

times: Lovers were being parted, and the mood was sentimental. Billie Holiday's 1941 "All of Me" became a favorite of countless homesick G.I.s, and a re-release of Harry James's 1939 "All or Nothing at All" became one of the first big hits for Frank Sinatra. When Sinatra moved from the James band to Tommy Dorsey's in early 1940, the bobby-soxers began to scream. By the time he bought out his contract in September 1942, his popularity was overshadowing Dorsey's. Booked into the Paramount Theatre in December 1942, he was a sensation. The girls screamed again, this time longer and louder; if some were paid to do so, thousands did it for free, and modern pop hysteria was born. (It is interesting to note that the phenomenon of young girls being bribed to misbehave at musical events was much older, dating back to at least Paderewski's sensationally successful American tours in the 1890s.)

But Sinatra's success marked a pivotal point in popular music. Singers were poised to replace the big bands in the popularity stake. However, Ella, the "plump chanteuse," looked set to be gradually sidelined by this new breed of romantic and photogenic songster. Much of her popularity was due to novelty numbers, but musical fashion was changing fast. She had not had a hit record since "The Muffin Man" in August 1941, and that had only made it to twenty-three on the charts for just one week. Now her career was being sustained by the memory of "A-Tisket, A-Tasket" and the following she had built up during her big band days, through radio, records, and personal appearances. Her career was kept afloat by her popularity at the major black vaudeville houses like the Apollo in New York, the Howard Theatre in Washington, D.C., the Earle Theatre in Philadelphia, and the Regal Theatre in Chicago, but that was hardly mainstream U.S.A.

Ella and the Three Keys, like most artists in Moe Gale's stable, spent a great deal of time working the military camps, and this further served to take her out of the public's eye. Thus the January 1943 *Metronome* readers' poll continued to reflect Ella's slipping popularity as she sank to eleventh position. In March 1943 she appeared at the Apollo, and it was clear that she had adjusted well to singing with a small group: "Much as one misses the old Chick Webb band," said *Metronome*, "the Keys' instrumental and vocal backing makes pleasant listening. They support her with sustained chords, occasional unison and riffing, and sometimes harmonize with her."[2]

Their repertoire included numbers like "Giddap Mule," "Craziest Dream," and the Ella Mae Morse hit, "Cow-Cow Boogie," a number

Ella herself would record eight months later. But of considerable interest was the fact that she was covering "Flying Home," Lionel Hampton's big 1942 hit. "'Flying Home' without words was good fun," *Metronome* reported. "Ella sang a scat chorus based on the famous tenor solo in Lionel Hampton's Decca version."³ Two years later she recorded it for Decca. When it was released it became a milestone in her career, acclaimed as a tour de force of scat singing.

In the course of 1943 the Furness brothers were gradually claimed by the draft board, forcing the Keys to disband. When Ella opened at the new Zanzibar Club in New York on July 1, she was booked in with her new pianist and musical director, Bill Doggett. The Zanzibar was once the ill-fated Frolics, which had a reputation for a series of flops before it was eventually forced to close its doors. When it reopened under a new name and new management, many predicted a similar fate, but Ella confounded the critics. With a mixture of her in-person charm and sheer ability, she did such good business that she was held over until October. "That was a great date," recalled Bill Doggett. "The Zanzibar at that time was a fabulous club on Broadway at Forty-ninth. They held us over. One of the shows they had was the boogie-woogie pianist Maurice Rocco; the bandleader was, I think, Don Redman. It was a fantastic show. Ella went down really well."

Meanwhile, in September, Decca became the first record company to reach agreement with the American Federation of Musicians to call off their strike. In November, Ella was back in the recording studios for the first time since July 1942. During those sixteen months there had been changes in Decca's Artist and Repertoire setup. The A & R department was responsible for deciding, among other things, what material their artists would record. At Decca these duties came under the strict supervision of the company's president, the autocratic Jack Kapp. By the end of 1943, however, Kapp began delegating these duties to Milt Gabler.

Gabler had originally joined Decca in 1941. He was the proprietor of the Commodore Record Shop at 144 East Forty-second Street in New York City. Through the 1930s it had become a mecca for both jazz fans and musicians. In 1938 he branched into recording, forming his own independent Commodore label and recording artists as diverse as Billie Holiday, Jelly Roll Morton, Eddie Condon, and Teddy Wilson, to create a body of music that represents one of the most significant repositories of mainstream jazz in the history of the music.

In 1941, Gabler was approached by Decca to examine their recently acquired Vocalian/Brunswick catalog and advise them on suitable jazz sides for re-release. His integrity and enormous knowledge of jazz were soon recognized by Jack Kapp, who appointed him to the permanent staff with an office next to his. Gabler was gradually given a free hand in determining Artist and Repertoire policy and producing the recordings for many of the artists in the Decca stable of stars.

However, simply turning up at the recording studio with a great performer is no guarantee of a great performance. Capturing those moments of recorded magic is as much about personal relationships as about technical skills, and a large responsibility lies with the record producer, who coaxes, encourages, and cajoles the best possible performance from the artist while keeping an eye on the technical end, ensuring that the recording engineer's aural vision of the proceedings coincides with his own. Gabler was one of the great unsung heroes of countless recording sessions during the 1940s and 1950s that produced some of the all-time classics of recorded jazz and popular music. When Gabler was profiled by Gilbert Millstein in the pages of *The New Yorker*, an anonymous musician described him at work: "There's a ray that comes out of him, you can't help doing something the way he wants. Here is this guy who can't read a note of music, and he practically tells you what register you're going to play in by the position of your head."[4] When Gabler assumed production and A & R responsibilities at Decca at the end of 1943, one of the artists who came under his control was Ella Fitzgerald.

The milieu in which Milt Gabler operated was very different from the music business of today. To all intents and purposes, songs were controlled by the music publishers, and when it came to recording new material, record companies were largely held in their sway. "When I started handling Ella," he said, "I made the decision what the company would invest in as a record—tunes, treatments. The material she sang, what all the artists on the label sang, came from the guys from the song publishers. They used to call on the record companies, and for the major labels like Decca, RCA, and Columbia it was mostly the owners of the music publishing companies who came around. Usually they had the writers of the song with them or sometimes a demonstrator, and they would sit down and play the songs and sing them.

"Some of the composers were very good demonstrators. They would say, 'This is the song we're going to work on from the first of

Above Just weeks after joining the Chick Webb band in the spring of 1935, a shy and awkward Ella is brought forward by Bardu Ali to take a bow at the Savoy Ballroom in Harlem. *(Malcolm Nicholson Collection)*

Below Ella's first-ever recording—"Love and Kisses," by Chick Webb and His Orchestra, vocal chorus by Ella Fitzgerald, June 12, 1935. *(Malcolm Nicholson Collection)*

Left The Apollo Theater, Harlem, in 1990, still running its famous Amateur Night—a long tradition dating back to the fall of 1934. Ella was its most distinguished graduate. *(Stuart Nicholson)*

Below Ella at the microphone with Chick Webb and His Orchestra at Randall's Island Stadium, May 29, 1938, appearing on Radio WNEW. The occasion was Martin Block's Outdoor Swing Session, a benefit for unemployed musicians. *(Max Jones Files)*

Right In 1932, at the age of fifty-two, Carl Van Vechten gave up his career as a critic and novelist to photograph black American writers, painters, and performers. His photograph of Ella probably dates from 1938–40. *(Carl Van Vechten Collection)*

Below Ella captured at the Barton Hall, Cornell, Ithaca, in 1938. *(Institute of Jazz Studies, Rutgers University)*

Above Ella's long friendship with Duke Ellington began during her days with Chick Webb. Here she shares a joke with him in 1938, along with bass player Alvis Hayes and Ellington's vocalist Ivie Anderson. *(Magnum)*

Below When Chick Webb died in June 1939, Decca quickly released a memorial album of 78s. By then Ella's name had become synonymous with the Webb band. *(Malcolm Nicholson Collection)*

Above Mario Bauza, who played trumpet in Chick Webb's band from 1933 to 1938, photographed in 1991. In the mirror is the author (left) and Phil Schaap. *(Malcolm Nicholson Collection)*

Right Charles Linton in 1991. Linton was Chick Webb's vocalist from 1933 to 1938. In 1934 he was asked by Webb's management to find a "girl vocalist" for Webb's band. He chose Ella Fitzgerald. *(Stuart Nicholson)*

Chick Webb and his Orchestra in 1938. Webb (drums) is flanked by
Bardu Ali (left) and Ella (right). *(Max Jones Files)*

Above Dancing to the music with (left to right) Taft Jordan, Beverly Peer, and Bardu Ali.

Right Ella singing with the Chick Webb Orchestra on the stage of the Apollo, fall 1936. (*Kansas City Museum, Kansas City, Missouri*)

Above When Chick Webb died, drummer Bill Beason replaced him, and the band continued under Ella Fitzgerald's name. Here they perform at the Savoy, Harlem, in 1940. *(Institute of Jazz Studies, Rutgers University)*

Below Ella and trio at the Rag Doll in Chicago, September 1948. The bass player is Ray Brown, whom she married on December 10, 1947; the drummer is Charlie Smith, the pianist Hank Jones. *(Wayne Miller/Magnum)*

the year for the first three months. First quarter we're going to work on this song.' And if, say, Shapiro-Bernstein was going to work on that song for the first three months of 1941, you knew you were going to hear that song on the air. So the reasons the publishers controlled what was made was [that] they had good staff in all the major cities and were going to get that song broadcast all over the United States.

"So if you were a producer, an A & R man, you'd listen to the composer play it on the piano. We'd say, 'That's a pretty damn good song Hoagy's playing there. We'd better make a record of it.' You then decide on the artist and who you're going to have arrange it, or maybe a bandleader might have it in his book, so we'd save on arranging costs. In those years the publishers would go to every record company with the same songs. There was no exclusivity (although exclusivity developed later), but in the beginning you had to figure out how to record a version of the goddamned song to make sure your version was the one that was going to be heard on the air.

"Singers didn't make too many decisions about what they recorded. It had to do with music publishers. We made the decision what actual songs we were going to invest in. If you were going to do the songs that were going to be the Shapiro-Bernstein plugs for the first quarter, you'd have made them in front and put them out two sides at a time. You knew the publisher's pluggers were going to work on it, but if it was a bomb or somebody on another label topped you, you'd put out another two sides. I used to say it was like playing poker or bridge. In other words, if Tommy Dorsey, say, made 'Once in a While' and it was a hit on Victor, we'd cover it with a band like the Ink Spots. You'd do a switch treatment and try and take the play away from them."[5]

When Ella recorded the Benny Carter composition "Cow-Cow Boogie" on November 3, 1943, it was one of the last numbers cut under Jack Kapp's supervision. Smooth and swinging, Ella's version was less frantic than the Ella Mae Morse version on Capitol, with the Ink Spots providing a simple vocal backing that had been previously worked out for the Keys. "'Cow-Cow Boogie' did very well," recalled Milt Gabler. "As a company, if the songs were big, you could do them with one of your own artists. Sometimes you took the play away from the original record, and sometimes you didn't. In that case we equaled Capitol or maybe did better because of our distribution."[6] Ella's "Cow-Cow Boogie" went to number ten on the charts when it was released in March 1944. Almost forty years later it could be heard on the soundtrack of the Martin Scorsese film *Raging Bull*, starring Robert De Niro.

Even though Ella's first chart success in three years put her back in the public eye, Moe Gale continued to book her as a single after the Zanzibar engagement. Making her own way on tour with just a maid, her cousin Georgiana Henry, for company, she had to use pickup bands of local musicians in whatever town or city she worked, and these were just as likely to be semi-pro as professional.

"I never liked the way Moe Gale handled Ella," said Milt Gabler. "I went to New Jersey one night to see her, to set up a recording session, and it was a very hot night. The musicians' dressing room was up the stairs and up at the back, and there were no screens in the damn windows, so the mosquitoes and bugs were flying around the light and all that kind of stuff. I went downstairs, and there was nobody to check the amplification or the balance of the little group that was going to play with her—the sound levels or anything. A great talent like that, and the son of a bitch didn't send a roadman to make sure she was treated properly and presented properly in the room when she got up to perform."[7]

Nineteen forty-four began with Ella's dropping almost out of sight in the *Metronome* poll: she placed thirteenth. However, in early January, Moe Gale put together a package comprising Ella, the Ink Spots, the Cootie Williams Orchestra, comedy dancers Moke and Poke, plus master of ceremonies Ralph Brown. Opening in Rochester, New York, on January 7, the "star-studded show of sepia entertainers," as *New York Age* dubbed them,[8] was billed as "a hit from the word go." They toured the theater circuit extensively, ending in Milwaukee, Wisconsin, on March 3. "We did about ten weeks," said Bill Doggett, who was then working as the pianist for the Ink Spots. "We traveled mostly by train but also by bus. Ella had Georgiana, her maid, with her. But we all soon got to know one another. She was real regular. . . . We used to play pinochle on our train trips—Ella, myself, and I think it was E. V. Perry, and I forget who our fourth partner was there. We used to play every day.

"Everybody had all the respect in the world for Ella. She wasn't lonely or anything like that on this tour because we in the band would be together practically all day. We'd be in town for maybe a week, and we'd get up in the morning and meet for breakfast. It was more like a family tour. Everybody knew and respected the fact that

Ella was headlining the show along with the Ink Spots. Cootie Williams and his band also backed up Ella. She never sang with the Ink Spots on the tour. Later, we got together for a couple of recording things."

In April the tour package was reconvened, and on May 1 they played the NBC Studios in Hollywood in a concert arranged by the Hollywood Victory Committee that was recorded for the Armed Forces Radio Service. "The program included the celebrated Ink Spots and Ella Fitzgerald," said the *Chicago Defender*,[9] which reviewed the program on coast-to-coast radio. The touring was grueling; Eddie "Cleanhead" Vinson, playing alto sax in the Cootie Williams big band, recalled: "We had this Ink Spots–Ella Fitzgerald show, you know, playing the entire RKO circuit. . . . By then we were making $100 [per week]. But there again you had to work hard for it, man, about four or five shows a day."[10]

In August they played New York, allowing Ella and the Ink Spots to go into the studios to cut "I'm Making Believe" and "Into Each Life Some Rain Must Fall" under Milt Gabler's supervision. "We had Bill Kenny do the ballad and Ella swing the jazz version on the same tune," said Gabler. "The Ink Spots were a formula presentation . . . having it straight and a swinging tempo. They weren't really duet records, they were two choruses, different ways, contrast."[11]

Almost from the start the Gabler-Fitzgerald combination paid off. Released as two sides of a 78 disc in November 1944, both songs went straight onto the charts at number one and stayed there for seventeen weeks, with "Into Each Life Some Rain Must Fall" going on to become a million-selling disc. "Ella really tears this one apart," said *Down Beat*. "She's never done anything quite like it, and her vocal is actually thrilling."[12]

In the fall the interminable touring continued with the Ella–Williams–Ink Spots package. Wartime travel restrictions meant that trains were always crowded. When the tour headed south, Ella couldn't find a seat in the blacks-only carriage and after hours of standing finally found a seat in the whites-only section as the train passed through Washington, D.C. When a railroad conductor tried to move her out, it was only the intervention of a group of white sailors who insisted she sit with them that enabled her to retain her seat.

When they arrived from Atlanta to play a military base in New Orleans, Ella was met by John Hammond, himself doing military service at the time. "I had lunch with Ella in a miserable black hotel while she told me her troubles. . . . The show played the open-air the-ater at the camp," he recalled. "Judging by the response, it was the best show the guys had seen."[13]

In November the package had returned to New York for a brief layoff, and Gabler seized the opportunity to bring Ella back into the recording studios to cover "And Her Tears Flowed Like Wine" with the Song Spinners. Released in January 1945, it reached number ten on the charts. "This is Ella in her most commercial vein," pronounced *Metronome*.[14] Before returning to the road with the Cootie Williams–Ink Spots package in early 1945, Ella saw in the New Year with the Ray Kinney Orchestra as part of a holiday vaudeville show in Chicago at the Downtown Theatre from Friday, December 29, to January 12, 1945. Her hit recordings were now beginning to turn the tide of her waning popularity; she was gradually moving back toward high-profile New York appearances.

A sure sign that her popularity was rising came in the January 1945 *Metronome* poll: She had moved back up to eighth position. She also picked up an eight-week sustaining radio slot early in the year. "I was her pianist and acted as her musical director," said Bill Doggett, "every Saturday afternoon on NBC here in New York. We used the house band from NBC as the backup band; I can't remember the name of the bandleader. It was shortly after I left the Ink Spots. I left them at the end of '44, and then I started playing for Ella, off and on, maybe for about a year."

Gabler was keen to follow up the success of "Into Each Life Some Rain Must Fall" and brought Ella and the Ink Spots together again to cover "I'm Beginning to See the Light" in February 1945. Released in April, it immediately went to number five on the charts. On the recording Ella is assured, weaving her own ear-catching melodic varia-tions in the second eight bars of the second chorus and effortlessly playing among the descending sevenths of the middle eight. The fol-lowing month Gabler used a different approach with the Delta Rhythm Boys to cover Nat King Cole's hit "It's Only a Paper Moon." Gabler said, "The Delta Rhythm Boys were a great quartet, but it was also like a formula date. You use them to do the humming and a halt chorus their way. They were really just accompanying Ella."[15]

The record charted at number nine in August. Ella's poise and sense of swing had now coalesced with the light, easy disposition of her voice to make the musically complicated sound easy. She had per-fected the art of concealing her art; through a combination of intu-ition and imagination she embellished the melody with clever and unexpected note choices within a crafty rhythmic logic that never sounded strained or hurried. Her gift of relative pitch ensured that every note was struck in tune, her range and delivery immaculate. In the final chorus of "It's Only a Paper Moon," her easy phrasing and note choices could well have come from the 1950s, 1960s, or even the 1970s.

The Ella–Williams–Ink Spots package continued to be very popular on Moe Gale's touring circuits throughout 1945. In July, Ella and Cootie were featured on the cover of *Down Beat*, a reflection of just what a popular attraction they had become. In between tours Ella was still being booked as a single by Moe Gale. "Well, Moe Gale's not spending any money on backing, and Ella could take care of herself" observed Gabler.[16] It was at one of these club appearances in the New York area that he saw her do her version of "Flying Home," which had been in her repertoire since early 1943. With Ella now reestablishing herself at Decca, Gabler felt he could take a chance on more adventurous material and called her into the studio with a pickup band directed by Vic Schoen on October 4, 1945.

"'Flying Home' is one we heard her do in a room," said Gabler. "She ran it down with the rhythm section in the studio, and then the arrangement was scratched out when we took a *long* five! It's almost like a head arrangement, the band parts. Of course all the guys were great studio men. It's like a club date—they could work out a 'Flying Home' arrangement in one rundown so it was easy to do the accompaniment, the riffs for her. I'm very proud of that record."[17]

Although she didn't realize it at the time, "Flying Home" was a watershed in Ella's career. It was the product of over two years' experimentation in extending the boundaries of jazz singing and remains among the finest jazz vocal records of all time. In it she harnessed scat singing for its musical potential, rather than exploring any subjective dimension of her singing. While on the one hand it was rightly hailed as a vocal tour de force, on the other, it showed, for those who would listen, that Ella was aligning herself with the new thing in music: bebop. It would turn out to be one of the most important career moves of her life, but one that would take a couple of years to be fully realized.

Four days after recording "Flying Home," Ella teamed up with Louis Jordan, then one of Decca's biggest names and one of the few black artists on their roster who appealed equally to black and white audiences. "Ella wanted to do 'Stone Cold Dead in de Market,'" recalled

Gabler. "She had heard the song at a beauty parlor where she went with a Jamaican lady. We'd done 'Stone Cold Dead' on Decca. I think it was written by Wilmouth Houdini, the West Indian calypso singer who was a Decca artist. She told me she had an idea on the song, and Jordan was in town—they knew each other from their Chick Webb days—and Jordan had such a great little band, plus he could do the Jamaican accent. It was a kick for them! And it's a classic record!

"Funny thing about 'Stone Cold Dead in de Market.' I used to get ... one-sided pressings from the factory to see if it was okay, for approval, before they'd go into production. I was playing it in my office, and Jack Kapp came in and said, 'What's that?' I said, 'It's Ella and Louis Jordan doing "Stone Cold Dead."' He said, 'I can't understand a word of it.' I said, 'You don't have to. The people like calypso, and it's a funny song.' He said, 'I can't understand it. You can't put it out. Do the date over.' You'll see that I did the date again, but it didn't come out because I didn't think it was as good as the first one I made. So I issued the first one, put out the original he had heard in the office, and it broke for a big, big hit! And he says, 'See, ain't you glad you remade that record?' I never told him I put out the original one!"[18] Released in July 1946 coupled with "Patootie Pie," it charted at number seven for six weeks.

"Stone Cold Dead" was a fun number, a frothy novelty that clicked with the public and presaged the calypso craze of a couple of years later. More engaging was the flip side, "Patootie Pie," with its allusions to bop in the introductory arpeggios reflecting the changing musical climate, while the rhythm section generates an easy, infectious swing. In the penultimate chorus, Ella trades scat with Jordan's sax, and the allusions to bop become stronger. While "Patootie Pie" is hardly a classic of American popular song, Ella nevertheless always excelled at novelty numbers; she swung, and her good humor was infectious. Gabler's choice of coupling cannot be faulted. While critics might later carp at the quality of the material Ella was given to record at Decca, this was a classic case of her being given a couple of numbers in which she would be outstanding and that she clearly enjoyed doing. "You know what I like?" said Benny Goodman in December 1946. "That record Ella and Louis Jordan made of 'Patootie Pie.' ... I've been playing it every morning now for about six weeks, almost as soon as I get up, and I still think it's great. That's a good test, isn't it?"[19]

In December 1945 the Ella–Williams–Ink Spots package was booked into Joe Howard's Zanzibar Club. They immediately began doing standing-room-only business. Ella and the Ink Spots shared the bill until the end of February 1946, but Cootie Williams left on January 25 to fulfill prior commitments and was replaced by Claude Hopkins and his orchestra. Ella's popularity was now firmly on the rise, which was reflected in the January 1946 *Metronome* poll when she came in fifth. This was due in no small part to the role Milt Gabler was now playing in the selection of her material for Decca. Although Ella had remained almost continually before the public in the ten years since her debut with Webb, she soon found that this was no substitute for the profile a hit record could provide. It was a lesson she would remember throughout her life, even into the late 1980s.

For Ella, one of the highlights of this period was sharing a record date with Louis Armstrong, a musician for whom she had unstinting admiration. On January 18, 1946, they cut two tracks together: "You Won't Be Satisfied" and "The Frim Fram Sauce." The coupling went to number ten on the charts three months later. Again the Gabler formula was one of contrast; in "Satisfied," Ella sings one sixteen-bar chorus relatively straight, and Louis follows with another chorus where he almost de-Satchmoes his voice near the top of his range. The last chorus is split between Louis's trumpet and a vocal duet. The scheme is simple, but the result has an endearing honesty and simplicity that few could fail to be moved by, something that would characterize all their subsequent work together. "The material is not great," observed *Metronome*, "but the singers are, and the result is delightful listening."[20]

In June, Ella appeared at the Apollo backed by the Willie Bryant band. Between an afternoon and evening show midweek she went downtown to make the final arrangements for several guest spots on radio. Time was tight, and she told the cab driver to wait outside the building. Three hours later the cabby was still waiting with the meter running. Ella had been trapped in the elevator between the twenty-first and twenty-second floors. The cabby received a $5 tip for waiting, but Ella missed the early evening show. "They caged the canary," said *Down Beat*. "Cost her fifteen bucks."[21]

Ella's show that week revolved around two big feature numbers, "Stone Cold Dead in de Market"—"in which she took over Louis Jordan's role on the record and did the whole thing alone in a superbly authentic Trinidad accent"—and "Lady Be Good," which was "notable for a long series of riff choruses, or scat singing in which . . . Ella's phrasing was entrancingly easy and instrumental."[22]

In August, Gabler rang the changes again, returning to another successful formula with the Delta Rhythm Boys. By now Ella had become a specialist at the jazz-influenced vocal, singing the melody relatively straight in the first chorus and embellishing it in the final one. "(I Love You) For Sentimental Reasons" adheres to this simple scheme, yet the result is so well done that it went to number eight on the charts when it was released the following December. "Other girl singers should listen and learn," commented *Metronome*. "She achieves a fine mellow mood. . . . Note that coda, it's so typically Ella."[23] "For Sentimental Reasons" was good-quality, easy-listening pop music, sung in an unfussy, unstylized, matter-of-fact way that allowed the melody to shine through as much as the lyrics. "That was a pretty good record," said Gabler. "It was a cover of one of the small Harlem labels. Savannah Churchill, I think, had a hit, and this was a cover. We took the play away from them."[24]

Ella returned to the Apollo in October, backed by her familiar touring companions, the Cootie Williams Orchestra. By now word had spread of her sensational virtuoso scat performances in "Lady Be Good," even though it would not be recorded until the following March. "Until Queen Ella walked onto this stage, this was just another good Apollo show," enthused *Metronome*. "After she had finished, the packed house was in an uproar. . . . The buxom gal is unquestionably the greatest singer of them all today. . . . The pièce de résistance was of course Ella's now famous vocal jam on 'Lady Be Good' and good for at least six sensational choruses. She has some set riffs that would make many top musicians' eyes bug out. . . . The whole thing packs more wallop than any music business specialty to be heard around today."[25]

Her "set riffs" would remain common to every performance of the song she gave for almost fifty years; they represented the building blocks around which she would construct her improvisation. This was a factor common to all her scat features. Probably as the result of her experience in singing with a big band, she developed "arrangements" for her scat features to which she generally adhered: "Like John Ford getting to work on yet another western or Chuck Jones directing his twelfth 'Roadrunner' cartoon," said Will Friedwald, "Fitzgerald uses formulas creatively, not only to precondition her audiences as to what they can expect, but to deliver the goods."[26]

In between recording sessions, including three V-Disc jam sessions with the drummer Buddy Rich, who reportedly got a great kick out of working with Ella,[27] Moe Gale continued to draw up tour schedules that included putting Ella out as a single. It was lonely work, with just Georgiana for company, and for someone with Ella's ability, it was also demeaning. One week she was playing with some of New York's finest musicians, and the next with a band of semi-pros in the boondocks.

Meanwhile, John Hammond, on behalf of the new independent label Keynote Records, came up with an offer of $40,000 if she signed with them. Gale declined, on the face of it doing his client a disservice by signing her again with Decca for the same $15,000 guarantee that she had received in the past.[28] But if Ella felt any grounds for dissatisfaction with Gale, she did not show it: In November 1946 she renewed her contract with him for an additional three years.[29]

During July 1946, Ella was at Virginia Beach, Virginia, backed by the house band, and from August 7 she spent two weeks at McVan's in Buffalo, New York. "Ella came into Buffalo as a single," the drummer Mel Lewis told author Jim Haskins, "and she brought all these arrangements from Chick Webb's band. My father's band at McVan's was only four pieces, and of course they couldn't do much with the arrangements done for a fourteen-piece band. . . . She was such a pain in the ass about it. My father came home and said to me, 'She's so good, but she's such a pain. She doesn't realize it's only four of us, and we can only do what we can.' These guys were some of the best show musicians in town. . . . I used to go down there every night and watch her, and I didn't think it sounded so bad. You could see she was lonely. . . . Ella just sat in her room between shows. She never really sat with the musicians and talked to them."[30]

Ella's career needed a boost. Her stage performances were a mixture of ballads, novelty numbers, current pop songs, and scat features. But there was no sense of any underlying aesthetic direction. Rather, her performances celebrated her talent by pushing in several directions at once with a childlike exuberance. "A standing quip in show business is: 'What is the Ella Fitzgerald style today?'" said *Ebony*. "The adaptability of the Fitzgerald voice to such a wide assortment of song forms has been perplexing to many of her . . . fans."[31]

But this childlike aspect of Ella's character was not confined to matters of repertoire. Ten years earlier, Chick Webb had said Ella would "never grow up," a point picked up by a *Chicago Defender* report in July 1945. While it acknowledged that her singing style had reached maturity, it said that in every other respect she still remained a kid at heart, skipping rope backstage to keep in shape and sitting by while her meals were selected and ordered for her.[32]

Even so, her talent was undeniable. Within the music business she was widely admired for her ability and adaptability; singers such as Bing Crosby, Perry Como, Mel Tormé, Dinah Shore, Peggy Lee, Dick Haymes, Judy Garland, Margaret Whiting, and Jo Stafford had all been quoted in the music press praising her talent. But a fickle public liked their idols to be labeled more plainly. Although it might sound surprising today, at the end of 1946 Ella was still not considered a jazz singer per se. The real big time still remained tantalizingly at arm's length, a situation that would not change until the racial climate in postwar America improved. Meanwhile, Ella's career needed fresh momentum.

CHAPTER SEVEN

1946–1947

Anyone who attempts to sing extemporaneously—that is, scat—will tell you that the hardest aspect of that kind of singing is to stay in tune. You are wandering all over the scales, the notes coming out of your mouth a millisecond after you think of them. . . . A singer has to work doubly hard to emit those random notes in scat singing with perfect intonation. Well, I should say all singers except Ella. Her notes float out in perfect pitch, effortless and, most important of all, swinging.

MEL TORMÉ[1]

WHEN ELLA CUT "Flying Home" in October 1945, jazz singing took a significant step forward. Scat had been used by jazz singers before, of course, but never with such dazzling creativity. Scat is vocal improvisation using phonetic sounds traditionally (but not always) similar to the instrumental sounds of jazz. Countless writers have credited Louis Armstrong as its originator; when singing "Heebie Jeebies" on a 1926 recording session, his music sheet is said to have fallen accidentally on the floor in the middle of his vocal, so he continued by improvising an onomatopoeic melody in place of the words—and lo! scat was born.

However, on the Library of Congress recordings for the Folklore Archives, Jelly Roll Morton gave credit to one Joe Sims of Vicksburg for creating scat, saying that New Orleans musicians took the idea from him. This dates scat to at least the turn of the century. Even Louis Armstrong (himself a New Orleans musician) had used scat on records well before "Heebie Jeebies." Brian Rust pointed out that he had previously scatted on records two years before, on Fletcher Henderson's "Everybody Loves My Baby," and saxophonist/arranger Don Redman got in a few bars on Henderson's "My Papa Doesn't Two Time No Time" from around then, too. Rust also cited a whole list of scat singing on records from the mid to the late twenties, including Johnny Marvin, Gene Austin, Lee Morse, and one of Fred Hall's Sugar Babies, who were using the technique quite independent of Armstrong's influence.[2]

In his book *Jazz Singing*, author Will Friedwald traced countless pre-Armstrong instances of scat, dating back as far as Gene Green in 1917. The most significant of these early scatters was Cliff Edwards, who, Friedwald points out, made his first disc in 1923 "with scat phrases that could have been played by trumpeter Joe Smith on a Bessie Smith record."[3] Everybody has heard Cliff Edwards's voice—he sang "When You Wish upon a Star" in Disney's movie *Pinocchio*. "Edwards was the first performer to make scat singing part of his act and developed it into a whole style," explained Friedwald later. "I guess the point there is that they are genuine scat improvisations. He's not just scatting the melody, he's really making up a tune, as far as I can tell, on the chordal structure. Bing Crosby said that he listened to people like Cliff Edwards. You don't have to guess, it's documented; he would have been very interested in anybody who was doing popular songs in a jazzy way in the early days."

Up until "Flying Home," Ella had been deep into singing pop songs with jazz inflections. She had used scat, but more for its novelty value, as in the few bars in "You'll Have to Swing It," recorded fifteen months after her recording debut with Chick Webb, in the eight bars tied rather awkwardly to the ground beat on "Organ Grinder's Swing" from the following month, and in her first outing in extended scat on "The Dipsy Doodle" in December 1937. But it was the popularity of Leo Watson with the Spirits of Rhythm in Harlem and the clubs on Fifty-second Street which showed Ella that scat need not remain in hock to Armstrong. It could be developed and personalized into a jazz act in its own right.

Leo Watson (1898–1950) was a significant influence on Ella. His surreal, uninhibited, fast-moving lines pointed a way of moving scat from swing to bebop. Watson's scat appears on just thirty-eight sides, a stream-of-consciousness legacy with his own groups, the Spirits of Rhythm, and with Gene Krupa, Artie Shaw, and Vic Dickenson, among others. His improvisations were at once highly sophisticated and slightly zany. Beginning with wide, attention-getting intervals, often archly humorous, he would drop in volume, narrowing his range with wildly offbeat phrases that paraphrased the melody until he reached the turnaround. This he often negotiated by inserting a hugely improbable quote. Then he would speed his line by subdividing the beat, making his ideas sound faster and faster, a technique that brought him almost to the door of bop. Watson's rhythmic freedom, his clever way of keeping the listener engaged with musical quotes—"horses, horses," borrowed by Ella on her version of "Flying Home," is an obvious one, for example—and his hornlike logic were years ahead of their time, although his brief career, a shooting-star flash of brilliance, remains largely forgotten in jazz today.

"Then there are also some Leo Watson things where he sounds pretty much like Crosby," added Friedwald, "'World on a String,' things like that, and definitely some of the Spirits of Rhythm were listening to Crosby. . . . I always think Leo Watson must have at some point listened to Cliff Edwards. It doesn't seem like he could have come up with all that entirely on his own. But Crosby listened to Edwards for sure, and out of that there's the connection between Crosby and Louis Armstrong to Leo Watson to Ella."

But it was not just the scat singers Ella absorbed to develop her style; instrumentalists also provided grist for her mill. "Ella has those extraordinary ears," Mel Tormé points out. "Remember, she did grow up in those wonderful years with the Chick Webb band, listening to Taft Jordan on trumpet and Dick Vance and all the people that she worked with, plus all the people that were playing at the time. She just kept those extraordinary ears open listening to the likes of Roy Eldridge and Coleman Hawkins and Lester Young and Joe Thomas of the Lunceford band. The list is endless.

"So she assimilated all of this . . . How do you describe it? . . . It's a God-given talent. It's the only way I can describe it—the fact that here is a woman who can run through chord patterns as deftly and with as much facility as any great tenor man or trombone player or pianist or trumpet player."

When "Flying Home" was released in 1947, coupled with "Lady Be Good," it caused a sensation. "Miss Fitzgerald comes on with two quasi-scat sides which will be listened to just as avidly ten years from now as they are today," said *Down Beat* prophetically. "Not only is her intonation perfect, her instrumental conception magnificent, the rhythmic effect climactic, but she tosses in some sly digs at Dizzy, Babs, Slam, Hamp, Leo Watson, and others by singing variations on their better-known ideas!"[4]

With "Flying Home" it was clear that Ella was aware of the fast-emerging bebop movement. After a brief introductory section, she begins by using the opening motifs from the famous Illinois Jacquet tenor sax solo from Lionel Hampton's 1942 Decca hit. It becomes the basis for her own improvisation, but as she moves further away from Jacquet's solo, she makes subtle use of notes that no swing era musician would use. For example, she sometimes uses a C on the "Flying Home" portion of the lyric to coincide with the *ing* of "flying." Since she sings the tune in the key of A flat, that C would be the thirteenth of the underlying chord of E flat major. As a general rule, swing era musicians tended to stay with thirds, fifths, sixths, sevenths, and, at a push, ninths.

Ella's affinity with bop goes beyond harmonic subtleties, however. You can actually hear her aligning herself with the bop movement through rhythmic choices that were directly colored by the bop musicians; frequently her scat uses the voiced consonant of "b" to begin phrases like "boy-dube-be," "blu-i-du," "blu-ya-do." These phonetic sounds are characteristic of the short, sharp phrases that were used by the bop instrumentalists; indeed, she also incorporates several "rebops" to underline the point.

Finally, like Leo Watson, Ella also incorporates musical quotations into her improvised line, a practice that she would follow for the rest of her life. At the same cadence point in the three "improvised" choruses, she successively inserts an extract from "Good Night Ladies" ("Merrily we roll along"), an extract from "Yankee Doodle," and "horses, horses."

"I think she brought scat singing to a new level of artistry," said Sonny Rollins, one of the greatest improvisers in the history of jazz. "Scat singing is an art, but the way Ella uses interpolations of different songs into different parts of the melodies is really high art. I have always loved the way she did that. It's one thing to put a melody of one song into another for effect, so the crowd likes it, but there's also an artistic level involved with these excursions. Ella really brought that to a high level." When she modulates into a new key for the final chorus, it not only climaxes a remarkable performance, but her impeccable timing and sure-footed pitch have the authority of a master.

Musically, bebop represented a focal point of evolution in jazz. It was a coming together of advanced rhythmic and harmonic ideas that had been worked and polished, both individually and collectively, by several young, highly sophisticated musicians over a number of years, to produce a new level of jazz expressionism. Bebop moved from the essentially diatonic conventions of swing to chromatic harmonies, thereby enlarging the number of possible note choices available to the improviser. Rhythmically, it broke free from the four- and eight-bar boxes within which prebop improvisers had contained their solos; bebop musicians used more angular, fragmented phrases that frequently crossed bar lines and began and ended in unexpected places.

Bebop evolved through the exchange of ideas among a group of brilliant young musicians who regularly gathered in Harlem's after-hours joints, such as Minton's Playhouse, to play together and put their theories for a new style of jazz into practice. Although it appeared that bebop emerged fully formed when the recording ban was lifted in 1944, it had actually begun to develop as early as 1940–41 at the hands of key musicians such as Dizzy Gillespie, Charlie Parker, Kenny Clarke, Thelonious Monk, Kenny Kersey, Charlie Christian, Joe Guy, Don Byas, Bud Powell, Max Roach, and others. When Dizzy Gillespie worked with Ella in 1941, she would have had the opportunity of hearing firsthand the new musical ideas from one of the music's architects.

As bebop developed in the Harlem clubs, Ella would also have become aware of the reputation being acquired by the young experimenters, most of whom were just a few years younger than she was. It is now clear that as early as 1942–43 she had begun to be drawn to the exciting musical challenge the music posed. She gradually incorporated elements of its rhythmic and harmonic characteristics into her act—for example, in the showpiece number "Flying Home," which she was performing years before she actually recorded it. "Bop musicians like Parker and Gillespie have stimulated me more than I can say," Ella later told *Ebony* magazine.[5]

Although bop was never destined to enjoy the widespread popularity of the swing bands of the 1930s and early 1940s, nonetheless by 1946 it was beginning to enjoy considerable interest in the music press and a fast-growing following among young, hip fans, particularly in New York and the northern cities. For the fans, the focal point of the music was trumpeter Dizzy Gillespie. Charlie Parker, the key figure of the era, remained in the background as far as the public at large was concerned, acclaimed by musicians and an inner circle of New York enthusiasts. Gillespie was bop's front man. A rare combination of clown and master musician, he was an ideal media person, someone who could be relied on for good copy; photogenic and witty, he would always oblige with a zany quote or a humorous pose.

In 1945, Gillespie was encouraged by his manager, Billy Shaw, to form his own big band, which was promptly booked into a touring package with comedians Patterson and Jackson, vocalist June Eckstine, and the Nicholas Brothers. Called the Hepsations of 1945, they were sent on a ninety-eight-day tour of the South. Gillespie's sidemen, several of whom had come from the recently disbanded Billy Eckstine band, viewed the prospect of touring the South with all the enthusiasm of a turkey contemplating Thanksgiving. Several left the band before the tour commenced, while others returned home en route, sickened by countless episodes of blatant racial prejudice. The promoters told Gillespie that the southern audiences couldn't dance to his music, and the tour laid one enormous egg.

Later in the year Dizzy Gillespie made another unsuccessful foray, this time into California with Charlie Parker, in an attempt to induct West Coast audiences into the rites of the new music. But gradually the tide began to turn, and by 1946 Gillespie's fortunes were beginning to improve. Voted Number One Trumpet Man in the *Metronome* poll, he returned to New York in March for a successful stay at the Spotlite Club on Fifty-second Street. Meanwhile, a marvelous series of small-group sides for the Victor label, recorded in February as part of a 78 album entitled *New Fifty-Second Street Jazz* (the company was not yet confident enough to call the music bop), went on to become a best-seller, while several brilliant sides for the Musicraft label in May further enhanced Gillespie's reputation.

As bop began to be seen as the latest "new thing" in the music business, Gillespie was seized upon by the music press, and as the year progressed he quickly became a public figure, with articles, reviews, and features in national publications. Mort Schillinger remarked in a lengthy profile: "Never before in the history of jazz has so dynamic a person as Dizzy Gillespie gained the spotlight of acclaim and idolization. . . . Few musicians have escaped the aura of Dizzy's music. . . . But the fad of copying Dizzy unfortunately has not stopped with the music; followers have been trying to make themselves look and act like Dizzy to boot."[6]

Gillespie affected a small goatee and often wore a beret and horn-rimmed glasses. By mid-1946, *Ebony* was carrying ads for "Bop Glasses—Real Gone Frames only $3.95," to which the bop devotee would add a paper goatee and a "bop cap," a beret with a peak. But despite the ephemeral lure of incidental trappings that separated the hip from the non-hip, bop was no longer an underground music played in Harlem clubs. It had now taken hold and was changing the face of jazz itself.

Gillespie's trumpet playing, like Parker's alto, exerted a profound influence on how bop was shaped; both had a sweeping influence on modern jazz. Like Parker, Gillespie was widely imitated, his pet phrases becoming stock licks for subsequent generations of trumpet players; they can even be heard in the playing of musicians, young and old, to this day. But it was not just trumpet players who came under Gillespie's spell; his ideas, so fresh and dramatic in the 1940s, could be heard in the work of countless saxophonists, pianists, and guitarists. An ideal proselytizer for the music, he would quietly explain the theory behind what he was doing to anyone who would listen, often demonstrating at a piano keyboard how the extended harmonies affected his note choices. He would spell out onomatopoeically bop rhythms that often became institutionalized as song titles, such as "Oo-Bop-Sh'Bam-a-Klook-a-Mop," "Ool-Ya-Koo," and "Oop-Pop-a-Da."

In the spring of 1946, Gillespie felt confident enough to try another big band venture. They made their first recordings for the Victor label in August, including a composition by their pianist John Lewis, "Two Bass Hit." A few years later Lewis would go on to form a prototype version of the Modern Jazz Quartet with fellow Gillespie sidemen Milt Jackson on vibes, Ray Brown on bass, and Kenny Clarke on drums. But at the time Lewis, fresh out of the army and having previously studied music at the University of New Mexico, was continuing his studies at the Manhattan School of Music and was eager to put his theories into practice in Gillespie's peripatetic musical laboratory.

Gillespie's band was pushing out the boundaries of jazz and was full of exciting young soloists. "I was in that *new* group," said Howard Johnson, "playing stuff that was very interesting and exciting. I was playing first alto chair. . . . Sonny Stitt had the alto solos at first, and John Brown took them after he left. We played dances, theaters, and everything, and then we went on the road in a package with Ella Fitzgerald."[7]

The touring package set off in November 1946 and continued through most of December. Once again it took in the South. Booked by Moe Gale, Ella had been added to create balance after the unrelieved diet of bop during the Hepsations tour in 1945 had confused and confounded the southerners. It was not very different the second time around, however. "They would look up at the bandstand as if we were nuts," said tenor saxophonist James Moody. "One time down South this guy was looking up, and he said, 'Where's Ella Fitzgerald?' He was mad because he didn't see Ella Fitzgerald."[8]

The public watched the band with a mixture of awe and confusion. "They'd listen, stand around and applaud, and try and pretend they dug it," said Johnson. "I think they appreciated the artistry of . . .

Dizzy because marvelous technique was involved. But the music wasn't really danceable."[9]

If Ella's reputation preceded her among the southerners, it also preceded her into Gillespie's band. "I spent some time with Ella when Dizzy's band started," said pianist John Lewis. "I first started working for the band in 1946. She lent Dizzy her prestige and went on a long tour with the band. At the time, in '46, along with the rest of the band, I was more interested in Sarah [Vaughan]. My appreciation for Ella wasn't as great as it should have been, although after Dizzy kept pointing it out to me every night, I got the message!" The Gillespie band saw Ella as a former swing era star, light-years removed from what they were doing, a palliative to help their music go down with the public.

However, if "Flying Home" revealed Ella's close affinity with bop, her tour with Gillespie allowed her to embrace the music wholeheartedly. When the tour started, she was an "outsider"; when it finished, she had earned the approbation of her peers, she was "in."

"We used to play theaters, what we used to call 'around the world,'" said Ella. "When the band would go out to jam, I liked to go out with Dizzy because I used to get thrilled listening to them when he did his bebop. That's actually the way I feel I learned what you call bop. It was quite an experience, and he used to always tell me, 'Come on up and do it with the fellas.' That was my education in learning how to really bop. We used to do 'Oo-Bop-Sh'Bam-a-Klook-a-Mop.' That's one of the first things I remember he used to do . . . and that fascinated me. When I felt that I could sing that, then I felt like I was in."[10]

"Oo-Bop-Sh'Bam-a-Klook-a-Mop" was one of the most popular bop songs, which Gillespie elevated to one of bop's anthems. It was also recorded by Machito and his Afro-Cuban Salseros as "U-BlaBa-Du," the connection being Gillespie's close association with Mario Bauza, Machito's brother-in-law and lead trumpeter, and a major influence on Gillespie's Afro-Cuban experiments at this time. The tune, like so much of the bop repertoire, was a contrafact, utilizing the chord sequence of a preexisting tune, often a standard—in this case, George Gershwin's "I Got Rhythm." The "Rhythm" changes were commonly used in jam sessions during the swing era, but Gillespie and Gil Fuller, the co-composers, created a line that was at stark variance with the original. The words "Oo-Bop-Sh'Bam-a-Klook-a-Mop" cover the first two bars of "I Got Rhythm," corresponding with the lyrics "I got rhythm," illustrating just how different bop's fragmented rhythmic line was from swing.

"Oo-Bop-Sh'Bam-a-Klook-a-Mop" was reharmonized so that in the first two bars Gillespie used four chords instead of Gershwin's two. At the middle eight of the tune that begins with the lyrics, "Old man trouble," there are four chords in eight bars. Gillespie uses sixteen. Although many swing era players could understand the harmonic changes the bop musicians introduced (Coleman Hawkins's 1939 "Body and Soul" was virtually an exercise in chromatic chord movement, for example), it was the combination of extended harmonies *and* a new rhythmic vocabulary that made bop appear so revolutionary.

For Ella, whose remarkable ear intuitively reacted to the subtle chord voicings, bop represented a challenge that linked her vocal technique to her powerful, propulsive rhythmic gift. The bop players preferred fast tempos. Instead of the dotted eighth note followed by a sixteenth that characterized the swing musician's approach to the basic beat unit, bop musicians used almost evenly accented eighth notes. They sped through bar lines with a gusto that left swing era players gasping, often taking flight in cascades of sixteenth notes that made the music appear to speed by twice as fast. Bop knocked listeners out of their diatonic comfort zones. It demanded the active participation of its audience, which had to *listen* to understand what was going on. Jazz was consciously moving out of the realms of popular entertainment and demanding acceptance as a true art form in its own right.

Such a stylistic Rubicon was too wide for the swing musicians to cross; they could only look on as bebop took over, establishing itself as the preeminent style in jazz by the end of the 1940s. For the swing era players, many then still young and at the height of their powers, such as Benny Goodman, Roy Eldridge, and Buck Clayton, it was a bitter pill to discover that almost overnight their style had become old hat. Some, like Coleman Hawkins and Don Byas, almost succeeded in adapting to bop, but only one—Ella Fitzgerald—successfully made the transition. In a music dominated by males, this was no mean achievement.

The tour with Gillespie was a happy one for Ella. After hours she went dancing with Gillespie and his musicians. "We would go into the towns and go to the clubs," she said. "There'd be a nightclub or somewhere to go, and the band would start playing and we would get up and that was it! We used to take the dance floor over. Do the lindy hop because we could do it. . . . We danced like mad. . . . We'd go with the old Savoy steps."[11] She still loved to dance, and with Gillespie in particular, because he also knew all the Savoy steps; but he was spoken for, having married Lorraine in May 1940.

As the tour progressed, Ella became romantically involved with the band's bass player, Ray Brown. One of the leading players of his instrument in bop, Brown, born in Pittsburgh in 1926, was nine years Ella's junior. They had originally met a year before when Brown arrived in New York and became part of Gillespie's combo on Fifty-second Street.

Romantic entanglements for a female singer among the fifteen to twenty men of the big bands with which they toured were not uncommon. "Just an observation on most professional singers I've worked with through the years," said Milt Gabler. "I've worked with a lot of them. One time I had on my roster Billie and Ella, Carmen McRae, Peggy Lee, Jeri Southern, and Sylvia Syms, and it was a pleasure. But singers generally ended up marrying someone in the band, the bass player or something.

"They're lonely people, and you go on the road, and what the hell can you do with your time? It's not just black singers like Ella, it's white girl singers, too. They marry somebody in the band. It's sad. We never talked about anything like that. It was all professional conversations. There's a certain distance, being the man who did her dates in the studio and who spoke to her about what material to record and all. But it was a lonely life."[12]

The list of singers who wound up with musicians from the same band is long: Doris Day married the Les Brown saxophonist George Weidner; Peggy Lee married the Benny Goodman guitarist Dave Barbour; Jo Stafford married Tommy Dorsey's arranger Paul Weston; Frances Wayne married the Woody Herman arranger-trumpeter Neal Hefti; Mary Ann McCall married the Herman saxophonist Al Cohn; June Christy married the Stan Kenton saxophonist Bob Cooper; and Ann Richards married Stan Kenton himself. And that's just a few of the better-known names!

Gradually Ella and Ray Brown grew closer, both personally and musically. After they returned to New York, they were seen together at the after-hours spots when their schedules permitted. They always went to where bop was being played. At her own appearances, Ella made a point of incorporating a couple of bop-oriented numbers into her act. But for her record-buying public she remained in the safe middle ground, exemplified by the release in 1947 of a 78 album of reissues entitled *Ella Fitzgerald: Souvenir Album of Vocal Foxtrots*. Scarcely in tune with the changing musical landscape, it was a collection of 1940–41 material intended to cash in on her rising success, which was reflected in the January 1947 *Metronome* poll where she had moved up to fourth position. However, the reissues inadvertently served to demonstrate the extent to which Ella had developed as an artist in the six or seven years since the numbers were originally recorded. "These records . . . [come] from a period when Ella was not singing as well as she is today," said *Down Beat* later in the year. "The phrasing isn't as sure, nor the tone as big."[13]

In January 1947, Ella was paired in the recording studio with pianist Eddie Heywood and his orchestra. "We cut 'Sentimental Journey,' a cover of the Les Brown hit, and 'Guilty,'" said Gabler. "The publishers were going to work on 'Guilty' again; it was a revival. In fact, I tried that with Billie Holiday but it didn't work, so I had Ella do it."[14] "Guilty" charted at number eleven the following April.

Gabler was as aware of Ella's interest in bop as of the rising popularity of the music itself. When he heard Ella perform "Lady Be Good" in a nightclub, he decided to record it. "I used to say to Ella, 'This one pays the rent' and 'This one's for us,'" said Gabler. "And 'Lady Be Good' was for us!"[15] The session on March 19, 1947, with a pickup band under Bob Haggart's musical direction, began with two commercial numbers, "A Sunday Kind of Love," covering Claude Thornhill's Columbia version of the tune, and "That's My Desire," using the Andy Love Quartet for vocal backings.

When the numbers were released in May 1947, *Down Beat* asserted: "Anyone who can listen to these two sides and not start revising up any estimates he may have had of Miss Fitzgerald's all-around singing ability is voice-deaf."[16] Although "That's My Desire" did not appear on the hit parade chart, it became very popular with disc jockeys across the country; one contemporary report claimed that it clogged radio programs nationwide.

The session that produced "That's My Desire" was fraught with difficulties, however; the Andy Love Quartet was a close harmony group that copied Mel Tormé's sensational but recently defunct Mel-Tones. "'That's My Desire' was a struggle, but we finally made it. It was tough getting the vocal group balanced. Sometimes when you don't have the complete 'A-team,' you have problems. It went down eventually and sold well," said Gabler.[17] Problems in a recording studio can easily upset an artist if things are not going well. Feelings can run high, people are on edge, nerves can fray. Yet, according to Gabler, after all the problems on the session, the band quickly worked out a head arrangement for "Lady Be Good," and Ella cut it in one take. It was a remarkable achievement.

"Lady Be Good" remained in Ella's repertoire for the rest of her life, a classic that in some ways surpassed "Flying Home" in its sheer exuberance and creativity. Once again the bop influence was readily apparent, as *Metronome* observed: "'Lady Be Good' . . . represents her awareness of the Gillespie school of jazz."[18] And as in "Flying Home," the building blocks are evident, the "arrangement" that would form the basis of subsequent versions over the years. Often Ella stayed relatively close to the original recording, but with the advent of the long-playing record her concert versions became longer and longer, leaving the original outline like a signpost glimpsed in the fog. "She pretty well stuck to that arrangement right down to the tee," said Tommy Flanagan, an accompanist who played extensively with Ella in later years, "almost exactly like the record. That is, when she was doing it a lot. But if she hadn't done it for a while, she didn't remember exactly how she had done it; then she would stretch out and do a little bit more, like getting away from how she used to do it. She'd try and find a better way."[19] In later years singer Mel Tormé based a brilliant scat version of his own on the number, which he dedicated to Ella.[20] It was a fitting tribute to one of the finest jazz vocal recordings of all time.

Outside the recording studios as well, Ella continued to immerse herself in bop. On April 5 she was one of the guests on Art Ford's "Saturday Night Swing Show" on Radio WNEW. The show was unusual in that the programs were unrehearsed and the choice and length of numbers were left to the musicians. Each show was entirely ad-libbed by Art Ford and his guests in front of a small audience of two hundred or so at WNEW's Studio 1 at 565 Fifth Avenue at Forty-sixth Street. Ella was paired with Buddy Rich, and the results were later issued on V-Disc. Rich emerged from behind his drums to exchange banter with Ford before joining Ella on "Blue Skies," which was later issued as "Budella." Rich puts in a creditable scat vocal before being swamped by a powerful, off-the-cuff performance from Ella that showed not only her mastery of bop but also just how instrumentally oriented her vocal improvisations were. Her line would have sounded just as convincing from a horn player.

* * *

The countless small clubs on Fifty-second Street between Fifth and Sixth avenues had been a hectic center of jazz since the late twenties. It became known affectionately as "The Street" by the 1940s and was host to the very first bop bands in 1944 when Dizzy Gillespie and Oscar Pettiford played the Onyx Club at about the same time Coleman Hawkins was playing just a couple of clubs down the block with fellow tenor saxophonist Don Byas, trumpeter Benny Harris, pianist Thelonious Monk, and drummer Denzil Best. Soon afterward Fifty-second Street became a major showcase for the burgeoning bop movement.

In June 1947, Louis Shanowitz reopened the Downbeat Club on Fifty-second Street (Rudy Breadbar had been forced to close its doors a couple of months earlier). To announce that the club was under new ownership and back in business, Ella was booked to headline the occasion. With her now regular backing trio led by Ray Tunia, she did standing-room-only business; in the first week alone she grossed $7,500, despite a rainy weekend. During her stay at the Downbeat, Ella, with her frequent after-hours companion Ray Brown, had her finger on the very pulse of bop.

The following month she was in the recording studios again, and although Milt Gabler supervised the session with the vocal group the Day Dreamers and a now forgotten combo, he did not select the material. "Some of those tunes were done for the Gale agency," he said, "someone trying to do a favor for somebody for something. Her boss said, 'Do this tune.'"[21] The results were not memorable; such were the vagaries of the music business. September saw Ella back on Fifty-second Street, this time at the third reincarnation of the Famous Door, reopened earlier in the year, followed by two weeks at the Downbeat Club with the Dizzy Gillespie big band.

From time to time throughout the year Ella continued to be booked as a package with the Dizzy Gillespie big band by Billy Shaw of the Gale office. It seemed natural, therefore, that when Dizzy was scheduled to make his big Carnegie Hall debut on September 29, Ella should also be included on the bill. The concert was presented by Leonard Feather, who co-sponsored the event. Dizzy and Ella were promoted, along with an "exclusive" appearance by Charlie "Yardbird" Parker, as a concert of "the New Jazz." It was evidence, if evidence was needed, of how, musically, bop was sweeping everything before it: "The bebop banner will be carried on this important date by the leading instrumentalist proponent of this new music and by the girl vocalist who has proved a great master of bop as she has of swing," said *Down Beat*.[22]

The concert was a sellout. *Metronome* magazine enthused that "a new era of jazz began in 1947, that modern jazz has come to stay."[23] Ella's program, for which she was paid $500, included six numbers. "Almost Like Being in Love," "Stairway to the Stars" and "Lover Man" were with the big band. "Lover Man" had a Gillespie solo where Ella interpolated, "Play pretty for the people, Dizzy," a line that would weary her accompanists for decades to come. On the now mandatory "Flying Home" and "Lady Be Good" she was backed by her own trio, and in another instance of her working out a scat feature prior to recording it, she included her version of the fast-rising bop anthem "How High the Moon," a number she would record three months later. Here she traded four bars over a couple of choruses with Gillespie that never quite got airborne; Gillespie was blasted by the critics for trying to steal the limelight from Ella. "While Ella Fitzgerald was singing . . . [he stood] with a bouquet of flowers meant for her doing mincing dance steps and in general stealing as much of the play from her singing as possible."[24] But despite Gillespie's clowning, a lifelong subtext to his performances, the Carnegie concert was an unqualified success, described as one of the freshest things since Duke Ellington's legendary 1942 concert. After praising Gillespie, *Down Beat* proclaimed "musical honors to Parker followed by Miss Fitzgerald."[25]

Down Beat had given the concert front-page treatment. On the same front page a bold byline announced "JATP Concert Opens Jazz Season at Carnegie" and continued: "The torrid squeal of the tenor sax rent the air for the first time this season September 27 at Carnegie Hall when Norman Granz's Jazz at the Philharmonic played a midnight concert to a practically full house."[26] Granz's jazz circus had hit town. Star of the show was vocalist Helen Humes, who stopped the show cold twice and finally had to be begged offstage by Granz. Among the musicians participating was Ella's boyfriend Ray Brown, who was back with Dizzy's big band two days later. So, too, was Norman Granz, this time as a member of the audience that witnessed the coming of age of the "New Jazz" in America's premier concert hall.

During the fall of 1947, Ella became involved in a mission that would last throughout her life: that of helping orphaned and disadvantaged children. She was asked by Edna Blue, the outgoing chair of the Foster Parents Plan, to succeed her in helping to develop a scheme to support orphanages and disabled children in war-ravaged Europe. Ella's own contribution was to fund a place in a home for a young orphan in Naples. Over the years Ella became noted for her love of children, her pro bono concerts, and her charitable donations to all kinds of deserving causes, culminating in The Ella Fitzgerald Child Care Center in the Lynwood section of Watts in Los Angeles, which she helped establish in 1977. In the later years of her life her principal social concern was child abuse, and the center became the focal point of her work to help sufferers, to whom she brought Christmas presents every year. Hundreds of thousands of dollars have been raised over the years by the annual dinner-dance benefit that, because of Ella's involvement, has attracted some of the finest entertainers in jazz and popular music: Frank Sinatra, Sammy Davis, Jr., Bill Cosby, Count Basie, John Denver, Quincy Jones, Tom Jones, Cleo Laine, Oscar Peterson, Joe Pass, the Pointer Sisters, Sarah Vaughan, and, annually, Ella herself.

Meanwhile, Ella continued working with Dizzy's big band, appearing at the Apollo in October and on a road trip of one-nighters that took in a week at Detroit's Paradise Theatre beginning on November 14. Ella had now been immersed in bebop for over a year, spending a lot of that time with Dizzy Gillespie. It was no coincidence, therefore, that Ella's scat style had developed similarities with Gillespie's trumpet playing.

Gillespie was endowed with a formidable technique, and a characteristic of his playing was that the ideas expressed were more important than the emotional content. Also, Dizzy's approach to bop was different from Charlie Parker's; Parker's was based on time, Dizzy's more on harmony. Ella followed Gillespie's, rather than Parker's, approach: "She learned . . . after she went with me, going on the road," Gillespie said.[27] Like Gillespie, too, Ella was less concerned with emotion, which was unusual for a vocalist. Her phrases never had the sophisticated rhythmic complexity of Parker; instead, her infallible ear responded to bop's complex harmonies, and her clear, light, flexible tone translated its fast-moving lines with ease.

As the end of 1947 approached, it was becoming increasingly clear that the American Federation of Musicians was once more reaching an impasse over the proliferation of shows on radio that played recorded music; it claimed these shows were depriving musicians of work. When a strike was called for January 1, 1948, Ella, in common with most recording artists, joined a rush to the recording studios to stockpile titles for release during the duration of the strike. She was scheduled for three sessions at the end of December. On the twentieth she managed to get her boyfriend Ray Brown in on the date to cut her version of "How High the Moon."

"That was another one we heard her doing in a room," said Milt Gabler. "I had her do that, and we taped it in my office on a little tape machine. We had the arrangement written from that, then she came in and did it. 'How High the Moon' was another great one, the bebop thing creeping in there."[28] After the piano pickup, the studio band immediately paraphrases "Bird"'s "Ornithology" as a background figure, the Charlie Parker contrafact that uses the same chords. Ella sings the theme straight for one chorus before doubling tempo and leading the listener by the hand into the improvisation section:

How High the Moon is the name of this song,
How High the Moon though the words may be wrong

(The lay listener is alerted to the fact that "scat" looms.)

We're singin' it 'cause you asked for it

(Subtle psychology. How can you dislike anything you asked for?)

So we're swingin' it just for you.

(The personal touch: It's just for me!)

At bar sixteen of the second chorus Ella returns to the lyrics, finishing with a reminder before the turnaround, "Though the words may be wrong to this song/We're asking how high, high, high is the moon." The listener, suitably preconditioned, is led into a superb improvisation that is wholly colored by bop. Indeed, as Ella goes into the second chorus of the improvised section, she quotes twelve bars from Parker's "Ornithology" lest there be any mistaking the musical territory, underlining the fact a few bars on with an emphatic "Bebop!"

Her Ella-ing of "How High the Moon" made her improvisation acceptable for broad popular consumption. Her improvised line tended to smooth out the angular contours of bop and, by pruning away its sharp edges, paved the way for broader public acceptance of the music. She was not alone in this; musicians such as George Shearing, Charlie Ventura, and Stan Getz also enjoyed a degree of popularity with a less angular style. For Ella it meant she could move with equal ease between supper club audiences and the bop cognoscenti of Fifty-second Street.

The final elements of her style were falling into place. With her virtuoso scat performances she was appealing to the public's love of vocal display, something that dates back at least to the Italian operatic *verismo* school that made the idiom so popular. Just how successful she was in charming both jazz and non-jazz audiences can be judged by the fact that "How High the Moon" has remained a lifelong staple in her repertoire.

All was not sweetness and light during 1947, however. Despite her obvious popularity and regular hit records, Ella was seldom heard on the radio that year. "Ella kills everybody—musicians, other singers, fans, hard-boiled recording men—but somehow or other she has been unable to get on the radio with a program of her own or a regular spot on a big show," wrote Bob Bach in *Metronome.*" Pointing out that the airwaves at the time were full of singers, all of whom were white, such as Milena Miller, Dorothy Lamour, and Dorothy Shay, Bach continued, "Need we draw any neon arrows to lead you to the large and disgraceful spectre of Jim Crowism behind American radio? If you want one small example of the malodorous color line in radio today, I will simply cite the answer I was given by one advertising big-wig when I suggested Ella for an opening on a big network show: 'She wouldn't look so good for pictures.'"[30]

CHAPTER EIGHT

1947–1949

I don't know another promoter in the country that can promote like me. The reason is simple: I spend more loot. You don't have to be a genius to be a promoter, you just take bigger ads than anybody else.

NORMAN GRANZ[1]

AT THE END OF NOVEMBER 1947, Ella was back on the road with her trio, this time with Hank Jones at the piano. She shared the bill with Illinois Jacquet at the Regal Theatre in Chicago for a week ending on the 27th, then was at the Merry-Go-Round nightclub in Youngstown, Ohio, until December 14. During their stay, Ray Brown popped *the* question. Ella's answer was an enthusiastic "Yes!" and on December 10 they applied for a marriage license and were married the same day before Clifford M. Woodside, probate judge. For the purposes of the marriage Ella said she was a resident of Youngstown, giving an address at 608 North Avenue and her year of birth as 1918.

Why 1918? Perhaps the marriage license provides the answer: "Said Ray Brown is 21 years of age on the 13 day of Oct 1947," it read. Maybe it was vanity that made Ella want to keep her age within the twenties and thus adjust it down a year to make the certificate read: "Said Ella Fitzgerald is 29 years of age on the 25 day of April 1947." Brown clearly knew she was an older woman, but did he know precisely how much older?

When Ella and Ray returned to New York for Christmas, they set up home together in apartment number 47 at 104 Ditmars Boulevard, East Elmhurst in Queens. But almost as soon as they had moved in, Brown was confronted with a conflict of interest. As one of the leading bassists in bop, he considered his job with Dizzy Gillespie the gig of a lifetime. But at the same time that Dizzy's big band was to embark on a major European tour, the new Mrs. Brown was sched-

Heer Ptg. Co., Cols., O. CD20633

In the Matter of
Ray Brown
and
Ella Fitzgerald

Colored

Probate Court, Mahoning County, Ohio
No..............
MARRIAGE LICENSE APPLICATION
To the Honorable Judge of the Probate Court of said County:

The undersigned respectfully makes application for a Marriage License for said parties, and upon oath states:

That said *Ray Brown*
is 21 years of age on the 13 day of *Oct* 19 47
his residence is *New York N.Y.*
his place of birth is *Pittsburgh Pa*
his occupation is *Musician*
his father's name is *Clifton Brown*
his mother's maiden name was *Margret Morton*
that he was *Not* previously married
and that he has no wife living.

That said *Ella Fitzgerald*
is 29 years of age on the 24 day of *April* 19 47
her residence is *608 North* Ave.....Mahoning County, Ohio
her place of birth is *Newport News. Va.*
her occupation is *Singer*
her father's name is *Fitzgerald*
her mother's maiden name was *Temple Fitzgerald*
that she was *once* previously married
and is *Now* a widow or divorced woman, her married
name being *Benjamin Kornegie*
and that she has no husband living. *New N.Y.*

That neither of said parties is an habitual drunkard, epileptic, imbecile, or insane, and is not under the influence of any intoxicating liquor or narcotic drug. Said parties are not nearer of kin than second cousins, and there is no legal impediment to their marriage.

It is expected that..is to solemnize the marriage of said parties.

Sworn to before me, and signed in my presence, this 10 day of *December* 19 47

Ella Fitzgerald
Ray Brown

Clifford Newoodside Probate Judge
By *Gomer Evan* Deputy Clerk.

Consent..................................

Medical Certificates of Applicants Filed.....................19........

ENTRY
Probate Court, Mahoning County, Ohio, *Dec 10* 1947
Marriage License was this day granted to *Ray Brown* and
Ella Fitzgerald
Clifford Newoodside Probate Judge
By *Gomer Evans* Deputy Clerk

MARRIAGE CERTIFICATE
No........
The State of Ohio, Mahoning County, ss:
I Do Hereby Certify, That on the 10 day of *December* A. D. 194 7, I solemnized the Marriage
of Mr. *Ray Brown* with Miss *Ella Fitzgerald*
Filed and Recorded *Dec. 12* 1947
Clifford M. Woodside Probate Judge
Bruce R. Black
Justice of the Peace

Although there has never been any doubt about Ella's marriage to Ray Brown, the actual date of the nuptials has always been shrouded in mystery. In fact, she was married on December 10, 1947, in Ohio, as this copy of her marriage certificate reveals. The designation "Colored," top right, is another reminder of the racial climate at the time.

uled to undertake a major tour of eastern cities with tenor saxophonist Illinois Jacquet and his band.

In mid-January 1948 the Dizzy Gillespie orchestra set sail for their tour of Scandinavia, Belgium, and Holland without Ray Brown. "When I left Dizzy, the band was getting ready to go to Europe, and I couldn't go," he said. "I'd just gotten married to Ella Fitzgerald. At that time I was in a bit of a curl between her wanting me to travel with her as well. She wanted me to travel with the trio; she had Hank Jones playing piano. So I finally decided I was going to stay in New York."[2] Not unnaturally, Ella was reluctant to be parted from her husband, for both personal and professional reasons. For a while a compromise seemed likely; *Metronome* even suggested that Ella would fly to Sweden for a few dates with Dizzy.[3] In the end, promoter Ernie Anderson refused to give Ella any leeway, and the idea fell through.

The tour with the Illinois Jacquet band opened on January 16, 1948, in Washington, D.C., and was followed by a series of one-nighters ending in Minneapolis on February 2. The Ella-Illinois combination proved to be an outstanding box office draw. Jacquet had been building the reputation of his "little big" band since 1944, although until 1947 the band had existed only in the recording studios. Signed to the Apollo label, he had a big hit with "Robbins' Nest," which Ella herself had just covered, adding her own lyrics, prior to the recording ban.

When Jacquet decided to put a band on the road in mid-1947, he was touring with Count Basie. Taking with him fellow Basiemen Joe Newman on trumpet, J. J. Johnson on trombone, and Shadow Wilson on drums to form the nucleus of the group, he added John Malachi on piano, Al Lucas on bass, Leo Parker on baritone sax, and his brother Russell on trumpet. From the very start the band became one of the hottest draws in jazz.

"We had the flexibility of a small band with the power of a big band," recalled Jacquet. "When I formed the band, everybody started memorizing the charts. So all of a sudden we didn't need charts because everybody could play them without looking. That was the astonishing thing about this band, that they could memorize the whole book. When that band started playing, the rest was history. The band was breaking records everywhere just in public appearances. A tremendous drawing card. Even Carnegie Hall. Then we went on tour with Ella Fitzgerald and broke all records in blizzard weather in January."[4]

In fact, when they played Carnegie Hall on Saturday, January 17,

New York had just endured its third heaviest snowfall in a three-week period. But despite the weather, all the house seats were sold out for the midnight concert, including two hundred seats on stage. The box office take was a remarkable $7,500; in comparison, the Ella-Gillespie concert there the previous September had grossed only $5,300. The tour turned out to be an enormous success: Their Detroit date was sold out three days before their arrival, grossing $13,900, and lesser dates ran as follows: Hartford, $3,965; Philadelphia, $4,250; Boston, $5,600; Washington, D.C., $4,000; Cleveland, $5,100; Buffalo, $4,400; Pittsburgh, $4,800; and Indianapolis, $4,650. This was big money in postwar America.

When Ella had completed the tour—over two weeks of grueling one-night stands—she was booked straight into Oakland from February 10 for a week, followed by a week at Billy Berg's nightclub on Vine Street in Los Angeles. The Berg booking was in lieu of a scheduled appearance at Hollywood's Meadowbrook that had fallen through the previous October because the price was too low.

Just five years earlier, Ella had been taking whatever bookings she could, even if it meant being backed by semi-pro musicians in dingy clubs. Now Moe Gale could afford to turn down a plum Hollywood booking because the fee offered was too low; he was confident he could get her fee elsewhere. It was a remarkable turnaround in Ella's fortunes. Her earnings were higher than she had ever dreamed possible, and she had successfully weathered the most difficult period in her career. Hank Jones recalled that when he joined her in the last weeks of 1947, they were always booked into good venues, and when they were out of town, they stayed at first-class hotels.[5]

Ella was now well on her way to gaining universal recognition as one of the great jazz and popular singers. During her week at Berg's, for example, the club was filled with celebrities every night. One evening during her week-long stay, Ella invited Peggy Lee to come out of the audience to sing the Benny Carter composition "Lonely Woman" in honor of the composer, who was sitting in the audience with conductor David Rose. "The 'First Lady of Song' stepped up on her present eminence as the result of the greatest skein of smash hits the singing industry ever witnessed," said the *Pittsburgh Courier*.[6]

At the end of April, Ella returned to the recording studios, once again circumventing the recording ban by using fellow non-union members, the vocal group the Song Spinners, to provide her backing. The Song Spinners sang heavenly-host chords while a baritone provided a slightly shaky bass line. Normally a session produced three or four 78 sides, but "My Happiness" and "Tea Leaves" took a session apiece because the Song Spinners had difficulty learning the material in the studios.

"'My Happiness' was a Jon and Sandra Steele hit we were covering," said Milt Gabler. "It was a two-part harmony song, and finally I had the singers singing unison behind Ella."[7] When the disc was released the following June, "My Happiness" peaked at number six, staying on the charts for a total of twenty-one weeks. "In spite of inept assistance from the Song Spinners," said *Metronome*, "Ella's singing is already in high jukebox demand. The limitations of postban noninstrumental recording and the songs themselves do not altogether efface Ella's lovely voice and professional polish."[8]

Although her appearances on network radio had become infrequent, Ella appeared as a guest on the "jubilee" show hosted by Ernie "Bubbles" Whitman on May 25 and June 1. These programs were transcribed for the Armed Forces Radio Service, and the norm was two slots per show for the second guest, three for the "star." Ella was allocated two spots on each, identifying with the bop movement on both programs with "Lady Be Good" on the first show and "My Baby Likes to Re-Bop," a grisly novelty number she had stockpiled for Decca in December, on the second.

From June 1, Ella and the trio were back in New York for four weeks at The Three Deuces at 77 West Fifty-second Street. They did incredible business; the four-week option clause was renewed in June and July, and they finally ended their stay there on August 31. On July 21, however, they took time off to make a high-profile appearance at the World Fair of Music being held at New York's Grand Central Palace. Featured as part of the "Contrasts in Modern Music" series, Ella stuck to the routine she had worked up for her nightclub act, a mixture of past hits, novelty numbers, and ballads, including "A-Tisket, A-Tasket," "Cow-Cow Boogie," "Lady Be Good," a cover version of the current chart topper "Nature Boy," popularized by Nat King Cole, "Summertime," and "The Woody Woodpecker Song."

The inclusion of "The Woody Woodpecker Song," and before it numbers such as "Giddap Mule," was a throwback to Ella's big band days when she was renowned for her handling of novelty numbers, epitomized by "A-Tisket, A-Tasket." Much has been written about the quality of material given to her by Decca to record. However, it is interesting to note that these songs were ones Ella herself had chosen to perform in her nightclub act, not once or twice but night after night for about two years. At various points in her career she included "Mule Train" and "Hernando's Hideaway" in her repertoire, and even pestered Milt Gabler into allowing her to record a cover version of Rosemary Clooney's "Come On-a My House." In later years the influence of Norman Granz would keep Ella's lack of artistic scruples under wraps, although even he succumbed to her request to record the appalling "Ringo Beat."

After her record-breaking stint at The Three Deuces, Ella played Chicago's Rag Doll Club on Western at Devon during the first week in September. Outside, the billboard read, "Last Appearance Before European Tour"; inside, it was clear that Ella had shifted the emphasis in her repertoire in favor of ballads. For some, her performance was a bit lukewarm: "What Ella sang . . . was mostly sweet. . . . The phrase 'something sweet and gentle' from 'Robbins' Nest' typified her mood. . . . But you can't be gentle with a jump tune, and Miss Fitzgerald was feeling very gentle indeed. How long this lasts we have no way of knowing," commented *Down Beat* magazine.[9]

When pressed on the issue, Ella retorted, "I don't like to sing bop most";[10] when the audience clamored for "Flying Home," she sang "Nature Boy." The reason for this change of emphasis, although it would have been somewhat infra dig for Ella to have admitted it, was that she was trying out some new numbers for her forthcoming English trip. Warned that she would be singing in English variety halls for audiences to whom the concept of jazz was as remote as the teachings of King Ramses III, she turned the emphasis to ballads at the expense of scat. However, in so doing, she brought to the surface a problem that had been gnawing at her for quite a while.

Always a little envious of the critical acclaim laid at the feet of Billie Holiday for her slow-burn classics on the Commodore and Decca labels, Ella felt she was not getting the recognition she deserved for her own ballad singing. She considered ballads a specialty and, seemingly oblivious of the profile her high-flying scat had earned her, thought she was being sold short at the expense of what she called "riffin'." But this was what her audiences loved: "As far as the audience is concerned I could sing 'How High the Moon' all night," she complained.[11] It was a theme that would resurface time and again throughout her career.

Ella's first trip overseas began when she embarked on the *Queen Mary* from Manhattan for Southampton, England, on September 15, 1948. It was a significant visit for Ella and for the United Kingdom. For years the British Musicians' Union insulated themselves from

American jazz by imposing a ban on visiting American musicians unless there was reciprocity of employment. It was a nearsighted view that in the long run would contribute to relegating jazz to the cultural margins of the country. Ella was considered a musical "act," however; she was booked into variety theaters and as such did not form part of the ban, although she was not allowed to bring her own drummer.

On arrival she was disconcerted to learn that her appearance at the London Palladium on the 27th had been canceled because Betty Hutton had been held over a week. She was scheduled instead for the Empire Theatre in Glasgow. Nervous, she used the same repertoire she featured at Chicago's Rag Doll—a mixture of hits, the dreaded "Woody Woodpecker Song," and plenty of ballads, including "Don't Worry 'Bout Me" and "Nature Boy." When she was called back for an encore, the crowd was shouting for "My Happiness."

"'My Happiness' was not jazz, it was just a pop song I had her do," said Milt Gabler. "When she went to England, our record was out here, and it was also out in England on Brunswick or some label or other, and the audience started to call for the song. She hadn't realized the record had been released there, but when it was requested, they went out and got the record. Then she remembered it—it was a simple song to remember—and put it in her act. She told me the story; she said, 'Milt, I didn't realize the power of a pop song like that one—until I got over there and they called out they wanted me to do that song for them.' And I said, 'Ella, that's what I say. This one pays the rent!' Because in those years when you did something that was jazz-oriented, like those first riff tunes, it would sell maybe 180,000 to 200,000 records tops. But if you did a song like 'My Happiness,' it would sell 500,000 to 600,000 records. So I said, 'That pays for all the good things we want to do, and you'll be in the black.'"[12]

The following week Ella went into the London Palladium, Europe's premier variety house, second on the bill to one of Britain's top variety artists, Gracie Fields. But just as at the Rag Doll, where her revamped repertoire failed to impress a jazz-oriented reviewer, this time for London's *Melody Maker* the response was much the same: "We who know her voice so well and admire it so much felt . . . that for some reason we were not seeing Ella at her best."[13]

During her stay in London, the English jazz writer Max Jones got to know Ella and sowed the seeds of a friendship that was to last over forty years. "She seemed friendly from the beginning," he said. "She had this little-girl voice, little-girl way of talking as well as singing.

She was amiable and approachable. At that time my son was just a couple of months old, and Ella took a great interest in him. On every subsequent visit she wanted to know 'How's that baby?'"

Ella and Ray, on what Max Jones called their "honeymoon trip," were booked into a different hotel from pianist Hank Jones. "I had only joined the *Melody Maker* in 1945. But getting to know Hank Jones— The first time I met him, I called at his hotel in Bloomsbury Square. He was in one of those private hotels, and when I called to interview him, he said he was getting 'the treatment'—looks in the bar and in the restaurant. The kind of situation where he 'felt a draft,' as he put it. We had a big house in Primrose Hill and some spare rooms, so we put him up for that period; about a fortnight he resided with us. He was wonderful company, and I learned a lot from him during our conversations."

On the final Sunday of her engagement, Ella, Ray Brown, and Hank Jones were invited to appear on bandleader Ted Heath's Sunday Swing Session at the London Palladium. Heath, Europe's top big-band leader, drew sellout crowds for his Sunday Swing Sessions. "For two weeks before the concert," reported *Metronome*, "Ella had been confined to pretty commercial stuff as she sang for the family type of audience at the Palladium. Her concert with the Heath band, about which she raved with enthusiasm, finally gave her an opportunity to show the Englanders what she could do. Suffice to say, after a half-hour of encores she had to beg off."[14]

At last Ella had an opportunity to pull out her bop charts of "How High the Moon," "Lady Be Good," and "Flying Home," to the crowd's delight. "Again and again she was recalled by the bop-hungry crowd," said *Melody Maker*.[15] She left England on the *Queen Mary* on October 30 and, said Max Jones, "continued to speak warmly of the initial exposure to the English public, of friendships she came to value, and of a feeling that England was a second home."

From November 24, Ella and her trio were booked into the Royal Roost for a two-week engagement alternating with the Lester Young Quintet. The Roost had a radio wire at the time, and several airchecks of their performances have become available over the years. There was the eminently forgettable "Old Mother Hubbard" and the novelty number "Mr. Paganini," dating back to her days with Chick Webb, which Ella never allowed to sink into the obscurity it deserved; her persistence in resurrecting the tune from time to time finally made it a hit among the party faithful a few years later. The rest of her repertoire was biased toward the strictly jazz policy of the Roost, and Ella clearly enjoyed herself. Singing a mix of ballads and uptempo numbers, she sounded comfortable and confident.

The new year of 1949 opened with a trip to the winter sun in Miami where she was booked into the Monte Carlo Club. When she opened on January 18, she discovered that the club's future booking policy toward black artists rested on how she was received by the white patrons. Ella rose to the challenge, and, as was perhaps inevitable, her stay was a success; the club continued to book black artists, a controversial move in the South.

Ella was now a successful and accomplished nightclub singer. Virtually everywhere she went she played to standing-room-only houses. To continue growing as an artist she needed fresh challenges and new horizons. The time was ripe to move on to a larger stage. Although she didn't realize it at the time, when she walked into Carnegie Hall's solo spotlight on February 11, 1949, her career was about to take off in a new and unexpected direction.

Norman Granz was born on August 6, 1918, in Los Angeles. He was raised in the Boyle Heights neighborhood, graduated from high school in 1935, and went on to the University of California at Los Angeles. Forced to work his way through school, he took a job as a board marker for a brokerage house, starting work at 6 A.M. and continuing his studies late into the night. He entered the armed forces in 1941, originally as a member of the Army Air Corps but later he was transferred to Special Services. After a medical discharge in 1942, he took a job as a cleaner at Warner Brothers Studios for a dollar an hour.

Since his time at UCLA as a philosophy major, Granz had developed an abiding interest in jazz. He was an avid record collector and habitué of the Los Angeles jazz scene, fascinated by the music and yet appalled by the rule of many large clubs of excluding black patrons. Taking advantage of a new ruling which insisted clubs that regularly employed musicians give them one night off per week, in July 1942 he talked the owner of the Trouville Club into staging a series of Sunday jam sessions when the regularly employed musicians were resting. He soon developed a circuit of clubs, each with a different "off" night, including a weekly session for Hollywood's leading nightclub operator, Billy Berg. Full of confidence, he was able to insist on three conditions: that the musicians be paid formally instead of given tips at the end of the evening (the norm at such events); that tables be placed on the dance floor to create a listening-only policy; and finally, that black patrons be admitted.

Musicians were drawn from whatever touring bands happened to be in town plus a pool of Los Angeles regulars. Nat King Cole was often house pianist, and Lester and Lee Young, who had a band on the coast at the time, were regular features alongside visiting musicians from the bands of Duke Ellington, Jimmie Lunceford, and Count Basie. In 1944, Granz took the ambitious step of arranging a promotion at Los Angeles' Philharmonic Auditorium to raise funds to provide a defense for a group of Mexican youths arrested in the so-called zoot-suit riots in the city. The whole case reeked of prejudice, and a number of Hollywood notables, including Orson Welles and Rita Hayworth, organized what was called the Sleepy Lagoon Defense Committee.

Granz had to borrow money to stage the show, which turned out to be a sellout, and the "Jazz at the Philharmonic" concept was born. During the rest of 1944 he presented his Jazz at the Philharmonic concerts as monthly events. But, significantly, he had reached an agreement with the Armed Forces Radio Service to record the first concert to beam to American G.I.s. After the concert they presented him with sixteen-inch acetates of the proceedings, which, after some difficulty, he managed to get released by Moe Asch on his Asch label. At the time, the concept of live recordings for commercial distribution was resisted by recording company executives who thought the crowd noises intrusive.

Because the Asch label was poorly distributed, Granz struck a deal with Mercury Records, which agreed to distribute the recordings on their label. This arrangement continued for the next four or five concert recordings, at which point Granz formed his own label, Clef, which released subsequent concerts through the Mercury distribution network. It was the beginning of what writer John McDonough described as "a selling reciprocity between box office and record sales that no one imagined possible. The albums leveraged the concerts. The concerts generated more live records. And within a few years the JATP was a national phenomenon."[16]

Granz had seen a hole in the marketplace and exploited it. By 1952 he was grossing a million dollars a year and claiming, "I give people in Des Moines and El Paso the kind of jazz they could never otherwise hear."[17] Through a mixture of concerts and recordings he was able to provide enough work to attract some of the top musicians in jazz to his banner. "His salaries are probably the highest in the history of jazz," remarked *Metronome*. "It's safe to say that his men average two and three times as much a week working for Granz as they would playing in nightclubs elsewhere. It's been said that one performer's nightly salary with Granz equalled one week's work at a top nightclub."[18]

But Granz's popularity was not acquired without controversy. A hallmark of the Jazz at the Philharmonic concerts was "The Battle." Trumpeters, saxophonists, and drummers were presented head-to-head in so-called cutting contests. The crowd yelled and cheered for their favorite musicians, some of whom were not beyond resorting to histrionics to get the crowd's reaction. The music press latched on to the yellers and screamers, indignant at "the lowest class of swing enthusiasts . . . [who] are heaven-sent only when a tenorman squeaks and yowls his way to C above high."[19] But Granz never expected the audience to react as if they were listening to chamber music; this was *exciting* music, he said.

Undoubtedly the crowds yelled and egged on some performers who, as recordings of the time reveal, gave them what they wanted, but those same recordings also present a lot of very good solos from some of the top musicians in the business. Granz, who would stop the concert if it got too noisy and even went as far as having brochures printed giving instructions on "how to act at jazz concerts," today feels reviewers concentrated too much on those musicians who did work the crowd, at the expense of some sublime contributions from players such as Coleman Hawkins, Benny Carter, and Charlie Parker, who did not. The whole point of a Jazz at the Philharmonic concert, he says, was to present good, happy, swinging jazz.

It was what the public wanted. The JATP concerts continued to grow in popularity, and by the fall of 1948 Granz had built a sophisticated operation. In advance of the JATP's two concerts in San Francisco, for example, Tony Valerio, a big record distributor in the Bay area, had made sure that ads appeared in newspapers and on the radio for five weeks before the concert, and he had aroused such interest among disc jockeys that twelve local radio stations were regularly featuring JATP recordings. Consequently, ticket buyers knocked each other over in the rush when the box office opened at San Francisco's Opera House. No matter what the critics said or thought, or how unruly the crowd reaction, JATP had become big box office.

In the four years since his first Jazz at the Philharmonic production in 1944, Norman Granz had become probably the most astute promoter of jazz in the world. An exceptionally able businessman, he had it all: negotiating skills, commercial instinct, and an endless reservoir of energy and determination. He once boasted that he knew more than any man alive about scaling a hall: "I've got a sixth sense about it," he said.[20] No other promoter had his finger closer to the pulse of jazz than Granz.

Over the years he had become well aware of what a crowd-puller Ella Fitzgerald was. Details of her successful engagements and her sellout concerts and reviews of her in-person appearances appeared frequently in the music press. Her records regularly charted on the hit parade and were favorites of record stations across the country. Discs such as "Flying Home," "Lady Be Good," "Air Mail Special," and "How High the Moon" were widely admired by musicians and jazz fans alike. Although at the time Granz's favorite singer was Billie Holiday (he voted for her in the annual *Esquire* awards), he was nevertheless amazed at the crowd response one night when, realizing Ella was in the audience watching her husband Ray Brown perform, he invited her onto the stage to sing a few numbers. From that point on there was no doubt in his mind about Ella Fitzgerald's commercial potential or the drawing power she would have in any JATP package. He was also well aware of the value of a vocalist in leavening the instrumental mix. Since 1946 he had been booking Billie Holiday or the ex-Basie singer Helen Humes. However, he never considered Humes a major jazz singer, and by 1947 Holiday's drug addiction had landed her in the federal reformatory for women at Alderson, West Virginia, for a year and a day.

Ella seemed a natural choice for JATP, but it was not easy to secure her services. While musicians were delighted with the fees Granz could offer them, she was a popular Decca recording artist and a star in her own right, and for the first few years of JATP productions she remained tantalizingly beyond the reach of his budget. Also, she had a longstanding management arrangement with Moe Gale and would not be able to record for Granz's Clef label because of her contract with Decca.

Although the first JATP package had ended in disaster in 1945 when the troupe became stranded in Victoria, British Columbia, by the end of 1948 it was an established success, able to outdraw attractions such as Duke Ellington, Nat King Cole, and the popular Stan Kenton band on the West Coast. Granz now felt that his gross was sufficient to add Ella to his roster without cutting too deeply into his profit margin. During the fall of 1948 he contacted Tim Gale, Ella's booking agent at Gale Inc., and entered negotiations to add her to his

1949 tour, set to open with a big concert at Carnegie Hall on February 11.

Machito and his orchestra were brought across from the Clique Club for the night of the concert to perform with Charlie Parker, while the touring members—Coleman Hawkins, Fats Navarro, Shelly Manne, Flip Phillips, Tommy Turk, and Ella and her fellas, Ray Brown and Hank Jones—were each featured throughout the evening. "With a Hoot and a Howl JATP Kicks Off" headlined *Down Beat*. "Against a background of hoots and howls from the hoodlum section . . . JATP launched another coast-to-coast tour before an almost capacity house. . . . Ella Fitzgerald, registered as the showstopper she always is, . . . obliged with two sets of tunes."[21] Ella was quietly on her way to becoming one of the stars of the JATP firmament; Granz's predictions about adding her to the roster were already coming true.

When the troupe reached the West Coast in mid-March, Tony Valerio had done his advance publicity work well. It was impossible to turn on any of the Bay area radio stations without hearing the DJ talking about the two JATP concerts on the 17th and 22nd: "The magic name of Ella Fitzgerald had every platter spinner in the Bay area mad with joy. Add to that the other promotion work Valerio . . . lined up, and you'll have some idea why they're predicting that Norman Granz will gross a fine, fat five-figure sum for the two dates."[22]

When they reached Chicago on the 25th, Hank Jones was down with the flu. But Ella simply went on and performed her usual two sets with just bass and drums, in an impressive display of musicianship. However, her lack of artistic direction was beginning to catch up with her: "Ella Fitzgerald sang what was generally regarded as a crummy selection of songs with delicacy and personal appeal," said *Down Beat*'s Chicago reviewer. "Just how 'Old Mother Hubbard,' 'Mr. Paganini,' and 'A Little Bird Told Me' got into her repertoire we don't know."[23]

Granz, who watched every performance by Ella throughout the tour before it finally ended at the Brooklyn Academy of Music on March 30, was in a dilemma. Much as he wanted to step in and suggest she change her program, he was prevented from doing so by Ella's longstanding association with Moe Gale. As a concert promoter he could no more insist she sing certain songs than any other promoter or club owner she worked for. If he pushed too hard, Moe Gale would clearly take exception. He could suggest, he could ask a favor here and a favor there, but ultimately he was convinced that what Ella needed was active management and artistic direction. Then she could become a major concert artist rather than a popular night-club singer.

On April 14, Bop City, New York's newest jazz club, opened its doors, a highly publicized event. On opening night, customers with-out reservations waited hopefully in a line that extended two blocks. It was estimated that three thousand got in and five thousand were turned away. Much publicity had been given to the return to the bandstand of Artie Shaw, who—incredibly—had brought a forty-piece symphony orchestra into the club to play the works of Debussy and Ravel. Needless to say, in a venue that aspired to be bop's newest headquarters, Shaw blew it. Asked to play two forty-five-minute sets, Shaw took an hour and a half to wade through his wares. "Bop City Books in Muzak," said *Billboard* wryly. The fans were not amused. After bearing Shaw's badly rehearsed offerings with fortitude for about an hour, they started heckling with calls of "Let's jump!" "Give us a break!" and cries of "Ool-ya-koo!" Adding to the collective angst was the failure of the air-conditioning. Men stripped to shirt-sleeves; women used the program notes as fans.

In all the confusion and turmoil, Shaw's co-headliner took the stage. Ella Fitzgerald didn't have to be told what had to be done. She pulled out her bop repertoire and saved the evening from disaster. "Despite the turmoil . . . [she] held the house on all her appearances. She was in wonderful form and was obviously what the paying ele-ment of the crowd had come to see."[24] Spotting Billie Holiday in the audience, she interpolated her usual "Lady Be Good" routine with "Oh, Lady Day be good."

Also in the audience watching Ella triumph in adversity were exec-utives from Time-Life-Fortune, America's most important documen-tary filmmakers, who were responsible for the "March of Time" series. Delighted with what they saw, they arranged for a shoot with Ella and her trio at the Decca offices on West Fifty-seventh Street, with a release date scheduled for June 10. Also in the film were Guy Lombardo, Bing Crosby, Eddie Duchin, and the Corn Cobblers. Ella flew back with her trio especially for the filming, and after it was over, the producers wanted to thank her for doing a highly profes-sional job. Unable to find her, they discovered that she had jumped into a waiting car with Ray Brown's trio in tow and raced back to La Guardia Airport. When the film was released, the spoken intro-duction to the film said: "As long as this country has artists like Ella

Fitzgerald making records, the recording industry will turn out millions of records annually which will find their way into American homes."

On a hot and sultry afternoon in June 1948, Columbia Records invited the press to a briefing at the Waldorf-Astoria Hotel to tell them about a "revolutionary new product." It turned out to be a nonbreakable microgroove disc with a playing time of about twenty-three minutes a side. Columbia called it the long-playing record. A new era was born.

However, the transition to microgroove was by no means as fast as the CD revolution in recent times. Initially the LP appeared cautiously in a ten-inch format, then gradually the industry norm became the familiar, but now extinct, twelve-inch platter. Decca, in 1949 still the largest record company uncommitted to the format, finally declared itself in favor of the LP in November of that year. By 1950 the 78-rpm shellac disc was no longer the industry standard but was rapidly giving way to microgrooved vinylite of either the 33⅓ rpm or the 45 rpm variety.

Although Ella did not know it when she went into the recording studios on April 28, the four cuts she made that day with Gordon Jenkins and his orchestra would not only be released as 78s but would later form part of the long-playing album *Miss Ella Fitzgerald and Mr. Gordon Jenkins Invite You to Listen and Relax*, released in 1954. Two cuts, "Happy Talk" and "I'm Gonna Wash That Man Right Outa My Hair," also went on to form part of a 78 album by several artists of the score of *South Pacific* in May 1949. Significantly, it was the *South Pacific* package that gave Milt Gabler the idea of a whole album of songs from the pen of a major Broadway composer.

If there was any doubting Ella's vocal skill, "I'm Gonna Wash That Man Right Outa My Hair" must have silenced her critics once and for all in 1949. "Could she have recorded . . . [it] for any other reason than to show off her rhythmic dexterity?" asked Will Friedwald. "Taking the central part of the refrain at a reasonably fast clip, she effortlessly dives into the bridge at double time. . . . The effect exhilarates."[25] Contemporary reviews were just as enthusiastic: "Ella sings *really* well," confirmed *Metronome*.[26]

The two non–*South Pacific* numbers cut on April 28 were released the following September: "Black Coffee" and "Lover's Gold." Both were awarded B ratings by *Metronome*: "As usual . . . [we] enjoy the quality of her voice. All agree she does remarkably well with the lugubrious . . . ['Lover's Gold']."[27] Then, at the end of a productive session with Gordon Jenkins, Ella crossed the corridor of the Decca studios to join Louis Jordan and his Tympany Five for two cuts, "Baby, It's Cold Outside" and "Don't Cry, Cry Baby." It was a fun session, and there could be no mistaking the fact that Ella really did enjoy doing novelty numbers. "Baby, It's Cold Outside" was another good example of this; well crafted, it went to number nine on the hit parade in November and stayed on the charts for a total of thirteen weeks. "George is knocked out by Ella's dainty way with the second chorus," said reviewer George T. Simon in 1949.[28]

Ella was out on the West Coast in June and July; in June she was booked into San Francisco's Ciro's Club. Critic Ralph Gleason went to the club's Starlight Roof to see her perform and, hardened pro that he was, was completely bowled over by her performance: "Ella was just simply and grandly grand. She captivated the audience, not only with her singing, but with her grace and showmanship."[29] Ray Brown's trio was also impressive in the instrumental slots, and the management was so pleased that it decided to make the band a feature in its own right. The only snag was management's insistence on a tenor player, which upset the group's rapport. There were no such problems in July, however, when Ella returned to San Francisco for a stay at the Tivoli, patronized by a college crowd; in live performance Ella had become such an accomplished performer that she could seemingly work her spell irrespective of situation or age group. At the end of her first week at the Tivoli, on July 20, she went into Decca's Los Angeles studios to cover "A New Shade of Blue" and "Crying," both of which had been recorded by other artists on other labels. *Metronome* rated them B and B+, respectively: "Ella does fine . . . [and] impressively."[30]

Ella's continued run of success with her recordings and in her personal appearances was pushing her earning capacity ever upward. Her earnings for 1949 were projected to be $150,000.[31] If she took a week's break, it could cost her almost $3,000 in lost earnings, so she remorselessly kept working. However, her unceasing schedule created a strain that slowly began to be felt within Ella and Ray's relationship, which would be tested to destruction over the next three years. "It was a good marriage," Ella said later, "but it's hard for two people in show business. You have to learn to really understand somebody."[32]

CHAPTER NINE

1949–1952

Ella really seemed to thrive under Norman Granz's leadership or agency. She really made it when he put her with
those JATP things. Ella's career just went up in leaps and
bounds after that.

                                        BILL DOGGETT

WHEN NORMAN GRANZ put together the musicians for his fall 1949
touring schedule, Ella Fitzgerald was at the top of his list. Her first
JATP tour earlier in the year had gone well. She was popular with the
crowds, and she added prestige to his promotions. Granz was sensitive to the music press, and Ella's presence meant that the JATP concert reviews were now no longer an unrelieved diatribe about honking
saxophones and shrieking crowds.

More important, though, Granz was now convinced that neither
Moe Gale nor Decca had capitalized on Ella's full potential. He
believed she was the greatest singer in jazz, and earlier in the year had
taken to introducing her as such. As a first step in determining her
artistic direction, he included her in the jam session that ended each
half of the show. By the time her first tour was over, Ella jamming
with the horns was already well on its way to becoming standard
JATP fare. Ella had already enjoyed success in her own right with
numbers like "Air Mail Special," "Flying Home," "Lady Be Good,"
and what Granz called the signature tune of Jazz at the Philharmonic,
"How High the Moon." These were the very numbers used by the
JATP musicians as vehicles for their improvised jams. It was almost
as if it had been preordained. Ella slotted in perfectly with the JATP
formula. When, in "How High the Moon," she went through her
"we're swinging it because you asked for it" routine, the crowds
loved it. It worked as well in nightclubs as on the concert stage.
Standing shoulder to shoulder with the instrumentalists, Ella traded

choruses with them just as Granz had seen her do on the stage of Carnegie Hall back in September 1947. Granz reasoned that if this did not prove she was on a par with the greatest male improvisers in jazz, nothing would.

The fall tour began with a sellout concert at Carnegie Hall at midnight on Sunday, September 18, 1949. Ella received star billing. She had a set to herself in each half of the program, whereas instrumentalists—even the big names—had to content themselves with just one or two feature numbers at various points during the show. In addition, her participation in the jam sessions helped raise her profile even further. Her star billing paid off: "Ella Fitzgerald was a smash success, broke it up with a whole gamut of songs," said *Down Beat*.[1]

Prior to the concert, Roy Eldridge, the featured trumpet player, entered an empty Carnegie Hall through the front door. He was, as usual, early. Seeing a lone soul sitting at the front of the hall, he introduced himself to the young man, who said his name was Oscar Peterson. He explained he had been flown in from Canada to be a surprise guest at this important concert. He admitted he was nervous. Eldridge said he must be some kind of piano player if Norman had gone to all this trouble and that he was eager to hear him. Peterson thanked Eldridge but said the real thrill for him was going to be hearing all the great names in jazz perform.[2] Along with Eldridge were Charlie Parker, Lester Young, Coleman Hawkins, and a rhythm section of Buddy Rich, Hank Jones, and Ray Brown. In any event, Peterson's U.S. debut was somewhat contrived in order to circumvent the regulations imposed by the Bureau of Immigration and the Local 802 of the American Federation of Musicians. He had to wait in the audience for Granz to "invite" him onstage to perform, as if he were there entirely fortuitously. Had Granz booked him through normal channels there would have been all kinds of paperwork and administrative problems for such a brief cameo performance. When Peterson did go onstage, he "stopped the . . . concert dead cold in its tracks."[3]

After the concert the troupe was launched into a series of one-nighters that lasted for almost two months. When the tour reached the South, Norman Granz was presented with a radio transcription by "Evelyn Fields." He was amused to find that this was Ella singing under another name (see page 271, note). Previously it had been assumed that the only time she had strayed from the Decca label was when she cut a couple of sides with Benny Goodman in the 1930s.

* * *

With the decline of the big bands, ballrooms all over the country were closing their doors for good. Jazz, for the most part, could only be heard in clubs. With his JATP concert tours, Norman Granz almost singlehandedly made the presentation of jazz on the concert platform a commonplace. In so doing he would elevate the status of both Ella Fitzgerald and Oscar Peterson to that of international concert artist.

They were the key musicians around whom he would build his recording business and concert promotions. Through them he would make his fortune, but he would also make them millionaires in the process. Mel Tormé said, "I give great credit to Norman Granz for saying to Ella, 'You are far more than a cult singer. You should be a national treasure, and you should be able to draw people in Las Vegas and the biggest nightclubs in New York.' And that's what he did for her, and I give him full credit for doing that. I just think it was a phenomenal job."

The more popular JATP became, the more tireless Granz became in using his commercial clout to combat racial injustice. Promoters seeking to book his concerts had to sign a contract that expressly forbade any kind of racial discrimination. This resulted in a JATP concert that played to the first integrated audience in the history of Charleston, South Carolina. Also, when Granz learned that a concert in New Orleans was being segregated into black-only and white-only sections, he canceled. Reflecting in later life on his groundbreaking work, he said it was simply a matter of principle. He wanted to prove it was possible to go into the deep South and present an integrated concert before an integrated audience, irrespective of any financial considerations.

At the time, racist custom in the South was institutionalized. Contracts for most venues there included the clause "The concert will be segregated/non-segregated." When Granz deleted "segregated," he was under no illusions as to what he was taking on. In some cities, however, where the concept of black sitting next to white in the same audience was a step too far, he introduced integration gradually by playing an unsegregated dance. But as the drawing power of JATP increased, he threatened to sue if a concert was blocked on racial grounds, as on one occasion in Kansas City, Missouri. In 1949, as a result of his unswerving dedication to the breaking down of racial barriers, he received the Russwurm Award for contributions to race relations. (The award was presented by the National Negro Publishers Association.)

Initially the JATP tours went by bus, just like every other touring band, but as soon as he was financially able, Granz ensured his artists traveled first class, flying from engagement to engagement. All his artists were booked into the best hotels and were among the best paid in jazz. Rightly, he inspired great loyalty and trust among his musicians, and Ella was no exception. She respected his wishes implicitly; on opening night of her second JATP tour, at Carnegie Hall, she stepped in to correct the tempo of "How High the Moon," cutting across her male confrères, asserting, "*He* [Granz] wants it up, *he* wants it up," and snapping her fingers to a brighter beat over the slower tempo until Buddy Rich on drums picked it up. If *he* wanted "How High the Moon" *up*, then Ella was going to make sure *he* got it. So when Granz began to suggest to Ella that he would give her much better material to record than Decca if she signed with him, she listened.

Moe Gale would hear none of it, however. He had turned down a lucrative deal put together by John Hammond on behalf of Keynote Records to sign Ella, and was proved right when the small independent failed. Similarly, he was wary of Granz's operation, which in his eyes was yet another independent, a one-man operation with hardly any track record, an outfit that would benefit immeasurably from the sales and prestige of signing Ella. She was an established star and an important cog in the Decca hit-making machine, and it made sense for her to stay with a major recording company that had sophisticated channels of distribution and promotion.

Nevertheless, Granz was undeterred by Moe Gale's stance. He was determined to sign Ella. When he recorded his JATP concerts, as he did at Carnegie Hall on September 18, he was frustrated by having her on disc yet being unable to release the portions of the concert in which she participated because it infringed her contract with Decca. At the end of 1949 he had already reached volume ten of his JATP series, extracts from his concerts spread over albums comprising four 78 sides, featuring Illinois Jacquet, Howard McGhee, Flip Phillips, and Bill Harris. His most popular release had been the first, a set containing the bop anthem "How High the Moon" that had notched sales in excess of 150,000. Compared to Ella's Decca sales, this was peanuts, but having seen how popular she was on tour, Granz was certain that her jazz sets with JATP were just what the public was waiting for. And there could be no doubt about Ella's popularity in 1949. In the September edition of *Metronome* she came second only to Billie Holiday in their first All Time All Star Poll.

Granz began maneuvering in earnest to secure Ella's release from Decca. Initially he contacted them over Moe Gale's head to see if they would entertain such a possibility. "Norman called me one day when he started to use Ella on his JATP tours," said Milt Gabler. "He said, 'Milt, I'll buy Ella's contract from Decca.' He offered me—the company—$25,000 to buy the contract. She had about a year left, maybe a year and a half. So I said, 'Norman, I love Ella just as much as you do, and I wouldn't sell her contract for any money in the world. I'm not even going to tell the president of our company, Milt Rachmil, that you offered $25,000. If you want her, you'll have to call him yourself. He's liable to take it because there's only twelve months or so left. So I won't sell her contract for any money in the world, but I can't stop you from calling him directly.' But he never did!"[4]

While he waited for Ella's contract to run out, Granz expressed his frustration at some of the material she was being given to record in the trade press. "Norman tried everything to get Ella away from me at Decca," continued Gabler. "He used to have pieces in *Down Beat* saying how I was destroying her, giving her bad material and all that kind of stuff. Sure, I used to give her pop material to do. I remember I once gave her 'Crying in the Chapel,' which was a cover of a country hit; she didn't like those songs, and neither did I. But that was a pretty big seller, a surprising one for Ella; it sold records, which was good for Ella and good for the company. She did very well when she did that kind of material, and we were reaching for the black market with those songs, like a crossover. And I used to like doing switch treatments, you know, for a different audience. Years later it came true with Ray Charles with probably the biggest album he ever made, and it was country music."[5]

Toward the end of 1949, Ella, too, began airing her feelings of artistic frustration about Decca in the press. In an interview with George Hoefer of *Down Beat* during the winter 1949 JATP tour, she made it clear that her preference was for ballads "rather than blues, scat, or bebop," and blamed Decca for "some poor choices of tunes."[6]

Elsewhere, critics without Granz's vested interest in trashing Decca did not see things that way at all. With the release of four discs that Ella cut between September 1949 and March 1950, Fred Reynolds, in his long-running review column in the *Chicago Tribune*, said:

There is so much ordinary on records these days that the various vocals of Ella Fitzgerald are as refreshing as *South Pacific*. Here is a singer who is the closest to a complete artist that popular music knows. . . . She is richly sincere as she sings Ray Noble's . . . "I Hadn't Anyone 'Til You." Listening to this you wonder somehow whether Noble didn't have Ella tucked away in the back of his mind when he wrote it. "I Got to Have My Baby Back" is one of the sweetest blues of 1950 or any other year. . . . When it comes to "Sugarfoot Rag," the first lady of song has herself a ball. . . . Her last chorus of "Sugarfoot" is pure improvisation, the voice in place of the instrument. This is a big affair, joyful and loaded with fine jazz. Then there's "Basin Street Blues," a wonderful thing indeed. . . . When you get down to it, there's no substitute for talent. Ella Fitzgerald proves it on these records.[7]

For Ella's session in New York on September 20, 1949, Gabler used the arranger Sy Oliver to act as musical director. Oliver, born in 1910, was brought up in Zanesville, Ohio, where he learned trumpet and worked as a casual employee in local bands. He began writing and arranging as a member of Zack Whyte's Chocolate Beau Brummels, a territory band with a big reputation, and he also put in a spell with another name territory band, one led by Alphonso Trent. In 1933 he joined the Jimmie Lunceford Orchestra, which quickly developed into one of the most important bands of the swing era, substantially helped by Oliver's compositions and arrangements. By 1934, Oliver was even arranging for bands other than Lunceford, while at the same time establishing himself as a fixture in the trumpet section. In 1939, Tommy Dorsey persuaded him to join his staff as an arranger and occasional singer, and although he subsequently led his own band briefly in 1946, his skills as a musical director were soon in demand by several record companies. By the end of the 1940s he had built a reputation with Decca as an arranger and musical director, acting for many of their major artists.

On Oliver's first session with Ella, they did her version of "Basin Street Blues" with a tongue-in-cheek impersonation of Louis Armstrong in the last chorus. "The idea just happened in a Las Vegas club when business was dull around closing time," reported George Hoefer shortly after the session. "Ella was kidding around with the band and . . . began imitating Louis. It killed the four customers in the place and is now a regular number."[8] Before recording it for Decca, Ella even tried it out on a JATP tour that was recorded by

Granz but not issued until the early 1980s; the audiences loved it. But George T. Simon noted that "she has had several occasions to regret that night when, for some reason or another, she first decided to do her Satchmo stunt, for although it has gone over big ever since, it has wreaked havoc with her vocal cords."[9]

On September 21, 1949, Ella was back in the studios with Gordon Jenkins as musical director, and two sides from the session were released the following month. "In her current Decca release, 'A Man Wrote a Song'—'Foolish Tears,' Ella gives her best and simplest performances," said the *Chicago Tribune*.[10] After a session with the Mills Brothers in November 1949, she was in the studios again for another session with Oliver as her musical director, this time with a pickup band he built around her regular accompanists Ray and Hank to cut "Don'cha Go 'Way Mad," a number that would stay in her repertoire for over thirty years.

Oliver, who died in 1988, loved working with Ella. He never had any problems with her as an artist. "Sy used to say to me, 'I'd make a suggestion to Ella, and she'd look at me as if she didn't know one word I was saying,' said his wife, Lillian Oliver-Clarke. "Then she'd go right over to the microphone and, first time, there it was!"

Throughout her marriage to Sy Oliver, Lillian Oliver-Clarke pursued her own career as a singer. Still active as a voice coach in the 1990s, she was once one of a select band of "studio" singers who were able to read anything at sight; she was in demand for record sessions and radio shows, including several years on the Perry Como Show. As a member of the Ray Charles Singers plus any number of ad hoc vocal groups assembled in the studios for their sight-reading abilities, she was on call for as many recording sessions as she could handle. Often she found herself in the Decca studios backing Ella, and from her unique vantage point observed her at work.

"We never rehearsed before the actual session, and neither did Ella, to my knowledge. We did it right on the session in those days. A session would have been, in general, three hours, and we would do at least four sides during that time. We would come in, actually when the date started, and run down the tunes. Sy would run the music down with the orchestra or band, and we might go quietly through our parts on mike. We would rehearse it all in front of the band, do it once or twice for balances, and then we'd be ready to cut.

"And Ella would be ready to cut. Now whether she'd gone through it before, I doubt it. I don't remember Sy ever spending time with Ella before a session at all, but there was never any hangups whatsoever. I mean, if we had to do four sides in three hours, we did four sides in three hours. And, do you know, they were all wonderful, near perfect. No overdubbing or anything like that in those days. They were done from beginning to end, no breaks."

In August 1950, Ella was in the studios twice. On the 15th she did another session with her ex-flame from Chick Webb days, Louis Jordan, who together with his Tympany Five came up with "'Tain't Nobody's Bizness If I Do" and "I'll Never Be Free" for Decca's "Sepia" series. In those days Decca still had difficulty in calling Jordan's music "rhythm and blues," a problem solved by *Billboard* in 1949 when they changed their black music chart from "race" to "rhythm-and-blues," responding to the success of independents such as Savoy and King.

On August 25, Ella was reunited with Louis Armstrong under Sy Oliver's musical directorship. A photo taken at the session shows Ella and Louis beaming with laughter. Their good humor was infectious; when "Can Anyone Explain? (No! No! No!)" was released in November 1950, it charted at number thirty and was a successful, if minor, hit. Whatever they performed, both artists' sincerity seemed to shine through.

Meanwhile, Ella, still without a radio show of her own, appeared reasonably frequently as a guest on other people's shows, often with Bing Crosby, a self-confessed Ella fan. And with the rise of television in 1949 she appeared on one of the first jazz shows to be televised, produced by Esme Sarnoff and put out under host Eddie Condon's name.

But despite the general consensus that she was one of the finest singers in popular music and jazz, Ella, for all her public profile, remained an enigmatic figure. George T. Simon interviewed her for the April 1949 edition of *Metronome* magazine and said later, "I had talked with Ella many times before and I have talked with her many times since, and the graciousness, the kindness, the enthusiasm have always been there. But so has the self-doubt. I kept wondering why."[11]

Ella's self-doubt has remained with her throughout her career. While some artists sought release from the inevitable buildup of stress by turning to drink or drugs, she turned to eating; she could afford to eat well, and she did. She ate regularly at expensive restaurants and prepared huge meals at home. She ballooned. Although it caused her embarrassment when she performed, she simply could not stop eating. It was a problem she battled throughout her life, alternately dieting and going on eating binges until ill health in the 1970s forced her to lose weight for good. She also compulsively bought expensive gowns, as if to compensate and to conceal and deflect attention from her excesses. "She used to go to Fifth Avenue and Fifty-seventh Street. There was a store there that sold beautiful gowns," said Charles Linton. "If they got dirty, if they dragged on the floor, she'd take them off and stuff them in the waste can. Back in those days $150 for a dress, that was a lot of money to just stuff them in the garbage can!"

Ella also suffered from profound performance anxiety, something that remained with her throughout her life. Even in the autumn of her years, when she had been acclaimed in concert halls throughout the world for over three decades, she remained in its grip. "I was in the relief band playing alongside Ella in London in 1984," recalled John Chilton. "It was a four-night season that provided dinner and Ella with an orchestra directed by Nelson Riddle. I was there every evening, of course, and had a good chance to witness her behavior prior to her going onstage. I've talked about this subsequently to other musicians who have worked with her, and they say it's been much the same with Ella for decades. In the dressing room area she was pleasant but quiet. But then a few minutes before she went on, she would go to the same spot on the side of the stage, and she seemed to go through a series of movements, a pattern of behavior where she was literally psyching herself up to go onstage. No one went within yards of her because this was a definite ritual. Then when she was announced, she literally catapulted onstage; she was very ebullient, totally in command, and an entirely different person. It was then that one could tell that the quietness before the show was worry or concern about the impending performance, because once it was over—and naturally she was a great success—she was quite euphoric and speaking at a different speed with different speech patterns. It made me realize that after all those years she never lost this nervous quality, yet she was singing stuff she knew back to front!"

Equally, at social gatherings she would become deeply worried that people were talking about her or, more particularly, about her weight. Unless she was in the company of friends, she became distinctly nervous, aware that she was lacking in social graces. Perhaps she had suffered abuse at the hands of her stepfather, and this played a part in these complex emotions. But whatever the reason, it is clear that beneath the little-girl image was a little girl at heart. It was something her management acknowledged and strove to play down. This duty fell to her press agent, Virginia Wicks (whose clients included Harry

Belafonte) and, in later years, Mary Jane Outwater, both of whom became very protective of their charge. Knowing how much Ella disliked being interviewed, they tried to keep reporters and journalists at arm's length and limited press access to her to the barest minimum, issuing instead a series of bland and innocuous press releases that, in the absence of more specific details, have shaped the "Ella Fitzgerald Legend" over the years.

When Ella and Ray's trio was in Chicago over the 1949–50 holiday season, for example, her press office released this typically trite story that, while providing copy for journalists, kept the real Ella under wraps:

> Ella Fitzgerald, in her appearance at the Marbro and Uptown theaters, was rarely allowed to leave the stage without singing "Lady Be Good" or "Flying Home," two bebop numbers she hates, preferring to do ballads. "But," says Ella, "as long as they ask for them, I have to do them. Recently in Texas I thought I'd get by without them for at least one set. It just about got to closing time, and there was no one in the place except two elderly ladies, gray-haired, sedate, neither the bop type. They were a lovely audience, and I was so happy to be singing soft songs. For my last number I asked them if there was anything special they wanted to hear, and they asked for "Lady Be Good"![12]

Sometimes events that had occurred years before were used to preserve an uncontroversial, endearing image, such as this early March 1949 release, resurrected from 1937 (see page 50): "Portly Ella Fitzgerald was a bit late for a recording date last week when she was caught in the escape hatch of an elevator. The infernal machine stalled between floors and Ella, already late for a recording date, endeavored to escape through a trapdoor in the top of the cage. It took three strong men to rescue the 220-pound songbird. Ella opens March 28 at the Blue Note."[13]

When Ella was persuaded to give interviews, she was frequently ill at ease. "[She] has a certain hesitancy offstage," said *Metronome* staff writer Bill Coss in 1953, "revealed by a certain turn of words or posturing of body. . . . The shy, inordinately modest woman who sings 'How High the Moon' on the nation's biggest stages is not much different from the young girl who wrote 'A-Tisket, A-Tasket.'"[14] Yet to people she knew and trusted, Ella was disarmingly straightforward and frank. "You will never meet a star more completely unpublicity conscious than Ella," Virginia Wicks told the writer and journalist Leonard Feather. "She can come over to the house and we'll exchange small talk, and she's just as sweet and charming as can be. Then I'll gingerly try and ease the conversation around to, say, a *Life* or *Time* man who wants to see her, and her face will fall and she'll stomp her foot and say, 'Gosh darn it, Virginia, I can't do it. I have to go *shopping!*' And she'll stay crotchety, but finally very reluctantly she may say, 'Oh, all right.'"[15] Feather himself observed that "when Ella is sulky, her manner and expression are identical with those of the little girl she becomes in the song when, in answer to the line, 'Was it green?' she pouts and answers, 'No, no, *no*, no.'"[16]

In reality, Ella cared only about her music. She was happy to delegate the running of her professional life to others; Moe Gale even had power of attorney and could sign contracts on her behalf. "She's a very simple person. I don't mean that derogatorily at all," said Mel Tormé. "Her needs are simple. Her approach to life is simple."

September 1950 saw Ella in the studios again to cut a series of numbers that would comprise the ten-inch long-playing record, *Ella Sings Gershwin*. However, with long-playing records still tentatively feeling their way in the market, Ella's Gershwin set was originally issued on all three turntable speeds. Accompanied only by pianist Ellis Larkins, they remain for many the high spot of Ella's work for the Decca label. "I set that up," said Milt Gabler. "I always wanted to do Gershwin with her. And they were in the days of ten-inch LPs when we recorded them originally. Later we wanted to make a twelve-inch LP so I added 'Lady Be Good' and 'Lucky So-and-So,' and with a little help from Duke we got the LP out! I always loved Ellis accompanying singers. They were just happy sessions. She loved singing with Ellis."[17]

With *Ella Sings Gershwin* Ella's talent is seriously and conscientiously employed on material with which she was in total sympathy. She sings with confidence and a total lack of artifice, without flights of virtuosity or exercises in complexity. And, significantly, she does not attempt to impose an emotional dimension on what she sings, throwing the subjective interpretation fairly and squarely into the listener's corner. She lets you do the thinking.

The success of these numbers lies in the way that they sound detached yet at the same time intimate. Ella achieves this through a combination of impeccable diction (in which she took great pride), the clarity and purity of her voice, and precise intonation that allowed her to project her voice quietly into the microphone, totally confident of pitch.

But equally important is the powerfully creative duality between singer and accompanist. While Ella shapes and reshapes the song with inch-perfect precision, Ellis Larkins's apposite accompaniment frames her talent so that from wherever the song is viewed, it sounds its best. He creates a setting in which her voice sounds profound; through allusion and elision he fragments the song and reassembles it, thus assuming a greater logic as a backdrop to Ella's voice. "Technically he is a marvel," said composer Alec Wilder, "accomplishing his infinitely fine musical embroidery by means of wholly relaxed fingers, a musical mind, and a loving heart. . . . He is a masterly accompanist. . . . He achieves his musical points always by means of understatement. His economy is as brilliant as a Simenon sentence. He is strong and direct without ever spilling over into aggressiveness. His left-hand harmonic inventions and sinuous bass lines are marvels of ingenuity and unexpectedness."[18]

If *Ella Sings Gershwin* represented one of the artistic highs of Ella's career with Decca, then just as surely followed a couple of sessions that, in Gabler's words, had to "pay for all the good things we want to do." Also in September she recorded "Molasses, Molasses" and "Santa Claus Got Stuck in My Chimney," which in later years would be hung around her neck as typical of the sort of number she was given during her Decca period. The date was the last for a while with Ray Brown, who, after working with Oscar Peterson as a duo, had been invited to join his new trio, along with Irving Ashby on guitar, for a Canadian tour. Although neither Ella nor Ray realized it at the time, Ray's increasing involvement with Oscar Peterson would be another factor in exacerbating the gradual deterioration of their relationship.

If the five sessions after the Gershwin album produced only commercial numbers, Gabler consistently tried to balance the ledger with material that reflected Ella's jazz sensibilities. June 1951 recordings included her now classic "Smooth Sailing," yet paradoxically, at her own insistence, she recorded a cover of the Rosemary Clooney hit "Come On-a My House" the same day. Needless to say, it is "Smooth Sailing" that is remembered today.

"There was a small group for 'Smooth Sailing,'" recalled Lillian Oliver-Clarke. "We did three tunes on that particular session. I can't believe Sy chose 'Mixed Emotions,' which we did also on that session, so I'm sure it was chosen by Milt Gabler. Only Ella could make a tune like that sound great. Again, there was no rehearsal. We did it right on the session. Everybody could read music, of course, and 'Smooth Sailing' was marvelous. It was funny because when Ella appeared in the

JVC Festival here in New York in 1991, I went along, and I said, 'My God, she's doing "Smooth Sailing," after all those years!'"

"Smooth Sailing" is another virtuoso scat performance, less frantic than its predecessors, and contains the earthy feel of the emerging hard-bop movement, the then current mutation in the evolution of jazz. The back-to-the-roots feel is exemplified by Bill Doggett's churchified organ and simple call-and-response patterns between voices and instruments. Sounding part big band and part gospel—a correlation that has always existed in big-band music—a strong gospel-type back beat gives the performance a swinging groove that is sustained from beginning to end. Doggett's organ and the Ray Charles Singers act as the saxophone and trumpet sections, around which Ella weaves her improvisation. This is safe, user-friendly scat over an engaging down-home feeling, and it clicked with the public. When it was released in September 1951, it went onto the charts for six weeks, peaking at number twenty-three before going on to enjoy a second life as a popular favorite in the jukeboxes around Harlem. "That went well, that session," said Bill Doggett. "Ella and all of us had a *good* time." It was a session that Ella herself would not forget.

In April, Ella had a run at the Regal Theatre in Chicago costarring with the Buddy Johnson Orchestra, and on June 21 she was booked into New York's Café Society with Hank Jones's trio. Mild controversy surrounded Ella's voice at this time. Some critics were accusing her of being soulless—for example, *Metronome*'s Barry Ulanov, who commented, "The voice is still there, but the soul is gone." Bill Coss, reviewing her performance at Café Society for *Metronome*, concluded, "Something that was Ella may be missing . . . but the phrasing, intonation, and projection remain. And Ella remains the greatest."[19] Ella's fans didn't have any complaints, however. Her original four-week stay was extended; she was still there in September.

It was during that month, September 1951, after almost fifteen years of rave reviews, regular appearances on the hit parade charts— in itself a rarity since black artists seldom crossed over from the "race" charts—Ella had her first write-up in *The New York Times*. A note of period condescension was unmistakable, however:

As she prances into the spotlight your impression may be of a large cheerful child . . . [said Carter Harman]. Like any sensitive performer, she immediately feels what kind of audience she has before her. When she sees that her listeners are pleased, she smiles her winsome smile and gives them what they like. . . . One time she sang ballads "all night" for a receptive crowd. On other occasions she indulges her delightful talent for mimicry. She can growl a chorus that sounds for all the world like Louis Armstrong, or twitter and chirp in a devastating imitation of Rose Murphy, the "chee-chee girl."[20]

Ray Brown returned from his tour with Oscar Peterson just after Ella had finished her extended run at the Café Society. At the beginning of October, she decided she wanted to move. Shortly after their marriage the couple had adopted a little boy, born to Ella's half-sister Frances, whom they christened Ray, Jr. They needed more space, and in late 1951 they moved to apartment number 7 at 179 Murdock Avenue in St. Albans, a quiet neighborhood in the New York borough of Queens. Ray, Jr., was cared for by Ella's aunt Virginia, the same aunt who had taken Ella under her wing after Tempie died and who was now installed as nanny-cum-housekeeper. Ella, who had once said, "The only thing better than singing is more singing,"[21] enjoyed her role as a part-time mother but never allowed her son to come before her career. As Ray, Jr., grew up it became clear to him that he was not the most important thing in his adoptive mother's life, and this later became a source of tension between them. By the age of sixteen (when he was over six feet tall) he was swept along by the sudden rise of rock music in the 1960s. He began studying drums with Bill Douglass, but to Ella's horror he joined a beat group. She wanted him to do more than just play "that Ringo beat," as she put it, and insisted he continue his formal studies.

But as with so many children, music became the forum of adolescent protest for Ray, Jr. The feelings of neglect that he had been nursing for so long came spilling to the surface. He dropped out of high school in his final year, another blow to his mother, and moved to Seattle, joining the local American Federation of Musicians in order to pursue a career as a drummer and singer. There was nothing Ella could do, and contact between them became intermittent; for example, by the early 1980s Ella had still not heard her son sing. When Ray, Jr., decided to marry, Ella had not even met the bride-to-be before the service: "I was waiting for this little colored girl to come down the aisle," she told Leonard Feather in 1983, "and I looked and saw this redhead! I think she's Scottish or Irish. A very sweet girl. They were supposed to come down last Christmas, but he had a job in Portland."[22] With the arrival in 1985 of Ella's first granddaughter, Alice, family ties began to be restored; Ella doted on the child. Ray, Jr., and his family eventually left Seattle in 1990 to be closer to his mother's home; his union membership lapsed, and his flirtation with music was over.

Despite Ella and Ray's move in late 1951 to a new home with their new child, tensions within their relationship were never far from the surface. Ella felt strongly that both professionally and personally, Ray's position should be at her side. Ray felt equally strongly that he should pursue his career with Oscar Peterson, and this time he was adamant about the direction it would take. But at least they were together for their fourth JATP tour, which closed at the end of 1951 in the Russ Auditorium in San Diego, California.

When Ella went into the Decca Studios in January 1952, three sessions and twelve sides separated her from her "Smooth Sailing" date. It was time to balance the ledger, and Milt Gabler decided on "Air Mail Special," one of her crowd pleasers with JATP, plus an alter ego of "Smooth Sailing," "Rough Ridin'." She was accompanied by Ray Brown and his trio, and it was not Hank Jones on piano, as all the discographies say, but Teddy Wilson.[23] To simulate the big-band feeling of "Smooth Sailing," Bill Doggett and the Ray Charles Singers were again on hand. "Air Mail Special," like all of Ella's big scat vehicles, follows a set pattern. In this instance it is based on the outline of the orchestration used by Count Basie (although unrecorded by him on either Decca or Columbia, appearing only on a film short). Again, it is a number Ella had worked up in live performance and is similar to the version she used at Carnegie Hall on September 18, 1949, which was recorded by Norman Granz.

Ella immediately impresses with her rhythmic momentum, soaring over the introductory pedal tones sung by the Ray Charles Singers and then fairly launching herself into the "orchestrated" section with a zeal that seems to leave her accompanists in her wake. In contrast, "Rough Ridin'" uses the same medium bounce of its predecessor and is pure riffing and improvisatory scat. Both numbers fly in the face of critical opinion that would have us believe Ella's Decca output was an artistic no-go area. As if to emphasize the point, her version of "Goody Goody" from a session the following month remained in her concert repertoire for decades.

Ella's weakness for singing novelty material meant that "Mr. Paganini" was never left for dead. On her next recording session in June she recorded the definitive version of it, "You'll Have to Swing It (Parts 1 and 2)," finally elevating it to the realms of a pop classic through Sy Oliver's arrangement and her own obvious love of the tune.

"She did so many wonderful things with Sy," said Lillian Oliver-

Clarke. "'Mr. Paganini,' which I remember as my favorite thing she did, I thought was a tour de force. That was one of her memorable recordings from those days, and of course she continued to perform it for years and years." Spread over two sides of a 78 and later reissued on the *Sweet and Hot* LP from the end of 1955, "it was originally a Martha Raye number from a Bing Crosby picture, one of her first movies," said Milt Gabler. "Ella had already done it in the early days with Chick Webb, and this was a remake of it. It was a great record!"[24]

Meanwhile, Norman Granz's most ambitious JATP undertaking to date finally got under way when the troupe left for its first European tour on March 26 from Idlewild Airport. Granz had been putting out feelers for a European venture since 1948; he even went to Europe himself in 1950 to promote the idea but was unsuccessful. However, in 1952, through the offices of Nils Hellstrom, a tour beginning in Scandinavia was arranged, kicking off at Stockholm's Concert Hall on March 30.

When the tour reached Paris they all had a welcome three-day break. It was ironic that Granz, Oscar Peterson, and Flip Phillips visited London on a day trip to take in the sights. The English public had the British Musicians' Union to thank for preventing them, as well as Ella, Ray, Hank, Lester Young, Roy Eldridge, Irving Ashby, and Max Roach, from performing on English soil. While the postwar culture of continental Europe was being enriched by Ella and the JATP and countless other touring American groups, the British Musicians' Union ban had the effect of keeping jazz firmly out of sight and out of mind of the arts establishment in the U.K.

For Granz, the outstanding feature of the tour was the lack of racial prejudice. Only two incidents occurred, and, curiously, both involved United States citizens. The first was in Amsterdam's Victoria Hotel. Ella and her maid, Georgiana Henry, entered the small bar and remained seated at the bar talking and sipping their drinks. Two American soldiers walked in and headed for the bar; the moment they saw Ella and Georgiana, they turned away and headed for a table. It was so blatant that everyone went and joined Ella at the bar. Even the singer who was working in the bar turned his back to the soldiers who, shamed, bought drinks all around. The second incident involved trumpeter Roy Eldridge. After a show in Frankfurt, he was taken by friends to a club where he was refused service by the American headwaiter. But these were only minor incidents compared to what was around the corner.

CHAPTER TEN

1952–1955

Every year I wait for the tour. It's pretty rough sometimes, but I think that my being with Jazz at the Philharmonic helps me win fans.

ELLA FITZGERALD[1]

ELLA WAS BACK ON THE ROAD in September and October 1952, this time for a stateside tour with JATP. Opening with a midnight concert at Carnegie Hall on September 13, they covered fifty-seven cities throughout the United States and Canada and for the first time included Hawaii and Alaska in their itinerary. The autumn troupe consisted of Ella, Buddy Rich, the Gene Krupa Trio, the Oscar Peterson Trio, Lester Young, Flip Phillips, Roy Eldridge, Charlie Shavers, Ray Brown, Barney Kessel, and Hank Jones.

With all the press and radio coverage Norman Granz's traveling jam sessions generated, plus the vast audiences the concerts attracted, Decca made sure they had an Ella release in the shops to coincide with the tour. Their marketing paid off. The coupling of "Trying" and "My Bonnie" went on the hit parade chart at number twenty-one for four weeks at the end of September. "My Bonnie," a curious choice for a pop number, has cropped up from time to time in all kinds of versions by all kinds of artists, but perhaps the most unusual place to stumble over it was on Ray Charles's hit album *What'd I Say*, one of the important rhythm-and-blues albums of the fifties.

Ella had recorded the titles in August of 1952. When they were released, they were awarded a five-star rating by *Down Beat* (five stars is their maximum rating: one is "poor," five "excellent").[2] Also from that same August session came "Ella's Contribution to the Blues." In one of her few forays into the twelve-bar idiom, she used the blues as a set of chord changes to scat through, rather than singing the blues per se, with their inimitable three-line stanzas. From start to finish her conception is purely instrumental, just like a trum-

139

pet or saxophone "blowing" through the blues changes. Her scat is effortless; ideas are developed logically and coherently and, as ever, she swings powerfully with Hank Jones, a model of sympathetic support, behind her.

For Ella, the blues always remained an enigma. "Ella Fitzgerald can't do it; I've never heard Ella Fitzgerald do it," Dizzy Gillespie once asserted.[3] There's an earthy, primal quality to the blues vocal that doesn't sit well with her light tone. And while it may be slick to suggest a contra-argument, that John Lee Hooker or Lightnin' Hopkins singing Cole Porter might not work either, the fact remains that several important female jazz singers—not the least Billie Holiday, Anita O'Day, Carmen McRae, and Dinah Washington— could, when they chose, sing the blues as convincingly as they did the American popular song.

It is certainly possible, however, that with Ella's gift for mimicry, she could have imported sufficient blues hues and rasps to sound suitably mean or lowdown, either "instrumentally," like Baby Cox (with a similar lightness of tone) over the slightly longer form of sixteen bars on Duke Ellington's 1928 *The Mooche*, or "vocally," as she herself did on the introduction to "Why Don't You Do Right?" with the JATP in November 1953. Instead, Ella aimed for purity. Like other musicians of her generation, she considered the blues genre to be beneath her. Self-conscious to the point of being embarrassed by her humble origins, she strove to improve herself socially. When she was dating Heywood Henry, for example, part of his attraction was the savoir faire of a college-educated young man. To him the blues were low-class, and any connotations that might imply were precisely what Ella was trying to escape from. "In those days blues wasn't proper like they are now," said Henry. "Strange as it may seem, we musicians who had studied music looked down on that kind of entertainment. We thought *nothing* of it."[4]

If, on one level, Ella was seeking to avoid the social stigma implied by the blues, then on a musical level it is interesting that the main influences who shaped her non-scat style—Armstrong, Boswell, and Holiday—are primarily remembered for their interpretations of the American popular song. Also, of the important influences in shaping Ella's "instrumental" approach to singing, the first, Leo Watson, was no blues singer. And when the time came for Ella to absorb bop—"It felt as if I was being left behind, and I was," she once said[5]—it was not to the blues-drenched playing of Charlie Parker that she turned but to the clean, intricate lines of Dizzy Gillespie.

* * *

November 1952 saw Ella's version of "Walkin' by the River" enter the charts at number twenty-nine, giving her her second hit parade success of the year. Recorded in September with the Leroy Kirkland Orchestra, a pickup group built around her pianist Hank Jones, it was another example of a pop tune of the day performed with almost perfunctory ease by Ella. But despite her continuing run of successes with Decca, Norman Granz had made it plain by 1953 that he wanted Ella signed to his own record company. Although neither Milt Gabler nor Moe Gale had changed his stance, Granz was well aware that in 1953 Ella's contract with Decca came up for renewal, and he prepared to begin negotiations in earnest.

"Moe Gale was officially her booking office," said Milt Gabler, "but actually he really deserved to lose her. She was getting all her work through Norman, who was effectively managing her. But Moe Gale had Ella's power of attorney, and he signed her with Decca for three more years, which was one reason Norman was very unhappy with me. We signed her for three more years, and we took up all the options, which he was able to agree to because he had power of attorney. So I got Ella for a few years longer than Norman liked, and I wouldn't give her up."[6]

In fact, Gale was getting Ella work, but it was Granz who was providing her with a profile. Although in 1953 Gale booked her into La Vie en Rose, Birdland, the Paramount, and the Chicago Theatre, and arranged a tour for her with the Woody Herman band (after which she raved about Herman's drummer Art Mardigan), it was the JATP tours that were adding to Ella's reputation. In February and March the troupe returned to Europe and even played two concerts in London. Granz circumvented the absurd musicians' union ban by offering to play two charity concerts for flood victims in Devon. Afterward the *New Musical Express* reviewer was amazed that Ella was almost in tears, convinced she had performed poorly, despite the fact the audience had "cheered her to the echo."

In June, Ella was back in the recording studios to cut "Crying in the Chapel," her biggest hit for Decca during the fifties, charting at fifteen for four weeks in September. But despite the success of her career, her marriage to Ray Brown was finally disintegrating. Ray remained adamant that he would pursue his career with Oscar Peterson, and the couple had begun to see less and less of each other. Finally, they decided to bring their marriage to an end and filed for a "quickie" divorce in Juárez, Mexico, which came through on August

28, 1953. Ray Brown moved out of their home, leaving Ella with custody of Ray, Jr.

"[When] my husband and I broke up, I got a little bit despondent," Ella told Clancy Sigal in 1990. "I cried and cried, and my cousin said, 'Oh, take her to a bar. I can't stand her crying.' So I went into this bar, and there was this pleasant bartender. 'What'll you have?' he asked. I jumped and said, 'I'll have a Manischewitz!' The whole bar said, 'Manischewitz?' The bartender said, 'If she wants it, she'll get it.' That's how much of a drinker I was."[7]

Ella and Ray's musical association would continue off and on throughout their lives. In October and November, JATP was again touring, and along with Ella was Oscar Peterson and his trio with Ray on bass, Benny Carter, Willie Smith, Roy Eldridge, Charlie Shavers, Ben Webster, J. C. Heard, and Ella's new pianist, Ray Tunia. Tunia had replaced Hank Jones in the summer when Jones, tired of the road, decided to freelance in New York. Tunia had worked with the bands of Lucky Millinder and Tab Smith in the forties and would later act as accompanist to Pearl Bailey and Mae Barnes before emigrating to Japan.

Beginning with a cross-country tour of North America, the troupe again visited Hawaii, from where they flew to Japan to perform twenty-four concerts. The visit was the first by an American touring jazz unit to play before civilian audiences. In April of the previous year Gene Krupa had taken his trio to Japan to play U.S. service bases and was amazed to discover a huge interest in jazz among the civilian population. It was as a result of Krupa's enthusiasm that Japan was added to Granz's autumn itinerary.

When the troupe arrived, the welcome they received was nothing short of sensational. They drove through Tokyo in open cars and were given a ticker-tape reception that was reported in all the newspapers. On the musicians' arrival at their hotel, the staff turned out to greet them, and Ella was given a huge bouquet of flowers. It was extraordinary; just eight years before, America and Japan had been deadly adversaries in the most vicious war witnessed by mankind, culminating in the use of the atom bomb at Nagasaki and Hiroshima. Now American musicians were being feted.

The tour was also a significant milestone in Ella's career in another way. While in Japan, Granz put it to Ella that since he was sending so much work her way, it might make sense for him to become her personal manager. Ella's initial response was not to jump for joy—the reverse, in fact. Granz recalls that Ella was very conservative about making any changes in her life. She had heard what he said and would think about it. Granz did not push the issue. If she was interested, he said, there would be no contract between them. If for any reason either party felt it was not working out, he or she would then be free to walk away without any messy legal consequences. (Granz operated in this way with all the musicians for whom he acted, then and later, including Duke Ellington, Count Basie, and Oscar Peterson.)

Granz arranged to have the concert at the Nichigeki Theatre in Tokyo's Ginza district recorded. The Japanese audience was remarkably well informed, so much so that during one of Ella's ballad features, a voice from the audience called out for "Lady Be Good," in just the annoying fashion of JATP audiences back home. Ella was clearly elated by the enthusiastic crowd, laughing at things that went bump in the background. She judiciously mixed ballads—"Body and Soul," "I Got It Bad and That Ain't Good," "My Funny Valentine"— with her usual JATP fare, the uptempo "How High the Moon" and "Lady Be Good," and included a couple of Decca hits, "Smooth Sailing" and "Frim Fram Sauce."

It is with "Frim Fram Sauce" that we get perhaps the most revealing insight into Ella as entertainer on record. When she originally recorded the number in 1946 it was with Louis Armstrong; here she gave a brilliant impersonation of Armstrong, capturing his inimitable syncopations, inflections, and humor with stunning accuracy. What's more, Ella loved every minute of it. It was done with such genuine affection that it broke up audience and musicians alike, and Ella, aware that the number was going down well, milked it for all it was worth.

It is difficult, perhaps impossible, to imagine Lady Day or Carmen McRae or Anita O'Day hamming it up like this for laughs. Yet this is precisely what Ella was doing, and it suggests an affinity between Ella and Armstrong that was closer than mere imitation. Armstrong, as Gary Giddins has pointed out, was an artist who happened to be an entertainer and an entertainer who happened to be an artist. Ella, in her own way, was just as much an entertainer as Armstrong. She was always concerned with "how she went down" with the audience, always keen to give them what they wanted; if it was nine or ten successive encores, the inclusion of the dire "Hernando's Hideaway" for a whole JATP season because she felt "the people liked it," or a request for a corny pop tune like "Mule Train," then Ella would give it to them. And if Armstrong suspected his audience would roar at fifty high C's climaxed by a double high C or his eye-rolling act, or if film producers put him in incongruous (and by today's standards unseemly) surroundings, then he would oblige for the greater good of the paying public. Both artists had an endless appetite for applause, which from time to time overshadowed any artistic considerations.

In December Ella recorded another novelty, "Somebody Bad Stole de Wedding Bell," but it was the flip side that received the praise: *Jazz Journal* called "Melancholy Me" a "lovely performance."[8] In fact, it was "Melancholy Me" that charted in March 1954 for one week at number twenty-five.

December 1953 marked an important milestone in Ella's career. Her four-year contract with Moe Gale expired that month, and she appointed Norman Granz her personal manager. "Moe Gale believed the manager was king," said Milt Gabler. "That's why Granz was able to take her over. He got her when her contract expired—it didn't go on forever!"[9] It was an inevitable parting of the ways. Gale had been indispensable to Ella in the early days. Without a white manager, she would not have gotten anywhere in an entertainment infrastructure dominated by white businessmen, and Gale was well aware of this. "He impressed me with having good connections," observed Gabler. "Black acts didn't have big [radio] shows, but he could get them to guest on various programs. His big connection was with NBC. He liked to hobnob with people of power, and he had enough income from the talent he booked and the Savoy Ballroom—Gale owned the lease up there, if not the building."[10]

Gale had always been rather complacent in handling Ella's affairs. As her personal manager he was responsible for negotiating her fees, but here Granz suspected she was not getting the best possible deal. Moe Gale, as her personal manager, would be negotiating with his brother Tim Gale, who handled the booking agency side of Gale Inc. In this scenario it was difficult to imagine one brother falling out with the other over the best possible fee for Ella. But what made the split inevitable was Gale's handling of Ella's finances. To her horror she learned that she had amassed a large tax debt, and the Internal Revenue Service was pressing for settlement. By 1953, *Time* magazine reported that Ella was grossing $50,000 a year from JATP alone,[11] but it seems that nothing had been put aside for taxes.

As soon as Gale relinquished his interest in Ella, Granz settled with the IRS from his own resources.[12] This was something Ella would never forget, and it formed the basis of a remarkable bond between artist and manager. "When Ella left Gale, it was cordial," said Bill Doggett. "A *lot* of things were happening. Seemingly there was something going on where Ella felt she should be getting more and better jobs, better money. So I guess their relationship wasn't that great. When Norman Granz came along, he swept her right away from Moe, as soon as her contract ran out. Ella wasn't the type of person to do anything backhanded."

In early 1954, after topping the *Metronome* and *Down Beat* polls for the third consecutive year, Ella was rushed to the hospital. "It was just after she went with Norman," said George Wein. "It was serious. At the time it was thought she'd never work again. Trouble with her throat. It was kind of hushed up, but it was serious." Just as Ella's career was marching on to ever greater heights, all seemed set to crumble around her. She had a node on her vocal chords. But unlike Miles Davis, whose voice was reduced to a husky rasp as the result of shouting during the recovery period for a similar operation, Ella took no chances. For six weeks following the operation she barely spoke, and by the end of March she had achieved a full recovery. On March 24 she was back in the recording studios and raring to go. The session with Gordon Jenkins produced "I Need," which turned out to be her last hit with Decca when it went onto the charts for one week at number thirty in May 1954.

Five days later Ella was reunited with Ellis Larkins for another duet session. "I had her pick her twelve favorite tunes," said Milt Gabler. "I had her do an LP of her favorite tunes. She might have given me a lot of titles, and we boiled them down to the twelve we were going to put out on the album. Norman was picking on me in the press, so I let Ella choose the numbers and we did them with Ellis!"[13]

The album was released as *Ella—Songs in a Mellow Mood*, and in many ways it is the equal of her much-praised Gershwin set, even though one or two numbers might seem strange choices, such as "Imagination," which she originally recorded with her big band in 1940. In June 1954 she was in the studio to record "Lullaby of Birdland." "I wanted to put out an album of her bop things," said Gabler, "so we had her do 'Lullaby of Birdland' and put out an LP album, *Lullabies of Birdland*, of her bop numbers, all her riff numbers she'd done over the years."[14] Also during the "Lullaby of Birdland" session, Ella did another scat on the blues, a number called "Later," which she had worked up in live performance during her JATP tour, continuing her arm's-length handling of the genre. Even so, this is perhaps her most exuberant performance for Decca, with tenor saxophonist Sammy Taylor good for a couple of JATP-style squeals.

Decca, initially cautious with the move to 33⅓ rpm, had convinced itself by 1954 that the medium would be popular with the public. To complement Ella's "riff" numbers on *Lullabies of Birdland*, the company put out another compilation album called *Listen and Relax*, featuring a selection of titles made with Gordon Jenkins, the musical director who would turn out to be one of Frank Sinatra's finest collaborators.

In June, Ella was booked into Basin Street, a gloomily lit cavern at Fifty-first Street and Broadway. The purpose was to celebrate her nineteenth year in show business. And if nineteen years seems like a strange number to celebrate, it also baffled *New York Times* reporter Howard Taubman: "An odd number, but how are you going to fence in a press agent with tidy round numbers?" But it didn't seem to matter. By midnight on June 1 the place was packed with stars from Broadway, the theater, radio, television, and the record industry. Among the organizations that sent representatives to honor Ella were Le Jazz Hot of France, Musica Jazz of Italy, Club Deritmo of Spain, Bladid Jazz of Iceland, Blue Rhythm of India, and Tempo of Australia. There were onstage tributes from Pearl Bailey, Eartha Kitt, Dizzy Gillespie, and Harry Belafonte. There were cables and telegrams from Lena Horne (in Paris), Billy Eckstine (in London), Benny Goodman, Fred Waring, Rosemary Clooney, Ray Anthony, Guy Lombardo, the Mills Brothers, Lionel Hampton, Louis Armstrong, and countless others. Audrey Hepburn arrived late, and the management struggled to find her and her party a table. It was that kind of occasion.

During the evening Ella was presented with a total of eighteen awards, but the highlight of the evening was the presentation of a plaque from Decca Records commemorating the sale of 22 million Ella Fitzgerald records. When Steve Allen, the master of ceremonies, asked her to sing, Ella began by saying, "I guess what everyone wants more than anything else is to be loved. And to know that you love me for my singing is too much for me. Forgive me if I don't have all the words. Maybe I can sing it and you'll understand."[15] Then they played her first recording, "Love and Kisses," and her current, 237th recording, "Who's Afraid?" This was followed by her first big hit, "A-Tisket, A-Tasket," and without ado she joined in. She wept a little. "Miss Fitzgerald was simple and unaffected. Of course she has knowhow as an entertainer, but her personality is warm and she is not afraid of emotion," said the *New York Times*.[16]

Ella's achievement in selling some 22 million discs since her recording debut with "Love and Kisses" with Chick Webb's band in June 1935 was, in terms of the recording industry at the time, remarkable. Here was a plump, middle-aged black artist who defied the convention of popular beauty at work in the field of popular music who managed to achieve widespread popularity in a United States that was still two years away from legislating that segregation in streetcars and buses was unconstitutional. "Other popular singers tend to become identified with a particular musical groove," said *Newsweek*. "Ella Fitzgerald plays the field, exerting a talent which, in addition to its unmatched pliability, has demonstrated an uncommon staying power. . . . Through the sundry demands of swing, dixieland, calypso, ballad, and pop, Miss Fitzgerald has moved with imperturbable ease."[17] But amid all the glitz and the glamour, observers who had been following Ella's career for years suspected that she had begun to coast a little in her nightclub sets. George T. Simon, reviewing her stay at Basin Street, said, "I do have one complaint to register. . . . That is Ella's lack of freshness, especially in her case when it comes to riffing. . . . I wish then that she would let go of those 'sure things,' those choruses such as in 'Lady Be Good' that she has repeated verbatim thousands of times, and ad lib in the true sense of the word. Too many of us . . . have heard those exact choruses many times before."[18]

During the spring of 1954, Ray Tunia left Ella's group and was replaced by John Lewis. "Norman Granz asked me to come," Lewis said. "It wasn't the first time, it was the second time he asked me. Before, he asked me in 1950, and then I decided to go back to music college. In 1954 the members of the Modern Jazz Quartet were making up their minds whether or not to pursue the venture full-time, give it their total commitment. So I took the job with Ella. So for the short time before the MJQ became serious about what they wanted to do, I developed a greater appreciation of her talent, and also of *her*. She commanded great respect from all the musicians I went on the road with—the JATP, anything that came up. She was subtle and as good as you could be."

On Saturday, July 17, Ella and her new trio, with Lewis on piano, Jimmy Woode on bass, and Shadow Wilson on drums, played the first Newport Jazz Festival. Produced by George Wein, the concept would eventually be institutionalized around the world and was another significant step in taking jazz out of the nightclubs and presenting it as a concert attraction. Ella and her trio was the last group before the all-star jam session that wound up the evening. As she sat talking quietly backstage to John Lewis, she became more and more nervous—not of the crowds this time but of the musicians who preceded her on the bill and who would be around afterward listening to her perform. When the time came to go onstage, however, she had the audience in the palm of her hand from the start: "Nervous or not, Ella Fitzgerald had the crowd in a frenzy. At the end of her performance, the roar was deafening," said photographer Burt Goldblatt, who was covering the festival.[19]

Just two days later, with the roar of the Newport Festival crowd still ringing in her ears, Ella went from the best to the worst a black artist could experience in America. She was confronted by racism. Booked on a first-class flight to Australia with her maid, Georgiana Henry, and accompanist John Lewis, Ella and her small party flew from San Francisco on Monday, July 19. They were to play a series of concerts in the Antipodes that was organized by Norman Granz, who had arranged to join them en route. When they reached the scheduled stopover for refueling in Honolulu, Ella and her party were bumped from their seats to make room for some white patrons. Since they were forced to stay in Honolulu for three days before making another connection, their concerts in Sydney had to be canceled.

Norman Granz was immediately outraged. This was precisely the situation he had been campaigning long and hard to stamp out. It was blatant, institutionalized racism. He immediately put legal proceedings into motion; when the matter finally came to court in December, his complaint read: "The refusal was willful and malicious and was motivated by prejudice against the plaintiffs, Fitzgerald, Lewis, and Henry, because of their race and color, and this conduct subjected the plaintiffs to unjust discrimination and undue and unreasonable prejudice."[20] Not only was the incident both humiliating and embarrassing but matters were made worse by Pan-Am's refusal to allow them to collect their clothes and other personal items left on their seats during the stopover. Ella asked for $25,000 damages plus $50,000 punitive damages, while John Lewis and Georgiana Henry asked for $10,000 damages plus $50,000 punitive damages. A spokesman for the airline said it was an "honest mistake." The suit was eventually settled out of court for an undisclosed sum.

In February and March 1955, Granz experimented with a miniature JATP concert tour, taking Ella and the Oscar Peterson Trio to Europe. On her return she was delighted to hear that Granz had successfully negotiated a part for her in the forthcoming Hollywood feature *Pete Kelly's Blues*. On a bright spring morning in late March 1955 she boarded a flight at La Guardia Airport for Hollywood with Georgiana Henry and pianist Don Abney, who had recently replaced John Lewis. At the time Ella considered her role in the Warner Brothers movie the biggest thing ever to have happened to her. Star-director-producer Jack Webb of *Dragnet* fame was cast in the role of a cornet-playing musician battling against prohibition-era Kansas City mobsters. Peggy Lee, who played Rose Hopkins, an alcoholic gangster's moll, picked up an Academy Award nomination, while Ella, as Maggie Jackson, had a cameo role as a nightclub singer.

The film preserves a superb Ella performance in a nightclub setting and is a glimpse of what it would have been like to see her at work in 1955; "Hard Hearted Hannah" simply surges with rhythmic momentum as Ella turns in a quite outstanding vocal performance. "The wonderful Ella Fitzgerald . . . fills the screen and soundtrack with her strong, mobile features and voice," said the *New York Times*.[21]

Three Ella tracks from the film came out on Decca, where she is accompanied by Don Abney, Joe Mondragon on bass, and Larry Bunker on drums. "'Ella Hums the Blues,' 'Pete Kelly's Blues,' and 'Hard Hearted Hannah' we took off a tape," said Milt Gabler. "They were from *Pete Kelly's Blues* out of L.A. . . . We got the tape and put them out from that."[22] While on the West Coast, Granz had booked Ella into the Mocambo, a big upper-crust nitery in Hollywood. This was done with the help of Marilyn Monroe, who, while recuperating from minor surgery in November 1954, went to hear Ella at a club near her Hollywood home and became a devoted fan. Between them, Granz and Monroe put pressure on the Mocambo's owner Charlie Morrison to open the doors of one of America's most exclusive night spots to a "jazz singer." On opening night Monroe ensured that the audience was liberally sprinkled with celebrities, including Judy Garland and Frank Sinatra. The engagement was a huge success, and night after night of full houses encouraged Morrison to extend Ella's run there. When she finally completed her stay, Granz booked her into the huge Fairmont Hotel in San Francisco, where she became the first-ever jazz performer to entertain in the hotel's Venetian Room.

From mid-September 1955 Ella was committed to the now annual fall JATP tour, which had scheduled concerts in Houston and Dallas Texas. Granz knew when he set up the Houston date that he might encounter problems. It was a city in which segregation was enforced by custom rather than by law. When they played the city's Music Hall on October 7, in case there should be any trouble, Granz hired eight policemen, headed by the mayor's chauffeur, Lieutenant Sam Clauder, at the then princely sum of $25 per man. During the concert, however, five members of Houston's vice squad—Officers E. L. Kennedy, E. F. Thomas, A. J. Burke, and Robert Schultea, and Sergeant W. A. Scotton, who was in command—tricked their way into the backstage area by showing their shields and claiming to be lifelong jazz fans. Their intention was to show Granz just what Houston thought of his "liberal" ideas. Law enforcement could not have been further from their minds. They were looking for trouble. They found it in the most innocuous of circumstances in, of all places, Ella's dressing room. Ella and Georgiana were having a snack while they watched a dice game between Dizzy Gillespie and Illinois Jacquet. Granz, another spectator, was just leaving as the law enforcement officers arrived. Brandishing their firearms, Houston's Finest found just the infraction of the law they needed.

As one officer headed alone for the toilet, Granz immediately brushed past the other officers to follow him. It was transparent that the raid was intended as a "drug bust," and Granz could see that the officer was seeking an opportunity to make a plant away from the general melee. Frustrated by such quick thinking, the officer turned on Granz: "I ought to kill you," he said menacingly, pushing a gun into Granz's stomach. Finally Ella, Georgiana, Dizzy, Illinois, and Granz were forced to go to the police station where they were charged with being party to an illegal dice game. By a remarkable coincidence the press was on hand to witness what the Houston police had hoped would be a major news coup. Instead it turned out to be a rather pathetic example of police harassment. But at least Granz had averted the unthinkable—headlines screaming, "Black JATP Musicians Caught in Drug Bust." Instead, the incident was given just a couple of column inches: The *Daily News* said "Houston Dice Cops Give Ella and Boys a Bad Shake," while *Variety* said it all in the last two words: "Granz and Co. Play 'Guys and Dolls' Dice Bit for Houston Cops; Aud Unsegregated." The *Houston Post* seemed bemused by the whole incident: "Miss Fitzgerald, wearing a décolleté gown of blue taffeta and a mink stole, was one of the most handsomely dressed women ever to visit the Houston Police Station."[23]

Not unnaturally, the press wanted to know why so many men had been used to such modest effect, culminating in each of the accused being posted with a $10 bail bond. Police Chief Jack Heard was reported as calling his men "a little overzealous. We could have used the manpower to more advantage elsewhere. We want to enforce the law, but common sense should apply."[24] On October 24, Judge W. E. Bell dismissed all charges against Ella, Norman Granz, and Georgiana Henry.

This was not good enough for Granz; he subsequently put his lawyers on the case until they finally got the charges against Dizzy Gillespie and Illinois Jacquet dismissed. It eventually cost him over $2,000 to recover the $20 posted for the bail bonds, but he had made his point. "I was the innocent one!" said Ella later. "Yeah, sitting up eating pie," she said with a laugh. "They took us down, and then when we got there, they had the nerve to ask for an autograph."[25]

Meanwhile, Milt Gabler was experiencing great difficulty in arranging for Ella to fulfill her contract with Decca. It seemed as if Granz was making all sorts of excuses to make it impossible to get her into the recording studios. In reality it was simply pressure of work getting in the way; Ella's remarkable appetite for performing meant she had bookings stacked up all over the country months in advance. But for Gabler, trying to arrange Ella's recording sessions had become a frustrating experience. "It wasn't pleasant those last years when he kept her from us. Too-long gaps between sessions, then you would just have to record what you could. He kept her from being available to me. She'd come into New York, and I'd have like two days to get a record session with her. I couldn't have any real discussion with her about what she was going to make. In fact, at one stage we picked up something she had done for Bing Crosby to fill out her contractual commitments. She had recorded something in the studios, a transcription of a Bing Crosby broadcast with John Scott Trotter accompaniment. We would never use John Trotter to accompany Ella, but she had done some standards on the show and we just took it from the transcriptions."[26]

In any event, Ella's contract with Decca never ran the full three years. "We gave her up a year early," continued Gabler. "Our contract called for a minimum of twelve tunes a year and three sessions of four each—a minimum of twelve. The way it worked out, he got her when we did *The Benny Goodman Story*. Norman controlled some of the acts, some of the musicians who appeared on the film. I had to put out the soundtrack album of the film on Decca, a double album, and he wouldn't give us the rights to his artists. So we made a deal where he let me record the twelve songs she was going to record during the year, and when she finished them—she finished them in four, eight weeks, or whatever—he got her."[27]

Having reached an agreement with Gabler, Granz continued to find it difficult to get Ella into the studios to complete her contract, even though it was now in his own interest to do so. Ella's unremitting schedule was now as frustrating to him as to Gabler. "There were two sessions when we had to finish up our contract, because we wanted to put out the Benny Goodman soundtracks; Sonny Burke produced those out on the West Coast, one with Benny Carter's band and another with André Previn," Gabler recalled.[28] The Carter and Previn tracks were eventually released at the end of 1955, together with the extended version of "You'll Have to Swing It" with Sy Oliver's orchestra, plus two numbers with John Scott Trotter, on the LP *Sweet and Hot*. With the exception of the Oliver track, all the numbers were standards; in concept and execution the album could well have come from Ella's subsequent period on the Verve label.

This is Ella revving her engines in readiness for the epic *Songbook* cycles that would consume her recording career for the next few years. Numbers like "It Might as Well Be Spring," "Thanks for the Memory," and "You'll Never Know," with their deliciously slow tempos, show the exemplary control of intonation, enunciation, and dynamic range that was so admired by singers from Crosby to Sinatra. The tracks with Carter represent the "hot" side of the album and include a superb "Old Black Magic" and "Old Devil Moon." This album stacks up well against most of Ella's orchestral albums with Granz and, like all her LPs for Decca prepared for release by Gabler, is an excellent representation of her Decca period.

"Finally we finished with two sessions in New York. I did those with Tutti Camarata," continued Milt Gabler. "Then, yes, I was sorry to see her go. Norman finally got her away from me! During all that time I only had a problem with her once. She strained her throat. She was playing a seashore joint, I can't remember the name offhand, but they used to have to sing out in the open there. And during this period I had one session I had to do over a couple of times. We didn't even get the sides in because she got hoarse after about thirty minutes, and I had to call the session off. I had to call the band back the next week and we tried again, and for the second time her voice didn't come back.

"She was working every night at that place and strained her vocal cords, but she had an audience. But at the record session you could hear it in the mike immediately. I called the date off and paid all the guys; all the guys got paid in the band. Three sessions to do it. It really wasn't her fault; the date should have been canceled. That was the only problem I ever had with her in the studio.

"But I don't know. When he took her away to his label, he didn't do as well or any better than I did for her. I didn't think so. He went in and did his Gershwin album, those big albums with her, and he got a lot of credit for that. I had really started that with her with the Ellis Larkins stuff. He started to do what I did, but he didn't have a pop record company where he had to worry about covering tunes.

"We could get her an audience from somebody who had a hit on another label. She would get a good piece of the business. The choice of material, getting her to do pop things and her jazz things, created an audience for her with a huge pop base. I did that with all the acts I handled. I made Billie a real pop singer. I didn't have to make her, that was right in her. It gave her a bigger audience. Ella too, she had a big following when she went to Norman."[29]

By 1954, Ella had sold over 22 million records for Decca. And Norman Granz's outbursts in the press notwithstanding, her recordings had almost always attracted good reviews in the music press, in the music columns of magazines, and in the national dailies. Indeed, reading those contemporaneous reviews, it is almost impossible to imagine the extent to which those same recordings would be dismissed by critics in later years.

Today Milt Gabler's influence is almost totally neglected, eclipsed by the huge success of Ella's work on the Verve label under the aegis of Norman Granz. But as the man responsible for almost all of Ella's recorded output between 1943 and 1955, Gabler played a crucial, if uncredited, role in her career. Not only was he largely responsible for rehabilitating her flagging fortunes, at a nadir in 1943, with a series of hits, he also laid the foundation for her later triumphs in the fifties and sixties by building a huge popular audience for her, far beyond that customarily associated with a jazz singer.

Although Ella's wide public following might have been bought at the expense of commercial pops, as early as 1945 Gabler realized Ella's capabilities as an improvising jazz singer, and he made a point of recording several scat features whose popularity would later seal her success with JATP and, incidentally, provide some much-neglected classics of jazz singing along the way. In contrast, it was also Gabler who recorded Ella with Louis Armstrong and discovered a wonderful empathy between them, while her fun sides with Louis Jordan still retain a freshness and vitality, despite their period charm. But it is Ella's work with Ellis Larkins that finally represents something that the singer herself wanted to do. They are sides of great honesty and humanity; they reach out across the decades and represent an artistic plateau that was surpassed only by her very best work on Norman Granz's Verve label.

Although it might be argued that Gabler's handling of Ella's talent lacked direction or a unified vision, it is important to remember the context of the times. Gabler handled her in an era of the 78 rpm record, Granz in the era of the 33⅓ rpm long-playing record. Whatever major record label Ella might have been with during the forties and early fifties, be it RCA Victor, Columbia, or Decca, she would have found herself covering the song publishers' plugs and hits by other singers on other labels, just as she had at Decca.

Subject to such market forces, no singer—or, indeed, the big bands that preceded them—emerged with artistic integrity entirely intact. It is fortunate, therefore, that fate smiled on Ella in her association with Gabler and that she did not come under the control of someone like Mitch Miller at Columbia who almost succeeded in turning great artists like Frank Sinatra, Rosemary Clooney, and Tony Bennett into hacks.

The extent and success of Gabler's role, given the constraints under which he worked, have been obscured by Decca's seeming reluctance to re-release the majority of Ella's material from 1943 to 1955—the "Gabler Years"—so correcting the myth that practically everything she recorded on the label was poor-quality pop has been almost impossible. Until GRP leased the Decca catalog in the 1990s, MCA, which owns the rights, had for decades issued the worst Ella selections on anthologies titled her "greatest hits." This effectively meant that Ella's Verve recordings never had to compete with her past, a period that did contain some excellent but now sadly overlooked recordings. Even so, there certainly were, as Gabler freely admits, some "crap numbers." But so was "A-Tisket, A-Tasket," which if it hadn't been a biggie would fall simply and easily into that category.

Who knows what will strike a chord with the record-buying public? In the music business there are no certainties. In 1938 "Begin the Beguine" was a forgotten Cole Porter tune; it never made it until it was recorded by Artie Shaw, who had an outstanding hit with it. Ella, as a popular singer, had no scruples about taking her chances in the hit-parade lottery and pursuing that elusive hit with whatever material Decca chose to give her. What emerged during the Gabler years is a delicate balancing act between commercial necessity and artistic aspiration. And that artistic aspiration more often than not came from

Gabler himself. As Dan Morgenstern points out, "To say that Decca gave her such a terrible deal is really not true. She got to make a lot of nice things, and I'm not just thinking of the Gershwin thing with Ellis Larkins."

Ella, as Nat Hentoff observed in the mid-fifties, became a jazz singer less through fierce personal conviction than through gradual force of circumstances. "Left to herself," he said, "I think you would find Ella would pick many more of the pop hits of the day than she would material better suited to jazz."[30] When Ella said in February 1955 that she wanted to do "Teach Me Tonight" and "The Man That Got Away,"[31] her complaint was not so much that she was given commercial pops to sing but that they were not *her* choice of commercial pops.

CHAPTER ELEVEN

1955–1957

I don't think anyone would accuse Ella of having an intellectual relationship with the lyrics of her songs.

SYLVIA SYMS

IT TOOK NORMAN GRANZ several months to get Ella into the recording studios after he secured her release from Decca. He was setting up a new record label, which, with characteristic gusto, he called Verve. But clearing the way for his new label was complicated as well as long overdue. Apart from his Clef and Norgran labels, he also owned the Downhome label. Securing Ella meant an almost complete restructuring of Granz's recording activities; he intended to build Verve around his star signing, and the famous Verve "4000" series was initiated with her in mind. The venture was originally described as a "pop company"; he told the press, "Ella . . . will also cut pop singles for Verve."[1]

Two years earlier, in 1953, Granz had Oscar Peterson begin recording for his Clef label over 120 tracks for ten albums of tunes written by the finest songwriters of the previous three decades. These recordings became known as the *Peterson and the Composer Series* and included albums of songs by Cole Porter, Irving Berlin, George Gershwin, Duke Ellington, Jerome Kern, Richard Rodgers, Vincent Youmans, Harry Warren, Harold Arlen, and Jimmy McHugh. The theme, inspired by Milt Gabler's 1950 production, *Ella Sings Gershwin*, worked well. Having satisfactorily established the feasibility of the concept, Granz decided to transfer the idea onto a larger screen and once again work through the canons of the great jazz and Broadway composers, this time using his major new signing, Ella Fitzgerald, backed by a sumptuous orchestra. As soon as he pulled all his diverse recording activities together under one roof, he immediately announced he would record an album of Cole Porter songs with Ella, who meanwhile had just begun a long Christmas–New Year stay at the Venetian Room of the Fairmont Hotel in San Francisco with her trio comprising Don Abney on piano, Vernon Alley on bass, and Jackie Mills on drums. On January 21, 1956, however, she appeared at Los Angeles's Shrine Auditorium opposite the Dave Brubeck Quartet, where Granz dispatched a recording remote, although the eight numbers she recorded have to date remained unreleased.

When at last the time came for her to step into the recording studios under the aegis of Norman Granz on January 25, it was not, as it turned out, for Verve at all, and neither was it to record the Cole Porter album. Instead it was a date for the Clef label; when Verve was finally set up, Granz simply transferred the masters across. The numbers she cut that day were "Stay There," "The Sun Forgot to Shine This Morning," "Too Young for the Blues," and "It's Only a Man" with the Buddy Bregman Orchestra. Straightforward swingers in a post-swing-era vein, today they are merely interesting precursors to the main event, the *Cole Porter Songbook*, which Ella began recording on February 7.

Although originally intended as a single LP, it quickly became apparent that only a double album would do after Granz and his musical director, Buddy Bregman, began short-listing suitable Porter numbers for the project. Porter, an American playboy during the 1930s, was a composer of songs that in their day were considered the epitome of fashion and wit among the *beau monde*. As Alec Wilder observed, many of his songs were turned out for the special amusement of his social set: "They seldom risked or indulged in tenderness or vulnerability," he wrote. "Even when concerned with emotional stresses, they often managed to keep a polite distance from sentiment by means of a gloss, a patina of social poise."[2] Porter's songs create the illusion that we can live on the surface of our emotions; sincere and touching, their truth is only partial. Yet Porter's lyrics were set to astonishingly well crafted music. He was perhaps the most thoroughly musically educated of all the composers of the American popular song, and his compositions brought wit, sophistication, and complexity to the form.

It was therefore intriguing to conceive of Ella, with her impeccable pitch and diction but disinclination to impose her subjective imprint on the material at hand, recording the songs of a composer whose emotionalism was ironic, if not illusory, and certainly not a prime consideration in their interpretation. Yet of all Ella's recordings, the mystery of the Porter set is not how good they were but why, especially considering the brouhaha leading up to their release, they were not significantly better.

Part of the reason lies in Buddy Bregman's orchestrations. They are functional but unimaginative, replete with standard dance-bandisms. More than any other single factor, they fail to project Ella to the extent that, say, Nelson Riddle had achieved during the past two years at Capitol for Frank Sinatra. On the three albums Sinatra had recorded prior to Ella's entering the studios for the Porter set— *Songs for Young Lovers*, *Swing Easy*, and *In the Wee Small Hours*—the mutual admiration society of arranger and singer soared beyond the mechanical and achieved a union that was unique in popular music. Yet while Riddle's gifts as an orchestrator might have seemed the logical choice for Ella, too, he was under contract to Capitol Records. Granz would have loved to have used him from day one; when he *was* finally able to secure his services four years later, it ensured that Ella's Gershwin set would become perhaps the most enduring *Songbook* collection of all.

If on the one hand unimaginative orchestrations conspired to devalue the ultimate quality of the Porter set, on the other lurked the suspicion that Granz was watching the studio clock carefully. It was an expensive undertaking, to be sure, and like all recording enterprises, a speculative one. But there is a feeling of undue haste, of settling for a take that sounds good enough rather than going for gold. On "Too Darn Hot," for example, Ella's voice sounds a little frayed around the edges, as if it was the end of a long day in the studio. And there are just one or two fleeting moments when she sounds as if she has not quite worked out where she can breathe to best advantage.

"I first met Ella in 1956 when she first did the *Songbook* albums," said pianist Paul Smith. "Cole Porter, Rodgers and Hart, I did all those albums. I was not her accompanist then, I just did the record dates. I was on staff at NBC at the time. There were hardly any second takes. The Cole Porter and some of the other ones were just kind of *ground* out—that's the only way I can describe them. We'd run down the verse, just to make sure she knew it, and bang, we'd record it!"

When the album was released in the spring of 1956, it was with superb David Stone Martin artwork on the cover, an innovative idea that was initially featured on the Clef album sleeves and subsequently on many Verve releases, plus a press release announcing how Granz had played the tracks for the composer in his penthouse apartment in the Waldorf Towers. "What diction she has!" Porter was reported as saying. The publicity Granz shrewdly generated was such that the albums even got reviewed in the *New York Herald Tribune:* "She handles . . . [the songs] with a fine straightforward style, spiced here and there with nice little personal touches."[3] Unusual for a double album, it went to number fifteen on *Billboard*'s chart and was listed in the July 23, 1956, edition of *Down Beat* as second on the list of top best-selling jazz albums.

In Britain, one number from the set, "Ev'rytime We Say Goodbye," became a perennial selection on the BBC "Forces' Favourites" program, and for years hardly a week went by without its being played. During the fifties and sixties, this program, broadcast at lunchtime on Sunday, enjoyed widespread popularity, and as a consequence the number began to assume a life of its own. In a quaint example of British parochialism, a large portion of the English public now associates the name Ella Fitzgerald with that one number, more so than with any other song she ever recorded.

The Porter set ultimately went on to become one of the best-selling jazz albums of all time, remaining almost constantly in print since its release—originally on vinyl and subsequently on compact disc. And it played a significant role in establishing the viability of Verve records. "After I formed Verve, things began to change," said Granz later. "Almost immediately we had a hit with Ella's *Cole Porter Songbook*. It was the eleventh biggest LP of the year. That was insane for me. . . . Verve put me in the commercial market for the first time."[4] Ultimately, however, the success of the *Cole Porter Songbook* seems now more a testament to the strength of the album's concept than to the quality of the album itself.

In June 1956, Norman Granz continued his policy of featuring Ella in the nation's most exclusive night spots by booking her into the sumptuous Starlight Roof of the Waldorf-Astoria for a short season, sharing the bill with the Count Basie Orchestra. Throughout her career Ella had always been strongly attracted to Basie, both musically and personally. They now shared a warm friendship, and she got on exceptionally well with all the band members, who nicknamed her "Sis." For the Waldorf-Astoria patrons, who were used to supper club cabaret and society bands and most of whom would never be caught dead anywhere near a jazz club, Ella and Basie represented something of an unknown quantity. How would such an audience react to two jazz acts?

On opening night the changeover from Basie to Ella's trio took a long time, and the audience grew restless. Ella, aware of what was at stake, was clearly on edge, and to make matters worse she had problems with the microphone, which further unsettled her. For a while she struggled to win the crowd with her opening numbers, "It's De-Lovely," "I've Grown Accustomed to (His) Face," "Cheek to Cheek," and "Lady Be Good," which was normally a surefire crowd-pleaser. But after her versions of "Black Magic," "Caravan," and "Witchcraft," "Ella got 'em," as Gene Knight put it in his review column, "Knight Watch." "She got 'em some more with 'I Love You Porgy'—had 'em groggy with 'Angel Eyes' (her best number on my score card). Swung 'em for a loop with her scat talk on 'How High the Moon' and knocked 'em out with her final blues routine backed by Basie's band."[5] Ella's Waldorf-Astoria date was a major success and was a key factor in enabling Granz to book her into similar high-class night spots throughout the country.

While at the Waldorf-Astoria, Ella and the Basie band were united on record for the first time when they went into the studio as part of the *Metronome All-Stars 1956* album. Many of the poll winners for that year were assembled under the direction of editor Bill Coss. "The Basie men arrived in their usual good humor," he recalled, "reminiscing about last night's jokes and loudly calling for sandwiches and paper cups. Ella Fitzgerald, Count Basie, and arranger Ralph Burns came in shortly afterward, with Ella protesting that she wasn't really a blues singer and that she felt rather awed to be singing with the band anyway. Ralph began to show the band what he had done to 'April in Paris' . . . an engaging performance with the special kind of grace Ella can give to a lyric. . . . Then Joe Williams entered the picture, and confusion reigned for almost an hour because no one could decide what Joe and Ella should sing together."[6] In any event, Ella joined Williams on "Every Day I Have the Blues" and an improvised scat sequence on "Party Blues." "Joe and Ella scatting all over the place probably was symbolic . . . of the delightful informality which presided over this session and the summing-up that Joe, Ella, and the band produced of the more virile side of modern swing, of the heart of jazz."[7]

Ella and Basie crossed paths again at the Newport Jazz Festival. Basie closed the first night, Thursday, July 5, to a huge ovation, and Ella, with her trio of pianist Don Abney, bassist Bennie Moten, and new drummer Gus Johnson, closed the second. She was preceded by her idol, Louis Armstrong. However, Louis was panned by the critics: "Too much Louis, not enough Ella," rebuked *Down Beat*. "He demonstrated with finality that it takes more than rolling eyes, handkerchief on head and chops, and the same old Paramount Theatre act to warrant time at a festival of jazz."[8]

Ella, in contrast, had the crowd in the palm of her hand. "Singing in her astonishingly vivacious manner—which, combined with her exact diction and true pitch, makes her a phenomenon among jazz singers—she quickly captured the crowd's fancy. They had what they came for and refused to let her go," said the *Christian Science Monitor*.[9]

Maybe Ella's triumph at Newport would be better remembered today if the following night Duke Ellington had not lit the fuse that caused an explosion of new musical life in his by then fading band. The fantastic ovation he earned that night was one of the most significant events in jazz for years. It had such a rejuvenating effect on his career that Ellington would say in later years: "I was born at the Newport Jazz Festival on July 7, 1956."

For the remainder of July, Ella was at George Wein's Storyville Club in Boston. "We paid her $2,500 a week. Remember, in those days beer was only sixty cents and whiskey ninety-five cents a shot. She cleared it. She was incredibly popular," said Wein. That popularity was now beginning to astonish even her most seasoned observers. "Even the waitresses paused in their shuttles from bar to table when Ella sang," wrote Don Cerulli in *Down Beat*.[10]

The mesmerizing effect that this now extremely overweight, middle-aged lady had on audiences was amazing; with a remarkable combination of girlish charm and sheer ability, she could get away with anything. "For 'I Can't Give You Anything but Love' Ella chi-chied a chorus à la Rose Murphy and mugged a chorus in the Armstrong style," continued Cerulli. "Somehow she rang in 'Davy Crockett' and 'Blue Suede Shoes.'"[11]

The Storyville gig provided an opportunity for drummer Gus Johnson, who had recently left the Basie band and had been working with Lena Horne, to settle in with the group. Johnson, a strikingly good-looking man, had an immediate effect on Ella, and for a while they had an affair.

"I joined Ella in 1956," said Johnson in 1979, "and I was with her nine years, till 1965. I really loved working with her. . . . She had her little ways, too, you know. She's self-conscious . . . she's very sensitive, and if she saw you talking, she might think you were saying bad things about her. . . . She wanted people to love her. She's beautiful to me, but she was always trying to improve herself in everything she did. . . . Norman Granz, her manager, is a great cat, too. Everybody's got their ways, but I like him. He knows what he's listening to, and he knows his business. I never had any problems with him—no problems whatsoever."[12]

Shortly after the Storyville gig, at the end of July, Don Abney fell sick, and Ella found herself in need of a pianist at short notice. Tommy Flanagan was recommended. "I had just arrived in New York," he recalled. "This was 1956 and the first time I joined Ella. . . . She had about one more month before she went on vacation. I was recommended by a cousin of Ella's. Her husband was in Dizzy's band which was playing Basin Street, E. V. Perry. I think Billy Mitchell, who was also in the band, must have spoken to him, and I guess he said something about Ella needing a pianist. . . . I showed up, and 'Hey, Ella needs you,' or something like that. And I was available.

"It was about a month with Gus Johnson and the bass player Bennie Moten. I didn't work with her again until the sixties. She had charts for everything, a lot of stuff; she had a large book there. Not only did she have a trio book, but she had a book for band arrangements. When I played with her the first time, we didn't play any big band things—until the second time I joined her. To begin with," Flanagan said with a laugh, "I don't think she had that much confidence in me. She didn't know me. I was just recommended. I just tried to do my job."[13]

Flanagan's introduction to the world of Ella Fitzgerald was hair-raising, as Gus Johnson recalled: "When Tommy Flanagan came with the group, we were playing some club in Cleveland, and the first night he was doing the best he could when she turned around and like scared him to death. I saw it happen and just told her, 'Turn around!' I believe that pretty well shocked her, so afterward I walked right behind her, waiting to hear, 'You're fired!' But she had evidently gotten over it. 'This is his first night,' I told her. 'He doesn't know the numbers, and he's nervous.'"[14]

In August 1956, Ella flew out to the West Coast where she was booked into Zardi's, an extremely popular supper club. She also appeared at the Hollywood Bowl on the 15th, backed in each instance by a quartet headed by Paul Smith on piano. At the Hollywood Bowl she played a short set and then joined Louis Armstrong and his All Stars. Granz recorded her at both places,[15] but he only issued a couple of tracks from the Hollywood Bowl concert. However, Ella was reunited with Louis in the recording studios the day after the Hollywood Bowl concert to cut the enduring *Ella and Louis* album.

In contrast to Ella's Decca sides with Satchmo, they were both set to work on superior popular songs. But superior songs or not, the magic was just the same; curiously, the quality of the tunes did not seem to matter. Like Billie Holiday in her early period with Teddy Wilson, it was not so much that Ella and Louis could make a silk purse from a sow's ear as that they could make a silk purse out of *anything*. Ella and Louis join in a noncompetitive, easy-listening session that remains timeless in its middle-of-the-road appeal, despite the fact that Louis was apparently travel-weary from an exhausting schedule of one-nighters.

"When she made the album with Louis," Norman Granz told Leonard Feather, "she insisted that he select the tunes, and she sang them all in his keys even if they were the wrong keys for her."[16] What was interesting about Granz's *Songbook* cycle (which was well under way with a Rodgers and Hart session just a few days after the Louis date) and the Ella-Louis collaborations was the gap in the marketplace they filled. Definitely not for the whistlers and screamers at the JATP concerts, they had great appeal for a whole generation brought up in the era of big bands who were now feeling disenfranchised from popular music by successive waves of bop and rock 'n' roll. In their youth they lindy-hopped in the aisles of the Paramount and the ballrooms across middle America. Now they had sons and daughters of their own who were jiving to Elvis Presley or to Milt Gabler's latest signing, Bill Haley. The music was a million miles from the sounds of their youth. Still with an interest in popular music, they found it easy to identify with Ella's cool breeze or the engaging humor and charm of her duets with Louis. Unlike the music of the new generation, it was noncombative, nonthreatening, and the ideal accompaniment for a chat around the coffee table or a dinner party with friends. The songs of the Broadway composers from the late 1920s, the 1930s, and early 1940s were the pop music of their salad days, the music with which they identified. Now they could hear those numbers again, tastefully updated on LP by a singer who let the songs speak for themselves rather than imposing on them the subjective baggage of her own life experiences. By traveling light, Ella left the songs as she found them, untouched by the cult of personality.

In order to finish the *Rodgers and Hart Songbook* by the end of August 1956, Ella was in the studios almost daily with an orchestra directed once again by Buddy Bregman. When the album was released in 1957, it went to number eleven on the *Billboard* chart, chalking up another commercial success for Granz's stewardship of Ella's career.

Yet, as with its predecessor, the *Cole Porter Songbook*, interest waned because of the glossy superficiality of Bregman's writing. In only a couple of tracks, where Ella is accompanied by just a rhythm section led by Paul Smith on piano, does the album come alive. With the big band tracks there is a duality of man-versus-machine that works less well for Ella than, say, Frank Sinatra. His ring-a-ding-ding masculinity was at home among the blasts of trumpets and trombones that acted as a springboard to project his personality. Yet all that power is somehow at odds with the essence of Ella's style. Fundamentally a humble singer, she sang her songs simply and without artifice; the simpler her accompaniment, the greater seemed her humanity.

As with the Porter set, the *Rodgers and Hart Songbook* reveals flaws under close scrutiny. Changing "Miss" to "Sir" on "Have You Met Miss Jones?" is understandable for a female singer but nevertheless irritating, particularly since a knight's appellation precedes his Christian name, not his surname. And the Rodgers and Hart selection, more so than the Porter collection, highlights how Ella, in responding more to the inherent musical features of a song than to its libretto, never became part of a song's inherent drama. This exteriorization, of remaining on the "outside" of a song's meaning yet remaining faithful to its musical characteristics, works well in songs like "Manhattan" or "Mountain Greenery," but fails, for example, in a number like "Ten Cents a Dance." Here the lyrics demand internalization. The singer has to get inside their meaning and then project the song as if she *is* that blowsy dime-a-dance hostess. For that reason Chris Connor, a capable but less musically endowed singer, could make the song come alive in a way Ella could not. Other songs, too, fail through lack of the internalization they require: "Bewitched, Bothered, and Bewildered," the confession of a middle-aged sophisticate, first stimulated against her better judgment, then wryly disillusioned; "Give It Back to the Indians," a New Yorker's ironic listing of the city's follies; and "To Keep My Love Alive" (an added number in the 1943 revival of *A Connecticut Yankee*), the confession of a medieval murderess.

The dichotomy of the *Songbook* cycle is that while the majority of the material highlighted the strengths of Granz's star performer, there was always one, two, three, or perhaps more songs in every album that highlighted her weaknesses. Granz was perhaps less concerned with this. His contention was that the strength of the songs in themselves, complete with their seldom-heard verses, would ultimately provide the enduring quality of the *Songbook* series. Viewed from this perspective, his selection of material is almost faultless; the *Songbooks* remain a remarkable document of the American popular song.

Viewed from the singer's perspective, however, the *Songbook* cycle exposed both Ella's strengths and, on occasion, her limitations because of the problem of relating material to her individual vocal characteristics. Thus, the *Songbooks*, for all the hyperbole that continues to surround them, can never be anything more or less than good songs well sung. Never *more* because of the occasional limitations of what the singer sang as much as the way she sang it and never *less* because of the remarkably high standard of Ella's inherent and instinctive musicality. It's fortunate that for much of the time the latter was enough.

Yet it is worth reflecting on the contrast between Granz's thirty-eight-songs-and-you've-got-your-album approach and the way Frank Sinatra made his albums work as albums. Sinatra's emerged as complete, self-contained works, very like miniature suites, with each succeeding song complementing the previous one, each with a reason to be there, each succeeding in defining Sinatra's style. Examples of these albums include *Only the Lonely, In the Wee Small Hours, Come Fly with Me*, and *Songs for Swingin' Lovers*. It was ironic that when Capitol began disassembling these masterpieces in miniature and reassembling them in composer collections after Ella's *Songbook* cycle success, Sinatra sued to make them desist.

While the *Rodgers and Hart Songbook* was being completed in early September, Granz began putting plans in place to record a *Duke Ellington Songbook*. But getting Duke himself into the studios to complete the sessions proved difficult; his busy schedule seemed unceasing, and it was not until the end of June 1957 that Granz secured him and his orchestra for four days. Meanwhile, Jimmy Jones was sent out to get Ella's keys so that Duke could prepare special arrangements for the session. It was to no avail, however; when Duke arrived in the studios he had nothing prepared. "It was a panic scene," said Ella, "with Duke almost making up the arrangements as we went along. Duke is a genius—I admire him as much as anyone in the world—but doing it that way, even though it was fun at times, got to be kind of nerve-racking."[17]

Consequently, the *Duke Ellington Songbook* has a scissors-and-paste feel. "It was done under the worst conditions," said Granz in 1979. "He was under contract to Columbia, but I had Johnny Hodges. When Hodges rejoined the band in 1956, I managed to force a few concessions. I would have Duke for one LP, two if I used Ella. We planned far in advance, but in the end Duke failed to do a single arrangement. Ella had to use the band's regular arrangements. She'd do a vocal where an instrumental chorus would normally go. To stretch to four LPs, we padded it with various small-group things with Hodges, Ben Webster, and so on."[18]

On some tracks with the full orchestra, Ella improvises over standard Ellington arrangements, her scat soaring like Barney Bigard's clarinet obbligatos of years before. On others she simply sings to existing Ellington arrangements in place of an Ellington vocalist or instrumentalist. Only on a couple of tracks does Ellington actually manage to provide a couple of new arrangements in the session, such as "Caravan." But although it is an interesting album, it does have a feel of muddling through, and if some numbers were "all right on the night," so to speak, others are merely fillers. Once again, as with the Porter album, there is a feeling of what might have been.

For this reason it is impossible not to listen to some tracks and wonder how things might have turned out had Duke prepared for the session as he did just a few years later for his latter-day masterpieces such as *And His Mother Called Him Bill* and *The Far East Suite*. But Ellington worked in strange and obscure ways. Did he really want to prepare for the session? Did he really want to be playing, literally and metaphorically, second fiddle to a singer? The centerpiece of the album is not, as one might expect, established compositions from the Ellington canon featuring Ella but a wholly new four-part instrumental called *Portrait of Ella Fitzgerald*, featuring Ellington's own band. As a suite it could have been about anything; only the unusual feature of Ellington prefacing each piece with a spoken introduction, full of the characteristically gushing, love-you-madly charm he reserved especially for the opposite sex, gives the suite the Ella connection.

Perhaps this gives us a clue as to how Ellington viewed the project; even in his autobiography he repeats his eulogy to Ella.[19] It is almost as if he is apologizing to her for lousing up her session while at the same time asserting himself. An intensely proud and dignified man, Ellington did not like playing the role of second banana to anyone, and on the *Duke Ellington Songbook* it showed.

On her return from the fall 1956 JATP tour, Ella was booked into the upper-crust Mocambo on Hollywood's Sunset Strip in October. Immediately the effect of her best-selling Porter album was apparent: She outdrew Roberta Sherwood, who preceded her at the club, despite the fact that Walter Winchell conducted an almost unprecedented publicity campaign over the airwaves on Miss Sherwood's behalf. In contrast, Ella bowed into Charlie Morrison's "Mo" with a minimum of advance fanfare and played to turn-away business every night.

While at the Mocambo, Ella told John Tynan that on her JATP European tour in the early spring of that year she had borrowed Oscar Peterson's harmonica and had played it during a couple of her sets.[20] Mercifully, it was a direction she never subsequently pursued! At the Mocambo, Ella used a West Coast pickup group led by Barney Kessel on guitar and with Max Bennett on bass, Larry Bunker on drums, and Jimmy Rowles on piano. "I first worked with Ella when I played an engagement at a place called the Mocambo, a big, plush nightclub on Sunset Strip," said Rowles. "Then I played with her on some record dates during the sixties, and finally went to work with her in the eighties and was with her for about three years."

On January 14, 1957, Ella was in the recording studios for a singles session to cut "Hear My Heart" and "Hotta Chocolota," which are titles deserving of comment in view of Norman Granz's tirades about the quality of material during her Decca years. During the last week in January she appeared at New York's Paramount Theatre with Nat King Cole and Count Basie and his orchestra but was stricken in the middle of the Sunday show with acute abdominal pains. Rushed to the hospital, Ella underwent a seventy-five-minute operation for an abdominal abscess. It was a measure of just how important Ella had become to the success of the JATP tours that Granz canceled the whole March European tour because of her illness. But the outcry from European promoters was so great that the tour was rescheduled for mid-April despite all the expense and problems this involved. Ella, with that remarkable determination to overcome any medical ailment that periodically struck her down, was back in harness by the end of March when she guested on Ed Sullivan's TV show.

About this time Ella decided to relocate from her home in New York City to the West Coast. She was spending more time there than in New York, both recording and performing. It was a logical step to take, and the clincher was moving closer to Norman Granz, whose counsel she had come to rely on implicitly. Granz, very much a West Coaster, had never once considered relocating to New York, despite the success of JATP, and retained a suite of offices at 451 North Canon Drive, Beverly Hills. While recuperating from her operation, Ella bought a house at 3971 Hepburn Avenue, Los Angeles, and moved in right away. The large house, set back from the road, had a driveway on its left side and the front was dominated by three large bedroom windows. "I decorated the new house myself," she told Mary Okon shortly after she moved in. "I'd sure like to . . . spend more time with Ray, Jr. I don't think I'd ever give up the tours though. Being on the road gets rough sometimes, but I'd sure miss singing to the people."[21]

Fully recovered from her abdominal abscess, Ella joined Roy Eldridge, violinist Stuff Smith, the Oscar Peterson Trio with bassist Ray Brown and drummer Jo Jones, and her own accompanist, Don Abney, for a long JATP tour that took in Italy, Germany, Switzerland, Spain, France, Holland, and the Scandinavian countries. During their stopover in Stockholm, their concerts at the Konserthuset on April 28 and 29 were recorded by Swedish Radio. Ella's opening number was a cover version of the hit made popular by Guy Mitchell in the United States and by Tommy Steele in the United Kingdom, "You Got Me Singing the Blues," which no doubt raised a few eyebrows. Her set included "Angel Eyes," "Lullaby of Birdland," "Tenderly," "Do Nothin' Till You Hear from Me" from Duke's repertoire, and "April in Paris" from Basie's repertoire, complete with a scaled-down version of the Wild Bill Davis arrangement for voice and trio. Interestingly, she retained "I Can't Give You Anything but Love" in her set, along with impersonations of Louis Armstrong and Rose Murphy, something she had been doing for most of the fifties—it was a surefire crowd pleaser.

When Ella returned home in June, there was no letup in her hectic schedule as she faced a challenging engagement at New York's famed Copacabana. It was her most important booking since appearing at the Waldorf-Astoria, and a successful debut would open more doors to the country's exclusive night spots. The fact that she had not appeared there before had even caused speculation in the trade papers—"How come no Ella at the Copa?"—a cry that soon changed to "Now she's booked there, how will Ella do at the Copa?"

As the first black artist to headline at the club, she was walking into unknown territory. It was a fact emphasized by the Copa's caution in billing her second to a seasoned comedian. But the same set that had charmed audiences during her recent JATP tour worked equally well in the sumptuous surroundings of the Copacabana. At the end of Ella's run, the club's owner promised her top billing on her next appearance. Widely reported in the press, her success would play an important role in enabling Granz finally to persuade the huge Las Vegas clubs to open their doors to her.

In July, Ella appeared again at the Newport Jazz Festival. It was not such a happy engagement this time. Ella's backing trio of Don Abney on piano, Wendell Marshall on bass, and Jo Jones on drums did not play to her liking. "She showed obvious signs of displeasure with the musicians accompanying her," wrote Bill Coss. "Although it was true that the drummer was having time trouble, the real reason was a microphone that squealed once or twice and threw her into a nonprofessional panic."[22] In fact, Ella expressed her dissatisfaction by shaking her head and glaring at her accompanist. It was made good by a breakneck "Air Mail Special," finishing on a note so high it made the crowd wince. She rounded out the set with her Louis Armstrong imitation of "I Can't Give You Anything but Love," but it was a tribute that would shortly turn sour, amid some of the most extraordinary scenes ever witnessed at Newport.

The plan was for both singers to celebrate Louis Armstrong's birthday during his set, which followed Ella's. Mindful of his last appearance at Newport, organizer George Wein asked him to consider varying his repertoire and perhaps feature some numbers from his distinguished past, such as his old Hot Five and Hot Seven numbers, and maybe share a duet with Ella. This was not what Louis wanted. A cake had been prepared, however, and Ella, still with her gown on, was among the well-wishers who had assembled backstage to celebrate with him. When the moment came to wheel his cake on stage, he erupted in a rage. Boiling with anger, he abruptly played "The Star-Spangled Banner" and stormed off. Backstage he started shouting at the top of his voice for Wein, "that goddamn motherfucker. I'll kill that son of a bitch." He could be heard all over the park.

At this particular Newport Festival sensibilities were being offended left, right, and center. Norman Granz, delighted with a record deal that allowed him to record the whole concert, held a private party at the nearby Viking Hotel to celebrate. When asked why he had not invited the Lorillards, the patrons of the festival and the prime movers who had made it all possible, he said, "I don't care for society people, and I don't want them there for that reason."[23]

A week later Ella was appearing at Atlantic City with Lionel Hampton's orchestra and Louis again. In front of two thousand people a man leaped on the stage and caught Ella with a punch on the right side of her jaw, screaming, "You've got another man." Ella reeled back while police and musicians grabbed her attacker. He was later identified as William Edward Fitzgerald (no relation), aged twenty-nine, of Atlantic City, who had recently been treated for a mental disorder.

Tension was mounting in Ella's life. Despite her success, with its inevitable ups and downs, she had no one to share it with. She felt alone and vulnerable. In a revealing interview with Sidney Fields in the *New York Mirror*, she confided, "I want to get married again. I'm still looking. Everybody needs companionship." Fields concluded: "That's the missing note in her life. Ella is just lonely."[24]

CHAPTER TWELVE

1957–1959

Romance was an unfulfilled direction in her life. She had very normal feelings—even more normal feelings about desires—but it didn't pan out for her that way.

LOU LEVY

BY JULY 1957, Ella's career was reaching higher and higher. She was looking forward to two of the most prestigious one-nighters she had ever played: an Ella Fitzgerald Night at the Hollywood Bowl on July 20 and a fund-raiser for polio sufferers before royalty in Monte Carlo at the end of the month. On the surface it seemed as if she was riding the crest of a wave.

Then suddenly, on July 29, while en route to Monte Carlo, a Reuters dispatch from Oslo claimed that Ella had been secretly married to Thor Einar Larsen, a Norwegian. The *New York Post* picked up the story: "Ella Fitzgerald Secretly Wed to Norwegian. . . . Miss Fitzgerald, about 40, was reported staying in an Oslo suburb with Thor Einar Larsen. . . . The singer has confirmed the marriage. . . . Miss Fitzgerald's most recent appearance before she left on a European tour was at the Newport Jazz Festival early this month, the night Louis Armstrong was honored. There was no hint that the bouncy singer had married again."[1]

It was the beginning of a bizarre episode in Ella's life. Lonely, she had begun a transatlantic affair earlier in the year while touring Scandinavia with JATP. It seemed to have culminated in some sort of wish fulfillment; while in Oslo she and Larsen displayed a photo of them both which she had signed "To my beloved Thor, my love and my husband." Yet three days later she was in Copenhagen, Denmark, where she was interviewed by *Ekstra Bladet*: "The world-famous jazz singer Ella Fitzgerald was in Kastrup [International Airport] this morning en route from Oslo to Nice. It has been alleged she has been married for two years to Norwegian impresario Thor Larsen. [During

173

her stopover] she told *Ekstra Bladet* that she was not married to Thor Larsen, but it came with a big smile and joy in her eyes. 'It would be wonderful, but it's not possible for me to have married Thor Larsen two years ago because he was married to a Swedish girl. Now he is divorced from her.' Ella Fitzgerald gave the impression that the idea of marrying Thor Larsen would not be unwelcome. On the question of marrying in Nice, she said, 'That's what people might think, I suppose.' Thor Larsen is presently applying for a visa to visit the United States."[2]

It was almost as if Ella wanted the love songs she had sung for so long to become a reality. "There's a kind of naïveté about her," said pianist Paul Smith. "She's like a little girl. If she was unhappy, she'd pout like a little eight-year-old, which in a way she was. I always thought of her as a lady that never quite grew up. She always had that little-girl quality about her. Her feelings could be hurt very easily. She's a very tender lady. She loves kids and is kind of a kid herself, inside. She never had a romantic life. It was like *The Roman Spring of Mrs. Stone*, that film starring Vivien Leigh about an older lady who was in Italy going with the young studs. Ella was a lonely lady, and every once in a while one of these guys would come by and they'd have a live-in relationship for a short while, but I don't think she ever got married to any of them." Ella's naïveté permeated her relations with men. By no means a conventional beauty, she was flattered by the attentions of the opposite sex, which left her vulnerable to being taken advantage of. But perhaps even more naïvely, if she felt attracted to someone, she let it be known. "Ella had eyes," said Dan Morgenstern. "I once appeared with her on a television show. This is years ago down at WNYC which is a city television station. I was really surprised she'd go for something like that, but I imagine she was appearing at a club at the time and her press agent must have thought it was a good idea. There was this guy who had a jazz-oriented show we were on.

"Afterward Ella and I shared a cab going uptown. She was staying at the Americana. On the way she was getting very friendly. When we got there, it was, 'Why don't you come up? Come up to my room and have a drink.' She was warm for my form! Even if I hadn't said no, there was her press agent, or whoever, who would have definitely discouraged me. But I think it was very sweet. She was open and honest and very sweet."

On August 15, *Jet* magazine reported that Larsen had been convicted of stealing money from a young woman to whom he was engaged and had been sentenced to five months' hard labor in

Sweden. He was banned from entering the United States until January 1, 1963.[3]

Prior to leaving for her European sojourn, Ella had been very busy at work in the recording studios in Los Angeles, cutting *Ella and Louis Again* on July 23, a follow-up to the successful *Ella and Louis* which had reached number twelve on *Billboard*'s album charts. The following day she was involved in an all-day session with a string-heavy orchestra directed by Frank DeVol. On her return from the Monte Carlo benefit in aid of the polio fund, she completed *Ella and Louis Again* on August 13 and five days later began work on *Porgy and Bess*, once more with Louis Armstrong. As she immersed herself in her only true love, singing, her press office was working overtime to minimize any damage the ill-considered affair with Larsen might have had on her career: "Officials here discount [Ella and Larsen's] denials as being customary in the case of a secret marriage," said *Jet*, "and especially in this case where Miss Fitzgerald might have found it professionally unwise to be party to an interracial union."[4]

When Ella and Louis began work on *Porgy and Bess* on August 18, it was by far their most ambitious project together to date. Backed by an orchestra directed by Russell Garcia, it was a bold concept by producer Norman Granz. However, once again a gulf began to open between concept and execution. "I always got [Louis] under the worst possible conditions," said Granz. "We'd work for months to set everything up and then—like on the *Porgy and Bess* LP with Ella—at the last minute we'd find he'd have a concert somewhere that evening. Everything would have to be rushed."[5]

Granz, in recording highlights of Gershwin's opera, was forced to take a little poetic license, giving Ella all the female parts from the opera and Louis all the male, with the exception of "The Buzzard Song," which, although sung by Ella, was written for a male voice. Both Ella and Louis handle Gershwin's folk opera with great integrity. Ella, for example, is close to perfection in "I Wants to Stay Here." Armstrong's vocals are both inimitable and engaging, but his trumpet playing fares less well. Amid Garcia's glossy sheen his often heavy syncopations sound mannered.

At the end of September, Granz mounted what would be his last Jazz at the Philharmonic tour of America for some time. With Ella were the Oscar Peterson Trio, Roy Eldridge, Lester Young, Stan Getz, Coleman Hawkins, J. J. Johnson, Illinois Jacquet, Flip Phillips, Sonny Stitt, Jo Jones, and the Modern Jazz Quartet. At the end of

1957, Granz's gross for just one year was reputedly $10,000,000 from his concert and recording activities. Now a millionaire several times over, he gradually began to focus on semi-retirement after the 1957 tour. Having spent more and more time in Europe, he finally moved in 1959 to 13 rue Marignac, Geneva, Switzerland, where he assembled a greatly admired Picasso collection.

The bigger the Verve recording company became, the less interested Granz seemed to be in running it. "As the fortunes of Verve rose, the concert tours began to be less successful," he said. "The artists were the best, and they were paid accordingly. We always traveled first class, and expenses were getting high. Some performers were getting to be headliners. I couldn't afford Ella [for JATP] after 1957, even though I continued to be her manager. I still recorded a lot of jazz sessions, but after 1957 the subsidies came entirely from the sales of the commercial stuff on Verve."[6] By the end of 1960 he had accepted an offer for Verve of $2,750,000 from MGM, and by late summer 1961 the transition was complete, down to the integrating of offices. As he left he suggested to the president of MGM, Arnold Maxim, that he try to get Frank Sinatra and Ella into the recording studio together. It was a project he had attempted in the past without success, thwarted by Sinatra's complex contractual obligations to Capitol.

But Granz's interest in Oscar Peterson and Ella remained undiminished, and as far as Verve/MGM was concerned, he continued to supervise their recording careers. They were now international box office stars capable of generating considerable income in their own right. On tour, Ella and Oscar were presented as a unique double-header, with Oscar and his trio opening and Ella, introduced by Granz as "the star of our show," performing the second half.

As soon as the 1957 JATP tour was over, Ella immediately went into Paramount's Hollywood studios to film another cameo role, this time playing herself in the Robert Smith production of *St. Louis Blues*, directed by Allen Reisner. The film gave star billing to Nat King Cole as W. C. Handy, and other parts were played by Eartha Kitt, Pearl Bailey, Cab Calloway, and Mahalia Jackson. It was not a memorable film, although the music almost made up for the shortcomings in dialogue and plot. It opened at Loew's State in New York on April 11, 1958, to mixed reviews.

The 1957 JATP tour yielded the first of Ella's classic live albums for the Verve label, released in 1958. *Jazz at the Opera House* was the first live album to suggest—more so than her studio recordings—that the essence of Ella's art was as a no-frills, straight-ahead jazz singer plying her craft in front of her public. Her in-person recordings provide the most vital life study of Ella Fitzgerald the artist. "Music, singing is her life," said Paul Smith. "That's why she continued singing into the nineties. It was the time she came alive, when she went on that stage. The rest of her life, well, she didn't have any family to speak of. No matter how successful she was, and I don't think anyone could be more successful, she always had that little anxiety before she went on about whether people would like her. That was the challenge, whether people would like her. When we used to play the Fairmont Hotel in San Francisco, a very posh hotel, she broke all the records there. Yet every time we went there, she'd still look around the curtain and say, 'I hope they like me.' I'd say, 'How can they *not* like you!'"

Jazz at the Opera House was re-released on compact disc in 1986 and contained the complete Chicago Opera House performance of September 29, 1957, in stereo and Ella's performance at Shrine Auditorium in Los Angeles of October 7 in mono. Accompanied by the Oscar Peterson Trio, with Herb Ellis on guitar, Ray Brown on bass, plus Jo Jones on drums, it provides graphic evidence of Ella's remarkable consistency (several songs were recorded at both venues, and some vary in length by as little as one second). Moving from one song to the next with an almost compulsive eagerness, Ella, now forty years old, was reaching the peak of her abilities. "The best thing I can say about Ella is that she's an accompanist's dream," said Paul Smith. "Ella was always very consistent in what she did. She never speeded up when out of tempo. She never did anything that wasn't very musical. You knew where she was going to hold a note and where she was going; a lot of singers aren't like that. You have to bird-dog them; you don't know where the heck they're going. They're going to do it one way in rehearsal, and then they do it another way on stage. Ella was so musical she made it very easy to play for her. She wasn't always the same, but the general continuity was always very easy to follow. Usually, the worse the singer, the harder it is to play for them!"

In October 1957, Ella completed the *Ellington Songbook* and cut two albums of easy swingers with the Frank DeVol Orchestra, *Like Someone in Love* and *Hello Love* (completing the remaining tracks in March 1959). Another session with DeVol from November the following year produced *Ella Sings Sweet Songs for Swingers*, and these albums saw Granz finally looking over his shoulder at Sinatra's alternately moody or swinging Capitols. Borrowing the idea of a "concept" album, the Ella-DeVol collaborations, as the original liner notes of *Like Someone in Love* made clear, were aimed at "people in love," reminiscent of "our urban young people" of Sinatra's first Capitols. Although overshadowed by the *Songbook* cycle, they are a worthy second attraction and, like the *Songbooks*, are good songs well sung.

Ella was back on the road with her trio in November. However, Don Abney, weary of touring, had decided to hand in his notice in order to concentrate on freelancing on the New York scene. With characteristic directness, Norman Granz invited Lou Levy to replace him at a recording session on October 22, 1957. "I can remember it exactly," said Levy. "I was doing a record date at Capitol Towers in Hollywood with Stan Getz and Gerry Mulligan. It was called 'Getz and Mulligan in Hi-Fi.' At the time I was working with Peggy Lee, and Granz jokingly said—I think it was a serious joke—'How'd you like to work with a good singer!' That was the way he asked me, I remember that. I don't remember my answer exactly, but it worked out. I went with Ella for a couple of years, then I went back with Peggy Lee, then I went back with Ella again."

Ella began 1958 with a stay at Chicago's Chez Paree and was proudly announcing her forthcoming movie appearance by incorporating *St. Louis Blues* in her repertoire. The following month she was in Los Angeles' Moulin Rouge. Both places had no previous history of booking jazz artists, and in both cases disaster was predicted for Ella. Once again she won over her audiences against all expectations. "The thrush transacted all of her thirty minutes on stage from the stationary mike, making 'em keep their eyes on the voice," said one perceptive critic.[7]

In February, Benny Goodman was contracted for an hour-long TV special for the Texaco Company as part of their "Texaco Star Theater" series. The show, called "Swing into Spring," was given considerable publicity; a 45 rpm single was cut to promote it, and Goodman himself appeared in early April on Hy Gardner's TV talk show and Jack Paar's "Tonight Show," talking about his guests, which included Ella, Jo Stafford, Ray Eberle, and Harry James, plus an all-star big band assembled especially for the show.

The theme was a return to the halcyon days of the swing era. When it was screened on April 9, Ella, always a Goodman favorite, was the most highly featured guest, appearing in six numbers. "Swing into Spring" received rave reviews, and Goodman was contracted for an additional show, scheduled for televising in 1959. Unfortunately, Texaco did not renew their option after the second one, which included Ella and ex-Benny Goodman alumna Peggy Lee and was shown on April 10, 1959.

But perhaps Ella's most interesting television appearances were with Frank Sinatra. She guested with him on "The Frank Sinatra Show" on May 9, 1958, and in a "Timex Spectacular" on December 13, 1959, subtitled "Frank Sinatra: An Afternoon with Friends," that pointed the way to her featured role on Sinatra's now legendary telecast, "A Man and His Music." Sinatra's delight in performing with Ella is obvious in all their appearances together, as can be seen by his reaction to Ella's stunning version of "Body and Soul" in "A Man and His Music." It was a meeting of two greats of twentieth-century popular music, and the chemistry was perfect: two swinging singers, one modest, one extrovert, at the peak of their powers who together seemed to be able to move mountains.

It ought to have been a harbinger of great things to come. Instead, Ella Fitzgerald and Frank Sinatra were hardly ever heard together again. "I wasn't with them when they worked together," said Paul Smith, "but Ella loved working with him. Sinatra gave her his dressing room on that show ["A Man and His Music"] and couldn't do enough for her." But somehow that elusive album together remained tantalizingly beyond their grasp; once again complex contractual reasons were blamed by Granz, who, despite being a friend of Sinatra's, could not bring off this potentially great recording coup.

Over the years, the role of Norman Granz in Ella's professional life has been the subject of much speculation. "I would say that Norman Granz was almost like her Svengali," observed Paul Smith. Granz feels this frequently quoted statement is unfair. He saw his role as one of making life as easy as possible for Ella and presenting as good an image of her as he could, which was why, he said, God made personal managers. This often meant handling tasks the artist herself found difficult or simply did not want to do, from dealing with the press to hiring and firing musicians. He is quick to assert that none of his artists—Ella, Basie, Ellington, Peterson, and so on—were ever or even *could* ever be "forced" to do anything they did not want to do. But as a personal manager he felt he was entitled to express his views, particularly in matters of artistic direction.

"Musically, Norman had his dislikes. He made blanket statements. He once said he hated everything Stephen Sondheim ever wrote, which was a broad statement. If Ella ever did a Stephen Sondheim song, he would make an issue of it so she'd take it out of the show rather than have an argument with him," Paul Smith recalled.

Often Ella's accompanists would find Granz selecting the tunes for her sets. "He'd program everything," said Lou Levy. "He'd pick the songs and give me a list at the beginning of a concert if he happened to be there. She wouldn't pick them." However, Granz was very conscious of not wanting Ella to go stale. She had a demanding yearly worldwide schedule, and he had seen, to his frustration, how Ellington played much the same set night after night and the numbing effect it had on the band. He had even tried without success to persuade Ellington to include an occasional new number to keep the younger band members happy. Knowing Ella loved a musical challenge, he encouraged her to change her material to keep her fresh, even if it meant stepping on a few toes. "He would suddenly turn up in Europe and meet with her in her dressing room," Jimmy Rowles recalled. "Just before we went on he would wield his power, and it would turn out that he'd thrown out half the numbers we'd been coasting along with. We had a real nice show put together, and all of a sudden we'd have these numbers we had not played in six months. I didn't dig that."

He also appeared to be responsible for the hiring and firing of Ella's musicians. "Ella really didn't hire anybody in all the time she was out," said Paul Smith. "Everything went through Norman." In his complex role, Granz says he never made any changes unless he discussed them with Ella. Often he would consult Oscar Peterson for advice as to the best drummer or bassist or pianist for Ella's group. Although he appeared to be making the decisions, he points out that there was considerable behind-the-scenes consultation. Granz continually strived to get the best out of Ella, even into the 1980s when, to paraphrase the old gag, she could have sung the telephone directory and made it sound good. Certainly this resulted in tension from time to time over the years, but it was a creative tension on which Ella thrived.

In mid-April 1958, Ella and her trio plus the Oscar Peterson Trio combined in a Granz package for a series of concerts on the European circuit. On April 25 they appeared at the Teatro Sistina in Rome where, unknown to the musicians, Granz had arranged to have the concert recorded. This recording lay undiscovered in Polygram's vaults until Phil Schaap discovered it in 1987 and prepared it for release. When it was finally issued as *Ella in Rome: The Birthday*

Concert the following year, it topped the *Billboard* charts throughout the summer. "One of my goals is to find the best sound quality for reissue I can," said Schaap. "One of the things I discovered in the Polygram filing system is how oddly tapes get tucked away under wrong artists. One day I was working on a totally independent Oscar Peterson project, and there was a sealed box with a Rome postmark of April 28, 1958. Now the fact it was from Rome was interesting enough, but the thickness of the box was an eye-opener as it was a half-inch reel, molding tape. It doesn't exist all that often. It seemed to be a concert of Oscar Peterson, but then came a huge gap which I let run because somebody said Ella was going to come on for the second half of the concert.

"Then I had a problem getting the complete concert. There are 130,000 tapes in Polygram's vaults; they were color-coded, and thankfully I found nine boxes: Peterson on his sets, then Ella, all on three-track stereo, which was very rare for 1958. I eventually pieced everything together. I believe Norman Granz wanted to do a live album to follow up *Opera House*. The *Songbooks* were still going, and he'd done a lot of work on those, so now he wanted some live albums. He hired RCA in Rome to make the tapes, but when they sent them back to him, they were not mixed. So Norman put them to one side and forgot them . . . and thirty years later here's a classic Ella concert, a key document from her prime."

In all, Schaap discovered twenty-eight items taken from the afternoon and evening concerts. There were several duplications, and eventually eighteen tracks were prepared for release. It is a memorable album, not only because Ella is clearly in superb voice, but her backing trio of Lou Levy on piano, Max Bennett on bass, and Gus Johnson on drums had become a superbly cohesive unit. Bennett and Levy had combined the previous year on Levy's immaculate trio album *Lou Levy: A Most Musical Fella* (RCA), and their rapport with Johnson was such that they would all record together in 1958 as the Lou Levy Trio for Jubilee Records.

"I didn't even know they recorded *Ella in Rome*, I really didn't," said Levy. "When they put it out and I got a copy of the record, I thought, 'God! we were swinging our cans off.' It was just great! So much spirit and drive on it. You could never get it if you went into a studio. If you tried for it in the studio, it would be one chance in a million. We were on tour; you do it every night, and you're in great shape. You're like a sporting team—the more you play, the better it gets. And that was true of our group with Ella. It just got to be at fever pitch. It was great, Ella's great. And since we didn't know it was being recorded, we didn't even think about anything, we just played!"

More than any other album of this period, *Ella in Rome* defines her art; songs by the great songwriters such as Gershwin, Richard Rodgers, Cole Porter, her lighthearted "I Can't Give You Anything but Love" with her impersonations of Louis Armstrong and Rose Murphy, the scat features "The Lady Is a Tramp," "Stompin' at the Savoy," numbers taken from the forthcoming *Ellington Songbook*, and, to announce her appearance on celluloid, a version of "St. Louis Blues" complete with a scat interlude ("People are wondering what I'm singing. Believe it or not it's still 'St. Louis Blues'"). The old W. C. Handy song is her first number, yet it's a tour de force, the sort of thing a lesser singer might use to climax a set. Ella launches into the song cold and within seconds she is breaking it up.

It is tempting to put the Rome version of "I Loves You Porgy" among the very best Ella Fitzgerald on record. It is a fetching and sympathetic performance and a striking example of her having "internalized" a song, of having got inside a song's meaning, something she was not normally noted for doing. "I've seen her mesmerize people night after night," said Lou Levy, "huge audiences, eighteen thousand people, or whatever the size of the place was. What they heard if they closed their eyes was a fantastic singer; what they saw was a lady having a wonderful time." Perhaps more than any of her live albums, *Ella in Rome* is a celebration of the joy of music-making, with Ella's voice the perfect instrument to express that joy.

The troupe continued on their busy European schedule, and when they arrived in England for a fifteen-day tour, British customs attempted to prove a correlation between jazz musicians and drugs. After a long and protracted search they were mortified that there was no evidence to support their theory. Ray Brown had been stripped, Ella's baggage had been scrutinized and vitamin pills taken away for analysis, while a tube of toothpaste belonging to Norman Granz was solemnly split open during the hunt. The search took so long that a scheduled TV interview had to be canceled. "Search by Customs Makes Ella Fume," announced the *New York Post*. "'I have never been so socially insulted in my life, and I have done some traveling,'" commented Ella bitterly.[8]

In July 1958, Ella and Duke Ellington headlined for the first time together at Carnegie Hall to launch the *Ellington Songbook;* the *New York Times* was not impressed. However, it marked the beginning of an association between Granz and Ellington that would link the careers of Ella and the Duke over the next few years. Granz had begun representing the Ellington band as well: "It makes a lot of difference when the man doing the talking for you is a millionaire," said Ellington.[9]

In June, Ella had been headlining at Manhattan's brassy Copacabana, pitting her voice against six hundred nightclub meals and winning. It was apparent to all that she had lost weight. "I've lost thirty-two pounds," she said, "and I've been so complimented, I'm determined to lose ten more."[10] It never happened. Ella's nervous disposition saw to that.

Meanwhile, the *Songbook* cycle continued unabated. March had seen the completion of the Irving Berlin set with Paul Weston's orchestra. "Paul Weston had a set orchestra that he used on all his dates," said Paul Smith. "I did all Weston's dates at that time in the fifties, and Billy May's. Paul wanted his rhythm section to fit his style—kind of cool and polite, sophisticated commercial jazz. But when he was doing his thing with Ella, I suggested he use a cooking rhythm section, mainly the Billy May guys I also worked with—Alvin Stoller on drums, Joe Mondragon on bass, and Al Hendrickson on guitar—because that bland rhythm section would not serve Ella well. He did that, and I think the Berlin set is one of the better ones of the bunch."

Berlin's sometimes tortuous, voice-trapping lyric mountains ("I want to peep through the deep, tangled wild wood/Counting sheep 'til I sleep like a child would") are complemented by Weston's uncomplicated arrangements. If any set highlights Ella's masterful diction, this is it. The National Academy of Recording Arts and Sciences thought so, too, and in their 1958 awards Ella won a Gramophone Award (Grammy) for Best Vocal Performance—Female. She also won the Best Jazz Performance—Individual category for the *Duke Ellington Songbook*. But there again she was bound to. The other contenders for best "jazz" performance were Matty Mattock, *Dixieland Story*; Jonah Jones, *Baubles, Bangles, and Beads* and *Jumpin' with Jonah*; and George Shearing, *Burnished Brass*.

In November 1958, Granz tried yet another approach in recording Ella, this time combining her with Marty Paich's Dek-Tette. In 1956, Mel Tormé's "Lulu's Back in Town" caused a sensation among musicians as Paich and Tormé combined in a superb integration of voice and a small jazz ensemble. The Ella-Paich union fares less well; even Tormé had difficulty repeating the magic on *Sings Fred Astaire* and

Prelude to a Kiss prior to mounting a higher peak with *Swings Shubert Alley*. Paich and Tormé made the deceptively difficult sound deceptively easy, a unique combination of a singer with ideas and an arranger with imagination.

The Ella-Paich union was a more one-sided affair that lacked the thrill of discovery and musical wit Tormé brought to his performances. This was largely due to the choice of material—songs associated with the big bands. Unlike a song by, say, Cole Porter or Irving Berlin, which has an independent existence of its own, the big band material seems too strongly associated with a single, individual, and often memorable performance of it, such as Roy Eldridge in "Little Jazz" or "Knock Me a Kiss," Bon Bon on "720 in the Books," and Eddie Sauter's masterful arrangement for Benny Goodman of "Moonlight on the Ganges." In *Ella Swings Lightly* it became impossible to disentangle the song from the original recording of it, unlike the *Songbook* material where no single performance seems able to exhaust the meaning. The "non-big-band" tracks fare far better; for example, "Just You, Just Me" and "Little White Lies" help redeem an album that is weak in concept rather than execution.

In 1959, the *Songbooks* reached their high-water mark with the five-album Gershwin set under the musical directorship of Nelson Riddle. Lou Levy was the pianist. "I remember going in there. They were spread over several weeks doing those albums," he said. "Ella would come in and sing with her hand over her ear in that little isolation booth . . . and we would just crank them out, one after another. Funny thing, they never sounded as if they were cranked out. Riddle did a fantastic job. We actually did them pretty rapidly for the quality of music.

"We'd run through the arrangements to make sure there were no bad notes in them, then Ella would try them out. I don't ever remember having gone over the numbers at her home or anything, but it seemed to me she was rather well prepared. Ella could read music, not like a symphonic musician reads, she had her own little system, but she could work it out, and that was enough. Learn the melody line and the lyrics, and we were there in the booth with her, and that was it. She never had an intonation problem in her life, not one note.

"We got them out fast, which we had to do. She did them over a reasonably short period of time. There were a lot of songs on the Gershwin set—five LPs takes a lot of songs. There must have been fifty or sixty songs including that little EP that went with the set that had a couple of instrumental things on it, a prelude by Gershwin that

Nelson orchestrated which she didn't sing on. Just cranking them out. We didn't do a lot of takes because of mistakes; there were hardly any, the musicians were all great.

"I always loved Nelson because he had an identity. It showed up in Frank Sinatra's records and on Ella's, too. But I think we all identify Frank Sinatra and Nelson, and rightfully so. Nelson had a dry way about him but a great wit; he was a very intelligent guy. Very patient. A funny sort of conductor with a corky way of conducting. Not the usual studied way, but he got his point across."

The Gershwin set went to the *Billboard* charts immediately after it was released, a major feat for a five-LP set. "The Gershwin box . . . remains a matchless feat of intelligent, articulate consistency," wrote critic Gary Giddins in 1983. "[Ella] never wrings a false emotion, and although she isn't a profound interpreter of lyrics either, she never subverts their meaning."[11] The *George and Ira Gershwin Songbook* has often been hailed as Ella's towering achievement, praised for its scale, its ambition, or both. In fact it was not. Riddle's stamp of individuality was less evident on the Gershwin set than it was on his subsequent collaborations with Ella, such as *Ella Swings Gently with Nelson* and *Ella Swings Brightly with Nelson*. And as with the other *Songbooks*, the necessity of "cranking out" the songs—the conditions under which all the *Songbooks* were recorded—made it impossible to internalize all or even most of the material at hand. The consequent effect in certain songs was to open a gulf between singer and material.

Yet a great deal of Ella's Verve material was recorded like this. As in her Decca work, she rarely had more than a passing acquaintance with many—indeed most—of the songs in the *Songbook* cycles until she walked into the recording studio. Such circumstances could only serve to increase her emotional distance from the lyricist's intentions.

With the subsequent *Harold Arlen Songbook*, a composer whose leanings toward jazz were perhaps stronger even than Gershwin's, it is often only in the familiar tunes, such as "Blues in the Night" and "That Old Black Magic," that Ella presents a memorable performance. Here she is helped by Billy May's arrangement, which sounds less in awe of the occasion than Nelson Riddle's. However, on other Arlen songs, as Max Harrison has pointed out, Ella seems to misunderstand their meaning completely. "I'm afraid Miss Fitzgerald does have this tendency to lapse into an uncommunicative mode of singing when she is not quite sure what to do with a number."[12]

* * *

185

In the fall of 1958, Granz repeated his Oscar-Ella package for North American audiences, adding the fine trumpeter Roy Eldridge to Ella's trio, something he would do from time to time over the next seven years. Eldridge was limited to a mute all night, improvising obbligatos behind Ella, and on this tour was given two numbers, "I Can't Get Started" and a riff number based on the "I Got Rhythm" changes, to show off his prowess. In 1959, Ray Bryant took over the piano chair for three months. "Just myself, Wilfred Middlebrooks, and Gus Johnson. Sometimes Roy would join us. During that time I realized she was one of the greatest singers of all time, but human, too. She got very nervous before a show," he recalled. When Bryant left, guitarist Herb Ellis, who had left the Oscar Peterson Trio because of a drink problem, came in as leader of the group. Since leaving Peterson, Ellis had straightened himself out through the help of Alcoholics Anonymous, and Granz was keen to help him rehabilitate himself. "We did a Bell Television show with Gus Johnson and Wilfred Middlebrooks. I was the leader and the only white guy in the group," said Ellis. "So they told Norman Granz, 'Now we will want to use another guitar player,' and Norman said, 'What?' And he found out the reason."[13]

The reason was that the Bell Telephone executives did not want to have a white and a black on camera at the same time. "Norman found this out and said not only would I not do it for that reason, but they had to use me because I was the leader. Well, they diffused the picture with Vaseline on the lens so you couldn't tell who was back there. Norman took out a two-page ad in *Variety* about it, and he wiped them out."[14]

Granz was incensed by the incident. Throughout his life, he remained unequivocal in his abhorrence of racial injustice. There is no question that his advertisement in *Variety* and the crucial issues it raised had an important effect on how NBC handled its sponsored programs in the future:

> I manage Ella Fitzgerald. A few months ago I was approached by the representatives of Henry Jaffe, who packages a show called "The Bell Telephone Hour." I was asked if Ella Fitzgerald could appear on that show's "Tribute to Gershwin," and of course I readily assented. . . . I was asked if I would approve of Teddy Wilson's Trio appearing with Ella Fitzgerald, and I agreed to that.
>
> At that meeting I was told by Barry Wood about the difficulties he had with integrating Negro and white artists on this show and I

expressed my extreme bitterness about this policy, but I privately thought this question could be met if it arose again. I felt rather than pulling Ella off the show, which would accomplish nothing, it might be better to have Ella on the show and fight the problem if and when it came up again.

About a week before the show began its rehearsals, I was called by Al Lapin, the contractor for the show, and was asked if I would approve of Ella's bassist and drummer appearing with Teddy Wilson in place of the two regular members of Wilson's trio. When I agreed to this, I also suggested that Teddy could use Ella's guitarist because she had him as a regular accompanist. The contractor said it wouldn't be necessary because they intended to use only a trio consisting of Teddy Wilson plus the two aforementioned men. I said, "Well, that's all right, but in any case when the Wilson Trio backs Ella, it will have to be a quartet because the guitarist must appear with Ella." He said he would get back to me.

An hour later I received a call from Barry Wood, the producer, and his opening statement was, "If you insist on using the guitarist, okay, but it will have to be a Negro guitarist instead of a white one. . . ." I asked Wood why it was necessary, and he said the sponsor, the Bell Telephone Company, never allows a mixed group to be on its show. I can't for the life of me, even as a practical matter, understand why the Bell Telephone Company doesn't want a mixed group consisting of Negro and white artists to appear on its television show because I'm positive no person in the South is sufficiently prejudiced to take his telephone out because he saw a nonsegregated group on a TV show under the sponsorship of Bell.

I pointed out to Barry Wood that there was a principle involved about which I felt very strongly, and under no conditions would I drop the white guitarist. We argued for a while, and finally Wood said that though he was sympathetic to my point of view, nevertheless he would have to insist the white guitarist not be used because of sponsorship pressure. I said that if that was so, I would pull Ella off the show, and after further argument he finally consented to the white guitarist. Incidentally, he told me at the time that though I would win my point about using a mixed group, they would not be on camera together at any time. As all of you know who saw the show, this was true, and there remained only Ella Fitzgerald with Teddy Wilson and not with a nonsegregated group of accompanists playing with her. . . .

I submit that [NBC-TV] concern itself with the principles of human rights and human dignities [rather] than the fixing of quiz shows. They must concern themselves with sponsors' policies which foster racial prejudice—the worst kind of prejudice in America. It isn't even a question, as is often put, of the eyes of the world upon us; it's simply respect for our fellow men. . . .[15]

The letter was signed Norman Granz.

CHAPTER THIRTEEN

1960–1966

There is no guile about Ella. She is a large woman who per-
forms so unaffectedly and straightforwardly that she is
transformed into a little girl. A beautiful little girl. She has
the dignity of innocence and she sings innocently, her
roots solidly in jazz, the kind of happy, haunting jazz that
has almost been frozen to death by the cool young men.

HERB CAEN[1]

TWO OF ELLA'S FINEST ALBUMS came from 1960. One, *Mack the Knife:
Ella in Berlin*, became her best-known album outside the *Songbooks;*
the other, *Let No Man Write My Epitaph*, remains the least known.
Both dispensed with lavish orchestral trappings and allowed her intu-
itive, inventive spirit to roam. No longer boxed in by the arranger's
pen, she blossomed. While the *Songbooks*, with their frequent string-
laden accompaniments, defined Ella to a broad middle-of-the-road
market, in live performance she remained a straight-ahead, no-frills
jazz singer.

Yet it was the popularity of the *Songbooks* that enabled Ella to out-
grow the JATP, with a following that went beyond audiences usually
associated with jazz. "They will dress to the hilt and attend Ella's
opening night in this hotel room or that nightclub," observed Mel
Tormé. "Not because they understand or appreciate her superlative
singing or choice of material, but because it is an 'event,' a social happening, a chance to be seen and admired by peers."[2]

It had taken Norman Granz ten years to move Ella out of the jazz
clubs and into America's top night spots and concert halls. His next
step was to move her on to the world stage. Organizing her touring
schedules from Geneva, he increased her European touring apprecia-
bly. "The first time I went on the road with Ella was in 1960 for just
six months," said pianist Paul Smith. "I had worked the record dates,
and Norman liked the way I played, so I took a leave of absence from

my staff job at NBC. We did a European tour early in the year. In Germany, Norman had them record us. We recorded in Hamburg, Stuttgart, six or eight cities in all, just our usual set. But when we opened in Berlin, it was Ella's version of 'Mack the Knife,' the first time we played it in the Deutschlandhalle, that made the album *Ella in Berlin*, and that was the version Norman put out.

"It was the first version and the best, where she got kind of loused up with the lyrics, which was the charm of the thing. She could always ad lib her way out of anything, and that was the hook that got that record off the ground! 'Mack' was probably the biggest song she had from 1960 when we recorded it, and from then on it was in every show, along with hits like 'A-Tisket,' 'How High the Moon,' and so on."

In August 1960, Granz released a single of "Mack the Knife" that went on the charts for fourteen weeks, peaking at number twenty-seven. It ensured that *Mack the Knife: Ella in Berlin* became one of Ella's most enduring albums, winning two Grammys, one for Best Vocal Performance—Female (Single or Track) for "Mack the Knife" and the other for Best Vocal Performance Album—Female. From the opening bars of "That Old Black Magic," both Ella and her group— Paul Smith on piano, Jim Hall on guitar, Wilfred Middlebrooks on bass, and Gus Johnson on drums—swing with an eloquent and powerful dynamism that is sustained throughout the album. The twelve thousand fans who filled the Deutschlandhalle gave Ella a charge that could never be reproduced in the recording studio.

On "Gone with the Wind," for example, Ella constantly surprises with a subtle rhythmic twist or a sly variation in the melody line. Using melismata, slides, and swoops, the song hardly ever falls precisely as written, either rhythmically or melodically. It is a fascinating miniature of her art, almost a commonplace throwaway, yet it was something she tossed to her fans twice nightly.

Smith, a massively accomplished pianist who at the time was perhaps the studio musician most in demand on the West Coast, playing over three hundred sessions a year, sustains the momentum by cuing each tune on the piano. Just before "Lorelei" he breaks Ella up by teasing her about the speed at which she sings the verse—a standing joke among most musicians she worked with—by playing it at an elaborately fast tempo. "You sure had to know verses with Ella," recalled Lou Levy. "There were a lot of verses, and she tore through them! Take the verse for 'Just One of Those Things.' [Lou Levy gave an example by singing it at a fast tempo.] There are chords going by like bang, bang, bang, so you had to be on your toes! She was a rapid mover!"

Whether it was her touching version of "Misty," the way she some-how made "Summertime" appear fresh and new, or her heartfelt ver-sion of "The Man I Love," there was a rhythmic intensity that was just as apparent on slow tempos as on fast. She could swing with an abandon that very few *instrumentalists*, let alone other vocalists, in jazz could match, as in "How High the Moon" when she demon-strates her remarkable creative freedom within form. She had impec-cable voice control and infallible intonation that was the envy of every singer who heard her. But more than that, there was a joy that readily communicated itself. On "Lorelei" when she acts the sexy vamp, you know that with Ella it is going to be safe sex, and when she covers "Mack the Knife," a superb example of her thinking on her feet when she forgets the lyrics, incidentally, she does not miss the opportunity to do her impression of Louis, for years a proven crowd-pleaser. Such performances gave the audiences an indefinable "feel good" factor that added significantly to her in-person charm, and it can still be felt, decades later, on compact disc.

"Ella was a stunning performer," recalled Jim Hall. "She's very careful about the sequence of tunes and organizing a set of music. I learned a lot from her. I used to tune up to her. If it was a choice between her and the piano, I would go for her! Ella was awfully good musically, but we also had a lot of fun. The most relaxed I was with her was on the trains and on the buses. A lot of times I would just accompany her on guitar, just screwing around; that was fun. My first job was in Minneapolis, I think, and then we went to Europe, and we recorded the *Ella in Berlin* album, which I was on. Later, we went to South America on tour."

Ella's best live recordings, of which *Ella in Berlin* was certainly one, reveal the real Ella, bringing pleasure to others by bringing plea-sure to herself. But the creative sparks that flew in front of an audi-ence were rarely ignited in the studio. There is a distinction to be made here between the brilliantly gifted singer, a child of the record-ing studios since 1935, able to sing virtually anything on demand in the recording booth with what Whitney Balliett once described as a kind of "blank perfection," and the singer who gave herself so com-pletely to her audiences and found redemption in return.

Yet on very rare occasions the joy that only seemed to surface in live performance was harnessed, controlled, and brought into the recording studio. Then Ella achieved a level of performance that became a benchmark of excellence, widely acknowledged among her peers, from Sinatra to Crosby to Sarah Vaughan to Betty Carter. This union between singer and song was realized in the recording studio in *Ella Sings Gershwin* with Ellis Larkins, and it happened again with *Let No Man Write My Epitaph*.

Early in 1960, Ella was featured in a minor role for Columbia Pictures in the motion picture *Let No Man Write My Epitaph*. Starring James Darren, Shelley Winters, Burl Ives, and Jean Seberg, the film examined the social relationships of a group of characters on the fringes of society. A somber melodrama set in the slums of Chicago in the 1950s, the screenplay was based on a novel by Willard Motley. Ella played a tired junkie, and if her height-weight ratio suggested she had been miscast, she did get to sing "Reach for Tomorrow." To capitalize on her film role, Granz decided to issue an album of songs using the name of the film as a sales gimmick. When the film was released in November 1960, it bombed, and the album sank with it.

"It was finally re-released in 1991 on CD as *The Intimate Ella*," said Paul Smith. "We did it together, just her and piano. I would advise any singer to listen to that and see how *easy* she sang. She didn't make a lot of work out of it, she sang easily. She loved what she was doing, and she sang well. The average singer would have a helluva time making those songs sound good: 'Melancholy Baby,' 'September Song,' 'Who's Sorry Now?,' 'I Can't Give You Anything but Love, Baby,' 'Angel Eyes.'

"She sang only one, maybe two songs on the soundtrack of the film. At the time, Norman had the idea of making something of the publicity for *Let No Man Write My Epitaph*. We redid the one or two things she sang, and we just picked tunes, maybe twelve, to make up the album. It's one of the few albums she did where nobody got in her way. There wasn't a horn playing for sixteen bars or Oscar playing a solo between every chorus or 'Sweets' Edison or Roy Eldridge sharing the limelight. The thing was she just loved to sing ballads, and when she really got into that groove, she enjoyed it more than the 'up' tunes."

Cut on April 14 and 19, 1960, in Los Angeles, the album was particularly well recorded, and this adds significantly to its timelessness. Smith's accompaniment is faultless; he is supportive and ever sensitive to the needs of the singer. He never gets in Ella's way with the superfluous or superficial, yet he has the technique and the imagination to complement rather than complicate. Ella's singing, with its precise enunciation, perfect breath control that allowed her to sing low and high notes with equal ease in an 'intimate' *sotto voce*, subtle use of tonal inflection, and tasteful use of vibrato, especially of terminal vibrato, marks these performances as among her very best.

Although several tunes were in her current repertoire and had been recorded in live performance, such as "Angel Eyes," "Misty," and a burlesque version of "I Can't Give You Anything but Love," the *Epitaph* versions had a haunting purity, almost as if they had been scrubbed clean of the emotional thumbprints that she, or any other singer, might have left. As she holds each song up to the light, it gleams anew, as if being sung for the first time. "This isn't the Ella of the concert stage or of the marathon show-tune performances," wrote Max Jones in 1960, "but a rather different singer, closely involved with the slightly brooding spirit of the material. . . . Ella is not the most emotional of jazz singers, but this time she has got inside the songs in her own thoughtful, if untroubled fashion."[3]

In mid-1960 pianist Lou Levy rejoined Ella's backing group along with Herb Ellis. Together with Wilfred Middlebrooks and Gus Johnson they jelled into a formidable unit. Their touring schedule was exhausting, but as Levy pointed out, "I was still in my late twenties, so I really enjoyed it—a different city every day, wonderful hotels, wonderful meals, another experience, another sight. I suppose it was tough, but I didn't notice much. It was all new."

On January 20, 1961, Ella flew back from Australia to Washington, D.C., to sing for just five minutes. The occasion was President John F. Kennedy's Inaugural Gala held at the National Guard Armory. Ella had been invited to perform by Frank Sinatra, who was in charge of organizing the festivities. The gala was both to celebrate Kennedy's win and to recoup the depleted coffers of the Democratic Party, which had been left with a $4,000,000 deficit following the election campaign. The Gala raised a staggering $1,500,000. Not only had Sinatra succeeded in persuading Ella to fly in from Australia, but he also got Gene Kelly to come from Switzerland and Sidney Poitier from France. He obtained the release of Ethel Merman from *Gypsy* for one night and managed to close another Broadway show, *Becket*, for the evening to free Anthony Quinn and Sir Laurence Olivier. Other guests included Leonard Bernstein, Bette Davis, Nat King Cole, Jimmy Durante, Juliet Prowse, Mahalia Jackson, Harry Belafonte, Milton Berle, Helen Traubel, and the Nelson Riddle Orchestra. "Tonight we saw excellence," said President Kennedy.

In February, Ella was back in Europe for the eighth consecutive JATP tour and on the 11th appeared once more at the Deutschlandhalle. "Last year when we played our opening concert in Berlin, we were very lucky to have one of the biggest albums that the star of our show has ever had, and it seemed appropriate we called the concert 'Ella Returns To Berlin,'" said Norman Granz at the beginning of the concert. Released in 1991 for the first time, *Ella Returns to Berlin* numbers among her finest live performances on record. Her complete show is included, with encores and a jam session with the Oscar Peterson Trio.

Once again this previously unreleased material was prepared for reissue by Phil Schaap. "Finding *Ella in Rome* was much harder and was a unique and true find, and created interest with Polygram to issue more of the same. There were two copies of the *Berlin* concert; neither of them was the original tape, and I was underwhelmed with the sound quality of both at first. But by using both copies I was able to restore the concert for release. I would guess it was a radio recording. European radio was almost always covering such events, and Granz probably said it was a professional recording, it sounds okay, let's go with it. Clearly he does have the idea in mind, from his introductory remarks, to issue it. It probably wasn't released at the time because Verve was in transition. The MGM people had taken over, and their priorities were not Norman's priorities. It probably just got forgotten."

Levy's quartet provides Ella with a superb, swinging backing and locks into an impressive groove that is sustained throughout the show. It was a night when everything seemed to click; as in *Ella in Rome* and *Ella in Berlin*, these performances, with her jazz credentials uppermost, reveal the side of Ella that has remained for too long in the shadow of her *Songbook* persona.

"I think it was her honesty that got across to the audience," said Levy. "She had a wonderful *sound*, she swung real hard. She's probably the hardest-swinging singer I've ever heard, and I think most people agree on this. The crowd was tremendously enthusiastic, and being Ella, she got a real lift from them. The group was very tight; the program was very tight. Everything was on a sure footing. There was never any 'ifs, ands, or buts'; everything swung real hard. And she brought the house down. She enjoyed it, and watching her night after night, I'm sure she reveled in it. She'd be very shy and so on, but how could you not like it when the whole world is at your feet, even if you are blushing!"

Her February 1961 tour, in tandem with the Oscar Peterson Trio, was the most extensive to date. They filled Belgrade's largest music hall for a concert that was televised all over Yugoslavia, then went on to Greece, Israel ("We did a concert in Tel Aviv for the army and then one for the citizens," said Levy), Turkey, and Iran. On her return, with scarcely a break, Ella played at Basin Street East in New York until the end of April. When she returned to the West Coast in May, she was booked into Hollywood's Crescendo, where Granz again recorded her live.

Contrary to the album liner notes of *Ella in Hollywood*, there had been no change in personnel. It is not Jim Hall on guitar but Herb Ellis. "That was a mistake," said Lou Levy. "These things happen occasionally. I don't know how they slip by, but I don't ever recall working with Jim Hall with Ella. By then we'd played together a lot and really had it together. So it was fun doing that album. We were just playing our library; we didn't program it for the record. We played an opener and did our regular set, sort of an 'up' program.

"As good as Ella is in the studios, she's far better in front of an audience. She's a real live, improvising-type performer, much more than any other singer I've worked with. It's more programmed with everybody else—which can be great, too—but with Ella it's more like the jam session thing. Nothing very formal: Play the intro and you're in! You don't need a conductor. Straight in and enjoy the ride!"

Levy had begun to write arrangements for the group, and the album kicks off with his arrangement of "This Could Be the Start of Something Big" and goes on to include three numbers Ella had recorded earlier—and better—in Berlin. However, the album is memorable for her two scat features: "Take the 'A' Train" and "Air Mail Special." Martin Williams has called "'A' Train" "an astonishing, extended tour de force of scat."[4] In it Ella weaves extracts of Ray Nance's trumpet solo taken from the original Ellington recording of the tune with the assimilated wisdom of almost thirty years of trading choruses with some of the finest instrumentalists in jazz. Ideas, musical motifs, are developed as logically and cohesively as by any of the great improvisers with whom she had shared the stage. As she reaches the climax of her "solo," she returns to the very beginning of her career to recall the shouting riffs of the big bands that used to have people crawling up the walls with excitement.

Also included was another version of "Mr. Paganini." "She enjoyed singing it," said Levy. "It was sort of a challenge. It goes in and out of tempo so much; it's like a little symphony on its own, it's not just straight ahead. She seemed to enjoy the stop-go pattern to it. It kept constantly going back to the verse, then swing, the verse, and a chorus, and so on. But to me 'Mr. Paganini' was like Al Jolson singing 'Swanee' or something!"

The following month Granz brought Ella and her quartet into the recording studios for one of the few occasions in her career when she cut a "non-live" album with her regular working group. "That was an album I did with her that I was particularly proud of," said Lou Levy. "*Clap Hands, Here Comes Charlie* was my assignment. Norman said to me, 'Here's a list of songs. You and Ella pick out the ones you want to do, you make up the arrangements, and we'll put an album out.' I think it turned out really good. Like anyone in jazz, Ella usually sounded best when it wasn't too complicated around her."

Released in 1962, the album was awarded four stars in *Down Beat* and this perceptive review:

> Amid the flood of Fitzgerald albums, few stand as superior representations of the singer as a jazz interpreter. This set is one of her best. Too often her albums bear the sausage-factory stamp; they appear to grind on and on, and as a consequence this superlative artist—who never turns in a musically bad performance—occasionally conveys a slick superficiality and a blandness that is admittedly never too hard to take. Thanks to the superb rhythm section and Levy's sensitivity as accompanist, this session is light, airy, and swinging all the way. It is a distinct pleasure to hear Miss Fitzgerald groove with only four men rather than those ponderous orchestras with which she is so often encumbered.[5]

From the purely jazz point of view, Ella's albums with Paul Smith and Lou Levy represent the high watermark of her career on record. Both provided her with that exciting, driving style of accompaniment that seemed to make her voice take wing. And while she got equally fine support from Tommy Flanagan in the late 1960s and 1970s, her voice was by then beginning to slide into the inevitable decline that comes with advancing years.

With Smith and Levy she really seemed to enjoy what she heard and responded with some of her most expansive and creative performances on record. Her voice, now a mature instrument (compare it with her concert recordings in Japan in 1953, for example) was at the peak of its form, perfectly rounded, with a secure, centered tone, honed night after night with scarcely a break since 1935. As the years progressed, the strain would gradually begin to tell, but here and now Ella was at her best.

If Ella's voice was as good as it was ever going to be, then so, too, was the repertoire she chose to sing during these years. This is another factor that lifts the Smith-Levy albums to the forefront of her huge discography. In later years she would importune inappropriate pop songs as she became awed, like most jazz musicians at the time, with the rise of pop and rock, feeling compelled to include up to two or three numbers in every set from the modern lexicon "for the people." As she tired of singing "those same old songs," she cast around for anything that caught her ear: Latin American numbers, soap opera signature tunes, and, at one time, the theme for an advertisement for raisins.

The numbers she was using in live performance were some of the best from Tin Pan Alley and jazz that, at this point in her career, she interpreted with zeal. It was only in later years that she began to feel she had exhausted their meaning and looked for alternatives. In the late 1950s and early 1960s there was a thrill of discovery every time she sang: The singer, her songs, and her accompanists were in perfect balance.

In 1961, Ella began another affair. "She was hanging out with a guy from a Danish airline—a real young, blond, rosy-cheeked, blue-eyed Dane. He was from Copenhagen," said Lou Levy. On August 16, *Ekstra Bladet* and *Berlingske Tidende* reported Ella was in Copenhagen. "Ella Fitzgerald will stay in Denmark," said *Berlingske Tidende*. "She is seeking a flat, incognito."[6] Eleven days later the paper confirmed the story:

ELLA LIVES BY THE SEA! Ella Fitzgerald has gotten a flat in Copenhagen, and Norman Granz is often seen in town. We had Oscar Pettiford and we had [Eric] Dolphy for some time, and now we have Ella Fitzgerald in our midst. Ella has a flat in Copenhagen by the sea, and this will be her home, as much as touring people ever have a home. She took over the tenancy during the last few days and will shortly be moving in after staying several weeks at the Hotel Tre Falke. The great singer knows that Denmark is not the United States or Paris. Here is the peace and quiet she says she is looking for. She will not talk of future plans, however, but refers us to Norman Granz who is also in town. "Ella loves Denmark, and it is her intention to stay here between her many tours," says Granz.[7]

While looking for a suitable house, Ella jetted back to Forest Hills, New York, for a concert before an audience of eleven thousand at the West Side Tennis Club on August 6. "There's such a natural drive in her voice," said George T. Simon, "such an assured sense of swing that she swept all before her, while receiving, of course, the usual noble assistance from . . . tasteful pianist Lou Levy."[8] She was back in Copenhagen for the 25th, when she cut a couple of tracks with a Danish rhythm section plus Jimmy Woode on bass—for Verve. Afterward she retreated to her new property at Strandvejen 417, Klampenborg, a suburb of Copenhagen.[9]

Her phone number was not listed, but if any of her fans wanted to speak to her, she could often be seen performing the mundane chores of a housewife, shopping, gardening, and decorating. She kept the house for three years, using it as a rendezvous to continue her affair, which was a spectacular if naïve indulgence because within twelve months of the purchase, it was all over. "Her little Danish guy was much younger than she was," confirmed Paul Smith, "and he was about half her size. It was a kind of live-in boyfriend type of thing." Even so, Ella often returned, attracted to the very real people she had gotten to know in her immediate neighborhood. She had become very friendly with the lady next door who tried to teach her Danish; she referred to her affectionately as "my mother"[10]—shades of "my husband" with Thor Larsen.

In 1963, while still using her Klampenborg address, Ella seriously contemplated strengthening her ties with Denmark by purchasing a regular base in which to perform in the country: "Ella Fitzgerald . . . with Swedish showman Simon Brehm and American-Swiss impresario Norman Granz has recently seen the Copenhagen jazz club Montmartre with a view to purchasing it."[11] The proposed venture fell through, and within a few months Ella had sold up, taking her expensive Danish furniture back to her Los Angeles home.

In early 1962, Bill Doggett received a call from Norman Granz: "'Ella would like you to arrange and conduct an album for her,' Granz said. 'Do you think you can do it?' I said, 'Just send me the list of tunes and the keys, and I'll do it!' I had the pleasure of choosing the musicians on the session, and I got the best around. We did it in two days, and it's one of the better 'swing' albums she did—all good 'swing' tunes. The sessions went just great. I had played my ideas for her before and asked her, 'What about your ideas?' She said, 'You bring the arrangements, and I'll sing them.' That's exactly what happened. We'd play the arrangement down at the session, she'd sing along with it, then say, 'Fine, let's make it!' And that's what it was like all the way through. Any little nuances she did were right there and then, right on the money. She was quick as a wink!"

Rhythm Is My Business was released in the fall of 1962. Interestingly, the best track on the album was a return to Ella's Decca days, "Rough Ridin'." "The emphasis here is on swinging. Doggett's simple, driving arrangements provide an effective background for Miss Fitzgerald—who has no peer among rhythm singers when it comes to swinging. . . . She doesn't communicate this same degree of personal involvement on ballads, though her work is technically flawless," said *Down Beat*, awarding three-and-a-half stars.[12]

In November, Norman Granz became incensed with the Lincoln Center in New York because, he alleged, they would not allow Ella to perform there. A storm raged in the columns of the *New York Post*. Duke Ellington, also at the time under Granz's control, fanned the flames by saying that if Lincoln Center was not for Ella, it was not for him. The Center had said it wanted a written outline of her program to "weigh the appropriateness of what she proposed to sing." Meanwhile, the proposed date of November 11 went to Dizzy Gillespie and Mary Lou Williams who had applied for it a month earlier. In fact, the advisory panel on jazz and folk music never had a chance to turn Ella down. They had never been consulted. Granz assumed that Ella's name was enough. He was right, yet the Center's response in wanting to know what she was going to perform was given by its spokesman as: "We feel the hall should challenge the artist."[13] Ella, who during her European tour had played to Princess Grace holidaying at the ski resort of Gstaad and then went on to play in over thirty of the world's biggest concert halls, could reasonably be expected to have been above having her program "vetted."

In early 1962, the piano chair had revolved once again, as Paul Smith returned. "I went out with her for forty-six weeks. We did a European tour, played a few week-stands at the really big, posh nightclubs, but most of them were one-nighters. She literally worked the whole forty-six weeks with very little time off. The bass player was Wilfred Middlebrooks and Stan Levey was on drums, and at the end of it Stan Levey and I decided to burn our tuxedos after playing the last date in Seattle. We said, 'Boy, we don't ever want to work this hard again!' We could never understand how she did it. She had done it for years before, and she did it for years afterward. That's when she comes alive, when she goes onstage. When the show was over, she usually went back to her hotel with her maid. It was kind of a lonely life."

In July 1963, Ella was reunited in the recording studios with Count Basie, someone whose company she really enjoyed. "Our . . . special thing was our first album with the First Lady of Swing. It was released as *Ella and Basie*, and the tunes were Quincy's [Jones] arrangements. And as usual, when you're working with Ella, it was more like a ball than a job," said Basie.[14]

Ella and Basie: On the Sunny Side of the Street is a much more satisfactory union than the *Duke Ellington Songbook*. Ella fitted into the fabric of Basie's band well, with the specially commissioned arrangements uniting Ella and Basie's common vision of swing. Basie even took time out to play organ, a specialty he kept under wraps for most of his career, in "Dream a Little Dream of Me." "The essential charm of this set is the blending of the Fitzgerald sound with the completely masculine texture of the Basie band," said John Tynan in *Down Beat*.[15]

When an exhausted Paul Smith and Stan Levey handed in their notice after almost a year of constant touring, Granz approached Tommy Flanagan to take over the piano chair. "I guess I had a better reputation the second time I worked with her," said Flanagan wryly (by then he had recorded with some of the biggest names in jazz, including Miles Davis, Sonny Rollins, and John Coltrane), "because this time I got a call from Norman Granz. She was working at Basin Street East, and I was available. I had been working with Coleman Hawkins and he wasn't doing all that much, and it was a chance for some steady work, which I needed to do for a while."[16]

When Flanagan joined Ella's group, it consisted of Les Spann on guitar, Jimmy Hughart on bass, and Gus Johnson on drums. When Les Spann left, Granz once again began to use Roy Eldridge in Ella's little combo with increasing frequency. Eldridge (1911–1989) was a forthright and explosive trumpet player. He is usually portrayed as the link in the evolution of the trumpet in jazz, the man who expanded on the virtuosity of Louis Armstrong with highly mobile lines inspired by saxophonists such as Coleman Hawkins, and in so doing pointed the way to bop. For Norman Granz, as for countless jazz fans, he was the most exciting trumpeter in jazz.

Eldridge's role in Ella's group was not ultimately an artistic success, however. On the one hand it effectively gagged an important and vital instrumentalist, while on the other it detracted from the highly swinging lines of an expansive, freewheeling singer. Ella came to resent Eldridge's constant buzzing obbligatos behind her singing, yet Eldridge could do little else. "This is no fit role for a still very vital and creative musician, especially since Ella Fitzgerald, never the most secure performer, seems to resent any applause going to Roy and gives him progressively less to play," observed Dan Morgenstern, who was a close friend of Eldridge's.[17] Even so, to suit his own convenience, Granz continued to foster their uneasy alliance, off and on, until March 1965.

"Roy played with us when I was with Ella," said Paul Smith. "He'd just go along and play on a harmon mute all night behind her and maybe have a solo at the top of the show. It wasn't that he was needed. In fact, a lot of times it was kind of irritating to Ella. I never felt it was personal. It was enough she had the trio. We would stay out of the way, which all good accompanists should, so it was an irritant to have someone bugging around the back of her."

However, when Ella and Roy combined in the recording studios with a group comprising Wild Bill Davis on organ, Herb Ellis on guitar, Ray Brown on bass, and Gus Johnson on drums to record *These Are the Blues* in October 1963, their artistic shortcomings together were far from obvious. Roy's role was in the context of a Louis Armstrong or a Joe Smith playing behind a Bessie Smith. The problem was more that Ella was no Bessie Smith, as she showed on Smith's "Jailhouse Blues." But Ella never once in her career pretended to be a blues singer, and while these performances never had the earthy power that contemporaneous singers such as Dinah Washington and Helen Humes could bring (although Washington herself blew a Bessie Smith tribute with knock-kneed accompaniment), the album is by no means a travesty of opposing styles. What Ella sings, she sings well but without idiomatic authenticity, much like a romantic Italian tenor trying to sing Wagner. When the album was reviewed by John Tynan for *Down Beat*, it received four stars.

"Roy said it was very difficult doing that date where she was singing the blues," said Dan Morgenstern, "not only because she wasn't a blues singer but also because she only gave him one solo on the whole album. Roy didn't say those things with resentment, it was just the way she was. But he was very happy when he didn't have to work with her anymore." So why didn't Eldridge quit?

His role with the regular trio was not an easy one. "Roy made the most of it, we all made the most of it," recalled Lou Levy, "but in a situation like that I think it's questionable to have an extra soloist when you're trying to feature someone with just a rhythm section. I mean, the rhythm section hardly gets any solos anyhow. On *Ella in Rome* and *Ella Returns to Berlin*, I don't think I hardly had a solo. When you get another instrument, you have to deal with that, like where do you put it in? . . . But Norman and Roy were very close. He was one of his very favorites, and he sort of took him under his wing and made sure he was comfortable."

Eldridge appears on record with Ella and her trio on *Ella at Juan-les-Pins*, from July 1964, where he plays alongside Tommy Flanagan on piano, Bill Yancey on bass, and Gus Johnson on drums. Here, Eldridge's lines become annoying to the listener, distracting from Ella's elegant swing. "It was kind of strange how he was used," said Flanagan. "Kind of eye to eye. I don't know how far it went back or anything. . . . Any friction was completely between the two of them."[18]

Ella's *Juan-les-Pins* performance was nevertheless of a very high standard. Martin Williams cited "You'd Be So Nice to Come Home To" as an excellent example of her style.[19] Yet in the context of her *previous* live albums, that all-consuming exuberance is gone. It is replaced by the gloss of a consummate professional at work. Ella was the featured artist at Juan-les-Pins, and her appearance was filmed by Radio Télévision Française, which concentrated on her final concert of July 29. Phil Schaap, who prepared the tapes for compact disc re-release together with previously unissued material, points out that only mono second-generation tapes exist, which, he speculates, were taken from the original tapes recorded by RTF at the concert.

One number, "The Cricket Song," was an impromptu duet with the sound of crickets that could be heard all around the festival stage. Schaap thinks the impetus for including this forgettable morsel came from Ella herself, always keen for her "hit record." Quite possibly she thought the song might be the hook to lift the album's sales, like the botched lyrics for "Mack the Knife" from the Berlin concert. But it didn't.

In fact, from time to time Ella would come up with an original composition that she felt sure would provide that elusive hit. One number from earlier in the year, the awful "Ringo Beat" ("Don't knock the rhythm of the kids today/Remember they're playing the Ringo way"), inspired by the Beatles, was a case in point. "Some of the songs she wrote were, well, like awful," said Tommy Flanagan with a laugh. "Some of her stuff from way back, even with Chick Webb, was very commercially minded."[20]

In 1966 Ella's record contract with Verve/MGM came to an end when the company decided not to take up their option. For the first time in her career and at the peak of her abilities, Ella was without a record contract. Granz, who at the time was also representing Duke Ellington, presented a package of two Duke Ellington albums and an Ella album to John Hammond at Columbia Records. Hammond's written response to Granz said that "Ella is absolutely superb," but he expressed reservations about the Ellington material. Ellington had been with Columbia throughout the 1950s and, as Hammond pointed out, "the Ellington material is largely stuff we have in the can in better performances."[21]

As Hammond expected, the Columbia executives did not take up the package because of the Ellington tie-up, and Ella continued without a recording contract. "A specific package consisting of material cut with Duke Ellington and her trio was turned down because it entailed the purchase of two Duke Ellington LPs which should never have been tied together with Ella," Hammond wrote later.[22]

CHAPTER FOURTEEN

1964–1972

Ella would sing anything!
LOU LEVY

WHEN ELLA OPENED at the Flamingo Hotel in Las Vegas in October 1964, she was sporting, somewhat bizarrely, a blond wig. Dinah Washington had been wearing one, so Ella followed, and it became a personal feature for about two years. "[Her] new blond hair lent an eerie resemblance to Sophie Tucker," observed the *Toronto Globe and Mail*.[1] She was now, said *Time*, "a hypo-millionairess" and "can afford a Don Loper wardrobe and endlessly redecorate her house in Beverly Hills."[2] But the personal cost of accumulating her great wealth was beginning to take its toll. "Sometimes you can find you're way up on top and all by yourself," she confided to Leonard Feather. "It can get pretty lonely up there, and you can miss all the kicks."[3]

Ella's touring schedule continued unrelentingly through 1965, but she was fast approaching fifty and was overweight, to boot. Something had to give. "We did double concerts in Europe in different cities," recalled Paul Smith. "One concert from six to nine, then get on a plane and fly to another concert four hundred miles away at midnight. It didn't necessarily need to be that hard, you know; it could be more relaxed." In Germany the pressure finally exacted its price. While onstage in Munich, "the highest-paid singer in show business," as the *Houston Post* described her, suddenly stopped singing and looked in danger of collapsing. "In Munich I just went berserk," Ella recalled later. "My drummer had to grab me and take me off. The people guessed something was wrong, but they applauded and wouldn't leave the hall. Arlene [her assistant] got me calmed down a bit. Then I went back and tried to sing some more."[4] On doctor's orders several English concerts were canceled. While recuperating in London, Ella fired an uncharacteristic salvo fairly and squarely in the direction of her manager: "A concert artist would never agree to do as we do. It's too much hassle. You're afraid that if you say no, people will say you don't appreciate what they've done for you. Some people get very angry when you're ill."[5] To which a Granz representative responded: "We couldn't afford to pay her the salary we do if she didn't give two concerts a night."[6]

By July 1965, Ella was back in harness, playing Melodyland at Anaheim with Nelson Riddle and his orchestra. "Exuding the same old energy underneath a new blond wig . . . Miss Fitzgerald is without a peer in the art of jazz singing. There is no other vocal swinger on the scene who has her uncanny sense of time or her flawless intonation. Nor can anyone goose a combo, push a whole band, or generate as much excitement as she," enthused *Down Beat*.[7]

When Ella entered the recording studios with Duke Ellington that November, eight years had passed since they collaborated on the *Songbook* sessions. This time the session went smoothly. Granz was in an amiable mood with his new bride, Hanne, a former airline stewardess whom he had married on August 22. Even Duke, better prepared and with arrangements this time from Gerald Wilson, Jimmy Jones, and Billy Strayhorn, was moved to dance a soft-shoe shuffle with Ella between takes on "The Brownskin Gal in the Calico Gown." After the session Ella held a party for all the participants at her home.

The following month Tommy Flanagan left Ella's trio, but the dates he had played with Ella and the Ellington band had left an indelible impression. "That was a thrill for me to hear the band parts played by the Ellington band. It always sounded so much different; it sounded like everything was written by Ellington. Just the sound of that band made everything terrific. They transformed everything into the Ellington sound."[8] Ella's new pianist was Jimmy Jones, who with Joe Comfort on bass and Ed Thigpen on drums now formed her regular group. But again the strain of touring was making itself felt, and at the end of the month, suffering from fatigue, Ella checked into Mount Sinai Hospital to undergo a complete physical check-up.

When Ella had fully recovered, Granz took the Ella-Duke package to Europe, opening at London's Royal Festival Hall on February 12, 1966. When the tour reached Sweden, their concert was broadcast on Swedish radio from the Konserhuset in Stockholm. Granz obtained the tapes and subsequently released the Ella-Duke concert in 1984 as *The Stockholm Concert, 1966*. It is another example of how Ella responded to the live situation: with Duke's driving ostinato comping and the band powering behind "Imagine My Frustration," Ella's

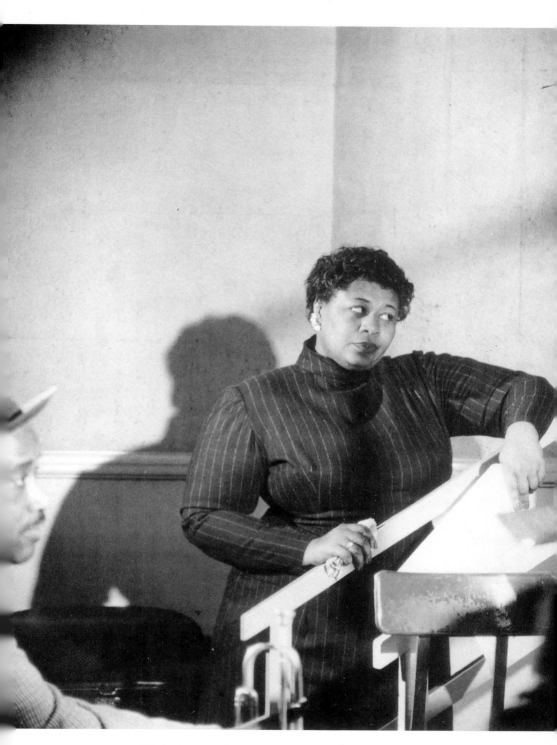

Ella in the recording studios, 1950. *(Max Jones Files)*

The following newspaper clippings appear:

Nab Ella Fitzgerald, Gillespie in Dice Game

Houston, Tex., Oct. 8 (AP)—B. (Dizzy) Gillespie, the trumpet

Houston Dice Cops Give Ella & Boys a Bad Shake

Houston, Tex., Oct. 8 (U.P.)—A vice squad broke up a dice game in the dressing room of singer Ella Fitzgerald but waited until the first performance was over before taking her to the station.

Vice officers at a one-night stand of "Jazz at the Philharmonic" walked into the singer's dressing room just as saxophonist Illinois Jacquet rolled his point.

But the officers, led by Vice Squad Sgt. W. A. Scotton, beat Jacquet to the pot and scooped up $185 and the dice.

Others Seized

Miss Fitzgerald, Jacquet, trumpet player Dizzy Gillespie, singer Georgianna Henry and producer Norman Granz were arrested.

At the station, Miss Fitzgerald, dressed in a decollete gown of blue taffeta and a mink stole, dabbed at her eyes with a wispy handkerchief.

"I have nothing to say," she said as she was booked for shooting dice. "What is there to say?" I was only having a piece of pie and a cup of coffee."

Not Actually Shooting

Sgt. Scotton agreed that Miss Fitzgerald was not actually shooting dice when they entered.

Play 'Guys & Dolls' Dice Bit on Cops; Aud Unsegregated

$10 Awaiting Singer At Police Station

Ella Lee Fitzgerald, dusky blues singer, whose recent Music Hall engagement included a brief interlude in the police station, has $10 waiting for her if she ever returns.

Ella Fitzgerald
But the show goes on.

Ella Fitzgerald, 4 Others Nabbed on Gaming Charge

MUSIC HALL RAID

'Jazz' Quint Seized For Crap-Shooting

HEARD SAYS DICE RAIDERS 'LITTLE BIT OVER-ZEALOUS'

Above When Jazz at the Philharmonic performed in Houston, Texas, in October 1955, Norman Granz insisted on no segregation. Houston police's response was a bungled drugs frame-up involving Ella and other musicians of the JATP. *(Malcolm Nicholson Collection)*

Below "Swing into Spring," a TV special sponsored by Texaco, April 10, 1959, featuring Benny Goodman. Special guests included Ella and Peggy Lee. *(Institute of Jazz Studies, Rutgers University)*

Ella in 1958. She preferred singing ballads to anything else. *(Dennis Stock/Magnum)*

Above Norman Granz (left) with Ella, Flip Phillips, and Buddy DeFranco backstage at JATP in the early 1950s. *(Irwin Kleiner/Max Jones Files)*

Below Ruby Dee (left) and Nat King Cole on the set of Allen Reisner's *St. Louis Blues* in 1958. *(Howard Lucraft/Paramount/Max Jones Files)*

Publicity shot for the *Cole Porter Songbook*, 1956. *(Aquarius)*

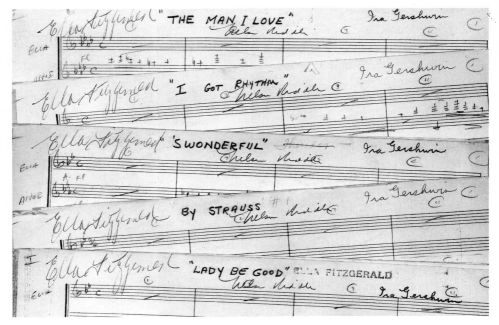

Above Ella's lead sheets from *Ella Fitzgerald Sings the George and Ira Gershwin Songbook*, arranged and conducted by Nelson Riddle, by common consent the best of the legendary *Songbook* cycle. *(State Historical Society of Wisconsin)*

Below A classy pair: Count Basie and Ella Fitzgerald during the late 1970s. *(Hans Harzheim/Max Jones Files)*

Ella's accompanists (from top right): Paul Smith *(Paul Smith)*, Lou Levy, Jimmy Rowles, Tommy Flanagan. *(Stuart Nicholson)*

Ella in the late 1970s. *(David Redfern)*

adrenaline level soars, and with it the listener's. Singing at a volume to compete with the band—something that would never happen in the controlled environment of the studios—this is a shouting, roaring performance by Ella as she takes on, and becomes part of, the Ellington instrument.

When she returned to the United States after the tour, her first stop was a triumphant opening at the Americana Hotel in New York City on March 14. To greet her that first night at the hotel's Royal Box were the ambassadors to the United Nations of the various countries she had just visited on tour. On March 23 she was received at the United Nations Building, where a reception was held in her honor. Later in the year the Ella-Duke package was reconvened for the Newport Jazz Festival and the Nice Jazz Festival. There were changes again: Joe Comfort was back on bass and Ed Thigpen on drums for Newport, and Grady Tate was on drums for Nice. The Newport concert went without a hitch. "This performance . . . [was] everything a jazz festival concert should be," said Dan Morgenstern in *Down Beat*. "A joyous and inspiring occasion."⁹

While at the Nice festival, however, Ella received news that her half-sister Frances had died suddenly. She immediately returned for the funeral, missing the July 25 concert, though she was back for the scheduled concerts on July 27, 28, and 29. But she was plainly distraught. The sisters had been very close since childhood, and Ella had even accepted financial responsibility for Frances and her family. Nevertheless, Norman Granz had decided to film the concert on the 27th. It was an ambitious attempt to capture the Ella-Duke collaboration live. Duke and the band were playing well that night. Ella, clearly upset, was frequently seen crying. Duke, aware of the situation, cut the first half of the concert short to save Ella further distress.

When he returned for the final set, he was under the impression that Ella would be unfit to perform again that night; however, Granz wanted to complete his film. As the band got into a powerful groove, he began shouting at Ellington to bring Ella on. Ellington's response was to play louder and longer, saying afterward that he was affronted by Granz's rudeness as well as by his lack of understanding of Ella's distress. There was a heated exchange between Duke and Granz, and their relationship was never the same again, culminating in a parting of the ways in 1967. "[Duke] asked me if I'd talk with Norman to try and smooth things over," said Renee Diamond, a close friend of Ellington's. "I did. For an hour, I suppose, Norman let me know just what he thought of Duke. Terrible things. At the end, though, most of the venom had gone. He said he was concerned that Ella hadn't been brought back on again. It would spoil the film he was making because Ella was billed as the star. I could understand his disappointment, but I couldn't see why he blamed Duke. Ella wasn't in any condition to perform, I thought."[10]

The following year Ella confirmed to Bent Henius: "When my sister died, I had to fly home to the funeral. It was hard to perform with Duke Ellington's band when I returned, but I said to myself, 'You have to go and sing for her. It's the only way you can express your feelings.'"[11] And on the double album *Ella and Duke at the Côte d'Azur* (awarded four stars in *Down Beat* when it was released in the spring of 1967), there's certainly a feeling of Ella's going through the pain barrier in some selections. She almost shouts parts of "Lullaby of Birdland" with her trio, as if to externalize her pain. Yet the performance is memorable for the incredibly powerful swing she generated. It could leave her accompanists in awe, as Tommy Flanagan recalled: "There were times that used to be exceptional. She could swing so hard. You'd think you were swinging, too, and she'd look at you and say, 'Oh, yeah? Is that swing?' and break it up!"[12] This was one of those occasions, as Ella immersed herself in her music to try to forget her loss. There is even a salute to Mel Tormé when she pinches a bit of scat from his version of "Lullaby," near the end. "The only thing I regret is that when I heard her in Las Vegas, I didn't hear more of this kind of thing," said George Shearing when he heard the recording of his composition the following year.[13] Despite Ella's personal tragedy, her European tour with Duke was acclaimed by public and critics alike as her most successful endeavor in years.

Ella would appear again with Ellington in Europe in early 1967, a collaboration that the London critic Derek Jewell described as a "mature masterpiece," and later in the year in the United States. Their appearances together were assuming almost legendary proportions. Henry Pleasants once described how Dietrich Fischer-Dieskau rushed to the airport immediately after a recital in Washington, D.C., to catch a connection to see Ella and Duke at Carnegie Hall, exclaiming, "Ella and the Duke together! One just doesn't know when there might be a chance to hear that again."[14]

However artistically satisfying their collaborations, Fischer-Dieskau was right in assuming they would not go on forever. Their association became intermittent after Granz blew his top over a misunderstanding about bookings with Ellington's sister. Among other things, he told her Ellington did not appreciate what he was doing for him. Ellington was less compliant than Ella, and this row with his sister finally motivated him to part company with Norman Granz. But despite their differences, both artist and manager held each other in high esteem. A reconciliation was effected and their friendship was restored, on both a personal and a professional level, during the last years of Ellington's life. Shortly before Ellington's death in 1974, Granz took him into the recording studios for *Duke's Big Four* (Pablo), a quartet album with Joe Pass, Ray Brown, and Louis Bellson, that featured Ellington's piano playing. When he died in New York on May 24, Granz was at his bedside.

On her return from Juan-les-Pins, Ella rested. In November 1966 she was booked into the Riverboat, a club located in the basement of the Empire State Building. On opening night she brought Tony Bennett onstage for a joint version of "I Left My Heart in San Francisco," to the delight of the celebrity audience that included composers Harold Arlen and Cy Coleman, federal judge David Edelstein, the legendary club owner and entertainer Bricktop, Connie Stevens, and John Hammond.

Hammond was greatly impressed by Ella's performance and returned the following week. Aware that Ella's recording contract with Verve/MGM had now expired, he tried to get his bosses to sign her to Columbia. He stated the following in an internal memo:

> During her engagement at the Riverboat, Ella Fitzgerald has broken every record for the room. So far I have been down there twice and am convinced that she is at the peak of her career and is without doubt the greatest popular singer in the business today. In the past there have been many talks between Columbia and her manager Norman Granz. These talks have broken down.... It is my recommendation that Columbia institute serious talks with Ella Fitzgerald as a star artist with no strings attached. In her field she is as unique an artist as Horowitz, Joan Sutherland.... I think we would literally be crazy not to sign her immediately.... She has years of creativity left.... I would urge immediate and serious consideration and the reinstitution of talks with Ella and Granz.[15]

Hammond was batting strongly for Ella, and his word counted at Columbia. He had been instrumental in the success of artists of the stature of Benny Goodman, Count Basie, Billie Holiday, and Teddy Wilson, and had recently signed Aretha Franklin and Bob Dylan to the label. In the 1970s he would sign Bruce Springsteen. Now that

Verve/MGM no longer wanted her, a move to Columbia might reju-
venate Ella's recording career. But the hoped-for and—from Ella's
point of view—very necessary deal never came to fruition.

In January 1967, Ella was one of nine Women of the Year chosen by
the *Los Angeles Times*. A presentation was made in the Times Building
to underscore her contribution to the status of women not only in
southern California but everywhere. It was ironic that the community
honoring her also had in place a set of so-called restrictive covenants
which were preventing her from living in certain white-only Beverly
Hills neighborhoods where she now wanted to move.

In March, Norman Granz decided to mount a Jazz at the
Philharmonic tour of America. "Those familiar letters JATP will be
seen on U.S. marquees beginning March 25," announced *Down Beat*.
"On that date Norman Granz who produced JATP in cities across
the U.S. from 1945 to 1957 will unveil the first domestic edition of
his touring concert in a decade (there have been three European tours
in the interim). At press time the following have been signed: Duke
Ellington's Orchestra, the Oscar Peterson Trio, trumpeters Roy
Eldridge and Clark Terry, saxophonists Benny Carter and Zoot Sims,
and vocalist Ella Fitzgerald."[16]

At the height of the 1960s' rock craze it was a courageous step to
take an ambitious, acoustic *jazz* touring package on the road. The
audience for the music—which ever since the 1920s had drawn heavily on successive generations of college students—was now being
lured away by the exciting new sounds of the Beatles, the Rolling
Stones, the Beach Boys, Janis Joplin, and countless groups that were
all part of the rise of rock music. The attrition was greatly assisted,
paradoxically, by jazz itself, as the "free jazz" movement had taken to
the barricades, rendering the music impossible to listen to for the vast
majority of its former audience. Although Granz was able to show a
modest profit for his endeavors, he claimed that the aggravation was
scarcely worth it. He returned to his lakeside retreat in Geneva.

In September 1967, Norman Granz signed Ella with the West
Coast Capitol label. In doing so, he relinquished all artistic control.
After twelve intensive years of dealing with Ella's recording career, he
feared he might be getting stale. He simply arranged the deal and
stood aside. Perhaps a new approach was what was needed. In
November producer Dave Dexter announced that he planned to
develop a "totally different sound"[17] for the singer. He did that all
right. The first album was a collection of religious songs, *Brighten the
Corner*, and was followed by an album of country music, *Misty Blue*,

and an album of Christmas songs, *Ella Fitzgerald's Christmas*. In fairness, she had done an album of Christmas songs for Verve under Granz, but that was far and away a more convivial affair. The Capitol years were not good ones for Ella; even a meeting with Benny Carter and a small combo, including Jimmy Jones, "Sweets" Edison, and Georgie Auld, on *30 by Ella* was as pedestrian as it was perfunctory.

In the spring of 1968, Ella visited Hungary for the first time, accompanied by the Tee Carson Trio with Keter Betts on bass and Joe Harris on drums. Her previous breakdown through exhaustion now forgotten, her nonstop itinerary also included Amsterdam, Basel, Berlin, Brussels, Dusseldorf, Frankfurt, Grenoble, Hamburg, London, Milan, Paris, Rotterdam, Stockholm, Stuttgart, Vienna, and Zurich—a whirlwind thirty-five-day tour that ended in Copenhagen on March 6. "I get a little tired sometimes," she said later, "but whenever I get on a stage and the public is there, I forget all the tiredness. Everything comes back and I feel good again."[18]

On her return to the United States she resumed her usual round-robin of the nation's top night spots: the Rainbow Grill in New York, the Flamingo Hotel in Las Vegas, the Cocoanut Grove in Los Angeles. When she returned to the Venetian Room of the Fairmont Hotel in San Francisco in November, Tommy Flanagan was with her again as pianist. "We worked forty to forty-five weeks out of the year," he said. "There wasn't much time for anything else. She would take a couple of weeks at Christmas and a month in the summer. She just loves it. There's nothing like applause."[19]

In January 1969 the press was given a preview of an upcoming TV special featuring Duke Ellington and Ella. After Ella's version of "Lady Be Good" there was such applause that the projectionist repeated the number. This was something that did not often happen with an audience of jaded press people. All the same, the show was not the triumph it could have been. Seen on KTLA in Los Angeles in January, it opened in the garden of Ella's home with her singing "People" to an audience consisting of Ray, Jr., and her two nieces. For the next hour Ella reminisced about the big-band days and the value of standards and alternated among a trio with Ellington at the piano, Duke's band, and a pickup band directed by Jimmy Jones that included strings.

In February, Ella was booked into the Royal Box of the Americana Hotel in Manhattan. "Duke and Pops [Louis Armstrong] came in one night," said Tommy Flanagan. "She had 'Hello Dolly' in the show. It was funny, I knew Pops would come up, but Duke was there and he came up and played 'Hello Dolly,' too! I won't say he wanted to do it, but he was a good sport! He loved everybody madly, and with Pops they had a thing. They had recorded all those things together, and they had a lot of rapport, friendship, I guess."[20]

In March, Ella was at the Fairmont Hotel again, and her trio had stabilized into a regular unit with Flanagan, Frank De Rosa from the Don Ellis band on bass, and Ed Thigpen from the Oscar Peterson Trio on drums. During the engagement she was recorded by the Prestige label, and *Sunshine of Your Love* saw the return of Granz to take care of production duties.

Throughout her career Ella had included at least one or two pop numbers in performances; with rock at its height she was now including chart successes, songs that did not really suit her style at all. "What she likes to do is really be current—do commercial things—but I don't care for that myself," said Flanagan.[21]

If *Sunshine of Your Love* included forgettable morsels like "This Girl's in Love with You" and "Hey Jude," she went whole hog on her subsequent two albums for the Reprise label, *Ella* and *Things Ain't What They Used to Be (and You Better Believe It)*. On numbers like "Got to Get You into My Life," "I'll Never Fall in Love Again," "Knock on Wood," "Mas Que Nada," "A Man and a Woman," and "I Heard It Through the Grapevine" Ella attempted to get with it.

When *Ella* was released for the year-end Christmas trade, Reprise advertised the album with an obvious swipe at Ella's dire Capitol output: "Isn't It Time Somebody Did *Something* with Ella?" But the problem of both the Prestige and Reprise recordings was that Ella, Norman Granz, and Richard Perry, who produced *Ella*, failed to realize that the days of "covering" hit tunes, as Ella had done in her Decca days, were over. In trying to "do" something with Ella, trying to cover contemporary pop, Ella's versions obscured the dimensions of the original hit songs that had made them both compelling and subversive. In covering, say, "Heard It Through the Grapevine," it was impossible to disentangle the memory of Marvin Gaye's original hit from the actual song itself. Singer and song had become bonded in a performance that exhausted the song's meaning. Pop and rock succeed in spite of mediocre lyrics and simplistic harmonic progressions because the performance achieves an autonomous character, an autonomy that embraces musical as well as nonmusical factors, such as style, fashion, and sex appeal. In contrast, the standards repertoire relied on interpretation, portraying the emotions contained in the lyrics or exposing their musical characteristics, or both. Ella failed to realize the distinction, with the result that her interpretations sounded like rationalizations after the main event.

Oblivious to the problems inherent in drawing from a contemporary repertoire, however, Ella now had her trio of Flanagan, De Rosa, and Thigpen billed as her "New Sound," in keeping with the times. "I don't want to be considered, as the song goes, 'as cold as yesterday's mashed potatoes.' I want to stay with it," she told interviewer Patricia Davis in 1968.[22] Her repertoire at the Nice Jazz Festival on July 21, 1971, contained a forgettable bossa nova medley, the Beatles' "Something," The Carpenters' "Close to You," and Del Shannon's "Put a Little Love in Your Heart." "A lot of times it got to be commercial and gimmicky stuff," said Flanagan.[23]

Ella at Nice comes as a shock if played back to back with her work with Levy and Smith from the early 1960s. Her voice was just beginning to show the inevitable effects of the aging process. She frequently used shorter, stabbing phrases, and her voice was harder, with a wider vibrato. Whereas earlier she could sustain notes with an effortless, bell-like clarity, now she made the mechanics of singing—the use of the diaphragm—more apparent. Before, notes floated by with reckless abandon; now, you sensed them being pushed, sometimes forced, out on a column of air.

Prior to flying out to Nice, Ella had been greatly distressed by the death of Louis Armstrong on July 6, 1971. She turned up at his funeral in dark glasses. George Wein greeted her and asked if she was going to sing. "She told me, very simply, 'I'm here to mourn,' because she loved him so much." But within days, she was back performing as part of a double feature with Oscar Peterson at Central Park's Wollman Rink. She impressed with an almost perfect "Body and Soul," yet ruined the effect with a slam-bang version of "Mas Que Nada," full of clicks, shouts, and assorted Latin-type effects. Benny Goodman was in the audience. When Ella realized this, she gave her accompanists heart failure by calling for the song she cut with him back in 1936, "Goodnight, My Love." "It was a remarkable display of total recall on her part and alert ad-lib backing by the Tommy Flanagan trio," said the *New York Times*.[24]

While at Nice in July, Ella had to shorten her stay because of problems with her sight. Dates in other parts of France and an appearance at the sixteenth annual Baalbek International Festival in Tunisia were canceled. Ella went first to a hospital in Paris and then to the Massachusetts Eye and Ear Infirmary in Boston for the removal of a cataract in her right eye and treatment of a hemorrhage in part of her left eye caused by her diabetes. After a long layoff she appeared for a month at the end of the year at the Flamingo in Las Vegas. During her enforced furlough she studied Portuguese to help with the pronunciation of the now mandatory bossa section of her act.

CHAPTER FIFTEEN

1972–1978

For all the people who say I over-recorded artists, my most profound regret is that I may not have recorded them enough.

NORMAN GRANZ[1]

MYSTERY AND DISAPPOINTMENT surrounded the last-minute cancellation of Ella's appearance at the Fairmont Hotel in San Francisco between May 24 and June 2, 1972. The only explanation offered by the Fairmont's management was a terse, "Cancellation due to a conflict of interest." Since the fifties Ella had become a regular attraction at the hotel's plush Venetian Room and had built up a considerable following among the affluent San Francisco crowd, with whom she was a special favorite.

Ella's "conflict of interest" was delicately put by the Fairmont. In fact it was a huge sellout concert at Santa Monica Civic Auditorium with Count Basie, mounted by Norman Granz, who was beginning to think his retirement had been premature. He had presided over a JATP reunion at the Monterey Festival in 1971 and liked it. Recently he had taken a Count Basie–Joe Williams–Roy Eldridge–Eddie Vinson package around Europe and liked it even more. But the Ella-Basie concert was a surprise on two counts: First, Granz announced he was going to record the concert; and second, he decided to include a ninety-minute jam session, JATP style, at the end.

"I don't know what possessed me to do it, but I decided to record it," said Granz later. "While I was at it, I decided to add a few surprise guests. Oscar Peterson was in town, and I brought in Stan Getz, Roy Eldridge, Harry Edison, Ray Brown, and some others. It was a lot of fun and went well, so afterward I thought I'd see how it might go as a record. I put out a small mail-order thing, and it was a disaster. Sold about 150. But a few got over to Europe, and I got a call from Polydor saying they would give me worldwide distribution if I went back into the record business. It was too good to refuse. I had bought all the Art Tatum sessions from MGM in 1972, and I also had a number of old JATP concert tapes that had not been part of the Verve sale in 1959. Since the musicians hadn't been paid, they were not mine to sell. Anyway, at least I had something to release until I could do some new sessions. I lined up a group of independent distributors to cover the U.S. market, and they served me well until I went with RCA in 1975. I named the label Pablo for my favorite artist, Pablo Picasso."[2]

When the concert was finally issued as a three-album box set, Ella had an album to herself; some tracks were with the Basie band (featuring mostly Marty Paich arrangements), some with Tommy Flanagan's trio, and the rest with a JATP-style jam band. Once again she goes into the province of current pops with "Theme from 'Sanford and Son'," Carole King's "You've Got a Friend," and Marvin Gaye's "What's Going On?" "I dig Marvin Gaye," Ella asserted. "When I sang his 'What's Going On?' some people said, 'Why are you doing that? It's a protest song.' I told them, 'I don't find it that way. To me it's good music.'"[3]

Ella's charming naïveté notwithstanding, these numbers are almost unlistenable today. The Basie band had by no means mastered the rock rhythm section patterns of the day and sounds like a hotel orchestra, and Ella sounds equally uncomfortable singing against the square rock patterns. Ironically, Granz said, "All the Las Vegas years have not affected her heart in soul and jazz."[4] Clearly they had. The Ella section of the concert was only good in parts.

Later, in June 1972, Granz took Ella, Roy, Oscar, Al Grey, and others to the Nice Jazz Festival once again. Following the festival Ella was scheduled to appear in Verona, and it was here that she noticed leakage from one eye and called a local surgeon who consulted her American specialist. When she arrived in St. Tropez, the recurrence of the eye problem forced her to cancel. Cars with loudspeakers rolled through the streets asking ticket holders to apply for a refund. Once again Ella returned to the Massachusetts Eye and Ear Infirmary where a spokesman confirmed that she underwent a laser operation for the removal of a cataract from her left eye.

Initially Ella's eye problems forced her to wear contact lenses, but she found them uncomfortable and so discarded them. She returned to active performance with a benefit concert for the Retina Foundation at Boston's Symphony Hall, which convinced her that she had recovered sufficiently to participate in what was billed as an "All-Star Swing Festival" at New York's Philharmonic Hall on October 23. The film of the concert, with Doc Severinson as master of ceremonies, was televised by NBC on November 29; it subsequently had wide distribution as a video in the 1980s. Sponsored by Timex, which had dabbled in jazz in the late 1950s with its "Swing into Spring" sessions, it was a memorable piece of jazz history, gathering together Duke Ellington and Count Basie and their respective orchestras, a reunion of the original Benny Goodman Quartet with Goodman, Lionel Hampton, Teddy Wilson, and Gene Krupa, the Dave Brubeck Quartet with Paul Desmond, plus guests such as Dizzy Gillespie, Bobby Hackett, and Earl Hines, and, of course, Ella with her trio. Slimmed down and wearing strong glasses, Ella was walked onstage by Count Basie to open the show and was greeted by a standing ovation. She scatted "Lady Be Good" with the Basie band and later appeared with her trio, performing "Goody Goody" and "Body and Soul." She said, "This is a wonderful evening for me with all the greats," and added mischievously, "Best of all, I'm the only girl!" During the tribute to the late Louis Armstrong, performed in front of his widow Lucille, Ella sang "Hello Dolly" to the delight of the audience, and afterward she joined in the finale, Basie's "One O'Clock Jump," with Basie and Ellington dueting on pianos. Suddenly Dizzy Gillespie walked out from the wings and had Ella join him for some of those "Savoy Steps" from way back. Both plump and in their mid-fifties, they were remarkably light on their feet in one of the few examples on film of Ella returning to her first love, dancing.

She was back in San Francisco with Basie where they took over the Circle Star Theatre for six nights in mid-December. Ella had not sung in northern California for two years, and the deterioration of her vision took the audience by surprise. She was helped on and off the stage, sometimes by Basie, but her famed ebullience was still very much in evidence. It was during this performance that Ella was persuaded to overcome her vanity once and for all and accept that she had to wear her glasses all the time, including onstage, which she hated.

Norman Granz had set up his Pablo operation by 1973, and in the summer of that year Ella's first project was an album of duets with guitarist Joe Pass, whom Granz also managed. "The first album I did with her, we went into a studio and Norman Granz brought a bunch of tunes in, lead sheets, songs," recalled Pass. "I had never met her before, and I had no idea whether she'd want to rehearse or what keys she sang in. But she just picked a tune like 'Gee Baby, Ain't I Good to You.' I said, 'What key?' She said, 'Well . . .' and just sort of hummed a little bit. I found the key, and we just did a whole album like that! Without any rehearsing, just sifting through tunes. 'Oh, I like this one,' she'd say. We'd try it and record it right away! On all the duet things we did together, four albums in all, there were no rehearsals. Just pick tunes out! I could change keys with her, anything I wanted to do. She's there, she hears it, no problem! It's like another musician. I play with her, and she's sort of like a horn player."

The Ella-Pass duets were not the first time she had sung with just guitar accompaniment; she had done it before on the verses of "They All Laughed" and "Nice Work if You Can Get It" on the *Gershwin Songbook*, and "Solitude," "Azure," and "In a Sentimental Mood" on the *Ellington Songbook*. Taken together, the four studio Ella-Pass albums ought to belong with the Ella–Ellis Larkins and the Ella–Paul Smith duos as among her finest work on record. But while the piano duos capture Ella at the peak of her powers, the Pass collaborations reveal the gradual effects of age on Ella's magnificent vocal equipment. Taken over a thirteen-year period—*Take Love Easy* from 1973, *Fitzgerald and Pass . . . Again* from 1976, *Speak Love* from 1983, and *Easy Living* from 1986—the decline in Ella's voice is plain. Yet there was a defiant beauty in her singing as with each successive album she was forced to maneuver her phrasing a little bit more so as not to expose the vocal shortcomings that were beginning to emerge.

"Ella has always sung on raw talent," said Paul Smith. "She never studied voice, she never took voice lessons. If you don't do it correctly and don't take it easy on the voice, there comes a time when the vibrato begins to go on you. You've stretched those vocal chords to a point where you can't really control them. That's pretty much what happened to her, and not only her but Sinatra as well. The same with Billy Eckstine; he also didn't sing correctly. Throughout the years his vibrato became so wide, you could drive a truck through it."

From 1972 the Newport Jazz Festival was transplanted to locations around New York. When Ella was invited to appear there in 1973 (she had last appeared at Wein's festival at Newport, Rhode Island, in 1970), it was decided to present her concert as a retrospective called "Salute to Ella." John Hammond negotiated a deal on behalf of Columbia Records to record the event. Ella appeared on the label courtesy of Pablo Records for an advance of $25,000 against royalties, payable to Ella's own corporation, Salle Productions (*Salle* is an inversion of Ella's), which was responsible for all musicians' costs. Salle Productions was run out of Granz's old Verve offices at

451 North Canon Drive, Beverly Hills, by Mary Jane Outwater, who was formerly on the Verve payroll.

A reconstituted Chick Webb band (all paid at union scale) was assembled under the direction of Eddie Barefield; Ellis Larkins was invited to re-create his memorable Decca duets with Ella (for a fee of $1,000); a jam band including Roy Eldridge, Al Grey, and Eddie "Lockjaw" Davis, dubbed the Jazz at Carnegie All Stars, re-created a typical JATP ensemble; and Ella's quartet of Tommy Flanagan, Joe Pass, Keter Betts, and Freddie Waits filled out the rest of the show.

The *New York Sunday News* previewed the Webb band—"Ella Revives the Savoy," showing the band rehearsing in a West Fifty-second Street rehearsal room. Ella did not attend any of the rehearsals, and the band had no idea what numbers she wanted to do with them. They ran down a few warhorses including Webb's theme "Let's Get Together," "A-Tisket, A-Tasket," and "Stompin' at the Savoy," plus "Indian Summer," a version of "Smooth Sailing," and an original ("Gemini") but were told that they were to perform five numbers only on the day of the concert.

In any event, only three Webb tracks were issued. "I'm eliminating most of the band stuff without Ella since it is clearly inferior to my memory of the old Chick Webb band," Hammond told Granz.[5]

Later, when he completed the album's production, he told Irving Townsend, "We had to pick up Ella from a hand-held mike, which was not of utmost quality. Even so, she never sounded better. At the actual concert, sides one and four comprise her appearance in the second half of the concert, whereas side two, where her voice is very nervous and sometimes very quavery, was her opening in the first half. I probably included too much of the JATP instrumentals, but at least Roy Eldridge is incredible and the rhythm section is the best she's had in a long time."[6]

When the album was released, the name of Panama Francis, the drummer who played in the Webb re-creation, was omitted from the liner notes. In Japan the album won the 1973 Swing Journal Gold Disc Award. "Obviously feeling ebullient, she swung and scatted effectively. But she was at her best at slow tempos," said the *New York Times* reviewer of the concert,[7] as good a summation as any of Columbia's *Ella Fitzgerald: Carnegie Hall 1973*. In a fragmented album, Ella does get in a memorable "Good Morning, Heartache" and an equally good "Miss Otis Regrets," which, compared to her *Songbook* version, highlighted the energizing effect an audience had on her. These two live performances have a quiet intensity that lifts them far above the workaday.

Ten days later Ella was in Houston, Texas, where she was caught in a candid mood by the *Houston Post*, underlining just how serious the problems were that she was encountering with her sight: "'I'm getting a little sight back in the right eye now. Let's hope the process continues.' She shook her head and lolled backward in the chair, her pained eyes squinted shut. Her right eye sometimes rolls upward, out of control. . . . 'You know I don't work at the furious pace I used to . . . ' she admitted, apologetically closing her eyes again. 'Mainly I'm doing scattered concerts, the usual summer routine, but right now it fits.'" Earlier she had told the packed audience in the Astrodome that it was her first trip there since "1955 when we had a little struggle. I wasn't shooting dice, of course, I was bobbing for apples!"[8]

With a less exhausting schedule, a new dimension had been introduced to Ella's performances. She was now singing with symphony orchestras. "It gives me a chance to do some of the tunes we've recorded but don't usually have a chance to perform in nightclubs, things with lush strings and horns," she said.[9] During 1973 she sang with six orchestras: the Boston Pops, Pittsburgh Symphony, New Jersey Symphony, Cincinnati Symphony, St. Louis Symphony, and Oklahoma Symphony. The following years saw an upsurge in demand for similar appearances, and by 1975 she had appeared with more than forty symphony orchestras throughout the United States, although curiously, Granz never recorded her in this context. Her performance with the Boston Pops under the baton of Arthur Fiedler was televised and included "That Old Black Magic," "Down in the Depths on the Ninetieth Floor," "Good Morning, Heartache," and "People." The Cole Porter number, "Down in the Depths," was from an album Granz had produced for Ella on the Atlantic label, recorded in June 1972 and just released as *Ella Loves Cole*, arranged and conducted by Nelson Riddle.

Meanwhile, Granz had begun to energize Pablo Records, signing several mainstream artists to the label. Many of them appeared on *Fine and Mellow: Ella Fitzgerald Jams*. It was what became a typical Granz mix-'n'-match session of the sort that began to proliferate on the label: "Jazz as I understand it—jamming," said Granz,[10] which broadly summed up the label's philosophy. Ella weaves her way through the instrumental traffic, much as she did with the JATP. But it was *Ella in London*, recorded live in Ronnie Scott's club, that provided the real-life study of the singer during this period.

For the past year Joe Pass (also managed by Granz) performed from time to time with Ella and Oscar Peterson. At the end of 1973 he left Oscar's trio suddenly and was replaced by Barney Kessel. In January 1974 he became a member of Ella's group, along with Tommy Flanagan, Keter Betts, and Bobby Durham, when the group went to Europe. Pass, however, was far from the supernumerary that Eldridge had been, the previous incumbent of the spot Granz seemed to use to keep certain selected instrumental clients working. Blending sensitively into the proceedings, Pass was the epitome of artistic discretion.

Ella in London came from a stay at Ronnie Scott's club in April 1974, during which time Ella was filmed in performance for BBC-TV. Her repertoire almost avoids the influence of the current hit parade, only Carole King's "You've Got a Friend" standing out as a disposable item against a strong jazz/standards selection of numbers. Indeed, when she performed the song at Avery Fisher Hall in New York City the following December, the *Village Voice* said, "She should not co-opt newer rock and/or pop material. . . . While she is forever immune to vogue, she is easily victimized by hostile musical idioms. For reasons of strained contemporaneity, Fitzgerald waded through Carole King's 'You've Got a Friend,' a song which should be banned from every repertoire for at least two decades."[11]

Ella's voice was now getting darker, and on some numbers, such as "Sweet Georgia Brown," sounds driven rather than effortlessly silken as in the past. Her great energy is still there, as "Sweet Georgia Brown" itself clearly shows, but her voice is now frayed around the edges: Phrases are snatched or shortened, and her vibrato has enlarged to almost alarming proportions, for example on "They Can't Take That Away from Me." "Her voice changed as it got older," confirmed Tommy Flanagan. "She'd always sing tunes like an instrumentalist. Like 'Body and Soul,' she used to do it in the key of F, but when I left, it was in the regular key, D flat!"[12]

On May 24, 1974, Duke Ellington died. Ella's friendship with Ellington stretched back to the days when she was the vocalist in Chick Webb's band, and she was asked to sing at his funeral service at New York's Cathedral Church of St. John the Divine. She sang Ellington's "Solitude" and a heart-wrenching "Just a Closer Walk with Thee," reading the lyrics, printed in two-inch capital letters, from a lectern in front of her. Ellington, who had once extravagantly promised to write a Broadway show featuring Ella, was a person whom she respected enormously, not, paradoxically, for his musical achievements but as a fatherlike figure to whom she occasionally turned for sage advice and counsel. His passing was a blow to her; at the funeral service she froze when singing and afterward said she could not remember if she had sung the words correctly.

The announcement in 1974 by the University of Maryland to call a new facility on campus the Ella Fitzgerald Center for the Performing Arts meant that it was one of the first buildings in the United States to be named after a black artist. At the time it was perhaps the most significant of the awards and citations that had started as a trickle and were now turning into a veritable flood celebrating Ella's achievements in jazz. But although approaching sixty, she was still capable of making history. In June she was part of a triumvirate with Frank Sinatra and Count Basie at Caesar's Palace in Las Vegas. The highlight of the show was their duet on "The Lady Is a Tramp" that earned a standing ovation every night. Sinatra, in the throes of making his comeback, was so encouraged by their reception that he wanted to take the package to New York to underline the message that Ol' Blue Eyes was indeed back. They opened at the Uris Theatre in September 1974 for two weeks. Billed simply as "The Concert," it was a triumph and a significant milestone on Sinatra's comeback trail. In two weeks the show grossed a stunning $1,088,000, a record for any show on Broadway. "[Sinatra] was at his easiest and his best when he joined Miss Fitzgerald for a finale in which they bounced lines off each other, she singing a gentle obbligato to his 'They Can't Take That Away from Me,' he belting out a lusty 'At Long Last Love,' and both of them swinging through 'Lady Is a Tramp,'" reported the *New York Times*.[13] But, sadly, an album by them both was never contemplated.

In May 1975, Ella collaborated with Oscar Peterson on *Ella and Oscar* in a series of duets and trios with the addition of Ray Brown on bass. Peterson, the consummate piano virtuoso, was also a superb accompanist. But his role was that of accompanist *and* soloist. His darting in and out of the limelight gave the album an unbalanced feeling; Peterson was like a miniature JATP and consequently robbed the album of the composure and natural ebb and flow that the self-effacing Paul Smith was able to bring to *Let No Man Write My Epitaph*.

That July, Ella was at the Montreux Jazz Festival with her regular trio for *Ella: Montreux, 1975*, an album distinguished by Flanagan's superb accompaniment. From the explosive opening of "Caravan," it was clear that one of jazz's major piano voices was at work. But "Caravan" revealed once more the decline of Ella's voice. Compared to the *Ella in Rome* version, with its effortless gliding between notes, flexibility of range and pixieish, side-slipping phrases, it is clear that Ella's voice was not the streamlined instrument it had been, even though her energy sought to shed the constraints imposed by age. "Teach Me Tonight" has an almost terrifyingly broad vibrato that is by no means attractive, and in "Wave," a nightmare for singers with its slowly unraveling theme that takes them both lower and higher than they appear to want to go, Ella struggles. Its range is almost too much for her to camouflage, which she attempts to do by introducing rococo Sarah Vaughan-isms. It is left to the breathtaking skill of Flanagan to paper over the cracks, something he does with inventive wit throughout the album.

On February 29, 1976, Ella won her eighth Grammy Award for *Fitzgerald and Pass . . . Again.* At the awards show Mel Tormé picked up a Grammy as Best Arranger for his *Gershwin Medley.* As part of the show Ella and Mel were invited to perform. "They got us together and we sang 'Lady Be Good,'" he said in 1991. "It was one of the highlights of my life. And I got a letter from the president of NARAS, the National Academy of Recording Arts and Sciences— I'm sure he sent one to Ella, too—that said, 'The standing ovation the two of you got is the single longest standing ovation we have ever experienced at any of the Grammy Shows. Thank you.' So on the heels of that, Ella said vocally and publicly, 'I want to make an album with Mel.' But Norman Granz wouldn't allow it.

"And yes, I'm pretty bitter about it because I've been referred to as Ella's male alter ego, and consequently as recently as 1990 she did a long, long interview with *USA Today* and again said, 'The one thing I want to do is make an album with Mel Tormé.' I guess he just doesn't think I'm good enough to sing with her. And you asked [about] control; if Ella really were her own lady so to speak, her own woman, from the standpoint of her career—I'm sure she is personally—but from the standpoint of her career she'd say, 'I'm sorry, Norman. I'm going over your head. I want to make this album with Mel.' But she won't because he is a kind of Svengali." And while it is true that Granz never saw a blend between Ella and Tormé, it is equally true that had Ella wanted to go ahead with an album, she could have done so. Norman Granz said he would not have stood in her way.

CHAPTER SIXTEEN

1978–1993

Ella Fitzgerald's voice isn't what it was when she was forty years old, that's obvious, but it's not the point. The point is that she has all this great wisdom and knowledge about performance, and that comes across even though she can't sing as high or as low as she did. I think that people who say Ella or Frank Sinatra should hang it up are totally foolish and irresponsible because we still have a lot to learn from the vantage point age and experience have brought them. I'd rather hear Ella Fitzgerald not at her peak than ten other singers at their peak.

LOREN SCHOENBERG

IN THE FALL OF 1978, Tommy Flanagan handed in his notice. He said he was driven to the decision by two days in Ella's summer itinerary when they went from Provence to Newcastle-upon-Tyne to Provence to Wolf Trap, Virginia. "It wasn't a contract or anything," he said, "it just ended up about ten years. It sounds like it was contracted, but we just came to a parting of the ways. For a long time . . . accompanying Ella I never thought I had enough technique as a soloist. But then I found I liked to put myself out there."[1] Wary of the pressures of travel after a mild heart attack earlier in the year, he was nevertheless taking a midlife risk by moving from the safe shadows as an accompanist into the vague spotlight provided by piano bars and foreign record labels. But he made it. In doing so he did the jazz world a great favor by finally revealing his great talent. "First-rate improvisation suggests that if one looked at the sheet music, one would find the notes the soloist has just played. That's what Flanagan does," wrote Whitney Balliett.[2]

Flanagan's replacement was Paul Smith. "I rejoined her in 1978," he said. "Then I was with her fairly consistently from 1978 to 1990. Twelve years just off and on. I'd be with her a couple of years, then there'd be one too many road trips and I'd quit, and come back when the road trips got less frequent.

"I hadn't worked with her for about sixteen years, other than a couple of commercials, so it was the first time we'd seen each other in a while. The first thing I did with her was a record date with Nelson Riddle called *Dream Dancing*. And I realized Ella's voice wasn't what it used to be. I hadn't heard it during those years, and I heard this little waver, her vibrato was a little bit uncontrollable. When I went into the booth, Ella herself had noticed it, and she said, 'I'm Mary McQuiver today.'"

The greater portion of *Dream Dancing* was recorded in 1972 by Norman Granz and leased to the Atlantic label and was released for a short while as *Ella Loves Cole*. It was intended as a new album of Cole Porter material and included some numbers not recorded in the *Cole Porter Songbook* sessions. Together with two additional tracks from 1978—the title track and "After You"—it was re-released on Pablo later that year. In a sense it gives a taste of what might have been. The Nelson Riddle arrangements frame Ella far better than the Buddy Bregman charts and make the album a sort of postscript for posterity.

Granz continued to record his two major clients, Ella and Oscar, prolifically for Pablo. The result created something of a critical ennui for both, which, it must be said, damaged neither career a bit. But for Ella, her Pablo albums, just as with many of the Billie Holiday Verves, chart the gradual deterioration of a legendary voice of jazz. What is fascinating, of course, is how both artists maneuvered their technical resources within the shrinking parameters of voice control at their disposal. As Granz points out, he would never have recorded either artist against such a background if they did not have anything to say.

If there was a feeling of casting around for a different context in which to feature Ella, however, it must be said that Granz did not lack imagination. *Lady Time* from 1978 placed Ella with Jackie Davis on Hammond organ and Louis Bellson on drums. But if creating a variety of context in Ella's output after almost half a century of recording was one problem, choosing material that Ella had not previously recorded was becoming another, as the subsequent *A Classy Pair* and *A Perfect Match*, both with Count Basie, revealed. Basie's band was now in its twilight years (he was to die of cancer in 1984) and not the force it had been in the 1950s and 1960s. Basie himself had recently suffered a heart attack and a viral infection. "Since these ailments began to slow the old sparrow down," he told Albert

Murray, "they know what I want, so when I start somewhere on the old keys . . . they know where I'm going and that's where they take it for me."[3] And if that sounds just a little too close to autopilot for comfort, then the presence of Ella had a remarkable galvanizing effect on the band. Singlehandedly she prompted them to play with some of the snap and crackle that characterized the best of Basie's postwar ensembles.

A Classy Pair, recorded in February 1979, and *A Perfect Match*, recorded live at Montreux the following July, do not lack energy on Ella's part. She throws herself into competition with the powerful brass and saxes, and if she sounds forced and strained in places, these valedictory meetings between two veterans of the swing era have a charm and piquancy of their own. *A Perfect Match* is continued on *Digital III at Montreux* with two more big-band tracks and a series of small-group sessions taken from Ella's performance on July 12, 1979, with the Paul Smith Trio, Joe Pass, and Pass plus bass phenomenon Niels-Henning Orsted-Pedersen. The voice is darker, and those flights of fancy that once came so easily now needed pumping up to become airborne: "I don't stand a ghost of a chance with you-hew-hew-hew-hew-hew-hewooooh."

Significantly, Ella had now returned almost exclusively to the standards repertoire. "As she got older there was less desire to go out and try and do something new," observed Paul Smith. "She did the things that were tried and true, which is what the people came to hear. The feeling was that new songs come out and last only a week or so on the hit parade, and then they're gone. And the songs aren't very good, generally. Once in a great while a good song would come up, but in the last twelve years I was with her, off and on, we didn't do a heck of a lot of new material. She realized it was the standards people came to hear her sing. They didn't want a Michael Jackson song!"

Earlier, in April 1979, Ella had appeared in Carnegie Hall with her trio, Pass, and Orsted-Pedersen, presaging their musical chairs at Montreux by three months. The *New York Times* noticed a change in her stage manner that had bemused critics and audiences for decades: "Despite her years of experience . . . she has never seemed at ease on stage. Her patter between songs often comes out as rote, and one got the feeling that she used her songs as a shield, as a means of escape from the audience. On this occasion, however, she seemed happily in command, moving from song to song with confidence and ease (despite the continued presence of some of the rote lines) and handling the logistics of frequent changes of accompaniment with charm and polish."[4] It was Orsted-Pedersen's U.S. debut. "I had previously played together with Ella in 1972 after I had left Oscar Peterson for the first time in 1971. I [substituted] for her regular bassist Keter Betts in the trio with Tommy Flanagan. Together with Oscar we had also done a Jazz at the Philharmonic. The first time I appeared in the States was as a duo with her in Carnegie Hall. As it was the first time I had played there, Norman Granz wanted to do something special about it; Joe Pass was there as well, and he also played duo with her. But the thing that impressed me the most was how she became turned on by an audience. As soon as she was onstage, she loved it."[5]

In September, Ella added another album to her *Songbook* canon, *The Antonio Carlos Jobim Songbook*. "Ella . . . displays her ear for foreign languages by singing some of the songs in Portuguese," said Granz;[6] Ella's studies had paid off. With Clark Terry, Zoot Sims, and Joe Pass, plus a rhythm section headed by percussionist Paulinho da Costa, the album fulfills Ella's ambition to do a whole album of Brazilian numbers, inspired by her love of the bossa medley she did in live performance. But by now she had become typecast by the standards of Tin Pan Alley rather than Brazil, which had the effect of making Jobim sound ephemeral.

In 1981, Smith took a leave of absence from the trio. "After I left, Norman ran into Jimmy Rowles on the street, and said, 'Hey! Do you want to play for Ella?' and that was it. Jimmy is a very good player, and he stayed with her a couple of years, then I came back," said Smith. Rowles is one of the great, but sadly underappreciated, pianists in jazz. "He's a consummate musician," said alto saxophonist Michael Hashim who recorded with him during the 1980s. "In a given set he might play an old warhorse like 'Limehouse Blues' and the very next number a very modern, sophisticated, pure jazz composition like Wayne Shorter's 'Momma G,' and there would be no feeling of discontinuity. He has such a powerful musical personality that he can literally play anything and it comes out as Jimmy Rowles."

Rowles, who had previously worked and recorded with singers such as Billie Holiday, Peggy Lee, Sarah Vaughan, Vic Damone, and Carmen McRae, and once gave singing lessons to Marilyn Monroe, fell easily and successfully into the role of Ella's accompanist. "I bumped into Norman, and he asked me if I wanted to work for Ella. So I took this first trip, and everything worked out. So I just stayed. I stayed for just under three years! No music except for a couple of special things. If she wanted to do something, we just did it. She didn't call out a song I didn't know, so we didn't have too much trouble. Just find a key, and that was that."

In February 1981 a party was held for Ella by Memorex. Ella was paid $500,000 for the first series of the "Is it live . . . " series of advertisements, her voice being used to shatter a wineglass as part of the blank-tape company's promotion that went on to win awards from the advertising industry. The Memorex ads were more than just a lucrative money-maker for Ella (the contract was renewed several times, on each occasion for a six-figure sum); they played an important role in keeping her name before a large, nonjazz public.

On the night of her birthday, April 25, Ella was the guest of honor again, this time in the plush New Orleans Fairmont Hotel. "Ella was performing in the Blue Room when fans carried in the cake after her show. Miss Fitzgerald is sixty-three," said the *Times-Picayune*. The story was also picked up by *Jet* magazine.[7] In fact, Ella was sixty-four and happy to perpetuate the myth of her date of birth. She still kept up an exhausting schedule, but the strain was becoming more apparent. "She was losing weight, and she was getting a little tired," said Jimmy Rowles. "I noticed when she finished a show you could tell she had worked. You could see when you were onstage and walked her off that she was tired. But she did a very long hardworking show. Then she'd come back and do about four or five encores! She did like a concert, and boy, she *did* one. She did a good one every time."

The only album Rowles recorded with Ella during his final stay with her was *The Best Is Yet to Come* with Nelson Riddle from February 1982. Two ensembles were used, one an enlarged jazz combo and the other an unorthodox string-horn ensemble. "Norman said he was tired of the conventional sound of the violin section," explained Nelson Riddle, "so we agreed on the use of four flutes, eight cellos, and four french horns. By superimposing the flutes or cellos on the horns I was able to create a sound similar to the blend Debussy achieved in *La Mer*."[8] The repertoire was a selection of solid standards; Ella and Rowles explore the verse of "Any Old Time," a tune written by bandleader Artie Shaw and recorded in 1938 with his then vocalist, Billie Holiday. Lady Day was again evoked with Ella's version of "God Bless the Child."

How, then, did Jimmy Rowles, from his unique vantage point as accompanist to both singers, feel Ella's and Billie's styles compared? "Well, Ella never impressed me as ever being *inside* a song, like with the *feeling* of the lyrics, like Lady. I don't think there's ever been a singer who could get inside a song and tell the tragic story of those love songs like her. Nobody could ever do that like Billie Holiday did. That's nothing against Miss Fitzgerald, but there are very few singers who could maintain that depth of performance and have it come off the way Billie Holiday did it, and that wasn't Ella's strong point, as far as I was concerned. She didn't have a conversational way of singing whereas Billie Holiday just sort of said what she was doing like the way Louis used to sing. He sang very much from the heart."

Jimmy Rowles, who regards Ella with great affection—"It was a pleasure to be performing with such a beautiful artist"—nevertheless articulates the debate among singers, musicians, critics, fans, and nonfans that has surrounded Ella's and Billie's quite different styles since they both began their singing careers in the 1930s.

In contrast, Paul Smith says, "Ella is a true *singer*. Billie was a *stylist*. If I had to listen to one or the other, I would never turn to Billie. You know, Billie had all her problems; she was a junkie, and people seem to thrive on scandal. But there's no scandal about Ella. She led a straight life, and you never heard anything about her getting high or looped. She was pretty much straight . . . and that doesn't make for exciting journalism."

And Lou Levy says, "I've heard people say she doesn't get inside a song, and I wonder about that. I think she's so good with all the other things that go with a song and singing it, maybe they might detract for some people. Maybe you can't sing that well and perfectly, and people see the point; maybe you have to make it easy for them, sound tragic like Billie. I think sometimes Billie overdid that—not purposely, but when she did, it had the reverse effect on me, it almost sounds funny."

Opinions will differ on the relative merits of Billie's and Ella's singing for as long as their recordings are played. But in comparing their contrasting styles, the key to Ella Fitzgerald's art emerges. For if Billie Holiday was both victim and accuser, then Ella Fitzgerald was the puritan in Bohemia, never imposing her emotions on a song or attempting to reveal its inner meaning. Perhaps the best way of illustrating this is by drawing a parallel with the distinction film critics make when analyzing the work of film directors in terms of the *auteur* principle. Given that the *auteur* and *metteur en scène* might both work from the same script, it is the latter who transfers, as faithfully as possible, the text to screen, while the former gives it emphasis that changes its meaning. The singer as *auteur* usually stamps a song's meaning in terms of his or her own personality and so imposes a further subjective dimension in its interpretation. In contrast, the singer as *metteur en scène* remains less concerned with interpretation and more with rendering accurately the musical features of the song.

To understand Ella Fitzgerald, therefore, is to understand her as a *metteur en scène*. Her voice never became enmeshed in the meaning of the lyrics but remained apart from them, as writer and critic Benny Green has pointed out: "Her vocal quality and her degree of tension are more or less the same no matter what she happens to be singing."[9] Ella projected a feeling of disarming honesty and, adding significantly to her broad appeal, a nonthreatening sexuality that was as attractive to women as to men. "That warm sound . . . is a part of her," observed singer Rosemary Clooney, "an extension of her personality. It's engaging and moving because she's open and childlike."[10]

Often, the singer as *auteur* obscures a more limited vocal endowment. "Billie Holiday had soul a yard wide and practically no voice in comparison to Ella," said the singer Sylvia Syms, a personal friend of both Billie and Ella. "But to me the things Billie sang came from the depths of the groin of life. It depends what you consider life is and what you home into, your personal bag. Technically, Ella is an incredible experience, but I don't think Ella made me go home and think of the depths of despair life can bring. We're dealing with two different sets of emotions here; Lady was the agony of living because of difficulties she had with addiction and life, and Ella was none of that. Ella was a bright shining little girl, and whatever personal hangups she may have had, you knew this was a clean-living, fun girl."

Billie Holiday, like many *auteurs*, had the ability to hijack a song by imprinting it with her own subjective stamp. This ability was so profound that in her later years she could take certain numbers and slot them into the autobiographical subtext of her performances. The same was true of Sinatra with his bar-stool performances, Piaf as the sparrow who remained unbroken by life, and Garland who was. These singers used the cult of personality to bring an additional dimension to their performances, and they learned how to trade off it. Their performances became a package deal of subjectivity and song. With Ella you got only the song.

On the other hand, some songs can be such a profound marriage of words, melody, and harmony that they arrive with a subjective dimension already built in. One reason, for example, that "My Funny Valentine" was recorded by practically everybody in the 1950s was that a relatively straight performance could end up sounding profound. The same thing happened when Ella sang "Ev'rytime We Say Goodbye," the song's subjective dimension papering over her arm's-length emotionalism.

Ella's voice had fewer limitations of range or tonal quality (listen to her air-bass solos or her Louis impressions and then her soaring scat, for example) than almost any other jazz or popular singer. Yet she respected the composer's and lyric writer's intentions with honest simplicity and humanity rather than with lyrical realism. At its simplest, lyrical realism means asserting a direct relationship between the lyrics and the social or emotional condition they describe or represent. The assessment of realism is an assessment of the *conventions* of realism; Holiday's cracked and broken voice at the end of her life was a direct manifestation of her life-style. The correlation was simple and direct and lent an "authenticity" to her performances that made her perhaps the finest of the *auteurs*. In contrast, Ella's singing is primarily concerned with the musical dimension of a song. While at her peak it meant that her singing could be the epitome of taste married to a superb technique, it also left no room for a chink of light that might allow a glimpse of her soul, as with a Piaf or a Garland or, indeed, a Billie Holiday.

But although Ella, the ultimate *metteur en scène*, never revealed anything of the inner woman, she also remained herself; her naïveté and her lack of affectation were there for all to see, but so also was the joy of making music. It was a joy she felt compelled to share with others. "Some people regard her as being too 'sweet' for jazz, comparing her to Billie Holiday as being the serious jazz singer," said Niels-Henning Orsted-Pedersen. "I've never felt this. Joy has the same right to be expressed as sadness. And having played with her, from my point of view Ella represents joy."[11]

If Ella remained less libretto-oriented than most contemporary singers, during the 1980s an even greater gulf began to open up between the inherent musical qualities of a song and its lyrics. In May 1982, for example, she was in Houston, where John Scarborough reviewed her concert for the *Houston Post*. "Significant was the presence of the hugely heralded but still relatively unsung Jimmy Rowles on piano. But Ella wasn't just into swinging jazz. At this stage of her legendary career she's beginning to have even more fun with material, to extend herself, to dissolve the literal meaning of the lyric where appropriate—not through deliberate abstraction but rather through total concentration on the purely musical aspects behind them."[12]

In fact, Ella's concern with abstraction, though modest compared to, say, Betty Carter's, was to conceal the continuing deterioration of her voice. Marshaling her vocal resources and remarkable imagination, she was using shorter phrase lengths to conceal her insecurities of pitch, vibrato, and breath control; rather than dwell too long on sustained notes, she would pump additional syllables into her line to jump back and forth from them, like stepping-stones across a wide brook. This technique showed up on "Nice Work If You Can Get It," with André Previn on piano and Niels-Henning Orsted-Pedersen on bass, from May 1983. In "A Foggy Day," for example, she oscillates between two notes on "A Fo-gog-gog-ey Day," yet despite her resourcefulness, her use of melismata, slides, and swoops, she was unable to disguise completely the inevitable effects of aging.

In the early spring of 1983, Jimmy Rowles handed in his notice. "The only thing I couldn't handle was all the traveling, and really, I don't know how she did. We did an awful lot of what you would call *serious* traveling. Brutal, like a one-nighter from New York to Caracas, Venezuela. A *one-nighter*! I didn't even get a chance to see the city! I was on the plane to come back home first thing in the morning. I'd get home and be resting . . . and the phone would ring, and we were leaving for twenty-five one-nighters through the Scandinavian states. I finally had to give up, I just had to throw in the towel."

Rowles was replaced by Paul Smith, and in June they appeared at the Kennedy Center. This was followed by a Carnegie Hall appearance for the 1983 Kool (formerly Newport) Jazz Festival: "The peerless vocalist delivered ninety minutes of standards . . . to sustained audience ovations."[13] Then followed a strange gig fifteen thousand feet up, aboard a Continental Airlines flight, to promote their new pub compartments. Ella, genial and unaffected as ever, was heard to exclaim mid-performance, "My stockings are beginning to fall down."[14]

In 1982, Norman Granz was contacted by Shin Watanabe, of one of the largest music publishers in Japan, who wanted to present a JATP concert to commemorate the thirtieth anniversary of the troupe's first Japanese visit in 1953. Once again Granz had Ella and Oscar Peterson to headline the show, but during the intervening years Charlie Shavers, Ben Webster, Bill Harris, Gene Krupa, and Willie Smith from the original group had died, and Roy Eldridge had retired. In attempting to preserve the same spirit of the 1953 group, Granz selected "Sweets" Edison and Clark Terry on trumpets, J. J.

Johnson and Al Grey on trombones, Zoot Sims and Eddie "Lockjaw" Davis on tenor saxophones, Joe Pass on guitar, Niels-Henning Orsted-Pedersen on bass, and Louis Bellson on drums, plus Ella's trio of Paul Smith on piano, Keter Betts on bass, and Bobby Durham on drums.

In October 1983 the group descended the steps of a Boeing 747 at Tokyo's airport. In contrast to their tumultuous welcome of 1953, nobody gave them a second glance as they were greeted by two soberly dressed representatives of the impresario. Times had changed: The JATP troupe was now just one of hundreds of American jazz groups who visited Japan every year. Their concert at Yoyogi National Stadium in Tokyo was recorded in its entirety and released in 1987 on two compact discs as *Return to Happiness: Jazz at the Philharmonic Yoyogi National Stadium, Tokyo, 1983*. Ella's portion of the concert took up the second half of the second compact disc; as usual, Granz presented her as the headliner at the top of the show. Ella, buoyed by an enthusiastic audience, contributes a typically hard-working set. Her version of "Manteca" suits the rhythmic orientation of her latter-day style, now emphasized in her ballads by moving into double time as soon as possible and dwelling less on sustained notes. Even though her voice is darker, her range smaller, and her vibrato less sure, there is a defiant courage in her singing that is perhaps most apparent in "All of Me" and the old JATP warhorse, "Flying Home," an over-the-shoulder glance at the days of yore when her voice was in total service to her imagination and she could look the horn players in the eye and say to herself, "Anything you can do, I can do better."

But the deterioration in Ella's health was closing in on her faster than she realized. In August 1985, complaining of shortness of breath, she was admitted to the George Washington University Hospital in Washington, D.C. Fluid in the lungs was diagnosed, yet within a month she was back performing at the Hollywood Bowl. She had lost weight and appeared to have breathing problems, but the hectic schedule continued.

In June 1986 she opened the inaugural JVC Jazz Festival in New York (formerly the Newport, then the Kool Jazz Festival) at Avery Fisher Hall. Trying to ring the changes from the "same old songs" that formed the basis of her repertoire, she included a *My Fair Lady* medley and the numbers she recorded with Benny Goodman back in 1936. But, as John S. Wilson in the *New York Times* pointed out, "It was the 'same old songs' that gave the program its high points. . . .

She delivered the songs with an inventive polish and an enthusiasm that, seemingly, has never flagged in all her years of singing them."[15]

Then suddenly, at 11 A.M. on July 27, having performed the night before at Artpark in Lewiston, New York, Ella was admitted to the nearby Niagara Falls Hospital suffering from what was initially diagnosed as heat exhaustion. Three days later she was released, after being reassured that she had not suffered a heart attack and that, as one doctor put it, she was "101 percent in spirit and almost 100 percent physically." But in early September came word that Ella was in a Los Angeles hospital with an undisclosed ailment. This was followed by the news that she had undergone open-heart surgery at Cedars-Sinai Medical Center, where she had been admitted on August 19. A hospital spokesman said that Miss Fitzgerald was making good progress. Later, Mary Jane Outwater confirmed to the press that Ella had canceled her engagements for the rest of the year.

Not even open-heart surgery could stop her determination to continue performing, however. In June 1987 she played El Camino College near Los Angeles. The audience response was overwhelming, prompting Ella to claim that it was as good as medicine. She played a few more dates and then in August was back in the hospital suffering complications from diabetes that resulted in the amputation of a toe. Recuperation took months, but she eventually returned to public performance in March 1988 at Palm Springs. This time she was hesitant about resuming her schedule, but *Ella in Rome: The Birthday Concert* had been released in the spring.

"Norman and Ella had a completely different reaction to *Ella in Rome* going to number one on *Billboard*," said Phil Schaap who produced the album for release. "Granz was unhappy that record came out. Now I don't know why exactly. She got her money according to the contract, and it is my understanding the agreements were maintained and that in the course of its success she got a nice bonus because it went to number one.

"It stayed number one for the whole summer, and I know she loved it. She used it in her concerts: 'I'm so happy to be back. Some little guy found a tape of me, and now I'm number one.' When I met her in June 1988, she was 100 percent positive the record was a catalyst to the reactivation of her career at this time. I was MC at the JVC Festival, and she was *positive* about it.

"She couldn't have made an album of that strength at that juncture in her career, and here was the past dovetailing with the present, giving her an incredible wealth of good publicity. The only time she appeared in print at that time was negative—that she was in the hospital and so on—and here was all this positive publicity. . . . I played it for her in Keter Betts's apartment the afternoon of the concert, and she agreed with me it was her best ever 'Porgy.' She liked the sound. She loved it!"

With the success of *Ella in Rome*, Ella's career once again gathered momentum. There were ups: In 1987 she was presented with a National Medal of Arts by President Reagan. And there were downs: At her July 1988 appearance at the Hollywood Bowl she took a tumble, joking, "It's okay. I'm okay. I'll just sing from down here," as Paul Smith leaped to her aid.[16] The incident showed Ella's determination to continue performing no matter what; many members of the audience had left for the second half, assuming that Ella would not be fit enough to continue. But continue she did, albeit seated, opening the second half with "I Fell for You."

Indeed, the more Ella performed, the more complete her rehabilitation seemed. "I worked with Ella for only one day as part of the sax section in Benny Carter's band backing her when she played Radio City Music Hall in New York in 1990," said Loren Schoenberg. "I mentioned to her road manager, Val Valentine, what a wonderful performer she was, and he said it was truly remarkable after this period of severe ill health. And remember, rumors had been rampant that either she had died, that she was very sick, that she had had a heart attack, or whatever, but she had been really sick and, it seems, she had been getting worse. She hadn't been singing, obviously, and then she did one concert, and she seemed a little better. So she started doing a couple of concerts, and her health started to come back.

"Only after she had been on the road singing did she really bounce back, so by protecting her and keeping her in her home in Beverly Hills, she was deteriorating. I think a lot of people are like that. Benny Carter is like that. These great artists who get to a relatively advanced age, playing and performing is so much a part of their makeup. It's so important to them to get out there."

Yet ever since the 1960s, when she began to enjoy international acclaim, Ella had progressively become a more isolated figure. She did have a boyfriend for a long while: "She had someone in Philadelphia she liked," said Lou Levy. "I don't know his name, but I think he was actually affiliated with the police force." However, Ella's office, Salle Productions, run by Mary Jane Outwater, worked hard to keep both the press and an adoring public at bay. Jim Haskins has written how

Mary Jane appeared to block fan mail just as much as letters from friends."[17]

But, as Norman Granz points out, it is well known that Ella is not the world's greatest party-goer. Close friends have her number and address, and she is particularly close to Peggy Lee. Although it may seem that she had become increasingly difficult to get to, appearing to be insulated by those who surrounded her, as friends on the West Coast came to report,[18] maybe it was because she wanted it that way.

Yet Ella is essentially a happy person, particularly with people she knows. "She has a great sense of humor," recalled Jimmy Rowles, himself a very witty man. "It came across great whenever she felt like it. She'd hear something or someone would tell her something, and if she liked it, she really enjoyed laughing at it. She loved to laugh, and she loved to talk about music and songs. That's the topmost subject she likes to talk about." But once the touring was over, so were the shared jokes and the fun shared with musicians on the road as she retreated to her ivory-towered luxury in Beverly Hills. Music also provided the social intercourse missing in her private life, maybe because it was the only time she felt confident and in control of things.

Perhaps the ultimate price of superstardom is loneliness. It becomes impossible to lead a normal life, to go to public places without being surrounded by a sea of well-wishers. As her social life became almost zero, her work provided interaction, another reason to keep performing. The British critic Max Jones, a friend since Ella's first appearance in the England in 1948, observed: "Ella was not gregarious by nature and tended to wait for people to seek her company. As she grew in fame and artistic stature, the less her fans and acquaintances, including me, felt free to intrude upon her uninvited.

"I don't think things were helped by her eyesight, which of course began to deteriorate at the end of the sixties. Norman Granz alerted us to this at one London concert when my wife had walked past the open door of Ella's dressing room, paused to nod to her as she was sitting there all alone, but received no greeting in reply. 'You should have gone in. You'd have been welcome,' Granz assured us. 'It wasn't a snub. She simply couldn't see you.' I took his advice, and it was clear no snub was intended. I concluded that although at times she preferred her own company, Ella often felt lonely, and not by choice."

On April 28, 1989, the Society of Singers created a trophy to honor a lifetime of achievement, dubbing it an "Ella." Its first recipient was, of course, its namesake. The idea was to raise money for singers who had fallen on hard times. Among the celebrity audience at the presentation ceremony were Mel Tormé and George Shearing (who later performed together), Bea Wain, Kay Starr, Kitty Kallen, Martha Tilton, Helen Forrest, Helen O'Connell, Carol Burnett, Dionne Warwick, Manhattan Transfer, Barbra Streisand, Quincy Jones, Clint Eastwood, Carol Bayer Sager, Burt Bacharach, Gloria Loring, Helen Reddy, Pat Boone, Gloria and Jimmy Stewart, Cyd Charisse, and Tony Martin; and the occasion was hosted by Bill Cosby. This was truly being honored by peers. The following night she received the prestigious George and Ira Gershwin Award for outstanding achievement.

In 1990, Ella presented her eponymous award to Frank Sinatra. "I saw her perform at the 'Ella' awards on December 3, 1990, when she presented the 'Ella' to Mr. Sinatra," said Sylvia Syms. "It was the second award given by the Society of Singers, and she sang 'The Lady Is a Tramp' with Mr. S., and my God, she blew everybody away. After she'd been so sick! I knew how bad she was because I had sent her a get-well card myself and saw her at that particular time—we were so glad to see each other—yet she could still get up there and sing and blow everybody away!"

In March 1989 she had ventured back into the recording studios. Ray Brown selected the music, which included a Jimmy Rowles composition, "Baby, Don't You Quit Now," plus a host of "good old good ones," including "My Last Affair," "Oh, Look at Me Now," "When Your Lover Has Gone," "The Nearness of You," "Little Jazz," "Dream a Little Dream of Me," "Just When We're Falling in Love" (a number that went back to her Decca output; she originally recorded it as "Robbins' Nest"), and the album's title track, "All That Jazz," a Benny Carter composition. As had been her wont in her later years, she also included some numbers associated with Billie Holiday: "That Old Devil Called Love" and "Good Morning, Heartache."

Norman Granz produced the session and selected the musicians, including many who had worked for him over the years: "Sweets" Edison, Benny Carter, Al Grey, and Clark Terry. It also included the debut of Mike Wofford, who had succeeded Paul Smith on piano. *All That Jazz* won a Grammy in 1991, to no one's surprise. Ella's voice was a shadow of her halcyon days, but the award seemed more for past triumphs than present aspiration. "There's a maturity and depth in her interpretations now that's better than ever, I think, in her approach to her material and repertoire," said Mike Wofford. "There's a new element in Ella that's beautiful to see and hear. That happened to Sass over the years. All the great singers, if they have continued over that many decades, become different singers than they were. They get deeper and better, with a touching quality."[19] Indeed, Norman Granz continued to record Ella and her trio, plus guests including Harry Edison and Joe Pass, for Salle Productions, which holds enough material for a further album.

When Ella appeared at the New York JVC Festival in June 1989, she received a rapturous welcome. She was now seen as a living legend and could do no wrong. "Ella Fitzgerald retains a remarkable artistic purity. The basic elements of her style were intact. Her primary qualities were a celestial sweetness, an unflagging rhythmic acuity, and a deep instinct for the melodic arc of a song," said the *New York Times*.[20] The following month she returned to the Hollywood Bowl and an adoring audience of 14,263. "In a performance that is certainly deserving of 'Triumph!' Fitzgerald showed that 71 is just a number and that a willing spirit more than compensates for a weakened body," said the *Los Angeles Times*.[21]

As she entered the 1990s, she continued to work under her doctor's supervision. Three concerts a month, because of her delicate health, eventually became one. Consequently, Ella spent more and more time at home. "She's not traveling so much anymore, but knowing Ella, I know she's a big fan of soap operas. She's always watching those things. That's how she kills most of her time," said Lou Levy. "She just watches television. Most of the time she's a lady of leisure. It doesn't take a lot to entertain Ella. I don't think she's a big reader. But she loves being out there, and she loves those accolades, I'm sure. That's what keeps her going."

Her need for applause was as insatiable in her seventies as it had been in her teens. In February 1990 she was feted at the "Hearts for Ella" concert. "Too often in tributes to the few jazz creators who are famous enough to transcend the jazz audience, jazz is left standing at the stage door," said Gary Giddins. "The hearts for Ella were in the right place—for which credit is undoubtedly due to producer Edith Kiggen, who booked a few show-biz personalities but did not let them hold sway."[22] In March, Ella again held sway, this time at the Royal Albert Hall in London, her first visit there in five years. In an interview for London's *Evening Standard* she said she'd heard a song on British television she wanted to do. It was a theme from the long-running Australian soap, *Neighbours*.

Despite having to pull out of the 1990 North Sea Jazz Festival, because of exhaustion in July, and the subsequent European tour, on her doctor's advice, Ella would not be stilled. She was back at the Hollywood Bowl on August 22, greeted by an audience of almost eighteen thousand fans. And so she continued, singing concert after concert, accepting award after award. By now those awards, honorary degrees, and citations, so much a part of being a living legend, were beginning to fill a whole room in her home, from floor to ceiling. "She doesn't know how good she is," said Mel Tormé. "I'm presenting an award to her on July 4, 1991, a Black Achievement Award, at the Palladium, and I consider it a signal honor. But believe me, when she gets that award it's going to be like all the other awards she has received: 'What did I ever do to deserve this?' That's the way she is."

In 1992, ASCAP gave a party in a Beverly Hills hotel suite to salute the achievements of Norman Granz, who flew in from Geneva for the occasion. Ella headed the guest list, of course, which included Benny Carter and composers Johnny Mandel and Alan and Marilyn Bergman. Ella was still performing—at the Hollywood Bowl, the Davies Hall with the San Francisco Symphony, and Radio City Music Hall in New York with Clark Terry's big band. "Singing is really her life," observed Paul Smith. "She doesn't have a lot of voice left, especially when it comes to singing ballads, but she can do the up tunes. She's still best at that. It's hard for her, with the health problems she's had, to sustain any kind of tone. She's had the heart problems, the amputation of the toe, but she still comes out and does a good show.

"She works about once a month, to keep her hand in the business. She wouldn't know what to do if she wasn't singing. That's when she comes alive, when she's onstage. The rest of her life, well, she doesn't have any family to speak of. What there is, she's kind of supported. She's the one who made it in the family."

Ella in those last years remained proud and unbowed. Although voice and body clearly showed the signs of aging, her spirit did not. It hungrily fed off the adrenaline charge that only a live performance can bring. To live is to perform; there is no other meaning or reason for being alive. At the 1990 JVC Festival in New York at the beginning of July, it was clear that she was being celebrated as much for hanging in there as for her performance. And even if she no longer achieves the level of excellence as in days of yore, then, as Gene Seymour in *Newsday* observed, there is still much to celebrate: "One didn't honor Fitzgerald for her ability to go ballistic so much as her singular ability to move horizontally with sly scat phrases and familiar lyrics that she can still twist into oblong or angular shapes. At one point in the first set she paid tribute to Billie Holiday with her own rendering of 'Rocks in My Heart.' Or was it 'Devil Called Love'? She couldn't remember all the lyrics. . . . Still, you can't help noticing that, just as Holiday's spirit often gave lift to her twilight performances even after her vocal performances declined, so does Fitzgerald retain an indomitable core of exuberance and invention."[23]

In 1989, Ella joined a cast of thousands assembled to participate on the Quincy Jones album, *Back on the Block*. She sang on three tracks: "Wee B. Dooinit," an a cappella groove number with Al Jarreau, Bobby McFerrin, Take 6, and Sarah Vaughan; "Jazz Corner of the World," a rap number; and "Birdland," with contributions from Miles Davis, James Moody, George Benson, Sarah Vaughan, Dizzy Gillespie, and the song's composer, Joe Zawinul. While her presence on the album seemed more in honor of who she was—Jones refers to her in his liner notes as "our most distinguished Grande Dame Ella Fitzgerald (past seven decades and still knocking us out)"—than for any specific musical contribution, the wheel had nevertheless turned full circle. She had begun her career singing commercial pop tunes, and in what was to be her final recording session, she was doing so again.

From the very beginning of her career during the swing era, Ella's voice, image, and body was never the site of sexual fantasy in the way many of the startling beauties that sang with the big bands did, such as Billie Holiday, Lena Horne, Peggy Lee, and Martha Tilton. Over the years female jazz and popular singing has tended to suggest femininity as something decorative and wistful, secret and available, addressed by its very nature to men. The effect of the voice, so intimately and intrinsically a part of the singer, makes sound and image virtually inseparable. Ella somehow transcended these conventions. Her voice seemed virginal and unsullied, speaking not of empty beds and unrequited love but of the modest hopes of pubescent romance. Her role as a singer was always that of a perpetual adolescent waiting to see what life will bring. She sounded too young to have had any sexual experiences of her own; the sheer innocent enjoyment she found in the music of sophisticated love songs contradicted the passion and pathos of their lyrics. This duality allowed her to leave a song very much as she found it, untarnished by subjectivity, so that in her vast discography there is no single version of a song that can be pointed to as the definitive Ella Fitzgerald. Instead, there are hundreds and hundreds of songs where her performances show a remarkable consistency; and the better the song, the better she appears as a singer. Ella's studio work is defined not so much by her performances as by the inherent musical characteristics of the songs themselves. Betty Carter, a brilliant jazz singer in her own right and herself the winner of a Grammy in 1989, observed: "Ella sings a ballad pretty much how the composer wants a ballad sung, because she's going to sing it straight, no doubt about that. She may twist it a little bit on the end—maybe. She's not going to deviate from the melody that much, but the way she approaches the melody is the important thing. Audiences liked that. They could always depend on Ella: on the way she approached the melody, the phrasing, the attack of the words, the way they *sounded* when she sang."

Outside the recording studio Ella was never more alive than with a band on stage and never more inventive than when she launched into a scatted improvisation. Then imagination, humor, and sheer talent earned her the respect of the jazz pantheon. This was the essence of Ella Fitzgerald.

But her wonderful voice and the priceless gift of being able to swing were in themselves no guarantee of success. To survive and thrive in the music business demands a determination to succeed that can withstand the most devastating blows to the ego. Ella, for all her performance anxieties and insecurities, has driven herself relentlessly. "She's worked hard all her life, and she's still working hard," said Betty Carter in 1992. "It's unreal how she's working so hard, being as ill as she is. You wouldn't be working in a wheelchair if you're not working for people. The woman's doing that now. So what's on her mind? It's not glamour. She just wants to do what she loves; she wants to hear the applause. It's her life, her reason for living."

It's ironic that Ella, who has so loved her audiences and who throughout her life has given unstintingly of herself, should have remained such a lonely figure. Apart from her marriage to Ray Brown, her life has been spent in a series of affairs that have never led to the security and happiness of which she sang and which she herself sought so desperately. But she has found fulfillment through her music and in the warmth and joy she has received from her audiences. This helps to explain why Ella has concerned herself less with the quality of her material than with the effect it has on "the people." She loves to sing, but it must be what she thinks her audiences want to hear. Sometimes she has appeared to make no discrimination between good and bad. The key has been the audience reaction: If they liked a number, then it was in. This policy has occasionally led to raised eyebrows among both her musicians and her more jazz-oriented fans. "I think she lays so much stress on being accepted in music because this is the one area of life into which she feels she can fit successfully," said one musician who toured with her for years. "Her marriages have failed. She doesn't have an awful lot of the normal activities most women have, such as home life, so she wraps herself up entirely in music. She wants desperately to be accepted."

It took the *Songbook* cycle and Norman Granz's careful stewardship of her career for Ella to become an internationally renowned jazz artist. Under Granz's authoritarian direction she thrived. He imposed an underlying aesthetic in the choice of her repertoire, realizing that the twentieth-century American popular song represented an opportunity for interpretation and extemporization. These songs could be reinvented by whatever artist happened to be singing them. When Ella addressed the *Songbook* cycle—part jazz lieder, part cocktail music—not only did she revalidate the songs in terms that proved to be accessible to a wide public, she made her statements stick, enhancing her status as an artist beyond her wildest dreams. And in return it seemed that every time she sang those songs, they revalidated her.

Ella's odyssey has taken her from dire poverty to the luxury of Beverly Hills via dance halls, dingy nightclubs, and segregated accommodations in a country that still totters on the racial divide. In her own unassertive way Ella has defied the traditional expectations of a black person in a predominantly white society. She has endured discrimination with dignity and given herself equally to black and white audiences, who in their turn have taken her into their hearts. She has been feted by the highest in the land and showered with awards, medals, and honorary degrees as tangible evidence of her status as a performing artist. She has been acknowledged as a legend in her own lifetime, a legend who in her later years performed before audiences that wanted to consume the aura of the physical presence of one of the great and enduring figures of twentieth-century music. "It isn't where you came from, it's where you're going that counts," she once said. And if anyone can claim to have gotten there and to have embodied the whole American Dream in the process, then it is that enigmatic, self-effacing black lady who was born out of wedlock on April 25, 1917, in Newport News, Virginia.

NOTES

PREFACE

1. Gary Giddins, *Riding on a Blue Note*, Oxford University Press, New York, 1981.

PROLOGUE

1. *Newsday*, April 25, 1990.
2. Ibid.

CHAPTER ONE: 1917–1930

Author's interviews with Josephine Attanasio, Mario Bauza, Annette Miller (née Gulliver), Dan Morgenstern, Joe Pass, Mel Tormé, and George Wein.

1. *Jazztimes*, September 1991.
2. Joe Smith, *Off the Record*, Warner Books, New York, 1989.
3. Letter from Mrs. A. Tyrpolis, Historical Archivist, Yonkers Public Schools, 1992.
4. New York State census, 1925.
5. Ibid.
6. Letter to author, 1991.
7. Ibid.
8. Whitney Balliett, *New York Notes*, Da Capo, New York, 1977.
9. Letter from Mrs. A. Tyropolis, Historical Archivist, Yonkers Public Schools, 1992.
10. Dorothy Baker, *Young Man with a Horn*, Amereon, Ltd., Mattituck, NY, 1977.
11. Gary Giddins, *Satchmo*, Dolphin Doubleday, New York, 1988.
12. *Pulse*, April 1988.
13. Will Friedwald, *Jazz Singing*, Scribners, New York, 1990.
14. Gunther Schuller, *The Swing Era*, Oxford University Press, New York, 1990.
15. Liner notes, MCA MCFM 2739.

CHAPTER TWO: 1931–1935

Author's interviews with Josephine Attanasio, Benny Carter, Charles Gulliver, Charles Linton, Annette Miller (née Gulliver), Phil Schaap, Sylvia Syms, and Arthur Tracy.

1. Interview with Mrs. A. Tyropolis, Historical Archivist, Yonkers Public Schools, by Marsha S. Dennis, 1992.
2. Among many references: Leonard Feather, *From Satchmo to Miles*, Da Capo, New York, 1984
3. Liner notes Verve 517 898-2 by Gene Lees.
4. Interview with Charles Gulliver by Marsha S. Dennis, 1992.
5. Letter from Mrs. A. Tyropolis, Historical Archivist, Yonkers Public Schools, 1992.
6. *Los Angeles Times*, January 30, 1983.
7. Ibid.
8. Schomberg Institute, Harlem; Riverdale Children's Association Archive.
9. Ralph Moore and Steve Dougherty, *Showtime at the Apollo*, HarperCollins, New York, 1990.
10. Ibid.
11. Buck Clayton, *Buck Clayton's Jazz World*, Oxford University Press, New York, 1987.
12. Joe Smith, *Off the Record*, Warner Books, New York, 1989.
13. Moore and Dougherty, *Showtime at the Apollo*.
14. Ibid.
15. *New York Age*, November 24, 1934.
16. Letter to author, January 27, 1991.
17. Among many references: Smith, *Off the Record*; *Continental*, September 1984; Aspel and Co., ITV interview, March 1990.
18. *Newsday*, April 25, 1990.
19. Smith, *Off the Record*.
20. Walter Allen, *Hendersonia*, Monographs, Highland Park, NJ, 1974.
21. Moore and Dougherty, *Showtime at the Apollo*.
22. Among many references: *Down Beat*, November 18, 1965.
23. Among many references: a ghost-written article under Ella's name, *Continental*, September 1984; Smith, *Off the Record*.
24. Moore and Dougherty, *Showtime at the Apollo*.
25. Stanley Dance, *The World of Swing*, Scribners, New York, 1974.
26. *Metronome*, November 1947.
27. *New York Age*, February 9, 1935.
28. Allen, *Hendersonia*.
29. John Chilton, interview with author, 1991.

CHAPTER THREE: 1935

Author's interviews with Mario Bauza, Charles Linton, and George T. Simon.

1. Interview with Ram Ramirez by Loren Schoenberg, 1991.
2. Obituary, *Down Beat*, July 1939.
3. Garvin Bushell, as told to Mark Tucker, *Jazz from the Beginning*, University of Michigan Press, Ann Arbor, 1988.
4. Burt Korall, *Drummin' Men*, Schirmer Books, New York, 1990.
5. *Amsterdam News*, May 18, 1927.
6. *Down Beat*, December 1937.

7. *New York Age*, November 24, 1928.
8. Korall, *Drummin' Men*.
9. *New York Age*, April 1931.
10. *Amsterdam News*, October 5, 1932.
11. Korall, *Drummin' Men*.
12. *Amsterdam News*, May 17, 1933.
13. Ibid., June 21, 1933.
14. Ibid., August 13, 1933.
15. Ibid., January 3, 1934.
16. Ibid.
17. Liner notes, REB 655.
18. American Federation of Musicians card, William Webb, 1939.
19. "The Rise of a Crippled Genius," *Down Beat*, January 1938.
20. Interview with Teddy McRae by Ron Welburn, October 6–8, 1981, Jazz Oral History Project, Institute of Jazz Studies, Rutgers University, NJ.
21. Ibid.
22. Leonard Feather, *From Satchmo to Miles*, Da Capo, New York, 1984.
23. *Down Beat*, February 1938.
24. Interview with Hal Austin by Loren Schoenberg, 1991.
25. Feather, *From Satchmo to Miles*.
26. *Down Beat*, February 1938.
27. Clyde Bernhardt, *I Remember*, University of Pennsylvania Press, Pennsylvania, 1986.
28. *Metronome*, June 1935.
29. Interview with Teddy McRae by Ron Welburn, 1981.
30. *Amsterdam News*, June 1, 1935.
31. Korall, *Drummin' Men*.

CHAPTER FOUR: 1935–1938

Author's interviews with Mario Bauza, John Chilton, Charles Linton, and Dan Morgenstern.

1. Interview with Hal Austin by Loren Schoenberg, 1991.
2. Nat Shapiro and Nat Hentoff, *Hear Me Talkin' to Ya*, Dover, New York, 1966.
3. *New York Age*, July 25, 1935.
4. Jack Schiffman, *Uptown: The Story of Harlem's Apollo Theater*, Cowles, New York, 1970.
5. *Metronome*, January 1936.
6. Interview with Teddy McRae by Ron Welburn, October 6–8, 1981, Jazz Oral History Project, Institute of Jazz Studies, Rutgers University, NJ.
7. Ibid.
8. Ibid.
9. Ibid.
10. Ibid.
11. *Melody Maker*, December 26, 1936.
12. Ibid., February 6, 1937.
13. Jim Haskins, *Ella Fitzgerald: A Life Through Jazz*, New English Library, London, 1991.

14. Gene Lees, *Waiting for Dizzy*, Oxford University Press, New York, 1991.
15. Interview with Ram Ramirez by Loren Schoenberg, 1991.
16. *Down Beat*, October 1937.
17. Ibid., February 1938.
18. Interview with Teddy McRae by Ron Welburn, 1981.
19. *Down Beat*, November 1937.
20. Korall, *Drummin' Men*.
21. Garvin Bushell, as told to Mark Tucker, *Jazz from the Beginning*, University of Michigan Press, Ann Arbor, 1988.
22. Korall, *Drummin' Men*.
23. *Down Beat*, October 1937.
24. Phil Schaap archives.
25. Ken Whitten collection.
26. Interview with Hal Austin by Loren Schoenberg, 1991.
27. *Metronome*, June 1937.
28. Ibid.
29. News clipping from an unknown source, courtesy of the Institute of Jazz Studies, Rutgers University, NJ.
30. *Down Beat*, March 1938.
31. Ibid., April 1938.
32. Interview with Teddy McRae by Ron Welburn, 1981.
33. Haskins, *Ella Fitzgerald*.
34. Interview with Teddy McRae by Ron Welburn, 1981.
35. Ibid.
36. Liner notes, Swingtime ST 1007.
37. Interview with Beverly Peer by Loren Schoenberg, 1991.
38. Interview with Teddy McRae by Ron Welburn, 1981.
39. Bushell, *Jazz from the Beginning*.
40. Interview with Beverly Peer by Loren Schoenberg, 1991.

CHAPTER FIVE: 1938–1942

Author's interviews with John Chilton, Phil Schaap, and George T. Simon.

1. Interview with Teddy McRae by Ron Welburn, October 6–8, 1981, Jazz Oral History Project, Institute of Jazz Studies, Rutgers University, NJ.
2. *Down Beat*, January 1939.
3. News clipping from an unknown source, dated January 1939, courtesy of the Institute of Jazz Studies, Rutgers University, NJ.
4. Interview with Heywood Henry by Loren Schoenberg, 1992.
5. *Down Beat*, March 1939.
6. Gene Fernett, *Swing Out*, Pendell Publishing Co., Midland, MI, 1970.
7. *New York Age*, February 2, 1939.
8. News clipping from an unknown source dated February 1939, courtesy of the Institute of Jazz Studies, Rutgers University, NJ.
9. Interview with Teddy McRae by Ron Welburn, 1981.
10. Paul Eduard Miller, *Down Beat Yearbook of Swing*, Down Beat Publishing Co., Chicago, 1939.

11. Interview with Teddy McRae by Ron Welburn, 1981.
12. News clipping from an unknown source dated June 1939, courtesy of the Institute of Jazz Studies, Rutgers University, NJ.
13. Interview with Teddy McRae by Ron Welburn, 1981.
14. Ibid.
15. Stanley Dance, *The World of Swing*, Scribners, New York, 1974.
16. Garvin Bushell, as told to Mark Tucker, *Jazz from the Beginning*, University of Michigan Press, Ann Arbor, 1988.
17. Dance, *World of Swing*.
18. Jim Haskins, *Ella Fitzgerald: A Life Through Jazz*, New English Library, London, 1991.
19. Interview with Teddy McRae by Ron Welburn, 1981.
20. Ibid.
21. Dance, *World of Swing*.
22. Interview with Teddy McRae by Ron Welburn, 1981.
23. Interview with Ram Ramirez by Stanley Dance, 1992, Jazz Oral History Project, Institute of Jazz Studies, Rutgers University, NJ.
24. Dance, *World of Swing*.
25. Joe Smith, *Off the Record*, Warner Books, New York, 1989.
26. *Down Beat*, November 1, 1940.
27. Gunther Schuller, *The Swing Era*, Oxford University Press, New York, 1990.
28. Interview with Milt Gabler by Loren Schoenberg, 1992.
29. Whitney Balliett, *Goodbyes and Other Messages*, Oxford University Press, New York, 1990.
30. *Down Beat*, July 1940.
31. Haskins, *Ella Fitzgerald*.
32. Ibid.
33. Interview with Beverly Peer by Loren Schoenberg, 1991.
34. Interview with Teddy McRae by Ron Welburn, 1981.
35. Ibid.
36. Ibid.
37. Ibid.
38. Stanley Dance, *The World of Earl Hines*, Scribners, New York, 1977.
39. Interview with Teddy McRae by Ron Welburn, 1981.
40. Dizzy Gillespie with Al Fraser, *Dizzy: To Be or Not to Bop*, Da Capo, New York, 1985.
41. Interview with Teddy McRae by Ron Welburn, 1981.
42. Ibid.
43. Interview with Eddie Barefield, Jazz Oral History Project, Institute of Jazz Studies, Rutgers University, NJ.
44. Fernett, *Swing Out*.
45. *Orchestra World*, May 1942.
46. *Metronome*, May 1942.
47. *Music and Rhythm*, May 1942.
48. *Metronome*, June 1942.
49. Interview with Eddie Barefield, Institute of Jazz Studies.
50. Interview with Beverly Peer by Loren Schoenberg, 1991.

CHAPTER SIX: 1942–1946

Author's interview with Bill Doggett.

1. Whitney Balliett, *Night Creature*, Oxford University Press, New York, 1981.
2. *Metronome*, April 1943.
3. Ibid.
4. Quoted in Balliett, *Night Creature*.
5. Interview with Milt Gabler by Loren Schoenberg, 1992.
6. Ibid.
7. Ibid.
8. *New York Age*, January 15, 1944.
9. *Chicago Defender*, May 13, 1944.
10. Liner notes, Affinity AFS 1031.
11. Interview with Milt Gabler by Loren Schoenberg, 1992.
12. *Down Beat*, 1944.
13. John Hammond, *John Hammond on the Record*, Penguin Books, Harmondsworth, England 1981.
14. *Metronome*, January 1945.
15. Interview with Milt Gabler by Loren Schoenberg, 1992.
16. Ibid.
17. Ibid.
18. Ibid.
19. George T. Simon, *Simon Says: The Sights and Sounds of the Swing Era*, Arlington House, New York, 1971.
20. *Metronome*, April 1946.
21. *Down Beat*, July 1, 1946.
22. *Metronome*, July 1946.
23. *Metronome*, December 1946.
24. Interview with Milt Gabler by Loren Schoenberg, 1992.
25. *Metronome*, November 1946.
26. Will Friedwald, *Jazz Singing*, Scribners, New York, 1990.
27. Mel Tormé, *Traps the Drum Wonder*, Oxford University Press, New York, 1991.
28. Hammond, *John Hammond on the Record*.
29. *Metronome*, December 1946.
30. Jim Haskins, *Ella Fitzgerald: A Life Through Jazz*, New English Library, London, 1991.
31. *Ebony*, May 1949.
32. *Chicago Defender*, July 21, 1945.

CHAPTER SEVEN: 1946–1947

Author's interviews with John Lewis, Will Friedwald, and Sonny Rollins.

1. Mel Tormé, *It Wasn't All Velvet*, Viking Penguin, New York, 1988.
2. Letter to author, 1991.
3. Will Friedwald, *Jazz Singing*, Scribners, New York, 1990.
4. *Down Beat*, July 2, 1947.

5. *Ebony*, May 1949.
6. Quoted in *Down Beat*, July 2, 1964.
7. Stanley Dance, *The World of Swing*, Scribners, New York, 1974.
8. Dizzy Gillespie with Al Fraser, *Dizzy: To Be or Not to Bop*, Da Capo, New York, 1985.
9. Dance, *The World of Swing*.
10. Gillespie, *Dizzy: To Be or Not to Bop*.
11. Ibid.
12. Interview with Milt Gabler by Loren Schoenberg, 1992.
13. *Down Beat*, September 24, 1947.
14. Interview with Milt Gabler by Loren Schoenberg, 1992.
15. Ibid.
16. *Down Beat*, May 21, 1947.
17. Interview with Milt Gabler by Loren Schoenberg, 1992.
18. *Metronome*, November 1947.
19. Interview with Tommy Flanagan by Loren Schoenberg, 1992.
20. *Together for the First Time: Mel Tormé and Buddy Rich*, CJCD-833.
21. Interview with Milt Gabler by Loren Schoenberg, 1992.
22. *Down Beat*, September 24, 1947.
23. Quoted in Gillespie, *Dizzy: To Be or Not to Bop*.
24. *Down Beat*, October 22, 1947.
25. Ibid.
26. Ibid.
27. Gillespie, *Dizzy: To Be or Not to Bop*.
28. Interview with Milt Gabler by Loren Schoenberg, 1992.
29. *Metronome*, November 1947.
30. Ibid.

CHAPTER EIGHT: 1947–1949

Author's interviews with Norman Granz and Max Jones.

1. Leonard Feather, *From Satchmo to Miles*, Da Capo, New York, 1984.
2. Dizzy Gillespie with Al Fraser, *Dizzy: To Be or Not to Bop*, Da Capo, New York, 1985.
3. *Metronome*, February 1948.
4. Liner notes, ND 86571.
5. Jim Haskins, *Ella Fitzgerald: A Life Through Jazz*, New English Library, London, 1991.
6. *Pittsburgh Courier*, March 26, 1949.
7. Interview with Milt Gabler by Loren Schoenberg, 1992.
8. *Metronome*, August 1948.
9. *Down Beat*, September 22, 1948.
10. Ibid.
11. Ibid.
12. Interview with Milt Gabler by Loren Schoenberg, 1992.
13. Quoted in Sid Colin, *Ella*, Elm Tree Books, London, 1986.

14. *Metronome*, December 1948.
15. Quoted in Colin, *Ella*.
16. *Wall Street Journal*, September 5, 1989.
17. *Time*, March 2, 1953.
18. *Metronome*, November 1953.
19. *Down Beat*, November 18, 1946.
20. *Time*, April 6, 1953.
21. *Down Beat*, April 8, 1949.
22. Ibid., March 27, 1949.
23. Ibid., May 6, 1949.
24. Ibid., May 20, 1949.
25. Will Friedwald, *Jazz Singing*, Scribners, New York, 1990.
26. *Metronome*, August 1949.
27. Ibid., September 1949.
28. *Metronome*, August 1949.
29. *Down Beat*, July 15, 1949.
30. *Metronome*, October 1949.
31. *Ebony*, May 1949.
32. *Los Angeles Times*, January 30, 1983.

CHAPTER NINE: 1949–1952

Author's interviews with John Chilton, Bill Doggett, Charles Linton, Lillian Oliver-Clarke, Mel Tormé, and Norman Granz.

1. *Down Beat*, October 21, 1949.
2. Story from Phil Schaap's liner notes for the Verve 10 CD, *Charlie Parker on Verve* set.
3. *Down Beat*, October 21, 1949.
4. Interview with Milt Gabler by Loren Schoenberg, 1992.
5. Ibid.
6. *Down Beat*, February 24, 1950.
7. *Chicago Tribune*, May 8, 1950.
8. *Down Beat*, February 24, 1950.
9. *Metronome*, April 1950.
10. *Chicago Tribune*, October 17, 1949.
11. *Metronome*, April 1950.
12. Press release dated January 1950. Courtesy of the Institute of Jazz Studies, Rutgers University, NJ.
13. Press release dated March 1949. Courtesy of the Institute of Jazz Studies, Rutgers University, NJ.
14. *Metronome*, October 1953.
15. *Playboy*, November 1957.
16. Ibid.
17. Interview with Milt Gabler by Loren Schoenberg, 1992.
18. Alec Wilder, "Ellis Larkins: An Appreciation," *Down Beat*, October 26, 1972.

19. *Metronome*, September 1951.
20. *New York Times*, September 9, 1951.
21. (New York) *Sunday News*, August 1, 1954.
22. *Los Angeles Times*, January 30, 1983.
23. Phil Schaap archives.
24. Interview with Milt Gabler by Loren Schoenberg, 1992.

CHAPTER TEN: 1952–1955

Author's interviews with Bill Doggett, Norman Granz, John Lewis, Dan Morgenstern, and George Wein.

1. Ella Fitzgerald to John Tynan, *The New Yorker*, November 28, 1956.
2. *Down Beat*, October 8, 1952.
3. Dizzy Gillespie with Al Fraser, *Dizzy: To Be or Not to Bop*, Da Capo, New York, 1985.
4. Interview with Heywood Henry by Loren Schoenberg, 1992.
5. *Metronome*, October 1953.
6. Interview with Milt Gabler by Loren Schoenberg, 1992.
7. *Observer* magazine, February 25, 1990.
8. Stanley Dance, *Jazz Journal*, no. 228, 1954.
9. Interview with Milt Gabler by Loren Schoenberg, 1992.
10. Ibid.
11. *Time*, March 2, 1953.
12. Lou Levy to author, 1992.
13. Interview with Milt Gabler by Loren Schoenberg, 1992.
14. Ibid.
15. *Newsweek*, June 7, 1954.
16. *New York Times*, July 2, 1954.
17. *Newsweek*, June 7, 1954.
18. *Metronome*, August 1954.
19. Burt Goldblatt, *Newport Jazz Festival*, Dial Press, New York, 1977.
20. *New York Post*, December 30, 1954.
21. *New York Times*, August 19, 1955.
22. Interview with Milt Gabler by Loren Schoenberg, 1992.
23. *Houston Post*, October 8, 1955.
24. Ibid.
25. Gillespie, *Dizzy: To Be or Not to Bop*.
26. Interview with Milt Gabler by Loren Schoenberg, 1992.
27. Ibid.
28. Ibid.
29. Ibid.
30. Nat Hentoff, "Ella Fitzgerald: The Criterion of Innocence for Popular Singers." Reprinted in Dom Cerulli et al., *The Jazz Word*, Da Capo, New York, 1963.
31. *Down Beat*, February 23, 1955.

CHAPTER ELEVEN: 1955–1957

Author's interviews with Norman Granz, Jimmy Rowles, Paul Smith, Sylvia Syms, and George Wein.

1. News clipping from an unknown source dated February 8, 1956, courtesy of the Institute of Jazz Studies, Rutgers University, NJ.
2. Alec Wilder, *American Popular Song*, Oxford University Press, New York, 1972.
3. *New York Herald Tribune*, July 22, 1956.
4. *Down Beat*, November 1979.
5. News clipping of an unknown source dated June 5, 1956, courtesy of the Institute of Jazz Studies, Rutgers University, NJ.
6. Liner notes, MV 2510.
7. Ibid.
8. Quoted in Burt Goldblatt, *Newport Jazz Festival*, Dial Press, New York, 1977.
9. *Christian Science Monitor*, July 10, 1956.
10. *Down Beat*, July 14, 1956.
11. Ibid.
12. Stanley Dance, *The World of Count Basie*, Da Capo, New York, 1985.
13. Interview with Tommy Flanagan by Loren Schoenberg, 1992.
14. Dance, *The World of Count Basie*.
15. Phil Schaap archives.
16. *Playboy*, November 1957.
17. *Down Beat*, November 18, 1965.
18. Ibid., November 1979.
19. Duke [Edward K.] Ellington, *Music Is My Mistress*, Da Capo, New York, 1976.
20. News clipping from an unknown source, courtesy of the Institute of Jazz Studies, Rutgers University, NJ.
21. (New York) *Sunday News*, September 8, 1957.
22. Quoted in Nat Hentoff, "Ella Fitzgerald: The Criterion of Innocence for Popular Singers," reprinted in Dom Cerulli et al., *The Jazz Word*, Da Capo, New York, 1963.
23. Goldblatt, *Newport Jazz Festival*.
24. *New York Mirror*, June 26, 1957.

CHAPTER TWELVE: 1957–1959

Author's interviews with Ray Bryant, Norman Granz, Lou Levy, Dan Morgenstern, Jimmy Rowles, Phil Schaap, and Paul Smith.

1. *New York Post*, July 29, 1957.
2. *Ekstra Bladet*, August 1, 1957. Translated by Michael Krog.
3. *Jet*, August 15, 1957.
4. Ibid.
5. *Down Beat*, November 1979.
6. Ibid.
7. *Down Beat*, February 1958.
8. *New York Post*, May 4, 1958.
9. Duke [Edward K.] Ellington, *Music Is My Mistress*, Da Capo, New York, 1976.

10. *Newsweek*, June 23, 1958.
11. Gary Giddins, *Rhythm-A-Ning*, Oxford University Press, New York, 1985.
12. *Jazz Monthly*, February 1962.
13. Gene Lees, *Waiting for Dizzy*, Oxford University Press, New York, 1991.
14. Ibid.
15. *Variety*, December 30, 1959.

CHAPTER THIRTEEN: 1960–1966

Author's interviews with Bill Doggett, Jim Hall, Lou Levy, Dan Morgenstern, Phil Schaap, and Paul Smith.

1. *Houston Post*, January 7, 1962.
2. *Down Beat*, March 1, 1973.
3. *Melody Maker*, December 3, 1960.
4. Martin Williams, *Jazz Heritage*, Oxford University Press, New York, 1991.
5. *Down Beat*, March 1, 1962.
6. *Berlingske Tidende*, August 16, 1961. Translation by Michael Krog.
7. *Berlingske Tidende*, August 27, 1961. Translation by Michael Krog.
8. *New York Herald Tribune*, August 7, 1961.
9. Thanks to Michael Krog for researching this information.
10. *Berlingske Tidende*, January 15, 1967. Translation by Michael Krog.
11. Ibid.
12. *Down Beat*, November 8, 1962.
13. *Life*, November 8, 1962.
14. Count Basie and Albert Murray, *Good Morning Blues: The Autobiography of Count Basie*, Donald I. Fine, New York, 1985.
15. *Down Beat*, November 21, 1963.
16. Interview with Tommy Flanagan by Loren Schoenberg, 1992.
17. *Down Beat*, February 4, 1971.
18. Interview with Tommy Flanagan by Loren Schoenberg, 1992.
19. Williams, *Jazz Heritage*.
20. Interview with Tommy Flanagan by Loren Schoenberg, 1992.
21. Letter from John Hammond to Norman Granz, September 20, 1966. Courtesy of Yale Archives, New Haven.
22. Internal memorandum to William P. Gallagher from John Hammond, November 17, 1966. Courtesy of Yale Archives.

CHAPTER FOURTEEN: 1964–1972

Author's interviews with Norman Granz, Lou Levy, Joe Pass, Paul Smith, Mel Tormé, and George Wein.

1. *Toronto Globe and Mail*, January 27, 1965.
2. *Time*, November 27, 1964.
3. *New York Post*, October 17, 1965.
4. *Houston Post*, April 3, 1965.

5. Ibid.
6. Quoted in *Down Beat*, June 17, 1965.
7. *Down Beat*, September 9, 1965.
8. Interview with Tommy Flanagan by Loren Schoenberg, 1992.
9. *Down Beat*, August 11, 1966.
10. Derek Jewell, *Duke: A Portrait of Duke Ellington*, Norton, New York, 1977.
11. *Berlingske Tidende*, January 22, 1967. Translation by Michael Krog.
12. Interview with Tommy Flanagan by Loren Schoenberg, 1992.
13. *Down Beat*, August 10, 1967.
14. Henry Pleasants, *The Great American Popular Singers*, Simon & Schuster, 1985.
15. Internal memorandum from John Hammond to William P. Gallagher, November 17, 1966. Courtesy of Yale Archives, New Haven.
16. *Down Beat*, March 9, 1967.
17. Ibid., November 30, 1967.
18. *Philadelphia Inquirer*, July 4, 1971.
19. Michael Ullman, *Jazz Lives*, Perigree Books, New York, 1980.
20. Interview with Tommy Flanagan by Loren Schoenberg, 1992.
21. Ullman, *Jazz Lives*.
22. *Houston Post*, January 7, 1968.
23. Interview with Tommy Flanagan by Loren Schoenberg, 1992.
24. *New York Times*, July 14, 1971.

CHAPTER FIFTEEN: 1972–1978

Author's interviews with Norman Granz, Joe Pass, Paul Smith, and Mel Tormé.

1. *Down Beat*, November 1979.
2. Ibid.
3. *New York Times*, July 14, 1971.
4. Liner notes, Pablo 2625701.
5. Letter from John Hammond to Norman Granz, July 11, 1973. Courtesy of Yale Archives, New Haven.
6. Letter from John Hammond to Irving Townsend, August 8, 1973. Courtesy of Yale Archives.
7. *New York Times*, July 7, 1973.
8. *Houston Post*, July 16, 1973.
9. *New York Times*, November 24, 1974.
10. Ibid., November 26, 1974.
11. *Village Voice*, December 9, 1974.
12. Interview with Tommy Flanagan by Loren Schoenberg, 1992.
13. *New York Times*, September 10, 1974.

CHAPTER SIXTEEN: 1978–1993

Author's interviews with Betty Carter, Norman Granz, Michael Hashim, Max Jones, Lou Levy, Jimmy Rowles, Phil Schaap, Loren Schoenberg, Paul Smith, Sylvia Syms, and Mel Tormé.

NOTES

1. Michael Ullman, *Jazz Lives*, Perigree Books, New York, 1980.
2. *The New Yorker*, November 20, 1978.
3. Count Basie and Albert Murray, *Good Morning Blues: The Autobiography of Count Basie*, Donald I. Fine, New York, 1985.
4. *New York Times*, April 16, 1979.
5. Interview with Niels-Henning Orsted-Pedersen by Michael Krog, 1992.
6. Liner notes, PACD 26300-201-2.
7. (New Orleans) *Times-Picayune*, April 27, 1981; *Jet*, May 14, 1981.
8. Liner notes, PACD 2312-138-2.
9. Liner notes, Metro 2682 035.
10. *Jazz Times*, September 1991.
11. Interview with Niels-Henning Orsted-Pedersen by Michael Krog, 1992.
12. *Houston Post*, May 25, 1982.
13. *Village Voice*, June 29, 1983.
14. *Esquire*, 1983.
15. *New York Times*, June 22, 1986.
16. *Newsday*, July 22, 1988.
17. Jim Haskins, *Ella Fitzgerald: A Life Through Jazz*, New English Library, London, 1991.
18. Ibid.
19. *Jazz Times*, September 1991.
20. *New York Times*, June 27, 1989.
21. *Los Angeles Times*, July 14, 1989.
22. *Village Voice*, March 13, 1990.
23. *Newsday*, July 2, 1990.

DISCOGRAPHY

PHIL SCHAAP

Noted jazz historian, educator, and broadcaster Phil Schaap has been dubbed "The Dean of Jazz Radio" by the *New York Times*. His archival and restoration work in the vaults of Verve records is legendary in the jazz world, most notably for his award-winning compilation *The Complete Charlie Parker on Verve* and *The Complete Billie Holiday on Verve*. His discovery of a previously unknown, complete Ella Fitzgerald concert, *Ella in Rome: The Birthday Concert*, went to the top of the *Billboard* jazz charts after he prepared it for release in 1988.

This discography does not claim to be complete. The constraints of time and space has meant it has been impossible to include every known Ella Fitzgerald album, and the twilight world of bootleg issues is almost impossible to monitor. However, Phil's work is a significant advance on anything that has previously been published because of the wealth of new material he has discovered, much of which, at the time of going to press, has not been issued.

Where possible the order of recording has been preserved in the text. Compact disc issues have been noted in bold typeface.

ABBREVIATIONS

alt	alternate take	iss	issued
cpt	complete	mst	master
inc	incomplete	tk	take
vo	vocal	p	piano
tp	trumpet	kb	keyboard
tb	trombone	g	guitar
vtb	valve trombone	b	bass
fh	french horn	el-b	electric bass
as	alto sax	t	tuba
ts	tenor sax	d	drums
bs	baritone sax	v	violin
cl	clarinet		
(E)	English issue	(I)	Italian issue
(G)	German issue	(J)	Japanese issue

DISCOGRAPHY

THE DECCA YEARS 1935–1955

June 12, 1935

CHICK WEBB AND HIS ORCHESTRA; EF, vo
I'll Chase the Blues Away: Brunswick (E) 02602; **Decca Jazz GRD-2-618; Classics 500**
Love and Kisses: Decca 494; **Decca Jazz GRD-2-618; Classics 500**

October 12, 1935

CHICK WEBB AND HIS ORCHESTRA; EF, vo
Rhythm and Romance: Decca 588; **Decca Jazz GRD-2-618; Classics 500**
I'll Chase the Blues Away: Decca 640; Swingtime (I) ST 1006; **Classics 500**

February 19, 1936

CHICK WEBB AND HIS ORCHESTRA; EF, vo
Shine/You Hit the Spot/Darktown Strutters' Ball/Rhythm and Romance: Circle CLP-81; **Forlane International UCD 19007**

March 17, 1936

TEDDY WILSON AND HIS ORCHESTRA; EF, vo; Frank Newton, tp; Benny Morton, tb; Jerry Black, as, cl; Ted McRae, ts; John Trueheart, g; Lennie Stanfield, b; Cozy Cole, d
My Melancholy Baby: Brunswick 7729; Swingtime (I) ST 1006; **Classics 500**
All My Life: Brunswick 7640; Swingtime (I) ST 1006; **Classics 500**

April 7, 1936

CHICK WEBB AND HIS ORCHESTRA; EF, vo
Crying My Heart Out for You: Decca 785; Living Era (E) AJD 055; **Classics 500**
Under the Spell of the Blues: Decca 831; **Decca Jazz GRD-2-618; Classics 500**
When I Get Low I Get High: Decca 1123; **Decca Jazz GRD-2-618; Classics 500**

June 2, 1936

CHICK WEBB AND HIS ORCHESTRA; EF, vo
Sing Me a Swing Song (and Let Me Dance): Decca 830; **Decca Jazz GRD-2-618; Classics 500**
A Little Bit Later On: Decca 831 (7)9222; **Decca Jazz GRD-2-618; Classics 500**
Love, You're Just a Laugh: Decca 1114; **Decca Jazz GRD-2-618; Classics 500**
Devoting My Time to You: Decca 995; Living Era (E) AJD 055; **Classics 500**

October 29, 1936

CHICK WEBB AND HIS ORCHESTRA; EF, vo

(If You Can't Sing It) You'll Have to Swing It (aka *Mr. Paganini*): (tk 1 mst): Decca 1032; Living Era (E) AJD 055; **Classics 500**; (tk 2 alt): **Decca Jazz GRD-2-618**

Swinging on the Reservation (2 tks; tk 1 mst): Decca 1065; Living Era (E) AJD 055; **Classics 500**

I Got the Spring Fever Blues: Decca 1087; Living Era (E) AJD 055; **Classics 500**

Vote for Mr. Rhythm (2 tks; tk 1 mst): Decca 1032; **Decca Jazz GRD-2-618**; **Classics 500**

NOTE: The metal master for take 2 came apart while being processed for GRP's Decca Jazz release *Ella Fitzgerald, the Early Years—Part I: With Chick Webb & His Orchestra (1935–38)* (**Decca Jazz GRD-2-618**). What remained after the metal collapsed has apparently not been saved.

November 5, 1936

BENNY GOODMAN AND HIS ORCHESTRA; Ziggy Elman, Chris Griffin, Zeke Zarchey, tp; Red Ballard, Murray McEachern, tb; Bill DePew, Hymie Schertzer, as; Vido Musso, Art Rollini, ts; Jess Stacy, p; Allan Reuss, g; Harry Goodman, b; Gene Krupa, d

Goodnight, My Love/Take Another Guess/Did You Mean It?: RCA Victor 25461; Living Era (E) AJD 055; RCA Victor Bluebird AXM2-5532; **Classics 500**

November 18, 1936

EF, vo; Taft Jordan, tp; Sandy Williams, tb; Pete Clarke, Teddy McRae, reeds; Tommy Fulford, p; John Trueheart, g; Beverly Peer, b; Chick Webb, d

My Last Affair: Decca 1061; **Decca Jazz GRD-2-618**; **Classics 500**

Organ Grinder's Swing: Decca 1062; **Decca Jazz GRD-2-618**; **Classics 500**

November 19, 1936

EF, vo; Taft Jordan, tp; Sandy Williams, tb; Pete Clarke, cl; Teddy McRae, ts & bs; Tommy Fulford, p; John Trueheart, g; Beverly Peer, b; Chick Webb, d

Shine: Decca 1062; **Decca Jazz GRD-2-618**; **Classics 500**

Darktown Strutters' Ball: Decca 1061; **Decca Jazz GRD-2-618**; **Classics 500**

January 14, 1937

CHICK WEBB AND HIS ORCHESTRA; EF, vo

Oh, Yes, Take Another Guess: Decca 1123; **Decca Jazz GRD-2-618**; **Classics 500**

EF, Charles Linton, Louis Jordan, vo

Love Marches On: Decca 1115; **Classics 517**

ELLA FITZGERALD AND THE MILLS BROTHERS; EF, the Mills Brothers, vo; Bernard Addison, g

Big Boy Blue: Decca 1148; Living Era (E) AJD 055; **Classics 506**

NOTE: There will always be some question concerning at what point in the January 14, 1937, session "Big Boy Blue" was made. Apparently a ledger-keeping mistake accounts for the matrix number being used twice, clashing with "There's Frost on the Moon" from the following day.

January 15, 1937

CHICK WEBB AND HIS ORCHESTRA; EF, Charles Linton, Louis Jordan, vo

There's Frost on the Moon: Decca 1114; **Classics 517**

February 3, 1937

ELLA FITZGERALD AND THE MILLS BROTHERS; EF, the Mills Brothers, vo; Bernard Addison, g

Dedicated to You: Decca 1148; Living Era (E) AJD 055; **Classics 506**

February 8, 1937

CHICK WEBB AND HIS ORCHESTRA; EF, vo

Vote for Mr. Rhythm/Big Boy Blue: Twinkgost Rogo CWIS 37

March 24, 1937

CHICK WEBB AND HIS ORCHESTRA; EF, vo

You Showed Me the Way (2 tks; tk 2 mst): Decca 1220; **Decca Jazz GRD-2-618; Classics 506**

Cryin' Mood: Decca 1273; **Decca Jazz GRD-2-618; Classics 506**

Love Is the Thing, So They Say: Decca 1356; **Classics 506**

May 24, 1937

EF, vo; Taft Jordan, tp; Sandy Williams, tb; probably Louis Jordan, Teddy McRae, reeds; Tommy Fulford, p; either Bobby Johnson or John Trueheart, g; Beverly Peer, b; Chick Webb, d

All or Nothing at All: Decca 1339; Living Era (E) AJD 055; **Classics 506**

If You Ever Should Leave (2 tks; tk 2 mst)/*Everyone's Wrong But Me*: Decca 1302; **Decca Jazz GRD-2-618; Classics 506**

Deep in the Heart of the South: Decca 1339; **Classics 506**

October 27, 1937

CHICK WEBB AND HIS ORCHESTRA; EF, vo

Just a Simple Melody: Decca 1521; **Decca Jazz GRD-2-618; Classics 506**

I Got a Guy: Decca 1681; **Decca Jazz GRD-2-618; Classics 506**
Holiday in Harlem: Decca 1521; Living Era (E) AJD 055; **Classics 506**

November 1, 1937

CHICK WEBB AND HIS ORCHESTRA; EF, vo
Rock It for Me: Decca 1586; **Decca Jazz GRD-2-618; Classics 506**

December 17, 1937

CHICK WEBB AND HIS ORCHESTRA; EF, vo
I Want to Be Happy: Decca 15039; **Decca Jazz GRD-2-618; Classics 506**
NOTE: A different take is listed for the Australian 78 issue, Decca Z-778. Turk Van Lake says he was not the arranger. Van Alexander was probably the arranger on this date.
The Dipsy Doodle: Decca 1589; Decca (7)9223; **Decca Jazz GRD-2-618; Classics 506**
If Dreams Come True: Decca 1716; **Decca Jazz GRD-2-618; Classics 506**
Hallelujah!: Decca 15039; **Decca Jazz GRD-2-618; Classics 506**

December 21, 1937

EF, vo; Taft Jordan, tp; Sandy Williams, tb; probably Louis Jordan and Teddy McRae, reeds; Tommy Fulford, p; probably Bobby Johnson, g; Beverly Peer, b; Chick Webb, d
Bei Mir Bist Du Schoen/It's My Turn Now: Decca 1596; **Decca Jazz GRD-2-618; Classics 506**

January 25, 1938

EF, vo; Taft Jordan, tp; Sandy Williams, tb; probably Louis Jordan, Teddy McRae, reeds; Tommy Fulford, p; probably Bobby Johnson, g; Beverly Peer, b; Chick Webb, d
It's Wonderful/I Was Doing All Right: Decca 1669; **Decca Jazz GRD-2-618; Classics 506**

May 2, 1938

CHICK WEBB AND HIS ORCHESTRA; EF, vo
A-Tisket, A-Tasket: Decca 1840; Decca DL 4149; Decca (7)9223; MCA2-4047; **Decca Jazz GRD-2-618; Decca Jazz GRD-2-619; Classics 506**
Heart of Mine: Decca 2721; **Decca Jazz GRD-2-618; Classics 518**
I'm Just a Jitterbug: Decca 1899; **Decca Jazz GRD-2-618; Classics 518**

May 3, 1938

EF, vo; Taft Jordan, tp; Sandy Williams, tb; possibly Louis Jordan, Teddy McRae, reeds; Tommy Fulford, p; Bobby Johnson, g; Beverly Peer, b; Chick Webb, d

This Time It's Real: Decca 1806; **Classics 518**

What Do You Know About Love?: Decca 1967; **Classics 518**

You Can't Be Mine: Decca 1806; **Decca Jazz GRD-2-618; Classics 518**

We Can't Go On This Way/Saving Myself For You: Decca 1846; **Classics 518**

If You Only Knew (2 tks; tk 2 mst): Decca 1967; **Decca Jazz GRD-2-618; Classics 518**

May 29, 1938

RANDALL'S ISLAND JAZZ CONCERT, ELLA FITZGERALD WITH THE CHICK WEBB ORCHESTRA

A short scrap of newsreel—silent—exists from this event. The audio portion was broadcast live on WNEW-AM in New York City. It was recorded off the air by Bill Savory, who has responded to inquiries (as recently as 1991) that the discs still exist.

June 9, 1938

CHICK WEBB AND HIS ORCHESTRA; EF, vo

Pack Up Your Sins and Go to the Devil: Decca 1894; **Decca Jazz GRD-2-618; Classics 518**

Macpherson Is Rehearsin' (to Swing): Decca 2080; **Decca Jazz GRD-2-618; Classics 518**

Everybody Step: Decca 1894; **Decca Jazz GRD-2-618; Classics 518**

Ella: Decca 2148; **Classics 518**

NOTE: Taft Jordan also sings on "Ella."

August 17, 1938

CHICK WEBB AND HIS ORCHESTRA; EF, vo

Wacky Dust: Decca 2021; **Decca Jazz GRD-2-618; Classics 518**

Gotta Pebble in My Shoe: Decca 2231; **Classics 518**

I Can't Stop Loving You: Decca 2310; **Classics 518**

NOTE: This is not the same song that was made famous by Ray Charles.

August 18, 1938

EF, vo; Taft Jordan, tp; Sandy Williams, tb; Hilton Jefferson, as; Teddy McRae, ts; Tommy Fulford, p; probably Bobby Johnson, g; Beverly Peer, b; Chick Webb, d

Strictly from Dixie: Decca 2202; **Decca Jazz GRD-2-618; Classics 518**

Woe Is Me: Decca 2202; **Classics 518**

CHICK WEBB AND HIS ORCHESTRA; EF, vo

I Let a Tear Fall in the River: Decca 2080; MCA- 1348; **Classics 518**

DISCOGRAPHY

October 6, 1938

CHICK WEBB AND HIS ORCHESTRA; EF, vo

F.D.R. Jones: Decca 2105; MCA-1348; **Decca Jazz GRD-2-618; Classics 518**

I Love Each Move You Make: Decca 2105; MCA-1348; **Classics 518**

It's Foxy: Decca 2309; MCA-1348; **Decca Jazz GRD-2-618; Classics 518**

I Found My Yellow Basket: Decca 2148; MCA-1348; **Decca Jazz GRD-2-618; Classics 518**

Listed as February 10, 1939

CHICK WEBB AND HIS ORCHESTRA; EF, vo

Deep in a Dream/That Was My Heart: Twinkgost Rogo CWIS 37

February 17, 1939

CHICK WEBB AND HIS ORCHESTRA; EF, vo

Undecided: Decca 2323; Decca DL4446; Decca (7)9223; **Classics 518; Decca Jazz GRD-2-619**

'Taint What You Do (It's the Way That'Cha Do It): Decca 2310; MCA-1348; **Classics 525**

One Side of Me: Decca 2556; MCA-1348; **Classics 525**

My Heart Belongs to Daddy: Decca 2309; MCA-1348; **Classics 525**

March 2, 1939

EF, vo; Taft Jordan, tp; Sandy Williams, tb; probably Hilton Jefferson, Teddy McRae, reeds; Tommy Fulford, p; John Trueheart, g; Beverly Peer, b; Chick Webb, d

Once Is Enough for Me: Decca 2451; **Classics 525**

I Had to Live and Learn: Decca 2581; **Classics 525**

CHICK WEBB AND HIS ORCHESTRA; EF, vo

Sugar Pie: Decca 2665; MCA-1327; **Classics 525**

It's Slumbertime Along the Swanee: Decca 2389; MCA-1327; **Classics 525**

I'm Up a Tree: Decca 2468; **Classics 525**

Chew, Chew, Chew, Chew Your Bubble Gum: Decca 2389; MCA-1348; **Classics 525**

April 21, 1939

EF, vo; Taft Jordan, tp; Sandy Williams, tb; probably Hilton Jefferson, Teddy McRae, reeds; Tommy Fulford, p; John Trueheart, g; Beverly Peer, b; Chick Webb, d

Don't Worry 'Bout Me: Decca 2451; **Classics 525; Decca Jazz GRD-2-619**

If Anything Happened to You: Decca 2481; **Classics 525**

If That's What You're Thinking: Decca 2581; **Classics 525**
If You Ever Change Your Mind: Decca 2481; **Classics 525**

CHICK WEBB AND HIS ORCHESTRA; EF, vo
Have Mercy: Decca 2468; **Classics 525**
Little White Lies: Decca 2556; MCA-1327; **Classics 525**
Coochi-Coochi-Coo: Decca 2803; MCA-1327; **Classics 525**
That Was My Heart: Decca 2665; **Classics 525**

May 4, 1939

CHICK WEBB AND HIS ORCHESTRA; EF, vo
*New Moon and Old Serenade/I Never Knew Heaven Could Speak/If I Didn't
Care/Chew, Chew, Chew, Chew Your Bubble Gum*: Collector's Classics CC-11;
Tax CD 3706-2

NOTE: The surviving Chick Webb Orchestra broadcasts that feature Ella are difficult
to document. There are transcription recordings listed for February 19, 1936;
February 8, 1937; and January 9, 1939. There is the Randall's Island broadcast,
plus two known remotes listed for February 10, 1939, and May 4, 1939. Except
for the May 29, 1938, concert at Randall's Island, the exact dates may no longer
be possible to authenticate. I have tried to eliminate the multiple listing of titles.
There are ten verified titles. Most discographies repeat some or all of them for the
five possible dates (nothing has surfaced from the May 29, 1938, broadcast from
Randall's Island). The transcription recordings of February 19, 1936, have been
pinned down. I believe Ella was not part of the January 9, 1939, transcription.
Judging by when the song was current, when it was part of the Ella/Webb repertoire, and by the recordings' sonics, I have placed each tune with the date on
which I believe it occurred.

Chick Webb died on June 16, 1939. Some of Ella's last sides with Webb and
his band list her as the leader on the 78 label. Occasionally the Webb name is
credited on the labels of those 78s made by the Webb band under Ella Fitzgerald's
nominal leadership after Chick's death.

June 29, 1939

ELLA FITZGERALD AND HER FAMOUS ORCHESTRA
Betcha Nickel: Decca 2904; Swingtime (I) 1007; **Classics 525**
Stairway to the Stars: Decca 2598; Decca 4446; **Classics 525; Decca Jazz GRD-2-619**
I Want the Waiter (with the Water): Decca 2628; **Classics 525**
That's All Brother: Decca 2628; Swingtime (I) 1007; **Classics 525**
Out of Nowhere: Decca 2598; **Classics 525**

August 18, 1939

ELLA FITZGERALD AND HER FAMOUS ORCHESTRA
My Last Goodbye: Decca 2721; **Classics 566**

Billy (I Always Dream of Billy)/Please Tell the Truth: Decca 2769; Swingtime (I) 1007; **Classics 566**

I'm Not Complainin': Decca 3005; Swingtime (I) 1007; **Classics 566**

October 12, 1939

ELLA FITZGERALD AND HER FAMOUS ORCHESTRA
You're Gonna Lose Your Gal: Decca 2816; Swingtime (I) 1007; **Classics 566**
After I Say I'm Sorry (What Can I Say?): Decca 2826; **Classics 566**
My Wubba Dolly: Decca 2816; Swingtime (I) 1007; **Classics 566**
Moon Ray: Decca 2904; **Classics 566**

January 22, 1940

ELLA FITZGERALD AND HER FAMOUS ORCHESTRA
Traffic Jam: **Collector's Classics 17**
A Lover Is Blue: unissued
Dodging the Dean/'Taint What You Do/I'm Confessin': **Collector's Classics 17**
What's the Matter with Me?: unissued
I Want the Waiter (with the Water): **Collector's Classics 17**

January 25, 1940

ELLA FITZGERALD AND HER FAMOUS ORCHESTRA
This Changing World: unissued
Oh Johnny, Oh Johnny, Oh!: **Collector's Classics 17**
Thank Your Stars: unissued

January 26, 1940

ELLA FITZGERALD AND HER FAMOUS ORCHESTRA
Is There Somebody Else?: Decca 2988; **Classics 566**
Sugar Blues: Decca 3078; **Classics 566**
The Starlit Hour: Decca 2988; Swingtime (I) 1007; **Classics 566**
What's the Matter With Me?: Decca 3005; Swingtime (I) 1007; **Classics 566**

February 15, 1940

ELLA FITZGERALD AND HER FAMOUS ORCHESTRA
Busy as a Bee: Decca X-1937
Baby, Won't You Please Come Home: Decca 3186; **Classics 566**
If It Weren't for You/Sing Song Swing: Decca 3126; **Classics 566**
Imagination: Decca 3078; **Classics 566**

February 26, 1940

ELLA FITZGERALD AND HER FAMOUS ORCHESTRA
Sugar Blues/It's a Blue World/Is There Somebody Else?/One Moment Please: Sunbeam 205

March 4, 1940

ELLA FITZGERALD AND HER FAMOUS ORCHESTRA
Chew, Chew, Chew, Chew Your Bubble Gum/Sing Song Swing/Starlit Hour: Sunbeam 205

Late March 1940 (date unknown)

ELLA FITZGERALD AND HER FAMOUS ORCHESTRA
Oh Johnny, Oh Johnny, Oh!/I Want the Waiter (with the Water)/I'm Confessin': Jazz Trip 5

May 9, 1940

ELLA FITZGERALD AND HER FAMOUS ORCHESTRA
Deedle-De-Dum: Decca 3224; **Classics 566**
Shake Down the Stars: Decca 3159; **Classics 644**
Gulf Coast Blues: Decca 3224; **Classics 644**
I Fell in Love with a Dream: Decca 3199; Swingtime (I) 1007; **Classics 644**

September 25, 1940

ELLA FITZGERALD AND HER FAMOUS ORCHESTRA
Five O'Clock Whistle: Decca 3420; **Classics 644; Decca Jazz GRD-2-619**
So Long: Decca 3420; **Classics 644**
Louisville, K-Y: Decca 3441; Swingtime (I) 1007; **Classics 644**

November 8, 1940

ELLA FITZGERALD AND HER FAMOUS ORCHESTRA
Taking a Chance on Love/Cabin in the Sky: Decca 3490; **Classics 644**
I'm the Lonesomest Gal in Town: Decca 3666; **Classics 644**

January 8, 1941

ELLA FITZGERALD AND HER FAMOUS ORCHESTRA
Three Little Words: Decca 3608; **Classics 644**
Hello Ma! I Done It Again/Wishful Thinking: Decca 3612; **Classics 644**

The One I Love (Belongs to Somebody Else)/The Muffin Man: Decca 3608; **Classics 644**

March 31, 1941

ELLA FITZGERALD AND HER FAMOUS ORCHESTRA
Keep Cool, Fool/No Nothing: Decca 3754; **Classics 644**
My Man: Decca 4291; **Classics 644**

July 31, 1941

ELLA FITZGERALD AND HER FAMOUS ORCHESTRA
I Can't Believe That You're in Love with Me: Decca 18421; **Classics 644**
I Must Have That Man: Decca 18530; **Classics 644**
When My Sugar Walks Down the Street: Decca 18587; **Classics 644**
I Got It Bad and That Ain't Good/Melinda the Mousie: Decca 3968; **Classics 644**
Can't Help Lovin' Dat Man: Decca 18421; **Classics 644**

October 6, 1941

EF, vo; Teddy McRae, ts; Tommy Fulford, p; Ulysses Livingston, g; Beverly Peer, b; Kenny Clarke, d
Jim/This Love of Mine: Decca 4007

October 28, 1941

EF, vo; Eddie Barefield, cl & as; Tommy Fulford, p; Ulysses Livingston, g; Beverly Peer, b; Bill Beason, d
Somebody Nobody Loves/You Don't Know What Love Is: Decca 4082

November 5, 1941

EF, vo; Eddie Barefield, cl; Tommy Fulford, p; Ulysses Livingston, g; Beverly Peer, b; Bill Beason, d
Who Are You?: Decca 4291
I'm Thrilled/Make Love to Me: Decca 4073

March 11, 1942

EF, vo; accompanied by the Four Keys
I'm Getting Mighty Lonesome/When I Come Back Crying: Decca 4315
NOTE: At midnight on March 31, 1942, the American Federation of Musicians went on strike against the record business. Commercial recording was limited for over a year.

DISCOGRAPHY

April 10, 1942

EF, vo; accompanied by the Four Keys
All I Need Is You/Mama Come Home: Decca 18347

July 31, 1942

EF, vo; with small group accompaniment
My Heart and I Decided: Decca 18530
I Put a Four Leaf Clover in Your Pocket/He's My Guy: Decca 18472

November 3, 1943

EF, vo; accompanied by the Ink Spots
Cow-Cow Boogie (2 tks; tk 1 mst): Decca 18587; Decca 4129; **Decca Jazz GRD-2-619**

March 20, 1944

EF, vo; with studio unit
Time Alone Will Tell [mx C25135]/*Once Too Often* [mx C25136]: Decca 18605

August 30, 1944

EF, vo; accompanied by the Ink Spots
Into Each Life Some Rain Must Fall (2 tks; tk 1 mst): Decca 23356; **Decca Jazz GRD-2-619**
I'm Making Believe (2 tks; tk 1 mst): Decca 23356

November 6, 1944

EF, vo; Johnny Long Orchestra; the Song Spinners
And Her Tears Flowed Like Wine (2 tks; tk 1 mst): Decca 18633
Confessin' (2 tks; tk 1 mst): Decca 18633

1944–45

EF, vo; Bill Doggett, p; at times others
As recently as January 1992, Bill Doggett has confirmed the existence of eight EF radio broadcasts during the period that he was her regular accompanist. Each broadcast would contain several performances by EF, backed by at least Doggett's piano.

February 26, 1945

EF, vo; the Ink Spots; studio unit
I'm Beginning to See the Light/That's the Way It Is: Decca 23399

NOTE: This session was originally recorded for World Transcriptions (a prerecorded specialty music company similar to the Muzak suppliers still in existence today). EF recorded more than once for such organizations as well as doing at least two sessions for the Armed Forces Radio Service (AFRS). She also had her own radio show and was featured on both local and network programs as a guest, as is noted in the foregoing entry. Her non-Decca studio recordings of this period were occasionally filed or mislisted under different names, including those of known singers Evelyn Fields and Cass Daley.

March 27, 1945

EF, vo; the Delta Rhythm Boys; studio unit
It's Only a Paper Moon: Decca 23425; **Decca Jazz GRD-2-619**
Cry Out of My Heart: unissued, presumed to exist

March 28, 1945

EF, vo; the Delta Rhythm Boys; studio unit
Cry Out of My Heart: Decca 23425

August 29, 1945

EF, vo; Randy Brooks Orchestra
A Kiss Goodnight/Benny's Coming Home Saturday: Decca 18713

October 4, 1945

EF, vo; Vic Schoen Orchestra
Flying Home: Decca 23956; Decca 8149; **Decca Jazz GRD-2-619**

October 8, 1945

EF, vo; Aaron Izenhall, tp; Josh Jackson, ts; Wild Bill Davis, p; Carl Hogan, g; Jesse Simpkins, b; Eddie Byrd, d; Harry Dial, Vic Lourie, percussion
Stone Cold Dead in de Market (2 tks; tk 1 mst): Decca 23546; Decca DL8477; MCA (E) 1807; Bear Family BCD 15557; **Decca Jazz GRD-2-619**
Patootie Pie: Decca 23546; MCA (E) 1807; Bear Family BCD 15557

October 12, 1945

EF, vo; Charlie Shavers, tp; Lou McGarity, tb; Peanuts Hucko, cl; Big Al Sears, ts; Buddy Weed, p; Remo Palmier, g; Trigger Alpert, b; Buddy Rich, d
That's Rich: V-Disc 603; Jazz Society 511, Hep 12
I'll Always Be in Love with You: V-Disc 569
I'll See You in My Dreams: V-Disc 730; Jazz Society 511

January 18, 1946

EF, vo; with Louis Armstrong, tp & vo
You Won't Be Satisfied: Decca 23496; Coral COP-57397; **Decca Jazz GRD-2-619**
The Frim Fram Sauce: Decca 23496; Coral COP-57397

February 21, 1946

EF, vo; Billy Kyle, p; Jimmy Shirley, g; Junior Raglin, b; Vess Payne, d
I'm Just a Lucky So and So/I Didn't Mean a Word I Said: Decca 18814; **Decca Jazz GRD-2-619**

August 29, 1946

EF, vo; the Delta Rhythm Boys
(I Love You) For Sentimental Reasons: Decca 23670; Decca 8832
It's a Pity to Say Goodnight: Decca 23670

January 24, 1947

EF, vo; Idries Sulieman, tp; Al King, tb; Jimmy Powell, as; Eddie Heywood, p; Billy Taylor, b; Keg Pumell, d
Guilty: Decca 23844; Decca 8882
Sentimental Journey: Decca 23844; Decca 8477

March 1, 1947

EF, vo; Joe Mooney, accordion; Nick Tagg, p; Big Sid Catlett, d; Buddy Rich, vo
Budella (Blue Skies): V-Disc 775; Hep 12

March 19, 1947

EF, vo; Bob Haggart Orchestra; Andy Love Quartet
A Sunday Kind of Love: Decca 23866; Decca 4129
That's My Desire: Decca 23866; Decca 8695
Lady Be Good: Decca 23956; Decca 8149; **Decca Jazz GRD-2-619**

(circa) June 26, 1947

EF, vo

Eight titles (possibly 8 discs with less than 8 titles) with an entire record date or even a double session.

DISCOGRAPHY

July 11, 1947

EF, vo; Bob Haggart Orchestra
You're Breakin' in a New Heart: unissued
NOTE: The balance of this session survives on 4 acetates in the Decca vaults.

July 22, 1947

EF, vo; Bob Haggart Orchestra
Don't You Think I Oughta Know?: Decca 24157; Decca 8832
You're Breakin' in a New Heart: Decca 24157

September 29, 1947

DIZZY GILLESPIE AND HIS ORCHESTRA; EF, vo
Almost Like Being in Love/Stairway to the Stars/Lover Man/Flying Home/Lady Be Good/How High the Moon: Natural Organic 7000
NOTE: This was EF's Carnegie Hall debut.

December 18, 1947

EF, vo; the Day Dreamers
I Want to Learn About Love: Decca 24581
That Old Feeling: Decca 28049; Decca 8832; MCA 2-4016

December 20, 1947

EF, vo; accompanied by small group
No Sense: Decca 24538; MCA Coral PCO 7666
How High the Moon: Decca 24387; Decca 8149; Jasmine JASM 1027; **Decca Jazz GRD-2-619**
My Baby Likes to Re-Bop: Decca 24332

December 23, 1947

EF, vo; Illinois Jacquet, ts; Sir Charles Thompson, organ; Hank Jones, p; Hy White, g; John Simmons, b; J. C. Heard, d
I've Got a Feeling I'm Falling: Decca 24232; MCA Coral PCO 7665
You Turned the Tables on Me: Decca 24387; MCA 2-4016
I Cried and Cried and Cried: Coral 6.22178; MCA Coral PCO 7666
Robbins' Nest: Decca 24538; MCA 510.184/85

April 29, 1948

EF, vo; the Song Spinners
Tea Leaves: Decca 24446

April 30, 1948

EF, vo; the Song Spinners
My Happiness: Decca 24446; Decca DL4129; **Decca Jazz GRD-2-619**

May 25, 1948

EF, vo; personnel unknown
Have Mercy/Lady Be Good: AFRS Transcriptions Jubilee 281

June 1, 1948

EF, vo; personnel unknown
My Baby Likes to Re-Bop/The Gentleman Is a Dope: AFRS Transcriptions Jubilee 282

August 20, 1948

EF, vo; Illinois Jacquet, ts
It's Too Soon to Know: Decca 24497; MCA 2-4047
I Can't Go On Without You: Decca 24497

November 10, 1948

EF, vo; unknown orchestra
To Make a Mistake Is Human/In My Dreams: Decca 24529

November 27, 1948

EF, vo; Hank Jones, p; Ray Brown, b; Roy Haynes, d; Allen Eager, ts; Kai Winding, tb
Ool-Ya-Koo/Love That Boy/You'll Have to Swing It (aka *Mr. Paganini*)/*Too Soon to Know*: Jazz Live BLJ 8035

December 4, 1948

EF, vo; personnel as on November 27, 1948
Heat Wave/Old Mother Hubbard/Ool-Ya-Koo/Flying Home: Jazz Live BLJ 8035

January 14, 1949

EF, vo; unknown orchestra
I Couldn't Stay Away: Decca 24562
Old Mother Hubbard: Decca 24581
Someone Like You: Decca 24562; Decca DL4447

February 28, 1949

EF, vo; Louis Jordan and His Tympany Five; Aaron Izenhall, tp; Eddie Johnson, ts;
  Bill Doggett, p; unknown, g; possibly Dallas Bartley, b; Chris Columbus, d; Louis
  Jordan, as & vo
Don't Cry, Cry Baby (5 tks; tk 5 mst): Decca DL8477; Decca 24644; MCA
  510.184/85; Bear Family LJTy5
NOTE: It is possible that take 3 is the master and that there is no take 5.
Baby, It's Cold Outside (2 tks; tk 2 mst): Decca DL8477; Decca 24644; MCA Coral
  PCO 7666; Bear Family LJTy5

April 15, 1949

EF, vo; Hank Jones, p; Ray Brown, b; probably Roy Haynes, d
Old Mother Hubbard/You'll Have to Swing It (aka *Mr. Paganini*)/*There's a Small
  Hotel/How High the Moon*: Session Disc SES 105

April 23, 1949

EF, vo; personnel as on April 15, 1949
*Robbins' Nest/As You Desire Me/Thou Swell/Flying Home/Someone Like
  You/Again/In a Mellotone/Lemon Drop/I Hadn't Anyone Till You*: Session Disc
  SES 105

April 27, 1949

EF, vo; unknown orchestra
My Baby Likes to Re-Bop: Decca 24232

April 28, 1949

EF, vo; Gordon Jenkins and His Orchestra
Happy Talk/I'm Gonna Wash That Man Right Outa My Hair: Decca 24639; Decca
  DL8696
Black Coffee: Decca 24646; Decca DL8696; **Decca Jazz GRD-2-619**
Lover's Gold: Decca 24646; Decca DL8696

July 20, 1949

EF, vo; Sonny Burke and His Orchestra
Crying: Decca 34708; Decca DL4447
A New Shade of Blue: Decca 34708

September 18, 1949

JAZZ AT THE PHILHARMONIC; EF, vo; Hank Jones, p; Ray Brown, b; Buddy Rich, d.
On "Flying Home," "How High the Moon," and "Perdido" the following are
added: Roy Eldridge, tp; Tommy Turk, tb; Charlie Parker, as; Lester Young and
Flip Phillips, ts. "Ow" played by horns and rhythm was used as an instrumental fan-
fare to bring EF back on stage between "Basin Street Blues" and "Flying Home."
First set
Robbins' Nest: Verve 815 147-1
A New Shade of Blue/Old Mother Hubbard: unissued
I'm Just a Lucky So-and-So/Somebody Loves Me/Basin Street Blues: Verve 815 147-1
Flying Home (add 5 horns): Verve 815 147-1; **Verve 837 141-2**

Second set
Lady Be Good: unissued
Black Coffee: Verve 815 147-1
A-Tisket, A-Tasket: unissued
How High the Moon (add 5 horns)/*Perdido* (add 5 horns): **Verve 837 141-2**

September 20, 1949

EF, vo; Sy Oliver and His Orchestra
In the Evening (When the Sun Goes Down): Decca 24780; MCA Coral PCO 7667;
  Decca Jazz GRD-2-619
Talk Fast, My Heart, Talk Fast: Decca 24780; MCA Coral PCO 7667
I'm Waitin' for the Junkman: Decca 24868; MCA Coral PCO 7667
Basin Street Blues: Decca 24868; Jasmine JASM 1027; **Decca Jazz GRD-2-619**

September 21, 1949

EF, vo; Gordon Jenkins and His Orchestra and Chorus
I Hadn't Anyone Till You: Decca 24900; MCA2-4047
Dream a Little Longer: Decca 24900; Decca DL8696
Foolish Tears/A Man Wrote a Song: Decca 24773; Decca DL8696

November 7, 1949

EF, vo; the Mills Brothers
Fairy Tales: Decca 24813
I Gotta Have My Baby Back: Decca 24813; Decca DL8477

November 9, 1949

EF, vo; John Scott Trotter Kraft Show Orchestra

A Dreamer's Holiday with Bing Crosby, vo/*My Happiness*/*Way Back Home* with Bing Crosby and the Mills Brothers, vo: **Parrot PARCD 002**

1950 (date unknown)

EF, vo; unknown rhythm section of piano, bass, and drums

Don't Cry, Joe/*Laura*/*You Go to My Head*/*I'll Remember April*/*Run, Joe, Run*/*The Boy Next Door*/*My Old Flame*/*Night and Day*/*The Way You Look Tonight*/*The Hucklebuck* : all unissued

NOTE: This studio session is probably related to the unreleased motion picture short subject "Jazz at the Philharmonic."

February 2, 1950

EF, vo; Sy Oliver and His Orchestra

Baby, Won't You Say You Love Me?: Decca 24917

Don'cha Go 'Way Mad: Decca 24917; Decca DL8477

March 6, 1950

EF, vo; Sy Oliver and His Orchestra

Solid as a Rock: Decca 24958; MCA Coral PCO 7667

I've Got the World on a String: Decca 27120; MCA 2-4047; **Decca Jazz GRD-2-619**

Sugarfoot Rag: Decca 24958; MCA Coral PCO 7667

Peas and Rice: Decca 27120

May 3, 1950

EF, vo; John Scott Trotter Kraft Show Orchestra

Stay with the Happy People with Bing Crosby, vo/*I Hadn't Anyone Till You*: **Parrot PARCD 002**

May 9, 1950

EF, vo; Four Hits and a Miss

M-i-s-s-i-s-s-i-p-p-i/*I Don't Want the World*: Decca 27061

August 15, 1950

EF, vo; Louis Jordan and His Tympany Five

'Taint Nobody's Bizness If I Do: Decca 27200; **Decca Jazz GRD-2-619**

I'll Never Be Free: Decca 27200

August 25, 1950

EF, Louis Armstrong, vo; Sy Oliver and His Orchestra
Dream a Little Dream of Me: Decca 27209; Decca DL8477; **Decca Jazz GRD-2-619**
Can Anyone Explain?: Decca 27209

September 11, 1950

EF, vo; Ellis Larkins, p
Looking for a Boy: Decca 27369; Decca DL5300; **Decca Jazz GRD-636**
My One and Only Love: Decca 27368; Decca DL5300; **Decca Jazz GRD-636**
How Long Has This Been Going On?: Decca 27370; Decca DL5300; **Decca Jazz GRD-636**
I've Got a Crush on You: Decca 27370; Decca DL5300; **Decca Jazz GRD-636**

September 12, 1950

EF, vo; Ellis Larkins, p
But Not for Me: Decca 27369; Decca DL5300; **Decca Jazz GRD-636**
Soon: Decca 27371; Decca DL5300; **Decca Jazz GRD-636**
Someone to Watch Over Me: Decca 27368; Decca DL5300; **Decca Jazz GRD-636**
Maybe: Decca 27371; Decca DL5300; **Decca Jazz GRD-636**

September 26, 1950

EF, vo; Charlie Shavers, tp; Hank Jones, p; John Collins, g; Ray Brown, b; Charlie Smith, d
Santa Claus Got Stuck in My Chimney/Molasses, Molasses: Decca 27255

November 29, 1950

EF, vo; John Scott Trotter Kraft Show Orchestra
Basin Street Blues with Bing Crosby, vo; Red Nichols, t/*Can Anyone Explain?/Silver Bells* with Bing Crosby, vo/*Marshmallow World* with Bing Crosby, vo/*Memphis Blues* with The Firehouse Five + Two: **Parrot PARCD 002**

December 20, 1950

EF, vo; the Ink Spots
Little Small Town Girl/I Still Feel the Same About You: Decca 27419

January 12, 1951

EF, vo; the Ink Spots
Lonesome Gal/The Bean Bag Song: Decca 27453

DISCOGRAPHY

March 27, 1951

EF, vo; Sy Oliver and His Orchestra
Chesapeake and Ohio: Decca 27602
Little Man in a Flying Saucer: Decca 27578
Because of Rain: Decca 27602; Decca DL8832
The Hot Canary: Decca 27578

May 24, 1951

EF, vo; Hank Jones, p; Everett Barksdale, g; Sandy Block, b; Jimmy Crawford, d
Even as You and I/If You Really Love Me: Decca 27634; Decca DL4447
Love You Madly: Decca 27693

June 26, 1951

EF, vo; Bill Doggett, organ; Hank Jones, p (Teddy Wilson, p, on "Mixed
Emotions"); Everett Barksdale, g; Arnold Fishkin, b; Jimmy Crawford, d; the Ray
Charles Singers
Mixed Emotions: Decca 27680; Decca DL8832
Smooth Sailing: Decca 27693; Decca DL8149; **Decca Jazz GRD-2-619**
Come On-a My House: Decca 27680

July 18, 1951

EF, vo; Sy Oliver and His Orchestra
It's My Own Darn Fault: Decca 27948; Decca DL8695
I Don't Want to Make a Change: Decca 27948
There Never Was a Baby (Like My Baby): Decca 27724; Decca DL8892
Give a Little, Get a Little: Decca 27724; Decca DL8695

November 23, 1951

EF, Louis Armstrong, vo; Dave Barbour and His Orchestra
Necessary Evil/Oops!: Decca 27901
Would You Like to Take a Walk?: Decca 28552; Decca DL8477
Who Walks in When I Walk Out?: Decca 28552

November 28, 1951

EF, vo; John Scott Trotter Kraft Show Orchestra
Undecided: **Parrot PARCD 002**

December 26, 1951

EF, vo; Sonny Burke and His Orchestra
Baby Doll: Decca 27900; Decca DL8832
What Does It Take?: Decca 28034
Lady Bug: Decca 27900
Lazy Day: Decca 28034

January 4, 1952

EF, vo; Ray Brown and His Trio; Teddy Wilson, p; Bill Doggett, organ; the Ray
  Charles Singers
Air Mail Special: Decca 28126; Decca DL8149; **Decca Jazz GRD-2-619**
Rough Ridin': Decca 27948; Decca DL8149; **Decca Jazz GRD-2-619**

February 25, 1952

EF, vo; Sy Oliver and His Orchestra
A Guy Is a Guy: Decca 28049
Nowhere Guy: Decca 28707
Gee, but I'm Glad to Know: Decca 28131; Decca DL4447
Goody Goody: Decca 28126; Decca DL4129; **Decca Jazz GRD-2-619**

June 26, 1952

EF, vo; Sy Oliver and His Orchestra
Ding-Dong Boogie: Decca 28321
You'll Have to Swing It (Parts 1 and 2): Decca 28774; MCA 2-4047; **Decca Jazz
  GRD-2-619**
Angel Eyes: Decca 28707; Decca DL8149; **Decca Jazz GRD-2-619**
Early Autumn: Decca 29810
Preview: Decca 28321; **Decca Jazz GRD-2-619**
NOTE: On "Ding-Dong Boogie" and "Preview" Sammy Taylor, ts; Hank Jones, p;
  Everett Barksdale, g; Jimmy Crawford, d

August 11–13, 1952

EF, vo; Leroy Kirkland and His Orchestra
Trying: Decca 28375; Decca DL5443
The Greatest There Is: Decca 28930
Walkin' by the River: Decca 28433; MCA 2-4047
My Favorite Song: Decca 28433
My Bonnie: Decca 28375
Ella's Contribution to the Blues: Decca 29810; Decca DL8695

DISCOGRAPHY

October 15, 1952

EF, vo; the Lawson-Haggart Jazz Band
Basin Street Blues: unissued

November 30, 1952

EF, vo; Jerry Gray and His Orchestra
I Can't Lie to Myself/Don't Wake Me Up: Decca 28589

December 18, 1952

EF, vo; John Scott Trotter Kraft Show Orchestra
Medley: *Trying/My Favorite Song/Between the Devil and the Deep Blue Sea/Rudolph the Red-Nosed Reindeer* with Bing Crosby, vo: **Parrot PARCD 002**

January 1, 1953

EF, vo; John Scott Trotter Kraft Show Orchestra
Medley: *I Hadn't Anyone Till You/If You Ever Should Leave/I Can't Give You Anything but Love/Chicago Style* with Bing Crosby, vo: **Parrot PARCD 002**

February 13, 1953

EF, vo; Sy Oliver and His Orchestra
Careless: Decca 28671; Decca DL8695
Blue Lou: Decca 28671; Decca DL8695; **Decca Jazz GRD-2-619**
I Wonder What Kind of Man: Decca 28930

June 11, 1953

EF, vo; Taft Jordan, tp; unknown, organ; Sandy Bloch, b; Jimmy Crawford, d; the Ray Charles Singers
When the Hands of the Clock Pray at Midnight/Crying in the Chapel: Decca 28762

September 11, 1953

JAZZ AT THE PHILHARMONIC; EF, vo; Ray Tunia, p; Ray Brown, b; Herb Ellis, g; J. C. Heard, d
S'posin': unissued
My Bill: Verve 815147-1
Lover Come Back to Me/The Birth of the Blues/Angel Eyes/Love You Madly/Babalu: unissued
Why Don't You Do Right?: Verve 815147-1
One O'Clock Jump: unissued

NOTE: "One O'Clock Jump" was the finale of the concert. Granz called out the members of the JATP troupe to jam with Ella, but the tape runs out before anyone other than Ella and the rhythm section perform. Ella is heard (briefly) singing special lyrics about Jazz at the Philharmonic.

Ella Fitzgerald's JATP recordings listed here and for September 17 and 18, 1954, hail from underdocumented and/or misdocumented sources. Further complicating the pinning down of specific concerts and their dates is the odd coincidence of the September 11, 1953, material listed here and those items placed under September 17, 1954, both having a rare audio problem. Engineering logs that cite two Hartford JATP recordings (September 11, 1953, and September 17, 1954), plus two concerts recorded at Carnegie Hall (September 18, 1954), coupled with the surviving tape data and some educated guesses, have led me to these listings.

November 4–9, 1953

JAZZ AT THE PHILHARMONIC; EF, vo; Ray Tunia, p; Herb Ellis, g; Ray Brown, b; J. C. Heard, d. On "Perdido" and "After Hours Session": Roy Eldridge, Charlie Shavers, tp; Benny Carter, Willie Smith, as; Flip Phillips, Ben Webster, ts, are added, and Oscar Peterson replaces Tunia.

On the Sunny Side of the Street/Body and Soul/Why Don't You Do Right?/Lady Be Good/I Got It Bad and That Ain't Good/How High the Moon/My Funny Valentine/Smooth Sailing/Frim Fram Sauce: Pablo 2620-104

Perdido/After Hours Session: Pablo 2620-104; Verve (J) MV 9061-3

December 13, 1953

EF, vo; John Scott Trotter Kraft Show Orchestra
White Christmas with Bing Crosby, vo/*Moanin' Low*: **Parrot PARCD 002**

December 23, 1953

EF, vo; Sy Oliver and His Orchestra
Empty Ballroom: Decca 29259; MCA 2-4047
If You Don't, I Know Who Will: Decca 29259
Melancholy Me: Decca 29008; Decca DL4447
Somebody Bad Stole de Wedding Bell: Decca 29008

December 27, 1953

EF, vo; John Scott Trotter Kraft Show Orchestra
Someone to Watch Over Me/Istanbul with Bing Crosby, vo; Ziggy Elman, t/*Looking for a Boy*: **Parrot PARCD 002**

DISCOGRAPHY

December 31, 1953

EF, vo; John Scott Trotter and His Orchestra
Moanin' Low/*Taking a Chance on Love*: Decca 29475; Decca DL8155

February 14, 1954

EF, vo; John Scott Trotter Kraft Show Orchestra
That's a Plenty with Bing Crosby, vo/*Taking a Chance on Love*: **Parrot PARCD 002**

March 24, 1954

EF, vo; Gordon Jenkins and His Orchestra
I Wished on the Moon: Decca 29137; Decca DL8696; **Decca Jazz GRD-2-619**
Baby: Decca 29108; Decca DL8696
I Need: Decca 29108; Decca DL8696
Who's Afraid?: Decca 29137

March 29, 1954

EF, vo; Ellis Larkins, p
I'm Glad There Is You/*What Else Could I Do?*/*What Is There to Say?*/*Makin' Whoopee*/*People Will Say We're in Love*: Decca DL8068
Until the Real Thing Comes Along: Decca DL8068; **Decca Jazz GRD-2-619; Decca Jazz GRD-636**

March 30, 1954

EF, vo; Ellis Larkins, p
Please Be Kind/*Imagination*/*My Heart Belongs to Daddy*/*You Leave Me Breathless*/*Nice Work If You Can Get It*/*Star Dust*: Decca DL8068; **Decca Jazz GRD-636**

June 4, 1954

EF, vo; Sy Oliver and His Orchestra
Lullaby of Birdland: Decca 29198; Decca DL8149; **Decca Jazz GRD-2-619**
Later: Decca 29198; Decca DL8149

September 17, 1954

EF, vo; Ray Tunia, p; Herb Ellis, g; Ray Brown, b; Buddy Rich, d. On "Perdido," add Roy Eldridge, probably Dizzy Gillespie, tp; Flip Phillips, possibly another, ts; possibly other horns.
A Foggy Day: Verve 815147-1

Lullaby of Birdland: **Verve 314 517 898-2**
The Man That Got Away/Hernando's Hideaway/Later: Verve 815147-1
Perdido (add horns): unissued
NOTE: See note under listing for September 11, 1953.

September 18, 1954

JAZZ AT THE PHILHARMONIC; EF, vo; Ray Tunia, p; Herb Ellis, g; Ray Brown, b;
   Buddy Rich, d
That Old Black Magic/Hey There: unissued

April 1, 1955

EF, vo; André Previn and His Orchestra
*You'll Never Know/Thanks for the Memory/It Might as Well Be Spring/I Can't Get
Started*: Decca DL8155

April 27, 1955

EF, vo; Benny Carter and His Orchestra
Between the Devil and the Deep Blue Sea/That Old Black Magic: Decca DL8155;
   Decca Jazz GRD-2-619
Old Devil Moon/Lover Come Back to Me: Decca 29580; Decca DL8155; **Decca Jazz
   GRD-2-619**

May 3, 1955

EF, vo; Don Abney, p; Joe Mondragon, b; Larry Bunker, d
Hard Hearted Hannah (The Vamp of Savannah): Decca 29689; Decca DL8166;
   Decca Jazz GRD-2-619
Pete Kelly's Blues: Decca 29689; Decca DL8166
Ella Hums the Blues: Decca DL8166

August 1, 1955

EF, vo; Toots Camarata and His Orchestra
Soldier Boy: Decca 29648
A Satisfied Mind: Decca 29648; Decca DL8695

August 5, 1955

EF, vo; Toots Camarata and His Orchestra
My One and Only Love: Decca 29746; Decca DL8695; **Decca Jazz GRD-2-619**

The Impatient Years/But Not Like Mine: Decca 29665; Decca DL8695
The Tender Trap: Decca 29746; **MCA 2-2047**

THE VERVE YEARS 1955–1966

Mid 1950s (date unknown)

EF, vo; Nelson Riddle Orchestra
Beale Street Blues: Verve V10128

January 21, 1956

EF, vo; personnel unknown. EF appeared opposite the Dave Brubeck Quartet at Los
Angeles' Shrine Auditorium.
*And the Angels Sing/Joe Williams' Blues/Air Mail Special/'S Wonderful/Cry Me a
River/Lullaby of Birdland/Medley: Fools Rush In; Glad to Be Unhappy*: all unis-
sued

January 25, 1956

EF, vo; Buddy Bregman Orchestra
Stay There/The Sun Forgot to Shine: Verve 10012
Too Young for the Blues (7 tks; tks 4 to 8 exist; tk 7 and 8 iss): Verve MGV 2036
(tk8); Verve 10002 (tk 8); **Verve 314 517 898-2** (tk 7)
It's Only a Man (5 tks; tk 5 iss): Verve MGV 2036; Verve 10002

February 2, 1956

EF, vo; Don Abney, p; Vernon Alley, b; Frankie Capp, d
Recorded at Hollywood nightclub, Zardi's
*It All Depends on You/Tenderly/Why Don't You Do Right?/In a Mellotone/Joe
Williams' Blues/A Fine Romance/How High the Moon/Gone with the
Wind/Bernie's Tune/'S Wonderful/Glad to Be Unhappy/Lullaby of Birdland/The
Tender Trap/And the Angels Sing/I Can't Give You Anything but Love/Little
Boy/A-Tisket, A-Tasket/My Heart Belongs to Daddy/Air Mail Special/I've Got a
Crush on You*: all unissued

February 7, 1956

EF, vo; Buddy Bregman Orchestra
*Why Can't You Behave?/I Love Paris/Do I Love You?/Ev'rytime We Say Goodbye/I
Am in Love/Ridin' High/It's All Right with Me/From This Moment On/Just One
of Those Things/Too Darn Hot*: Verve 4001-2; **Verve 821 989/90-2; Verve 314 519
832-2**

EF, vo; Paul Smith, p; Barney Kessel, g; Joe Mondragon, b; Alvin Stoller, d

Miss Otis Regrets/Get Out of Town/Easy to Love: Verve 4001-2; **Verve 821 989/90-2; Verve 314 519 832-2**

NOTE: One other tune was recorded by EF and the rhythm section. It is presumed lost.

February 8, 1956

EF, vo; Buddy Bregman Orchestra

So in Love/You Do Something to Me/In the Still of the Night/Begin the Beguine/All Through the Night/Always True to You in My Fashion/It's De-Lovely/Ace in the Hole/Love for Sale (spliced take)*/Anything Goes/I Concentrate on You**: Verve 4001-2; **Verve 821 989/90-2; Verve 314 519 832-2**

*NOTE:This would be Verve master 20085-4, with the March 27, 1956, remake (20123-3). The March version remained unissued until the Complete Ella Songbook box (**Verve 314 519 832-2**); performed by EF and rhythm section only. With no other listings or leads, I'm making the assumption that the issued full band version comes from this session.

EF, vo; Paul Smith, p; Barney Kessel, g; Joe Mondragon, b; Alvin Stoller, d

Let's Do It

NOTE: Edited performance; at least the ending spliced in from March 27, 1956, version. Two other tunes were recorded by EF and the rhythm section. They are presumed lost. It is plausible that Verve 20085, "I Concentrate on You," was by EF and the rhythm section thereby making the rhythm section accompaniment a traditional four-titled session. But there is no paperwork or tape to document this scenario and the full orchestra version of "I Concentrate on You" must be accounted for, as noted just above.

February 9, 1956

EF, vo; Buddy Bregman Orchestra

I Get a Kick out of You/You're the Top/I've Got You Under My Skin: Verve 4001-2; **Verve 821 989/90-2; Verve 314 519 832-2**

What Is This Thing Called Love?: Verve 4001-2; Verve 10248; **Verve 821 989/90-2; Verve 314 519 832-2**

All of You/Don't Fence Me In: Verve 4001-2; **Verve 821 989/90-2; Verve 314 519 832-2**

March 27, 1956

EF, vo; Buddy Bregman Orchestra

Night and Day: Verve 4001-2; **Verve 821 989/90-2; Verve 314 519 832-2**

The End of a Beautiful Friendship: Verve 2036

EF, vo; Paul Smith, p; Barney Kessel, g; Joe Mondragon, b; Alvin Stoller, d

You're the Top/I Concentrate on You: **Verve 314 519 832-2**

EF, vo; Buddy Bregman Orchestra

I Had to Find Out for Myself (11 tks; tk 11 mst): all unissued

NOTE: Takes 1-8 are presumably lost; take 11, at a slower tempo, was designated as the preferred or "master" take.

EF, vo; Paul Smith, p; Barney Kessel, g; Joe Mondragon, b; Alvin Stoller, d

Let's Do It (3 tks): **Verve 314 519 832-2**

NOTE: Some of the ending (at least) to take 3 has been attached or intercut with the known version of February 8, 1956. There is an interesting studio conference with EF, the instrumentalists, and, I believe, Buddy Bregman over the purpose of this remake with its extra chorus and lyrics. The scraps have been saved and were issued on **Verve 314 519 832-2**.

June 25, 1956

METRONOME ALL-STARS/COUNT BASIE AND HIS ORCHESTRA; EF, vo; Wendell Culley, Reginald Jones, Thad Jones, Joe Newman, tp; Henry Coker, Bill Hughes, Benny Powell, tb; Frank Foster, Charlie Fowlkes, Bill Graham, Marshall Royal, Frank Wess, reeds; Freddie Greene, g; Eddie Jones, b; Sonny Payne, d; Joe Williams, vo on "Party Blues" and "Every Day I Have the Blues"; Count Basie, p. Ralph Burns replaces Basie on "Every Day I Have the Blues." An octet of T. Jones, Newman, Coker, Wess, Greene, E. Jones, Payne, and Basie back the singers on "Party Blues."

April in Paris: Clef MGC 743; Verve 8030; Verve (J) 2510; **Verve 314 517 898-2**

Too Close for Comfort: Verve 8288

Every Day I Have the Blues: Clef MGC 743; Verve 8030; Verve (J) 2510

Party Blues: Clef MGC 743; Verve 8030; Verve 8341; Verve (J) 2510

August 15, 1956

JAZZ AT THE HOLLYWOOD BOWL; EF, vo; Paul Smith, p; Barney Kessel, g; Joe Mondragon, b; Alvin Stoller, d

This Can't Be Love/The End of a Beautiful Friendship/I Could Have Danced All Night/Lady be Good: unissued

Little Girl Blue/Too Close for Comfort: Verve 8231

Love for Sale/Just One of Those Things: Verve 8231; Verve 603; **Verve 314 519 564-2**

Angel Eyes: probably lost

I Can't Give You Anything but Love/Air Mail Special: Verve 8231

NOTE: "Love for Sale" and "Just One of Those Things" were issued on the Verve ten-inch LP 603, which is a European issue of her February 13, 1960, Berlin concert. Yes, these August 15, 1956, recordings were issued as though they were part of the *Ella in Berlin* material! These two tracks were included on *Mack the Knife: The Complete Ella in Berlin*, which is **Verve 314 519 564-2**.

EF, vo; Trummy Young, tb; Edmond Hall, cl; Billy Kyle, p; Dale Jones, b; Barrett Deems, d; Louis Armstrong, vo & tp

You Won't Be Satisfied/When the Saints Go Marching In (no audible EF): Verve 8231

Undecided: Verve 8231; **Verve 314 517 898-2**

August 16, 1956

EF, vo; Oscar Peterson, p; Herb Ellis, g; Ray Brown, b; Buddy Rich, d; Louis Armstrong, vo & tp

They Can't Take That Away from Me/Isn't This a Lovely Day?/Tenderly/Stars Fell on Alabama/Cheek to Cheek/Under a Blanket of Blue/Moonlight in Vermont/A Foggy Day/April in Paris/The Nearness of You: Verve 4003; **Verve 825373-2**

Can't We Be Friends?: Verve 4003; **Verve 825373-2; Verve 314 517 898-2**

August 21, 1956

EF, vo; Buddy Bregman Orchestra

This Can't Be Love/The Lady Is a Tramp: Verve 4002-2; Verve V6-4022; Verve VST 10001/ST20010; Verve Ve2-2519; **Verve 821 579/80-2; Verve 314 519 832-2**

I've Got Five Dollars: Verve 4002-2; Verve V6-4023; Verve Ve2-2519; **Verve 821 579/80-2; Verve 314 519 832-2**

Lover (mono take): Verve 4002-2; **Verve 314 519 832-2**

Lover (stereo take): Verve Ve2-2519; **Verve 821 579/80-2; Verve 314 519 832-2**

The Silent Treatment: Verve MGV 2036

August 28, 1956

EF, vo; Buddy Bregman Orchestra

Ten Cents a Dance: Verve V6-4023; **Verve 314 519 832-2**

I Wish I Were in Love Again: Verve V6-4022; **Verve 314 519 832-2**

Mountain Greenery: Verve V6-4023; **Verve 314 519 832-2**

Johnny One Note: Verve V6-4022; **Verve 314 519 832-2**

Give It Back to the Indians: Verve V6-4023; **Verve 314 519 832-2**

NOTE: All August 28, 1956, titles also on Verve 4002-2; Verve Ve2-2519; **Verve 821 579/80-2.**

August 29, 1956

EF, vo; Buddy Bregman Orchestra

Blue Moon: Verve V6-4023; **Verve 314 519 832-2**

Thou Swell/Manhattan: Verve V6-4022; **Verve 314 519 832-2**

There's a Small Hotel/I Didn't Know What Time It Was: Verve V6-4023; **Verve 314 519 832-2**

EF, vo; Paul Smith, p; Barney Kessel, g; Joe Mondragon, b; Alvin Stoller, d

With a Song in My Heart/To Keep My Love Alive: Verve V6-4022; **Verve 314 519 832-2**

Bewitched/Wait Till You See Her: Verve V6-4023; **Verve 314 519 832-2**

NOTE: With Ella's Rodgers and Hart songbook, Verve began an audiophile release series on tape that was apparently an early attempt to offer stereo issues. The series is not documented.

August 30, 1956

EF, vo; Buddy Bregman Orchestra

My Romance: Verve V6-4022; **Verve 314 519 832-2**

My Heart Stood Still: Verve V6-4023; **Verve 314 519 832-2**

A Ship Without a Sail/Have You Met (Sir) Jones?: Verve V6-4022; **Verve 314 519 832-2**

Here in My Arms: Verve V6-4023; **Verve 314 519 832-2**

It Never Entered My Mind/Little Girl Blue/Spring Is Here: Verve V6-4022; **Verve 314 519 832-2**

My Funny Valentine/I Could Write a Book: Verve V6-4023; **Verve 314 519 832-2**

NOTE: All August 30, 1956, titles also on Verve 4002-2; Verve Ve2-2519; **Verve 821 579/80-2.**

August 31, 1956

EF, vo; Buddy Bregman Orchestra (smaller than previous studio bands; Barney Kessel definitely present)

Blue Room: Verve V6-4023; **Verve 314 519 832-2**

Dancing on the Ceiling/Where or When: Verve V6-4022; **Verve 314 519 832-2**

Isn't It Romantic?: Verve V6-4023; **Verve 314 519 832-2**

You Took Advantage of Me: Verve V6-4022; **Verve 314 519 832-2**

NOTE: All August 31, 1956, titles on Verve 4002-2; Verve Ve2-2519; **Verve 821 579/80-2.**

September 4, 1956

EF, vo; Ben Webster, ts; Stuff Smith, v; Paul Smith, p; Barney Kessel, g; Joe Mondragon, b; Alvin Stoller, d. On "Solitude," "Azure," and "In a Sentimental Mood," Ella is accompanied only by guitar. On "Ev'rything I've Got Belongs to You," Webster and Smith are out.

I Let a Song Go Out of My Heart/Rocks in My Bed/Cottontail/Just Squeeze Me/Do Nothing Till You Hear from Me/Solitude/Sophisticated Lady/Just a Sittin' and a Rockin'/It Don't Mean a Thing (If It Ain't Got That Swing)/Prelude to a Kiss/Don't Get Around Much Anymore/Satin Doll/Azure/In a Sentimental Mood: Verve 4010-4; Verve Ve2-2540; **Verve 837 035-2; Verve 314 519 832-2**

DISCOGRAPHY

Ev'rything I've Got Belongs to You: Verve 4002-2; Verve V6-4023; Verve Ve2-2519; **Verve 821 579/80-2; Verve 314 519 832-2**

January 14, 1957

EF, vo; Russ Garcia Orchestra
Hotta Chocolota (8 tks; tk 8 mst)/*Hear My Heart* (9 tks; tk 9 mst): Verve 10031

April 29, 1957

EF, vo; Don Abney, p; Herb Ellis, g; Ray Brown, b; Jo Jones, d
You Got Me Singing the Blues/Angel Eyes/Lullaby of Birdland/Tenderly/Do Nothin'
Till You Hear from Me/April in Paris/I Can't Give You Anything but Love/Love
for Sale/add Roy Eldridge, t; Stuff Smith, v; and sub Oscar Peterson for Abney, p,
on *It Don't Mean a Thing (If It Ain't Got That Swing)*: **Tax CD 3703-2**

June 24, 1957

DUKE ELLINGTON AND HIS ORCHESTRA; EF, vo; Cat Anderson, Willie Cook, Clark
Terry, tp; Quentin Jackson, John Sanders, Britt Woodman, tb; Harry Carney,
Frank Foster, Jimmy Hamilton, Johnny Hodges, Russell Procope, reeds; Billy
Strayhorn, p; Jimmy Woode, b; Sam Woodyard, d. On "Take the 'A' Train,"
Duke Ellington replaces Strayhorn on piano, and Dizzy Gillespie, Ray Nance, and
Harold "Shorty" Baker are added on trumpet. Ray Nance or Shorty Baker may
already have been playing on the date.
Day Dream/Take the "A" Train: Verve MGV 4010-4; Verve VE2-2535; **Verve 837
035-2; Verve 314 519 832-2**
NOTE: For the June 24–27, 1957, sessions with Ellington and His Orchestra, there
will always be some question about which days Frank Foster substituted for Paul
Gonsalves. Trumpeters Shorty Baker, Willie Cook, and Ray Nance were used
interchangeably in the trumpet section during these recordings.

June 25, 1957

DUKE ELLINGTON AND HIS ORCHESTRA; EF, vo; Cat Anderson, Willie Cook, Ray
Nance, Clark Terry, tp; John Sanders, vtb; Quentin Jackson, Britt Woodman, tb;
Harry Carney, Jimmy Hamilton, Johnny Hodges, Russell Procope, probably Paul
Gonsalves, reeds; Duke Ellington, p; Jimmy Woode, b; Sam Woodyard, d. On
"Lost in Meditation," Merce Ellington plays clave, Clark Terry plays cowbell, per-
haps others join the miscellaneous percussion. (Harold "Shorty" Baker may have
played trumpet on this date.)
Everything But You/I Got It Bad (and That Ain't Good)/Drop Me Off in
Harlem/Lost in Meditation/I Ain't Got Nothin' But the Blues: Verve 4010-4; Verve
VE2-2535; **Verve 837 035-2; Verve 314 519 832-2**

June 26, 1957

DUKE ELLINGTON AND HIS ORCHESTRA; EF, vo; Cat Anderson, Willie Cook, Ray Nance, Clark Terry, tp; Quentin Jackson, John Sanders, Britt Woodman, tb; Harry Carney, Frank Foster, Jimmy Hamilton, Johnny Hodges, Russell Procope, reeds; Duke Ellington, p; Jimmy Woode, b; Sam Woodyard, d

Clementine/I'm Just a Lucky So-and-So/I'm Beginning to See the Light/I Didn't Know About You/Rockin' in Rhythm: Verve 4010-4; Verve VE2-2535; **Verve 837 035-2; Verve 314 519 832-2**

June 27, 1957

DUKE ELLINGTON AND HIS ORCHESTRA; EF, vo; Cat Anderson, Willie Cook, Ray Nance, Clark Terry, tp; Quentin Jackson, John Sanders, Britt Woodman, tb; Harry Carney, Paul Gonsalves, Jimmy Hamilton, Johnny Hodges, Russell Procope, reeds; Duke Ellington, p; Jimmy Woode, b; Sam Woodyard, d; Billy Strayhorn took part in this session. Merce Ellington briefly fills in for one of the trumpeters during the rehearsal of "Chelsea Bridge."

Chelsea Bridge (rehearsal): partial **Verve 314 519 832-2**

NOTE: Part of this was to be included as a bonus track to **Verve 837 035-2**, but apparently was left out. A ten-minute excerpt, however, was included on *The Complete Ella Fitzgerald Songbooks* (**Verve 314 519 832-2**).

Chelsea Bridge (alternate): **Verve 314 519 832-2**

All Too Soon/Caravan/Bli-Blip/Chelsea Bridge (tk 8—mst)/*Perdido/The E and D Blues*: Verve 4010-4; Verve VE2-2535; **Verve 837 035-2; Verve 314 519 832-2**

July 4, 1957

NEWPORT JAZZ FESTIVAL; EF, vo; Don Abney, p; Wendell Marshall, b; Jo Jones, d

This Can't Be Love/I Got It Bad (and That Ain't Good)/Body and Soul/April in Paris/I Got a Crush on You/I Can't Give You Anything but Love: Verve 6022/8234; Verve (J) MV 2576

Air Mail Special: Verve 6022/8234; Verve (J) MV 2576; **Verve 314 517 898-2**

July 23, 1957

EF, vo; Oscar Peterson, p; Herb Ellis, g; Ray Brown, b; Louis Bellson, d; Louis Armstrong, vo & tp

Our Love Is Here to Stay/Autumn in New York/Let's Call the Whole Thing Off/They All Laughed (NOTE: no tp)/*Gee Baby, Ain't I Good to You?/ Stompin' at the Savoy*: Verve 4006-2; **Verve 825 374-2**

Learnin' the Blues: Verve 4006-2; **Verve 825 374-2; Verve 314 521 851–2**

NOTE: Satchmo left at this point, and the date continued with Ella and the rhythm section.

These Foolish Things/Comes Love/Ill Wind: Verve 4006-2

July 24, 1957

EF, vo; Frank DeVol Orchestra
Tenderly/Moonlight in Vermont/Stairway to the Stars: Verve 4034
A-Tisket, A-Tasket: Verve 10079; Verve 4063; **Verve 314 517 898-2**
You Turned the Tables on Me/Gypsy in My Soul: Verve 4036
Goody Goody: Verve 10079; Verve 4036
St. Louis Blues: Verve 10128; Verve 4036

EF, vo; possibly Ben Webster, ts; probably Sweets Edison, tp; probably Paul Smith,
 p; Barney Kessel, g; possibly Red Mitchell, b; unknown, d
Don'cha Go 'Way Mad (4 tks): all unissued
NOTE: After the break, EF suggests a fleshing out of the intro. She sings it, then the
 instrumentalists rehearse it.
Don'cha Go 'Way Mad (2 further tks; tk 6 mst): **Verve 314 517 898-2**
Angel Eyes: **Verve 314 517 898-2**
NOTE: "Angel Eyes" is a duet with Ella and guitarist Barney Kessel. I have deter-
 mined the personnel by ear. There are no solos. The familiar breathy tenor makes
 me think of Ben Webster, but it's difficult to claim that he's on this session.

August 13, 1957

EF, vo; Oscar Peterson, p; Herb Ellis, g; Ray Brown, b; Louis Bellson, d; Louis
 Armstrong, vo. On "I'm Putting All My Eggs in One Basket" and "I've Got My
 Love to Keep Me Warm," Louis Armstrong also plays trumpet.
I Won't Dance: Verve 4006-2; **Verve 825 374-2**; **Verve 314 517 898-2**
A Fine Romance: Verve 4006-2; **Verve 825 374-2**; **Verve 314 521 851-2**
*Don't Be That Way/I'm Putting All My Eggs in One Basket/I've Got My Love to Keep
 Me Warm*: Verve 4006-2; **Verve 825 374-2**

August 18, 1957

EF, vo; Russ Garcia Orchestra; Louis Armstrong, tp & vo
*Summertime/Bess, You Is My Woman Now/I Got Plenty o' Nuttin'/It Ain't
 Necessarily So*: Verve 6040-2/4011-2; Verve VE2-2507; **Verve 827 475-2**

August 28, 1957

EF, vo; Russ Garcia Orchestra
I Wants to Stay Here (aka *I Loves You Porgy*)/ *My Man's Gone Now/What You Want
 with Bess/Buzzard Song/Oh Doctor Jesus/Here Come de Honey Man/Oh Dey's So
 Fresh an' Fine (Strawberry Woman)*: Verve 6040-2/4011-2; Verve VE2-2507;
 Verve 827 475-2

September 29, 1957

JAZZ AT THE PHILHARMONIC; EF, vo; Oscar Peterson, p; Herb Ellis, g; Ray Brown,
 b; Jo Jones, d

It's All Right with Me: unissued

NOTE: The tape runs out on the surviving reel from the location recording of the early show.

EF, vo; Oscar Peterson, p; Herb Ellis, g; Ray Brown, b; Jo Jones, d. On "Them There Eyes" it is plausible that Connie Kay, not Jo Jones, is drummer; while on "Stompin' at the Savoy," Connie Kay is on drums and Roy Eldridge on trumpet; J. J. Johnson, tb; Sonny Stitt, as; Stan Getz, Coleman Hawkins, Illinois Jacquet, Flip Phillips, Lester Young, ts.

It's All Right with Me/Don'cha Go 'Way Mad/Bewitched/These Foolish Things/Ill Wind/Goody Goody/Moonlight in Vermont/Them There Eyes/Stompin' at the Savoy: Verve 6026; **Verve 831 269-2**

NOTE: The Chicago concert(s) of Sunday, September 29, 1957, are the ones recorded in stereo. The date—despite published references which all state October 19, 1957—is correct.

October 9, 1957

JAZZ AT THE PHILHARMONIC; EF, vo; Oscar Peterson, p; Herb Ellis, g; Ray Brown, b; Jo Jones, d. On "Stompin' at the Savoy" and "Lady Be Good": Roy Eldridge, tp; J. J. Johnson, tb; Sonny Stitt, as; Stan Getz, Coleman Hawkins, Illinois Jacquet, Flip Phillips, Lester Young, ts, are added. The drummer on "Savoy" is probably Connie Kay, but on "Lady Be Good" the drummer is definitely Jo Jones.

It's All Right with Me/Don'cha Go 'Way Mad/Bewitched/These Foolish Things/Ill Wind/Goody Goody/Moonlight in Vermont/Stompin' at the Savoy: Verve 8264; **Verve 831 269-2**

Lady Be Good: Verve 8264; **Verve 831 269-2; Verve 314 517 898-2**

NOTE: This long misdated concert (most discographies list October 25, 1957) was originally scheduled for October 7, 1957, but recent research pins it down as occurring on Wednesday, October 9, 1957. Recorded in mono.

October 15, 1957

EF, vo; Frank DeVol Orchestra. On "There's a Lull in My Life," "You're Blasé," "What Will I Tell My Heart?" and "Midnight Sun," Stan Getz on tenor sax is added and featured.

There's a Lull in My Life/You're Blasé/More Than You Know/Like Someone in Love/What Will I Tell My Heart?/We'll Be Together Again/Then I'll Be Tired of You/Close Your Eyes/I Thought About You/I Never Had a Chance/Midnight Sun: Verve 6000/4004; **Verve 314 511 524-2**

October 17, 1957

EF, vo; Ben Webster, ts; Oscar Peterson, p; Herb Ellis, g; Ray Brown, b; Alvin Stoller, d. On "Mood Indigo," Ben Webster lays out. "Lush Life" is a duet by Ella and Oscar Peterson.

In a Mellotone/Mood Indigo/Love You Madly/Lush Life/Squatty Roo: Verve VE2-2540; **Verve 837 035-2; Verve 314 519 832-2**

293

October 28, 1957

EF, vo; Frank DeVol Orchestra. On "Hurry Home," "How Long Has This Been Going On?" and "What's New?" Stan Getz (ts) is featured.

I'll Never Be the Same: Verve 4034; **Verve 314 511 524-2**

Night Wind/Hurry Home/How Long Has This Been Going On?: Verve 6000/4004; **Verve 314 511 524-2**

Lost in a Fog/Everything Happens to Me: Verve 4034; **Verve 314 511 524-2**

What's New?: Verve 6000/4004; Verve **314 511 524-2**

So Rare: Verve 4034; **Verve 314 511 524-2**

circa 1957–58

NOTE: There are two surviving performances from Nat King Cole's TV show of 1957–58.

circa 1957–58

EF, vo; Jazz at the Philharmonic rhythm section

Angel Eyes/Joe Williams' Blues: unissued

March 13, 1958

EF, vo; Paul Weston Orchestra

Isn't This a Lovely Day?/All by Myself in the Morning/Let's Go Slummin' on Park Avenue/I'm Putting All My Eggs in One Basket/Always: Verve 6005-2/4019-2; **Verve 829 534/35-2; Verve 314 519 832-2**

March 14, 1958

EF, vo; Paul Weston Orchestra

I Used to Be Color Blind/You Can Have Him/How's Chances?/No Strings (I'm Fancy Free): Verve 6005-2/4019-2; **Verve 829 534/35-2; Verve 314 519 832-2**

March 17, 1958

EF, vo; Paul Weston Orchestra

You Keep Coming Back like a Song/Suppertime/How Deep Is the Ocean/You're Laughing at Me/Russian Lullaby/Change Partners/Now It Can Be Told/How About Me?/Get Thee Behind Me, Satan/Reaching for the Moon: Verve 6005-2/4019-2; **Verve 829 534/35-2; Verve 314 519 832-2**

March 18, 1958

EF, vo; Paul Weston Orchestra (including Sweets Edison, tp)

I've Got My Love to Keep Me Warm/Heat Wave/Cheek to Cheek/The Song Is Ended: Verve 6005-2/4019-2; **Verve 829 534/35-2; Verve 314 519 832-2**

Blue Skies: Verve 4036; **Verve 829 534/35-2; Verve 314 519 832-2**

Lazy/Let's Face the Music and Dance/It's a Lovely Day Today/Puttin' on the Ritz/You Forgot to Remember: Verve 6005-2/4019-2; **Verve 829 534/35-2; Verve 314 519 832-2**

March 19, 1958

EF, vo; Paul Weston Orchestra (including Sweets Edison, tp)

Alexander's Ragtime Band/Let Yourself Go/Top Hat, White Tie and Tails: Verve 6005-2/4019-2; **Verve 829 534/35-2; Verve 314 519 832-2**

Teach Me How to Cry (2 tks; tk 2 mst): Verve 10130

EF, vo; Sweets Edison, tp; unknown, flute; unknown, p; unknown, g; unknown, b; unknown, d

Swingin' Shepherd Blues (3 tks; tk 3 mst): Verve 10130; Verve V6-8579; **Verve 314 517 898-2**

April 24–25, 1958

EF, vo; Lou Levy, p; Max Bennett, b; Gus Johnson, d

St. Louis Blues: **Verve 835 454-2**

EF, vo; Oscar Peterson, p; Herb Ellis, g; probably Ray Brown, b; Gus Johnson, d

Stompin' at the Savoy: unissued

April 25, 1958

Afternoon Concert

EF, vo; Lou Levy, p; Max Bennett, b; Gus Johnson, d

When You're Smiling/A Foggy Day/Midnight Sun/The Lady Is a Tramp: **Verve 835 454-2**

Just Squeeze Me/That Old Black Magic: unissued

Sophisticated Lady/Caravan: **Verve 835 454-2**

Angel Eyes/St. Louis Blues: unissued

EF, vo; Oscar Peterson, p; Herb Ellis, g; probably Ray Brown, b; Gus Johnson, d

Stompin' at the Savoy: unissued

Evening Concert

EF, vo; Lou Levy, p; Max Bennett, b; Gus Johnson, d

When You're Smiling/A Foggy Day: unissued

These Foolish Things: **Verve 835 454-2**

Midnight Sun/The Lady Is a Tramp: unissued

Just Squeeze Me/Angel Eyes/That Old Black Magic/Just One of Those Things: **Verve 835 454-2**

Sophisticated Lady/Caravan: unissued

I Loves You Porgy/It's All Right with Me/I Can't Give You Anything but Love: **Verve 835 454-2**
St. Louis Blues: unissued

EF, vo; personnel as afternoon "Savoy"
Stompin' at the Savoy: **Verve 835 454-2**

May 9, 1958 (telecast date)

EF, vo; "Frank Sinatra Show" Studio Orchestra
Moonlight in Vermont/I May Be Wrong: **Bravura BVRCD 105**

July 1, 1958

EF, vo; Lou Levy, kb; Dick Hyman, organ; Max Bennett, b; Gus Johnson, d
Travelin' Light (6 tks; tk 6 mst): Verve 10143; **Verve 314 517 898-2** (tk 6)
NOTE: "Travelin' Light" is Verve master 22290. Lou Levy plays celesta.
Your Red Wagon (7 tks; tk 7 mst): Verve 10143; Verve 8320
NOTE: "Your Red Wagon" is Verve master 22291. Lou Levy plays piano. The master takes of both tunes may have come out on a stereo single in the rare Verve 700 series.

August 10, 1958

EF, vo; Lou Levy, p; Max Bennett, b; Gus Johnson, d
Recorded at Mr. Kelly's nightclub in Chicago
Your Red Wagon/Nice Work If You Can Get It/I'm Glad There Is You/How Long Has This Been Going On?/Across the Alley from the Alamo/Perdido/The Lady Is a Tramp/Witchcraft (incomplete)/*Bewitched/Summertime/In the Wee Small Hours of the Morning/St. Louis Blues*: all unissued
NOTE: "Across the Alley from the Alamo" is not the famous "On the Alamo" but a novelty tune recorded by, among others, the Mills Brothers and Stan Kenton.
Witchcraft (2nd version)/*Love Me or Leave Me/Joe Williams' Blues/Medley* from *Porgy and Bess/How High the Moon/Exactly Like You/Come Rain or Come Shine/Stardust/'S Wonderful/Oo-Bop-Sh'Bam/You Don't Know What Love Is/Witchcraft* (3rd version)/*Perdido* (2nd version)/*In the Wee Small Hours of the Morning* (2nd version)/*My Funny Valentine/Anything Goes*: all unissued
NOTE: "Lover," "On the Sunny Side of the Street," "Willow Weep for Me," "My Heart Belongs to Daddy," "The Lady Is a Tramp" (2nd version), "Too Close for Comfort," unknown title, assigned Verve master 22352, are all presumably lost.

DISCOGRAPHY

November 22, 1958

EF, vo; Marty Paich Dek-Tette: Don Fagerquist, Al Porcino, tp; Bob Enevoldsen, vtb and ts; Vince De Rosa, fh; John Kitzmiller, tu; Bud Shank, as; Bill Holman, ts; Med Flory, bs; Lou Levy, p; Joe Mondragon, b; Mel Lewis, d

You Hit the Spot/Blues in the Night: Verve 6019/4021; **Verve 847 392-2**

What's Your Story, Morning Glory?: Verve 4021; **Verve 847 392-2**

Just You, Just Me/My Kinda of Love/If I Were a Bell/Teardrops from My Eyes: Verve 6019/4021; **Verve 847 392-2**

You're an Old Smoothie (3 tks; tks 2 and 3 iss): Verve 4021; **Verve 847 392-2**; (tk 2) **Verve 314 517 898-2**

As Long As I Live (3 tks; tk 3 mst): Verve 6019/4021; **Verve 847 392-2**

NOTE: An edited version of "Teardrops" was issued on Verve singles: VS-702 (stereo) and 10166 (mono).

November 23, 1958

EF, vo; Marty Paich Dek-Tette (same personnel as on November 22)

Knock Me a Kiss: Verve 6019/4021; **Verve 847 392-2**

It's Gotta Be This or That/720 in the Books: Verve 4021; **Verve 847 392-2**

Moonlight on the Ganges: Verve 6019/4021; **Verve 847 392-2**

Oh What a Night for Love (4 tks); tk 2 (Ella's version): Verve (J) J28J-25118; **Verve 847 392-2**; tk 4 mst (single version): Verve 10158; **Verve 847 392-2**

NOTE: Verve 10158, the mono 45 rpm issue, was probably paralleled by a stereo single in the Verve VS-700 series.

Little Jazz (2 tks); tk 1: Verve (J) J28J-25118; **Verve 847 392-2**; tk 2 mst: Verve 6019/4021; **Verve 847 392-2**

NOTE: An edited version was issued on Verve singles: VS-702 (stereo) and 10166 (mono).

Little White Lies (2 tks; tk 2 mst): Verve 6019/4021; **Verve 847 392-2**

You Brought a New Kind of Love to Me (3 tks; tk 3 mst): Verve 6019/4021; **Verve 847 392-2**

Dreams Are Made for Children: Verve 10158; **Verve 847 392-2**

NOTE: Verve 10158, the mono 45 rpm issue, was probably paralleled by a stereo single in the Verve VS-700 series.

November 24, 1958

EF, vo; Frank DeVol Orchestra (including Sweets Edison)

East of the Sun/Lullaby of Broadway/Let's Fall in Love Again/I Remember You/Sweet and Lovely/Can't We Be Friends?: Verve 6072/4032

Out of This World (7 tks; tk 7 mst): Verve 6072/4032

Makin' Whoopee: Verve 6072/4032; **Verve 314 517 898-2**

January 5, 7, and 8, 1959

EF, vo; Nelson Riddle Orchestra

Soon/I Got Rhythm/Our Love Is Here to Stay/They Can't Take That Away from Me:
Verve 6082-5/4029-5; Verve VE2-2525; **Verve 825 024-2; Verve 314 519 832-2**

How Long Has This Been Going On?: Verve 6082-5/4029-5; **Verve 825 024-2; Verve
314 519 832-2**

A Foggy Day/The Man I Love/I'm Bidin' My Time: Verve 6082-5/4029-5; Verve
VE2-2525; **Verve 825 024-2; Verve 314 519 832-2**

He Loves and She Loves/I've Got Beginner's Luck: Verve 6082-5/4029-5; **Verve 825-
024-2; Verve 314 519 832-2**

Somebody Loves Me: Verve 4036; **Verve 314 519 347-2; Verve 314 519 832-2**

Slap That Bass: Verve 6082-5/4029-5; **Verve 825 024-2; Verve 314 519 832-2**

Clap Yo' Hands: Verve 6082-5/4029-5; Verve VE2-2525; **Verve 825 024-2; Verve
314 519 832-2**

Cheerful Little Earful: Verve 4036; **Verve 314 519 347-2; Verve 314 519 832-2**

You've Got What Gets Me/Embraceable You/I've Got a Crush on You/But Not for Me:
Verve 6082-5/4029-5; Verve VE2-2525; **Verve 825 024-2; Verve 314 519 832-2**

NOTE: Verve VE2-2525, despite some listings, contains this version of "But Not for
Me."

Lady Be Good (11 tks; tk 11 mst): Verve 6082-5/4029-5; Verve VE2-2525; **Verve 825
024-2;** (tks 8 and 9) **Verve 314 519 832-2**

NOTE: This last tune was recorded January 8, 1959, according to logic and documentation.

March 18, 1959

EF, vo; Nelson Riddle Orchestra

I Can't Be Bothered Now/Of Thee I Sing (spliced take): Verve 6082-5/4029-5; Verve
VE2-2525; **Verve 825 024-2; Verve 314 519 832-2**

I Was Doing All Right/Funny Face: Verve 6082-5/4029-5; **Verve 825 024-5; Verve
314 519 832-2**

Fascinating Rhythm: Verve 6082-5/4029-5; VE2-2525; **Verve 825 024-2; Verve 314
519 832-2**

March 25, 1959

EF, vo; Frank DeVol Orchestra

*You Go to My Head/Willow Weep for Me/I've Grown Accustomed to His Face/Spring
Will Be a Little Late This Year/I'm Through with Love*: Verve 6100/4034

EF, vo; possibly Lou Levy, p; Herb Ellis, g; unknown b; unknown d

Pennies from Heaven (2 tks): unissued

NOTE: Take 2 was the preferred or "master" take.

It's a Good Day (4 tks): all unissued

Detour Ahead (2 tks; tk 2 iss): **Verve 314 517 898-2**
NOTE: "Detour Ahead" is a duet with Ella and Herb Ellis.

EF, speech, street calls, vo
Voice tracks for *Porgy and Bess*: Verve 6040-2/4011-2; Verve VE2-2507; **Verve 827 475-2**

March 26, 1959

EF, vo; Nelson Riddle Orchestra
My One and Only: Verve 6082-5/4029-5; **Verve 825 024-2; Verve 314 519 832-2**
Someone to Watch Over Me/Nice Work If You Can Get It: Verve 6082-5/4029-5; Verve VE2-2525; **Verve 825 024-2; Verve 314 519 832-2**
Love Walked In: Verve 6082-5/4029-5; **Verve 825 024-2; Verve 314 519 832-2**
But Not for Me: Verve VS-717/10180; **Verve 314 519 832-2**
NOTE: This version of "But Not for Me," and/or a number of the outtakes, may have been used by Paramount Pictures.
Let's Call the Whole Thing Off: Verve 6082-5/4029-5; Verve VE2-2525; **Verve 825 024-2; Verve 314 519 832-2**
Lookin' for a Boy/Let's Kiss and Make Up: Verve 6082-5/4029-5; **Verve 825 024-2; Verve 314 519 832-2**
They All Laughed: Verve 6082-5/4029-5; Verve VE2-2525; **Verve 825 024-2; Verve 314 519 832-2**

July 11, 1959

EF, vo; Frank DeVol Orchestra
My Old Flame/Gone with the Wind/That Old Feeling: Verve 4032
Moonlight Becomes You (spliced take): Verve 6102/4036
Moonlight Serenade: Verve 4032
You Make Me Feel So Young: Verve 6102/4036; Verve VS-717/10180

July 15, 1959

EF, vo; Nelson Riddle Orchestra
Shall We Dance?/That Certain Feeling: Verve 6082-5/4029-5; Verve VE2-2525; **Verve 825 024-2; Verve 314 519 832-2**
What Love Has Done to Me/Boy Wanted: Verve 6082-5/4029-5; **Verve 825 024-2; Verve 314 519 832-2**
"The Half of It, Dearie" Blues/Lorelei: Verve 6082-5/4029-5; Verve VE2-2525; **Verve 825 024-2; Verve 314 519 832-2**

July 16, 1959

EF, vo; Nelson Riddle Orchestra

'S Wonderful/Who Cares?: Verve 6082-5/4029-5; Verve VE2-2525; **Verve 825 024-2; Verve 314 519 832-2**

Treat Me Rough/Strike Up the Band/Sam and Delilah: Verve 6082-5/4029-5; **Verve 825 024-2; Verve 314 519 832-2**

By Strauss: Verve 6082-5/4029-5; Verve VE2-2525; **Verve 825 024-2; Verve 314 519 832-2**

July 17, 1959

EF, vo; Nelson Riddle Orchestra

My Cousin from Milwaukee/Things Are Looking Up: Verve 6082-5/4029-5; Verve VE2-2525; **Verve 825 024-2; Verve 314 519 832-2**

Stiff Upper Lip/Oh So Nice/Just Another Rhumba: Verve 6082-5/4029-5; **Verve 825 024-2; Verve 314 519 832-2**

July 18, 1959

EF, vo; Nelson Riddle Orchestra

Somebody from Somewhere/Love Is Sweeping the Country/For You, for Me, for Evermore/Aren't You Kind of Glad We Did?: Verve 6082-5/4029-5; **Verve 825 024-2; Verve 314 519 832-2**

Isn't It a Pity?: Verve 6082-5/4029-5; Verve VE2-2525; **Verve 825 024-2; Verve 314 519 832-2**

The Real American Folk Song (Is a Rag): Verve 6082-5/4029-5; **Verve 825 024-2; Verve 314 519 832-2**

September 3, 1959

EF, vo; Marty Paich Orchestra

Like Young/Cool Breeze/Beat Me Daddy, Eight to the Bar: Verve 6102/4036

The Christmas Song: Verve 10186

The Secret of Christmas: Verve 10186; **Verve 840 501-2**

NOTE: Verve 10186, the mono 45 rpm issue, was probably paralleled by a stereo single in the rare Verve VS-700 series.

December 13, 1959

EF, vo; "An Afternoon with Frank Sinatra" Studio Orchestra

Can't We Be Friends?: **Bravura BVRCD 105**

February 13, 1960

JAZZ AT THE PHILHARMONIC; EF, vo; Paul Smith, p; Jim Hall, g; Wilfred Middlebrooks, b; Gus Johnson, d

That Old Black Magic/Our Love Is Here to Stay: **Verve 314 519 564-2**

NOTE: Verve 603, the ten-inch LP version of *Ella in Berlin*, contained two tunes— "Love for Sale" and "Just One of Those Things"—which didn't appear on any other issue. They were, in fact, from the issued portion of Ella's performance at Jazz at the Hollywood Bowl recorded on August 15, 1956. "Love for Sale" and "Just One of Those Things" were, however, included on the CD issue *Mack the Knife: The Complete Ella in Berlin* (**Verve 314 519 564-2**).

Gone with the Wind/Misty/The Lady Is a Tramp/The Man I Love/Summertime/Too Darn Hot/Lorelei/Mack the Knife/How High the Moon: Verve 4041; **Verve 314 519 564-2**

April 14, 1960

EF, vo; Paul Smith, p

My Melancholy Baby/Angel Eyes/Black Coffee/I Hadn't Anyone Till You/I Cried for You/Misty: Verve 4043; **Verve 839 838-2**

April 19, 1960

EF, vo; Paul Smith, p

Who's Sorry Now?/I Can't Give You Anything but Love/I'm Getting Sentimental over You/Then You've Never Been Blue/September Song/Reach for Tomorrow/One for My Baby: Verve 4043; **Verve 839 838-2**

July 15, 1960

EF, vo; Frank DeVol Orchestra

Santa Claus Is Coming to Town/Jingle Bells/Frosty the Snowman (7 tks; tk 6 mst): Verve 4042; Verve VE1-2539; **Verve 827 150-2**

NOTE: Take 7 of "Frosty" has been listed as the issued master.

Medley: *We Three Kings of Orient Are/O Little Town of Bethlehem*: HMV (E) 45POP817

Christmas Island: unissued

Rudolph the Red-Nosed Reindeer: Verve 4042; Verve VE1-2539; **Verve 827 150-2**

The Christmas Song: unissued

July 16, 1960

EF, vo; Frank DeVol Orchestra

Winter Wonderland/What Are You Doing New Year's Eve?: Verve 4042; Verve VE1-2539; **Verve 827 150-2**

Let It Snow: Verve 4042; Verve VE1-2539; **Verve 827 150-2**; **Verve 314 517 898-2**

White Christmas: Verve 840 501-2

Have Yourself a Merry Little Christmas: Verve 4042; VE1-2539; **Verve 827 150-2**

DISCOGRAPHY

August 1, 1960

EF, vo; Billy May Orchestra

Hooray for Love/When the Sun Comes Out/As Long as I Live/It's Only a Paper Moon/The Man That Got Away/Ac-Cent-Tchu-Ate the Positive/I've Got the World on a String: Verve 4046-2; **Verve 817 527/28-2; Verve 314 519 832-2**

August 2, 1960

EF, vo; Billy May Orchestra

Get Happy: Verve 4046-2; **Verve 817 527/28-2; Verve 314 519 832-2**

Sing My Heart (4 tks; tk 4 mst): **Verve 817 527/28-2**

Ding-Dong! The Witch Is Dead (3 tks; tk 3 mst): **Verve 817 527/28-2**

Let's Take a Walk Around the Block (4 tks; tk 4 mst): Verve 4046-2; **Verve 817 527/28-2; Verve 314 519 832-2**

Heart and Soul (2 tks; tk 2 iss): **Verve 314 517 898-2**

August 5, 1960

EF, vo; Frank DeVol Orchestra

Good Morning Blues/Sleigh Ride/The Christmas Song: Verve 4042; Verve VE1-2539; **Verve 827 150-2**

White Christmas: Verve 4042; Verve VE1-2539; **Verve 827 150-2**; HMV (E) 45POP817

January 14, 1961

EF, vo; Billy May Orchestra

That Old Black Magic/Blues in the Night/I Gotta Right to Sing the Blues/Stormy Weather/One for My Baby/My Shining Hour/Ill Wind/Over the Rainbow/This Time the Dream's On Me/It Was Written in the Stars (spliced take): Verve 4046-2; **Verve 817 527/28-2; Verve 314 519 832-2**

January 16, 1961

EF, vo; Billy May Orchestra

Between the Devil and the Deep Blue Sea/Let's Fall in Love/Happiness Is Just a Thing Called Joe/Out of This World/Come Rain or Come Shine: Verve 4046-2; **Verve 817 527/28-2; Verve 314 519 832-2**

NOTE: "Blues in the Night," "One for My Baby," and "Come Rain or Come Shine" were also issued on Verve EP 5073, a release not cited in discography.

January 23, 1961

EF, vo; Lou Levy, p; Herb Ellis, g; Wilfred Middlebrooks, b; Gus Johnson, d

The One I Love Belongs to Somebody Else (7 tks; tk 4 mst): **Verve 835 646-2**

NOTE: The session reels and paperwork offer no take preference. The Verve master ledger cites take 7. My uncredited production work for the CD issue of *Clap Hands, Here Comes Charlie* (**Verve 835 646-2**) included a selection of the bonus material, and I picked the peppier take 4 over take 7 for issue.

I Got a Guy (8 tks; tk 5 iss; tk 8 mst): **Verve 835 646-2**

NOTE: This time my selection of take 5 over master take 8 was dictated by tape damage on the master take.

This Could Be the Start of Something Big (32 tks; tk 32 mst): **Verve 835 646-2**

NOTE: The high take number has no obvious explanation.

Stella by Starlight (4 tks): all unissued

NOTE: There were two attempts to complete take 4 of "Stella by Starlight" by inserts. These attempts are in themselves incomplete. The Verve master book lists take 1 as the preferred or "master" take. "Stella by Starlight" was remade, however, on June 23, 1961, and the issued master is from that session.

February 11, 1961

EF, vo; Lou Levy, p; Herb Ellis, g; Wilfred Middlebrooks, b; Gus Johnson, d

Give Me the Simple Life/Take the "A" Train/On a Slow Boat to China/Medley: *Why Was I Born?; Can't Help Lovin' Dat Man; People Will Say We're in Love/You're Driving Me Crazy/Rock It for Me/Witchcraft/Anything Goes/Cheek to Cheek/Misty/Caravan/(If You Can't Sing It) You'll Have to Swing It* (aka *Mr. Paganini*)/*'Round Midnight/Joe Williams' Blues*: **Verve 837 758-2**

EF, vo; Oscar Peterson, p; Herb Ellis, g; Ray Brown, b; Ed Thigpen, d
This Can't Be Love: **Verve 837 758-2**

Possibly April 5, 1961

EF, vo; with, conceivably, her working group; at Northwestern University
St. Louis Blues/(If You Can't Sing It) You'll Have to Swing It (aka *Mr. Paganini*): unissued

May 11, 1961

EF, vo; Lou Levy, p; Herb Ellis, g; Wilfred Middlebrooks, b; Gus Johnson, d.
Despite the album credits and all discographies, Herb Ellis, not Jim Hall, is the guitarist.
Second Set
(If You Can't Sing It) You'll Have to Swing It (aka *Mr. Paganini*): unissued

May 12, 1961

EF, vo; Lou Levy, p; Herb Ellis, g; Wilfred Middlebrooks, b; Gus Johnson, d

First Set

(If You Can't Sing It) You'll Have to Swing It (aka *Mr. Paganini*): Verve 4052; **Verve 831 367-2; Verve 314 517 898-2**

NOTE: The ledger is unclear. This performance might actually come from the second set of May 12, 1961.

Second Set

Lover Come Back to Me/You Brought a New Kind of Love to Me/Across the Alley from the Alamo/I'm Glad There Is You/'Round Midnight/Take the "A" Train: all unissued

Third Set

A-Tisket, A-Tasket: **Verve 831 367-2**

May 13, 1961

EF, vo; Lou Levy, p; Herb Ellis, g; Wilfred Middlebrooks, b; Gus Johnson, d

First Set

I Found a New Baby/On the Sunny Side of the Street/Am I Blue?/I've Got a Crush on You/It's All Right with Me/Caravan/Blue Moon/Lullaby of Birdland/A-Tisket, A-Tasket/Imagination/Mack the Knife/Joe Williams' Blues: all unissued

Third Set

Give Me the Simple Life/(If You Can't Sing It) You'll Have to Swing It (aka *Mr. Paganini*)/*'Round Midnight/Just Squeeze Me/This Could Be the Start of Something Big/'S Wonderful/In the Wee Small Hours of the Morning/Mack the Knife/How High the Moon*: all unissued

May 14, 1961

EF, vo; Lou Levy, p; Herb Ellis, g; Wilfred Middlebrooks, b; Gus Johnson, d

First Set

Just In Time: Verve 4052

Rock It for Me/'S Wonderful/St. Louis Blues: unissued

Second Set

I've Got the World On a String: Verve 4052

It's All Right with Me/(If You Can't Sing It) You'll Have to Swing It (aka *Mr. Paganini*): unissued

NOTE: The tune sequences for both sets represent educated guesses.

May 16, 1961

EF, vo; Lou Levy, p; Herb Ellis, g; Wilfred Middlebrooks, b; Gus Johnson, d

First Set
I Found a New Baby/Deep Purple: unissued
You're Driving Me Crazy/Blue Moon: Verve 4052

Second Set
This Could Be the Start of Something Big/Baby Won't You Please Come Home: Verve 4052
On a Slow Boat to China/Take the "A" Train: unissued
NOTE: Hereafter, the sequence is confirmed.
Li'l Darlin': unissued
NOTE: Ella introduces Gig Young, who was in the audience.
Caravan/In the Wee Small Hours of the Morning/Mack the Knife/Joe Williams' Blues: unissued
NOTE: "Slow Boat," "Caravan," and "Joe Williams" were given Verve master numbers 27043, 27046, and 27047, respectively, and were deleted from the album *Ella in Hollywood* before it went to press. "Joe Williams" dovetailed into the rhythm section's "Fanfare Music for Ella," which was also intended for issue and is part of Verve master 27047.

May 17, 1961

EF, vo; Lou Levy, p; Herb Ellis, g; Wilfred Middlebrooks, b; Gus Johnson, d
First Set
(If You Can't Sing It) You'll Have to Swing It (aka *Mr. Paganini*): unissued

Second Set
Satin Doll: Verve 4052
'S Wonderful: unissued
Air Mail Special: Verve 4052

May 18, 1961

EF, vo; Lou Levy, p; Herb Ellis, g; Wilfred Middlebrooks, b; Gus Johnson, d
First Set
The Lady's in Love with You/Our Love Is Here to Stay/Come Rain or Come Shine/Anything Goes/This Could Be the Start of Something Big: unissued
NOTE: Ella introduces Carl Reiner, who was in the audience, then spots songwriter Mack David and follows up with David's "Candy," although she has problems with the lyrics.
Candy/Little Girl Blue/You're Driving Me Crazy/Mack the Knife: unissued
NOTE: The tape ran out shortly after the performance started, and the balance is presumably lost.
Blue Moon/Joe Williams' Blues/'S Wonderful: unissued

Second Set

Give Me the Simple Life/On a Slow Boat to China/Am I Blue?/Lullaby of Birdland/But Not for Me/Take the "A" Train/In the Wee Small Hours of the Morning/Witchcraft/ A-Tisket, A-Tasket/Mack the Knife/I've Got a Crush on You/Joe Williams' Blues: all unissued

May 19, 1961

EF, vo; Lou Levy, p; Herb Ellis, g; Wilfred Middlebrooks, b; Gus Johnson, d

First Set

This Could Be the Start of Something Big/Witchcraft/Gone with the Wind: unissued

It Might as Well Be Spring: Verve 4052

Happiness Is Just a Thing Called Joe/It's De-Lovely/The Lady Is a Tramp/That Old Black Magic/Lullaby of Birdland: unissued

Second Set

Just Squeeze Me/(If You Can't Sing It) You'll Have to Swing It (aka *Mr. Paganini*)/*Stompin' at the Savoy*: unissued

Third Set

'S Wonderful/Nice Work If You Can Get It/I Can't Get Started/Give Me the Simple Life/Caravan/Little Girl Blue/One for My Baby/This Could Be the Start of Something Big/Lorelei/Across the Alley from the Alamo/A-Tisket, A-Tasket: all unissued

May 20, 1961

EF, vo; Lou Levy, p; Herb Ellis, g; Wilfred Middlebrooks, b; Gus Johnson, d

Either the First or Second Set

Lover Come Back to Me/Too Close for Comfort/Little White Lies/On the Sunny Side of the Street/Ac-Cent-Tchu-Ate the Positive/Little Girl Blue/Anything Goes/Take the "A" Train/(If You Can't Sing It) You'll Have to Swing It (aka *Mr. Paganini*): all unissued

NOTE: The tape ran out close to the end of the performance, and the ending is presumably lost.

Third Set

This Could Be the Start of Something Big/I Found a New Baby/On a Slow Boat to China/Medley: *Am I Blue?; Blue and Sentimental; Baby, Won't You Please Come Home*: unissued

NOTE: This is a short performance, perhaps intended as a novelty or a novel way of getting into "Baby, Won't You Please Come Home." Ella's laughter leads to her halting the performance, quickly followed with another "Baby, Won't You Please Come Home," this time without the other songs interpolated as an intro.

Baby, Won't You Please Come Home/My Heart Belongs to Daddy/Perdido/Witchcraft/In the Wee Small Hours of the Morning: all unissued

DISCOGRAPHY

May 21, 1961

EF, vo; Lou Levy, p; Herb Ellis, g; Wilfred Middlebrooks, b; Gus Johnson, d
Second Set
Love for Sale: unissued
Stairway to the Stars: Verve 4052
(If You Can't Sing It) You'll Have to Swing It (aka *Mr. Paganini*): unissued
Take the "A" Train: Verve 4052
Mack the Knife/Exactly Like You: unissued

June 23, 1961

EF, vo; Lou Levy, p; Herb Ellis, g; Joe Mondragon, b; Stan Levey, d
Stella by Starlight/Born to Be Blue/'Round Midnight/My Reverie: Verve 4053; **Verve 835 646-2**

June 24, 1961

EF, vo; Lou Levy, p; Herb Ellis, g; Joe Mondragon, b; Stan Levey, d
Cry Me a River/Signing Off/Clap Hands, Here Comes Charlie/The Music Goes 'Round and 'Round: Verve 4053; **Verve 835 646-2**
A Night in Tunisia: Verve 4053; **Verve 835 646-2; Verve 314 517 898-2**

August 25, 1961

EF, vo; Knud Jorgensen, p; Jimmy Woode, b; William Schiopffe, d
(If You Can't Sing It) You'll Have to Swing It (aka *Mr. Paganini*)/*You're Driving Me Crazy*: Verve (G) 90012
NOTE: Ella sings on this 45 rpm in German.

November 13, 1961

EF, vo; Nelson Riddle Orchestra
Darn That Dream: Verve 4055; **Verve 314 519 348-2**
Mean to Me: Verve 4054; **Verve 314 519 347-2**
Georgia on My Mind: Verve 4055; **Verve 314 519 348-2**
I Can't Get Started: Verve 4055; **Verve 314 517 898-2; Verve 314 519 348-2**

November 14, 1961

EF, vo; Nelson Riddle Orchestra
What Am I Here For?/Alone Together/I Only Have Eyes for You: Verve 4054; **Verve 314 519 347-2**
It's a Pity to Say Goodnight: Verve 4055; **Verve 314 519 348-2**
I Hear Music/When Your Lover Has Gone: Verve 4054; **Verve 314 519 347-2**

DISCOGRAPHY

November 15, 1961

EF, vo; Nelson Riddle Orchestra

Pick Yourself Up/The Gentleman Is a Dope: Verve 4054; **Verve 314 519 347-2**

Call Me Darling (LP take): **Verve 314 519 348-2**; (tk 3 single version): Verve 10248; **Verve 314 519 347-2**

Love Me or Leave Me: Verve 4054; **Verve 314 519 347-2**

All of Me: Special United Nations LP; **Verve 314 519 348-2**

December 27, 1961

EF, vo; Nelson Riddle Orchestra

I Won't Dance/I'm Gonna Go Fishing: Verve 4054; **Verve 314 519 347-2**

Don't Be That Way: Verve 4054; **Verve 314 517 898-2**

January 30, 1962

EF, vo; Ray Copeland, Taft Jordan, Ernie Royal, Joe Wilder, tp; Melba Liston, Kai Winding, Britt Woodman, tb; Carl Davis, Jerry Dodgion, Wilmer Shakesnider, Les Taylor, Phil Woods, reeds; Hank Jones, p; Mundell Lowe, g; Lucille Dixon, b; Gus Johnson, d; Bill Doggett, arranger and conductor

After You've Gone (2 tks; tk 1 mst): Verve 4056; **Verve 314 517 898-2**

Broadway/I Can't Face the Music/You Can Depend on Me/Hallelujah, I Love Him So: Verve 4056

If I Could Be with You (One Hour Tonight): unissued

January 31, 1962

EF, vo; same personnel as on January 30, 1962, but substituting George Duvivier, b. On "Rough Ridin'," Bill Doggett on organ.

Laughing on the Outside/Show Me the Way to Get Out of This World/No Moon at All/Runnin' Wild: Verve 4056

Rough Ridin': Verve 4056; **Verve 831 367-2**

Taking a Chance on Love (2 tks): unissued

NOTE: I believe this is the correct sequence for both January 30, 1962, and January 31, 1962, despite the master numbers. Bill Doggett believes he has more outtake material in his personal collection than the unissued items I have found and listed.

February 1962

EF, vo; West Coast Big Band

I'll Always Be in Love with You: Verve 4056

April 9, 1962

EF, vo; Nelson Riddle Orchestra including Ronnie Lang, ts

It's a Blue World/He's Funny That Way/Street of Dreams/Body and Soul: Verve 4055; **Verve 314 519 348-2**

April 10, 1962

EF, vo; Nelson Riddle Orchestra including Ronnie Lang, ts

I Wished on the Moon/Imagination/My One and Only Love/The Very Thought of You/Sweet and Slow: Verve 4055; **Verve 314 519 348-2**

June 29, 1962

EF, vo; Paul Smith, p; Wilfred Middlebrooks, b; Stan Levey, d

NOTE: On the anniversary of *Ella in Hollywood*, Verve tried it again. This time they recorded in three-track stereo, but apparently on just two nights, June 29–30, 1962. Songs asterisked received master numbers, presumably for LP issue. The album never came out, although "Ol' Man Mose" and "Bill Bailey" made it onto a single. The versions of "Ol' Man Mose" and "Bill Bailey, Won't You Please Come Home" are not on the surviving location recordings or the post-production reels, so I'll place them after the June 30, 1962, listing.

First Set

Misty (inc)/*Hallelujah, I Love Him So/Joe Williams' Blues/Bill Bailey/Mack the Knife*: all unissued

Later Set(s)

All of Me/It Might as Well Be Spring/The Lady Is a Tramp/Little Girl Blue/On the Sunny Side of the Street/My Heart Belongs to Daddy/Hard Hearted Hannah*/ Broadway/He's My Kind of Boy/It Had to Be You/All of Me (version 2)/*Bewitched/Exactly Like You/I've Got a Crush On You/How Long Has This Been Going On?*: unissued

Evening's End

C'est Magnifique/On the Sunny Side of the Street/Bill Bailey*: unissued

June 30, 1962

EF, vo; Paul Smith, p; Wilfred Middlebrooks, b; Stan Levey, d

NOTE: The sequencing at the end of June 29, 1962, and the beginning of June 30, 1962, contains some reaching on my part, through Verve's fudged ledgers.

First Set

He's My Kind of Boy*/Teach Me Tonight*/Exactly Like You*/C'est Magnifique: unissued

Later Set(s)

On the Sunny Side of the Street/When Your Lover Has Gone/Teach Me Tonight/Taking a Chance on Love*/Good Morning Heartache/Clap Hands, Here Comes Charlie/C'est Magnifique/It Had to Be You/Exactly Like You*/Hallelujah,

I Love Him So/Exactly Like You (version 2)/*Perdido*/Angel Eyes/Ol' Man Mose*/Bill Bailey/Bill Bailey* (encore)/*All of Me/He's My Kind of Boy/My Heart Belongs to Daddy/*(ballad begins, Ella stops)/*Too Close for Comfort/Teach Me Tonight* (version 2)/*Too Darn Hot* (stopped by Ella)/*Ella's Twist*: all unissued

NOTE: The Crescendo had an upstairs room with dancing. Although it doesn't bleed onto the tape, the upstairs dancing to different music was distracting Ella (note the ballad false start before "Too Close for Comfort"). So she created an impromptu parody, which I've arbitrarily entitled "Ella's Twist." The twist was very big during the 1962 rock 'n' roll scene.

Too Darn Hot/Bewitched: unissued

June 29 or 30, 1962

EF, vo
Ol' Man Mose: Verve 10288
Bill Bailey: Verve 10288; Verve 4063

October 1, 1962

EF, vo; Marty Paich Orchestra
Desafinado: Verve 10274; Verve 4063
Stardust (Bossa Nova): Verve 10274
Steam Heat: Verve 4059

NOTE: It is plausible that the lost "A Felicidade" is from this session, or perhaps the one of October 4, 1962. Discographies list "A Felicidade" for October 9, 1962, a recording date that is also listed (incorrectly) for the next session.

October 2, 1962

EF, vo; with unidentified studio orchestra
I Could Have Danced All Night/Whatever Lola Wants/Guys and Dolls: Verve 4059
Hernando's Hideaway: Verve 4059; **Verve 314 517 898-2**

October 3, 1962

EF, vo; with unidentified studio orchestra
Somebody Somewhere/No Other Love/Dites-Moi/Warm All Over: Verve 4059

October 4, 1962

EF, vo; with unidentified studio orchestra
Almost Like Being in Love/If I Were a Bell/Show Me: Verve 4059

January 5, 1963

EF, vo; Nelson Riddle Orchestra
I'm Old-Fashioned/A Fine Romance/I'll Be Hard to Handle:Verve 4060; **Verve 825 669-2; Verve 314 519 832-2**

January 6, 1963

EF, vo; Nelson Riddle Orchestra
The Way You Look Tonight/Can't Help Lovin' Dat Man/Yesterdays/Why Was I Born?: Verve 4060; **Verve 825 669-2; Verve 314 519 832-2**

January 7, 1963

EF, vo; Nelson Riddle Orchestra
You Couldn't Be Cuter/She Didn't Say Yes/Let's Begin/Remind Me/All the Things You Are: Verve 4060; **Verve 825 669-2; Verve 314 519 832-2**

July 15–16, 1963

EF, vo; with Count Basie and His Orchestra; Quincy Jones, arranger
Shiny Stockings/I'm Beginning to See the Light/Ain't Misbehavin'/On the Sunny Side of the Street/Satin Doll/Into Each Life Some Rain Must Fall/Honeysuckle Rose/Tea for Two: Verve 4061; **Verve 821 576-2**
'Deed I Do: Verve 4061; **Verve 821 576-2; Verve 314 517 898-2**

EF, vo; Joe Newman, tp; Urbie Green, tb; Frank Foster, ts; Freddie Greene, g; Buddy Catlett, b; Sonny Payne, d; Count Basie, piano and organ
Them There Eyes/Dream a Little Dream of Me: Verve 4061; **Verve 821 576-2**

July 16, 1963

EF, vo; Count Basie and His Orchestra; Quincy Jones, arranger
Robbins' Nest (14 tks): all unissued
NOTE: After slating take 11—the first of three quick false starts—the recording engineer (the date was done at A&R in New York City) does not slate his tape again. But the MGM ledger for this session lists all 14 takes.
My Last Affair (3 tks; tk 3 mst): Verve 4061; **Verve 821 576-2**

October 28, 1963

EF, vo; Roy Eldridge, tp; Wild Bill Davis, organ; Herb Ellis, g; Ray Brown, b; Gus Johnson, d
How Long, How Long Blues/See See Rider/Trouble in Mind/Jailhouse Blues/Heah Me Talkin' to Ya/Cherry Red: Verve 4062; **Verve 829 536-2**

DISCOGRAPHY

October 29, 1963

EF, vo; Roy Eldridge, tp; Wild Bill Davis, organ; Herb Ellis, g; Ray Brown, b; Gus Johnson, d

NOTE: It is unusual to have take numbers for Verve sessions during this period, but since they exist for the October 29, 1963, session, I have included them here.

You Don't Know My Mind (tk 6)/*Down Hearted Blues* (tk 4)/*St. Louis Blues* (tk 1)/*In the Evening (When the Sun Goes Down)* (tk 2): Verve 4062; **Verve 829 536-2**

Jailhouse Blues (beginning remake/tk 9)/*Private Jam Session* (tk 1): unissued

Late 1963

NOTE: An undocumented yet important part of Ella Fitzgerald's discography is the album *Ella in Nippon*, which has never been heard or heard of. Ella's fall 1963 tour of Japan was recorded by Verve. She was recorded backed by the Roy Eldridge Quartet, with a Japanese big band, on Japanese TV, and in a jam session with Japanese musicians. Back in the States, between February and August 1964, an incredible (for the time) amount of post-production work was done. LP masters were cut and test recordings were sent around. Yet the album—or albums, since a deluxe set was contemplated with over half an LP of the Roy Eldridge Quartet slated for issue—never came out. Unlike other aborted projects, *Ella in Nippon* vanished without a trace in standard references or vault files. The music still exists, with complete master LP setup reels. The music is listed below in two parts: first, material produced for issue; and second, the extra material.

Produced for Issue

Cheek to Cheek/Deep Purple/Too Close for Comfort/I Love Being Here with You/Fly Me to the Moon/'S Wonderful/I've Got You Under My Skin/Hallelujah, I Love Him So/Misty/Whatever Lola Wants/Bill Bailey, Won't You Please Come Home/Ella's Blues

Extra Material

Cheek to Cheek/Can't Help Lovin' Dat Man/Shiny Stockings/Bill Bailey/Take The "A" Train/A-Tisket, A-Tasket (all recorded at the Hotel Okura)/*Hallelujah, I Love Him So/Ella's Blues/Mack the Knife* (on Japanese television)/*Ain't Misbehavin'/My Last Affair/Perdido* (with a Japanese big band plus Roy Eldridge)

NOTE: The proposed LP side of Roy Eldridge's Quartet included "'Round Midnight," "I Can't Get Started," and "Undecided." There was also an instrumental jam session with Japanese players.

February 3, 1964

EF, vo; Roy Eldridge Quartet: Roy Eldridge, tp; Tommy Flanagan, p; Bill Yancey, b; Gus Johnson, d

You'd Be So Nice to Come Home To/I'm Beginning to See the Light/My Last Affair/Dream a Little Dream of Me/Goody Goody/I Love Being Here with

You/Ten Cents a Dance/Deep Purple/Witchcraft/Them There Eyes/Shiny Stockings/The Lady Is a Tramp/Bill Bailey/Perdido/Mack the Knife: all unissued

NOTE: The reel was flipped on my recording between "Bill Bailey, Won't You Please Come Home" and "Perdido," so the tape lacks the very end of "Bill Bailey" and much of the beginning of "Perdido."

March 3, 1964

EF, vo; Frank DeVol Orchestra including Zoot Sims, ts

There, I've Said It Again (4 tks): all unissued

How High the Moon (4 tks; tk 4 mst): Verve 4064

Pete Kelly's Blues (2 tks; tk 2 mst): Verve 4064

NOTE: A note survives documenting Ella's preference for this issued take. Producer Granz had voted for take 1.

Memories of You (11 tks; tk 11 mst): Verve 4046; **Verve 314 519 832-2**

March 4, 1964

EF, vo; Frank DeVol Orchestra including Zoot Sims, ts

Lullaby of the Leaves (4 tks; tk 4 mst): Verve 4064

I'll See You in My Dreams (5 tks): all unissued

My Man (tk 2 mst)/*The Thrill Is Gone* (tk 7 mst): Verve 4064

There Are Such Things (6 tks; tk 5 mst): unissued

Miss Otis Regrets (6 tks; tk 6 mst)/*Volare* (tk 3 mst): Verve 4064

April 7, 1964

EF, vo; no further details

Can't Buy Me Love/Hello Dolly/People/The Sweetest Sounds: Verve 4064

July 28, 1964

EF, vo; Roy Eldridge, t; Tommy Flanagan, p; Bill Yancey, b; Gus Johnson, d

Hello Dolly: unissued

Just a-Sittin' and a-Rockin': Verve 4065; **Verve J25J 25147**

Day In, Day Out: Verve 4065; **Verve J25J 25147**; **Verve 314 517 898-2**

I Love Being Here with You: unissued

People/Someone to Watch Over Me/Can't Buy Me Love/Them There Eyes: **Verve J25J 25147**

The Lady Is a Tramp/Summertime/Cutie Pants: **Verve J25J 25147**

I'm Putting All My Eggs in One Basket: unissued

St. Louis Blues: Verve 4065; **Verve J25J 25147**

Perdido: **Verve J25J 25147**

Mack the Knife: unissued

Honeysuckle Rose: Verve 4065; **Verve J25J 25147**

July 29, 1964

EF, vo; personnel same as July 28, 1964

Hello Dolly/Day In, Day Out/Just a-Sittin' and a-Rockin'/I Love Being Here with You/People/Someone to Watch Over Me/Can't Buy Me Love/Them There Eyes/The Lady Is a Tramp/Summertime/Cutie Pants/I'm Putting All My Eggs in One Basket/St. Louis Blues (EF can be heard laughing throughout but does not sing): all unissued

Goody Goody/The Boy from Ipanema: **Verve J25J 25147**

They Can't Take That Away from Me/You'd Be So Nice to Come Home To: Verve 4065; **Verve J25J 25147**

Shiny Stockings: **Verve J25J 25147**

Somewhere in the Night/I've Got You Under My Skin: Verve 4065; **Verve J25J 25147**

Blues in the Night/Too Close for Comfort/Mack the Knife: unissued

The Cricket Song/How High the Moon: Verve 4065; **Verve J25J 25147**

October 19, 1964

EF, vo; Marty Paich Orchestra

Travelin' Light (7 tks; tk 7 mst): Verve 4067; **Verve 314 519 832-2**

All the Live Long Day (4 tks; tk 4 mst): Verve 10338

I'm a Poached Egg (2 tks; tk 2 mst): Verve 10338

October 19–22, 1964

EF, vo; Marty Paich Orchestra

Too Marvelous for Words/Early Autumn/Day In, Day Out/Laura/This Time the Dream's on Me/Skylark/Single O/Something's Gotta Give/Midnight Sun/Dream/I Remember You/When a Woman Loves a Man: Verve 4067; **Verve 314 519 832-2**

October 22, 1964

EF, vo; Marty Paich Orchestra

Old MacDonald (11 tks)/*He Said No* (3 tks)/*When Sunny Gets Blue* (5 tks)/*I've Got Your Number/Thanks for the Memory/Spring Can Really Hang You Up the Most/Melancholy Serenade* (3 tks): all unissued

October 23, 1964

EF, vo; Barney Kessel and others

That Ringo Beat/I'm Falling in Love: Verve 10340

March 26, 1965

EF, vo; Tommy Flanagan, p; Keter Betts, b; Gus Johnson, d

Walk Right In/That Old Black Magic/Body and Soul/And the Angels Sing/A Hard

Day's Night/Ellington Medley: *Mood Indigo; Do Nothin' Till You Hear from Me*/*It Don't Mean a Thing*/*The Boy from Ipanema*/*Don't Rain on My Parade*/*Angel Eyes*/*Smooth Sailing*/*Old MacDonald Had a Farm*: Verve MGV 4069
Here's That Rainy Day: Verve MGV 4069; **Verve 314 517 898-2**

With Duke Ellington and His Orchestra
Duke's Place/*The Shadow of Your Smile*: Verve 10408

July 6, 1965

EF, vo; no further details
She's Just a Quiet Girl/*We Three*: Verve 10359

November 1965 (date unknown)

EF, vo; Duke Ellington and His Orchestra; Jimmy Jones, p (some tracks)
A Flower Is a Lovesome Thing/*Azure*/*I Like the Sunrise*/*Passion Flower*/*Cotton Tail*/*Imagine My Frustration*/*What Am I Here For?*/*Duke's Place*/*The Brown-Skin Gal*: Verve V6 4070
Something to Live For: Verve V6 4070; **Verve 314 517 898-2**

NO FIXED LABEL 1966–1971

Mid-January 1966 (date unknown)

EF, vo; Jimmy Jones, p; Joe Comfort, b; Gus Johnson, d; the Duke Ellington Orchestra
Imagine My Frustration/*Duke's Place*/*Satin Doll*/*Something to Live For*/*Wives and Lovers*/*So Danco Samba*/*Let's Do It*/*Lover Man*/*Cotton Tail*: **Pablo 98.819-2**

April 5, 1966

EF, vo; no further details
The Shadow of Your Smile (8 tks; tk 8 mst): Verve 10408
You're Gonna Hear from Me (23 tks): all unissued

July 27–29, 1966

EF, vo; Jimmy Jones, p; Jim Hughart, b; Grady Tate, d
Jazz Samba/*Goin' Out of My Head*/*How Long Has This Been Goin' On?*/*Misty*/*The More I See You*/*Lullaby of Birdland*: Verve MGV 4072-2

July 27, 1966

EF, vo; Duke Ellington and His Orchestra
Let's Do It/*Satin Doll*/*Cotton Tail*: all unissued

315

July 28, 1966

EF, vo; Duke Ellington and His Orchestra. Probably Jimmy Jones and not Ellington on piano.
Thou Swell/Satin Doll/Something to Live For/Let's Do It: all unissued

July 29, 1966

EF, vo; Duke Ellington and His Orchestra. Probably Ella's regular rhythm section play with the band.
Thou Swell/Satin Doll/Wives and Lovers/Something to Live For/Let's Do It/Sweet Georgia Brown/Mack the Knife/Cottontail: all unissued

EF, vo; Jimmy Jones, p; Jim Hughart, b; Grady Tate, d
Goin' Out of My Head/Jazz Samba/Lullaby of Birdland/The Moment of Truth: all unissued.
Add Ray Nance, t; Ben Webster, ts
Just Squeeze Me: Verve 4072-2
It Don't Mean a Thing: Verve 4072-2; **Verve 314 517 898-2**

August 1966 (date unknown)

EF, vo; Marty Paich and His Orchestra; Harry Edison, tp; Jimmy Rowles, b; Chuck Berghofer, b; Louis Bellson, d
Sweet Georgia Brown/Whisper Not/I Said No/Thanks for the Memory/Spring Can Really Hang You Up the Most/Old MacDonald Had a Farm: Verve MGV 4071; (E) SVLP 9148

August 1966 (date unknown)

EF, vo; Marty Paich and His Orchestra; Stu Williamson, tp; Bill Perkins, ts; Jimmy Rowles, p; Al Viola, g; Joe Mondragon, b; Shelly Manne, d
Time After Time/I've Got Your Number/Lover Man/Wives and Lovers/Matchmaker, Matchmaker: Verve MGV 4071; (E) SVLP 9148
You've Changed: Verve MGV 4071; (E) SVLP 9148; **Verve 314 517 898-2**

September 14 and 25, 1966

EF, vo; Duke Ellington and His Orchestra; Jimmy Jones, p; Jim Hughart, b; Ed Thigpen, d
I'm Just a Lucky So-and-So/The Moment of Truth/Satin Doll/These Boots Are Made for Walking/Something to Live For/Let's Do It/Sweet Georgia Brown/Baby, Bye-Bye/Mack the Knife/Cottontail/(possibly) *Stardust*: all unissued
NOTE: Duke Ellington discographies date this material September 24, 1966. The confusion over the date may be caused by the fact that this was a pretaped television show.

1966 (date unknown)

EF, vo; no further details
These Boots Are Made for Walking/Stardust: Stateside SS569; Stateside SE 1044
The Moment of Truth/I'm Just a Lucky So-and-So: Stateside SE 1044

1967 (live; date unknown)

EF, vo; no further details
Gone with the Wind/The Man I Love/Summertime/The Lady Is a Tramp/The Boy from Ipanema/That Old Black Magic/Just a-Sittin' and a-Rockin'/They Can't Take That Away from Me/I've Got You Under My Skin/Body and Soul/St. Louis Blues/ Stompin' at the Savoy: Verve V6-8748

February 1967 (date unknown)

EF, vo; Ralph Carmichael Chorus and Orchestra
God Will Take Care of You/What a Friend We Have in Jesus/God Will Be with You Till We Meet Again/Abide with Me/In the Garden/Brighten the Corner Where You Are/I Shall Not Be Moved/Just a Closer Walk with Thee/Throw Out the Lifeline/ The Old Rugged Cross/Rock of Ages Cleft for Me/I Need Thee Every Hour/Let the Lower Lights Be Burning/The Church in the Wildwood: Capitol T 2685; **Capitol 795151-2**

July 19, 1967

EF, vo; Ralph Carmichael Chorus and Orchestra
Silent Night/Hark the Herald Angels Sing/Angels We Have Heard on High/We Three Kings/O Little Town of Bethlehem/Away in a Manger/It Came upon a Midnight Clear/Sleep, My Little Lord Jesus/Joy to the World/O Holy Night/O Come All Ye Faithful/God Rest Ye Merry Gentlemen: Capitol T 2805

July 21, 1967

Session continues with: *The First Noel*: Capitol T 2805

December 20, 1967

EF, vo; Sid Feller Orchestra
I Taught Him Everything I Know/Don't Touch Me/Turn the World Around/Walking in the Sunshine: Capitol T 2888; **Capitol CDP7 95152-2**

December 21, 1967

Session continues with: *It's Only Love/Born to Lose/The Chokin' Kind/Misty Blue*: Capitol T 2888; **Capitol CDP7 95152-2**

December 22, 1967

Session continues with: *Evil on Your Mind/Don't Let the Doorknob Hit You/This Gun Don't Care*: Capitol T 2888; **Capitol CDP7 95152-2**

July/August 1968 (dates unknown)

EF, vo; Harry Edison, t; Benny Carter, as; George Auld, ts; Jimmy Jones, p, celesta; John Collins, g; Bob West, el-b; Panama Francis, d

Medley: *No Regrets; I've Got the World on a String; Don't Blame Me* (inst); *Deep Purple; Rain; You're a Sweetheart*/Medley: *On Green Dolphin Street; How Am I to Know?; Just Friends; I Cried for You; Seems Like Old Times; You Stepped Out of a Dream*/Medley: *If I Give My Heart to You; Once in a While; Ebb Tide; The Lamp Is Low; Where are You?; Thinking of You*/Medley: *My Mother's Eyes; Try a Little Tenderness; I Got It Bad (and That Ain't Good); Everything I Have Is Yours; I Never Knew; Goodnight My Love*/Medley: *Spring Is Here* (inst); *720 in the Books; It Happened in Monterey; What Can I Say After I Say I'm Sorry?*: all on Capitol T 2960; **Capitol CDP7 48333-2**

October 21, 1968

EF, vo; studio orchestra
A Place for Lovers (5 tks)/*Lonely Is* (11 tks): all unissued

May 26, 28, 29, and 30, 1969

EF, vo; studio orchestra directed by Richard Perry
Get Ready/The Hunter Gets Captured by the Game/Yellow Man/I'll Never Fall in Love Again/Got to Get You into My Life/I Wonder Why/Open Your Window/Savoy Truffle/Ooh, Baby, Baby/Knock on Wood/Try a Little Bit: Reprise RS 6354; **Reprise 9 26023-2**

Unknown Month, 1970

EF, vo; studio orchestra directed by Gerald Wilson
Sunny/Mas Que Nada/A Man and a Woman/Days of Wine and Roses/Black Coffee/Tuxedo Junction/I Heard It Through the Grapevine/Don't Dream of Anybody but Me/Things Ain't What They Used to Be/Willow Weep for Me/Manteca/Just When We're Falling in Love: Reprise RS 6432; **Reprise 9 26023-2**

Circa 1970 (date unknown)

EF, vo
Two titles on a 45 rpm on the Sable label.

318

DISCOGRAPHY

THE PABLO YEARS 1971–1989

July 21, 1971

EF, vo; Tommy Flanagan, p; Frank De Rosa, b; Ed Thigpen, d

Night and Day/Medley: *Get Out of Town; Easy to Love; You Do Something to Me*/Medley: *Body and Soul; The Man I Love; Porgy*/Medley: *The Girl from Ipanema; Fly Me to the Moon; O Nosso Amor (Carnival Samba); Cielito Lindo; Madalena; Agua de Beber*/*Summertime*/*They Can't Take That Away from Me*/Medley: *Mood Indigo; Do Nothin' Till You Hear from Me; It Don't Mean a Thing (If It Ain't Got That Swing)*/*Something*/*St. Louis Blues*/*Close to You*/*Put a Little Love in Your Heart*: **OJCD 442-2 (Pablo 2308-234)**

June 2, 1972

EF, vo; Tommy Flanagan, p; Keter Betts, b; Ed Thigpen, d; and the Count Basie Orchestra

Shiny Stockings/*You've Got a Friend*/*What's Going On?*: **Pablo 2625-701**

EF, vo; Tommy Flanagan Trio

Spring Can Really Hang You Up the Most/*Madalena*: **Pablo 2625-701**

EF, vo; Tommy Flanagan Trio and the Count Basie Orchestra

Medley: *Too Darn Hot; It's All Right with Me*/*"Sanford and Son" Theme*/*I Can't Stop Loving You*: **Pablo 2625-701**

EF, vo; Count Basie and the Jazz at the Philharmonic All Stars

C Jam Blues: **Pablo 2625-701**

June 9, 1972

EF, vo; studio orchestra directed by Nelson Riddle

I've Got You Under My Skin/*I Concentrate on You*/*My Heart Belongs to Daddy*/*Love for Sale*/*So Near and Yet So Far*/*Down in the Depths*/*Just One of Those Things*/*I Get a Kick out of You*/*All of You*/*Anything Goes*/*At Long Last Love*/*C'est Magnifique*/*Without Love*: originally issued as Atlantic SD 163 I/K 40 450; reissued as **Pablo PACD 2310-814-2** with two extra tracks from 1978.

July 5, 1973

EF, vo; with a re-created Chick Webb Orchestra directed by Eddie Barefield

A-Tisket, A-Tasket/*Indian Summer*/*Smooth Sailing*: CBS 68279

EF, vo; Ellis Larkins, p

You Turned the Tables on Me/*Nice Work If You Can Get It*/*I've Got a Crush on You*: CBS 68279

Second Set

EF, vo; Tommy Flanagan, p; Joe Pass, g; Keter Betts, b; Freddie Waits, d

I've Got to Be Me/Down in the Depths/Good Morning Heartache/What's Goin' On:
unissued

Miss Otis Regrets/Medley: Don't Worry About Me; These Foolish Things (with Joe
Pass, g)/*Any Old Blues/Medley: Taking a Chance On Love; I'm in the Mood for
Love; Lemon Drop; Some of These Days; People*: CBS 68279

August 28, 1973

EF, vo; Joe Pass, g

*Take Love Easy/Once I Loved/Don't Be That Way/You're Blasé/Lush Life/A Foggy
Day/Gee Baby, Ain't I Good to You?/You Go to My Head/I Want to Talk About
You*: **Pablo 2310-702-2**

January 8, 1974

EF, vo; Harry Edison, t; Clark Terry, t, fh; Zoot Sims, Eddie "Lockjaw" Davis, ts;
Joe Pass, g; Tommy Flanagan, p; Ray Brown, b; Louis Bellson, d

*Fine and Mellow/I'm Just a Lucky So-and-So/(I Don't Stand) a Ghost of a Chance
with You/Rockin' in Rhythm/I'm in the Mood for Love/'Round Midnight/I Can't
Give You Anything but Love/The Man I Love/Polka Dots and Moonbeams*: **Pablo
2310-829-2**

April 11, 1974

EF, vo; Tommy Flanagan, p; Joe Pass, g; Keter Betts, b; Bobby Durham, d

*Sweet Georgia Brown/They Can't Take That Away from Me/Ev'rytime We Say
Goodbye/The Man I Love/It Don't Mean a Thing (If It Ain't Got That
Swing)/You've Got a Friend/Lemon Drop/The Very Thought of You/Happy Blues*:
Pablo 2310-711-2

May 19, 1975

EF, vo; Oscar Peterson, p; Ray Brown, b (on last four songs)

*Mean to Me/How Long Has This Been Going On?/When Your Lover Has Gone/More
Than You Know/There's a Lull in My Life/Midnight Sun/I Hear Music/Street of
Dreams/April in Paris*: **Pablo 2310-759-2**

July 17, 1975

EF, vo; Tommy Flanagan, p; Keter Betts, b; Bobby Durham, d

*Caravan/Satin Doll/Teach Me Tonight/Wave/It's All Right with Me/Let's Do It/How
High the Moon/The Girl from Ipanema/'Taint Nobody's Bizness If I Do*: **Pablo
2310-751-2**

February 8, 1976

EF, vo; Joe Pass, g

I Ain't Got Nothin' but the Blues/'Tis Autumn/My Old Flame/That Old Feeling/Rain/I Didn't Know About You/You Took Advantage of Me/I've Got the World on a String/All Too Soon/The One I Love (Belongs to Somebody Else)/Solitude/Nature Boy/Tennessee Waltz/One Note Samba: **Pablo 2310-772-2**

July 14, 1977

EF, vo; Tommy Flanagan, p; Keter Betts, b; Bobby Durham, d

Too Close for Comfort/I Ain't Got Nothing but the Blues/My Man/Come Rain or Come Shine/Day By Day/Ordinary Fool/One Note Samba/I Let a Song Go Out of My Heart/Billie's Bounce/You Are the Sunshine of My Life: **OJCD 376-2 (Pablo 2308-206)**

February 13, 1978

EF, vo; studio orchestra conducted by Nelson Riddle

Dream Dancing/After You: **Pablo 2310-814-2**

June 19–20, 1978

EF, vo; Jackie Davis, organ; Louis Bellson, d

I'm Walkin'/All or Nothing at All/I Never Had a Chance/I Cried for You/What Will I Tell My Heart?/Since I Fell for You/And the Angels Sing/I'm Confessin' (That I Love You)/Mack the Knife/That's My Desire/I'm in the Mood for Love: **Pablo PACD 2310-825-2**

February 15, 1979

EF, vo; Count Basie and His Orchestra

Honeysuckle Rose/My Kind of Trouble Is You/Teach Me Tonight/Organ Grinder's Swing/ Don't Worry 'Bout Me/I'm Getting Sentimental over You/Ain't Misbehavin'/Just a-Sittin' and a-Rockin'/Sweet Lorraine: **Pablo 2312-132-2**

July 12, 1979

EF, vo; Count Basie and His Orchestra

Please Don't Talk About Me When I'm Gone/Sweet Georgia Brown/Some Other Spring/Make Me Rainbows/After You've Gone/'Round Midnight/Fine and Mellow/You've Changed/Honeysuckle Rose/St. Louis Blues/Basella: **Pablo 2312-110-2**

EF, vo; Paul Smith, p; Keter Betts, b; Mickey Roker, d; and the Count Basie Orchestra

(I Don't Stand) a Ghost of a Chance with You/Flying Home: **Pablo 2308-223-2**

EF, vo; Joe Pass, g
I Cover the Waterfront/Li'l Darlin': **Pablo 2308-223-2**

EF, vo; Joe Pass, g; Niels-Henning Orsted-Pedersen, b
In Your Own Sweet Way/Oleo: **Pablo 2308-223-2**

September 17–19, 1980, and March 18–20, 1981

EF, vo; Clark Terry, tp; Zoot Sims, ts; Toots Thielemans, harmonica; Henry Trotter, Mike Lang, Clarence McDonald, kb; Joe Pass, g; Oscar Castro-Neves, Paul Jackson, Mitch Holder, Ronald Bautiste, g; Abraham Laboriel, b; Alex Acuna, d; Paulinho da Cota, percussion
Dreamer/This Love That I've Found/The Girl from Ipanema/Somewhere in the Hills/Photograph/Wave/Triste/Quiet Nights of Quiet Stars/Water to Drink/Bonita/Off Key/Dindi/How Insensitive/One Note Samba/A Felicidade/Useless Landscape: **Pablo 2630-201-2**

February 4–5, 1982

EF, vo; studio orchestra conducted by Nelson Riddle
Don't Be That Way/God Bless the Child/I Wonder Where Our Love Has Gone/You're Driving Me Crazy/Any Old Time/Goodbye/Autumn in New York/The Best Is Yet to Come/Deep Purple/Somewhere in the Night: **Pablo 2312-138-2**

March 21–22, 1983

EF, vo; Joe Pass, g
Speak Low/Comes Love/There's No You/I May Be Wrong (But I Think You're Wonderful)/At Last/The Thrill Is Gone/Gone with the Wind/Blue and Sentimental/Girl Talk/Georgia on My Mind: **Pablo 2310-888-2**

Session continues and released as below, which also includes some additional tracks from February 25 and 28, 1986, as yet unidentified.
My Ship/Don't Be That Way/My Man/Don't Worry 'Bout Me/Days of Wine and Roses/Easy Living/I Don't Stand a Ghost of a Chance with You/Love for Sale/Moonlight in Vermont/On Green Dolphin Street/Why Don't You Do Right?/By Myself/I Want a Little Girl/I'm Making Believe/On a Slow Boat to China: **Pablo 2310-921-2**

May 23, 1983

EF, vo; André Previn, p; Niels-Henning Orsted-Pedersen, b
A Foggy Day/Nice Work If You Can Get It/But Not for Me/Let's Call the Whole Thing Off/How Long Has This Been Going On?/Who Cares?/Medley: I've Got a Crush On You; Someone to Watch Over Me; Embraceable You/They Can't Take That Away from Me: **Pablo PACD 2312-140-2**

October 1983 (date unknown)

EF, vo; Paul Smith, p; Keter Betts, b; Bobby Durham, d

Manteca/Willow Weep for Me/All of Me/Blue Moon/Night and Day/They Can't Take That Away from Me/Medley: *The Man I Love; Body and Soul/'Round Midnight*: **Pablo PACD-2620-117-2**

EF, vo; Jazz at the Philharmonic All Stars

Flying Home: **Pablo PACD-2620-117-2**

March 15, 16, 20, and 22, 1989

EF, vo; Harry Edison, tp; Benny Carter, as; Kenny Barron, p; Ray Brown, b; Bobby Durham, d; or Al Grey, tb; Clark Terry, tp; Mike Wofford, p; Ray Brown, b; Bobby Durham, d

Dream a Little Dream of Me/My Last Affair/Baby, Don't Quit Now/Oh, Look at Me Now/The Jersey Bounce/When Your Lover Has Gone/That Old Devil Called Love/All That Jazz/Just When We're Falling in Love (aka Robbins' Nest)/Good Morning, Heartache/Little Jazz/The Nearness of You: **Pablo PACD 2310-938-2**

Late 1980s (dates unknown)

EF, vo; (probably) Mike Wofford, p; Keter Betts, b; Bobby Durham, d; with guest appearances by Harry "Sweets" Edison, tp; Joe Pass, g; among others

Titles not known, but Norman Granz has confirmed he has recorded enough for one album for Salle Productions, who hold the masters.

1989 (date unknown)

EF, vo; Quincy Jones ensemble. Ella adds her voice by multitracking amid contributions from Sarah Vaughan, Miles Davis, Take 6, Bobby McFerrin, Al Jarreau, Dizzy Gillespie, James Moody, George Benson, et al.

Wee B. Dooinit/Birdland/Jazz Corner of the World: **Quest/Warner Bros. 926020-2**

TEN ESSENTIAL ELLA RECORDINGS
(ALL ON CD UNLESS INDICATED)

The author has chosen the albums, and the discographer confirms they are among his favorites, too.

Lullabies of Birdland: Jasmine JASM 1027 (LP)

Ella Sings Gershwin: **Decca Jazz GRD-636**

Ella Fitzgerald: Jazz at the Philharmonic, 1957: **Tax CD 3703-2**

Ella at the Opera House: **Verve 831 269-2**

Ella Fitzgerald Sings the George and Ira Gershwin Songbook: **Verve 825 024-2**

Clap Hands, Here Comes Charlie: **Verve 835 646-2**

Mack the Knife: The Complete Ella in Berlin: **Verve 314 519 564-2**

Ella Returns to Berlin: **Verve 837 758-2**

Ella Fitzgerald Sings the Songs from the Film Let No Man Write My Epitaph: **Verve POCJ 2067** (also available as *The Intimate Ella*)

Ella in Rome: The Birthday Concert: **Verve 835 454-2**

INDEX